Law and Society
Recent Scholarship

Edited by Eric Rise

A Series from LFB Scholarly

Race, Law, and the Desegregation of Public Schools

Peter William Moran

LFB Scholarly Publishing LLC
New York 2005

Library of Congress Cataloging-in-Publication Data

Moran, Peter William, 1964-
Race, law, and the desegregation of public schools / Peter William Moran.
p. cm. -- (Law and society : recent scholarship)
Includes bibliographical references and index.
ISBN 1-59332-039-6 (alk. paper)
1. Segregation in education--Law and legislation--Missouri--Kansas City. 2. Discrimination in education--Law and legislation--Missouri--Kansas City. 3. Kansas City (Mo.). Board of Education. 4. Kansas City (Mo.)--Race relations. I. Title. II. Series: Law and society (New York, N.Y.)
KFX1591.S34M67 2005
344.778'4110798--dc22

2004023823

ISBN 1-59332-039-6

Printed on acid-free 250-year-life paper.

Manufactured in the United States of America.

Table of Contents

Acknowledgements

This book is dedicated to Amy, Sarah, Matthew, my parents, and all of my family, near and far.

This project would not have been possible without the assistance of a number of people. I am deeply indebted to J. Glenn Travis who provided expert guidance through the archival collections of the Kansas City public schools. Recognizing the historical value of the statistical data and studies that he helped to compile, Mr. Travis had the foresight to file away many of the documents that crossed his desk during his long tenure with the school district. Had it not been for the efforts of Mr. Travis, much of the story of desegregation in the Kansas City schools would have been lost and this study would not have been possible. My thanks also to John Duncan, Glenn Travis's successor as the school district historian. Both men were always generous with their time and patient in clarifying developments that I did not fully grasp. I am also grateful to Cheryl Cousins, Jane Owen, and Lois Henderson for making the school board's meeting minutes available to me, and to the Desegregation Monitoring Committee for providing me with copies of their annual reports. Thank you to the many principals who allowed me to tour their schools, and thanks to the wonderful staff of the Missouri Valley Room at the Kansas City public library for their assistance with the newspaper clippings microforms and vertical files. I owe special thanks to Phil White, a phenomenal legal researcher who helped me with the court cases and legal developments. In those chapters dealing with the *Jenkins* litigation, two of the attorneys in the case, Arthur Benson and Shirley Ward Keeler, were extremely helpful in explaining the complicated development of *Jenkins*. The Missouri Department of Elementary and Secondary Education, and the Attorney General's office also provided documents related to the *Jenkins* case. I am most grateful for the guidance, encouragement, and invaluable editorial advice offered by Sue Zschoche, Lou Williams, Albert Hamscher, and John McCulloh. Their suggestions improved this work immeasurably. Parishioners of Immaculate Conception Catholic Church in Grinnell, Kansas were gracious in providing me with office space each summer so that I could write, and I owe a huge debt of gratitude to Christi Boggs and Suzie

Young for their help in overcoming the technical difficulties that I experienced in assembling this manuscript. I am also grateful to Leo Balk for his guidance and patience in helping me to complete the book. I am forever indebted to the members of my family for their encouragement and loving support throughout this project. Finally, none of this would have possible without my wife, Amy, and our children, Sarah and Matthew. Their unfailing support, occasional prodding, and many sacrifices allowed me to see this through.

Introduction

Public school integration has been a wrenching process in a number of American cities over the past fifty years. In few cities, however, has the process been so heavily litigated, so rife with controversy, so costly, so lengthy, or, ultimately, yielded results so mixed as in Kansas City, Missouri. More than four decades after the Supreme Court's *Brown v. Board of Education* decision, Kansas City continues to struggle to develop a successful integration program for its schools and provide an adequate education for its students. Despite decades of litigation and legal decisions that facilitated the creation of the nation's most expansive and expensive magnet school system, the Kansas City school district remains highly segregated and objectionable to a large portion of the city's population. This book analyzes the troubled course of integration in the Kansas City public schools and the numerous forces that influenced that course. In short, it is a study of one district's struggle to formulate an integrated school system and the manner in which changing legal standards, shifting demographic patterns, pressure from various community groups, financial limitations, and other political considerations have shaped public policy choices regarding racial integration in the Kansas City schools.

Integrating America's public schools following the 1954 *Brown* decision has been the subject of a voluminous literature. Yet, one is struck by the manner in which most scholars have approached school integration in a fragmented fashion, as if, for example, the legal issues could somehow be divorced from the social, political, and demographic setting of the city. There are several general treatments of race relations and the modern civil rights movement which recognize school integration and the *Brown* decision in particular, as developments meriting some analysis. Such studies, however, tend to treat school integration in an episodic manner and neglect much of the important local context which produced change.

Constitutional and legal historians have focused more directly on school integration. Although these scholars meticulously probe the evolution of the legal standards and constitutional interpretations concerning integration, they typically incorporate little analysis of the social and political context in which policy decisions at the local level were arrived at and implemented. Moreover, these studies generally provide only brief treatment of the demographic context and the shifting populations of the cities under discussion, and thereby fail to address factors that are essential to understanding school integration as a powerful social issue that mobilized thousands of concerned citizens.

Several other works analyze particularly sensational episodes in the history of school integration. Such a framework is well suited for examining the pressing issues for a particular school district at a particular moment in time, but this approach typically offers scant attention long-term change.

Urban historians, sociologists, and geographers have examined the changing demography of cities and the implications of demographic change for the city's social and political order. Yet, these scholars tend to minimize the importance of public policy decisions in spurring or responding to population shifts and generally eschew using school integration as a lens through which these important shifts might be viewed.

Finally, there are a great many policy studies that examine the success or failure of various desegregation remedies implemented in different locales. These studies provide valuable analysis of the impact of certain types of plans, such as the percentage of racial mixing produced through the adoption of a busing scheme or school pairing arrangements. Moreover, these works often include analysis of those variables that appear to influence the public acceptance of a desegregation scheme. However, they typically ignore the local circumstances and pressures which swayed school officials to adopt a certain plan in the first place. In many cases, understanding the local pressures that influenced the adoption of a specific plan are arguably as important as analyzing the degree of integration that a plan produced.

In the literature on school integration there is a dearth of long-term case studies of individual cities that place the subject in its complete context as an issue with legal, social, political, demographic, educational, and financial implications. This study synthesizes the approaches discussed above and applies them to a longitudinal analysis of integration in the Kansas City, Missouri, public schools. Obviously, the five-decade process of integration was experienced quite differently by different groups of the city's citizens. The focus here is not, however, upon any one individual or group of citizens, but rather upon the policy-making apparatus within the school district itself. In short, I have chosen to center this case study upon the two groups which, ultimately, were charged with making policy decisions, specifically, the Kansas City Board of Education and the district's central administration. In particular, I focus on the manner in which these two bodies fashioned and re-fashioned integration policy in the light of multiple and continually evolving social, political, financial, demographic, and legal considerations.

Clearly one important consideration in formulating school district policy was the need to adhere to the changing legal standards for integration. Between the 1950s and the 1980s, the legal standards that applied to Kansas City and other cities involved in school desegregation changed radically from separate but equal, to integration on a token basis at a handful of schools, to striving for racial balance at all schools through mass busing or other means. The evolving legal climate necessarily compelled school administrators in Kansas City to make numerous adjustments to the district's integration plans or risk litigation. Ultimately, the leadership of the Kansas City schools would embrace litigation as the only means through which massive change for the system could be effected. During the 1980s and early 1990s, a series of court orders provided the school district with the unprecedented opportunity to build a city-wide system of magnet schools in order to promote integration. However, when the magnet schools failed to fulfill the lofty goals set forth by the courts, subsequent legal decisions set in motion the dissolution of the magnet system. With the return of more traditional models of school organization, the school district was again confronted with the familiar problem of racial isolation in the schools.

Second, district administrators and Board of Education members struggled to formulate integration plans that would satisfy, or at least be tolerable to, the diverse ethnic and socioeconomic groups of the city. For more than four decades the district was plagued by difficulties in formulating policies in light of a wide variety of different, and often conflicting, sets of pressures and expectations from the various community groups representing the district's black, white and Hispanic patrons. Attempts by school officials to strike balances between these competing interests generally had the effect of alienating certain groups of patrons and on several occasions led to litigation. In the end, thoroughly satisfying these divergent interests proved impossible and remains so today.

Third, the school district had to apply its solutions in a city undergoing massive demographic change, and the changing demography of the Kansas City metropolitan area was a major source of frustration for school policy makers. Racially specific population shifts within the city necessitated annual adjustments to integration plans and led the district to adopt busing plans that may have actually aggravated the demographic problem by stimulating "white flight" to the suburbs. The school administration's inability to cope with these population shifts within an integrated school system goes far in explaining the decision in the late 1970s to resort to litigation as a solution.

Finally, it is imperative to recognize the fiscal restraints within which the school district operated. The abysmal financial standing of the school district placed strict limits on how much could be done to promote integration until the mid-1980s. During one period in the late 1960s and early 1970s, nineteen consecutive bond issues or tax levy increases failed to win the approval of the voting public. The cumulative result of so many failed fiscal measures was a badly deteriorating school system that satisfied very few of its patrons, be they black, white or Hispanic. The fiscal situation changed following the 1984 federal court ruling that provided for massive increases in state aid to the Kansas City schools in order to develop the magnet schools system. Even so, the uses of that money and the district's financial priorities were a significant source of tension between the school board and various community groups. Moreover, the funding formula and the uses of state monies were continually assailed in the courts by the State of Missouri throughout the period 1984 to 1995. Ultimately, a series of legal decisions during the late 1990s brought an end to the massive infusions of state money, and the school district, to its detriment, was again relegated to operating within a strictly limited budget.

Integrating the nation's public schools has certainly been a vexing problem in scores of American cities, and Kansas City's experience is no exception. The sources of tension vary from city to city and often include one or more of the following – the city's rapidly changing demographic composition, the fiscal constraints of the school district, rising black community activism demanding change, reactionary white responses to what were perceived as overly ambitious integration plans, the courts' prodding of unrepentant districts, or agencies of the federal government intervening to exert pressure on recalcitrant districts. In Kansas City all of these elements are present. For this reason Kansas City is an ideal subject for a case study on school integration. Kansas City's experience reveals the remarkable complexity of cause and effect in school integration as a social problem. Through this lens it is possible not only to gain a greater appreciation for the day to day trials of one city, but also to analyze how long-term national developments in the law, public policy, race relations, and demography influenced the course of integration in Kansas City, and how the city's experience influenced national developments, particularly in the legal realm.

Finally, Kansas City is an important case study because in analyzing the city's troubled course one may gain a deeper understanding of how one school district has been viewed by the courts, federal government and the larger public, and how those perceptions could shift radically over relatively short periods of time. Initially, the Kansas City public schools were praised as a model of compliance and the district's leadership roundly applauded by both blacks and whites for its initiative in integrating the schools. In the sixties, Kansas City's schools, like others around the country, struggled to walk the thin line of satisfying the city's black patrons without disaffecting the white community. Ultimately, the schools came under fire from civil rights organizations for the stilted pace of integration in Kansas City and the district fell out of favor with the federal government in the late 1960s and 1970s. Finally, as the school district implemented the magnet schools plans and sought to promote more extensive integration, it won the favor of most of the city's black community, the support of the federal government, and the endorsement of the courts. The state of Missouri and the communities surrounding Kansas City, however, roundly criticized the expense of the solution in Kansas City, attacked the court-imposed funding formula, and resisted any invitation to join voluntary student exchange arrangements proposed by Kansas City administrators. Five decades after integration began in Kansas City, the school district continued to search for solutions which would win the support of the district's patrons, the state, the federal government, the courts, and the city's suburban neighbors.

CHAPTER 1

Dismantling the Dual System

Implementing the *Brown* Decision in Kansas City, 1954-1960

In the early 1950s, five cases testing the constitutionality of "separate but equal" schools progressed through the nation's judicial hierarchy. The cases originated in Kansas, Delaware, Virginia, South Carolina, and the District of Columbia, and each involved school systems that either required segregated schools by constitutional or statutory mandate, or provided for permissive segregation at the discretion of local school boards. Each case was appealed to the Supreme Court, and the four state cases were heard collectively in 1952 and reargued in 1953 as *Oliver Brown et al. v. Board of Education of Topeka et al.*. Just before one o'clock in the afternoon of May 17, 1954, Earl Warren, Chief Justice of the United States Supreme Court, began to read the unanimous opinion in *Brown*, one of the truly monumental cases in the history of the Court.

"The plaintiffs," the opinion read, "contend that segregated public schools are not 'equal' and cannot be made 'equal,' and that hence they are deprived of the equal protection of the laws." The Court recognized that, "the Negro and white schools involved have been equalized or are being equalized, with respect to buildings, curricula, qualifications and salaries of teachers, and other 'tangible' factors." Therefore, the decision "cannot turn on merely a comparison of these tangible factors in the Negro and white schools involved in each of these cases. We must look instead to the effect of segregation itself on public education." Warren's opinion then posed and answered the central question: "Does segregation of children in public schools solely on the basis of race, even though the physical facilities and other 'tangible' factors may be equal, deprive the children of the minority group of equal educational opportunities? We believe that it does." The Court's reasoning was simple: separating children "of similar age and qualifications solely because of their race generates a feeling of inferiority as to their status in the community that may affect their hearts and minds in a way unlikely ever to be undone." In reaching this conclusion, the Court accepted the legitimacy of Dr. Kenneth Clark's controversial sociological evidence presented by the plaintiffs. Dr. Clark's studies explored the values and qualities black children associated with black and white dolls. The results, Clark concluded, indicated that segregation instilled a feeling of inferiority in black children that scarred the child's self-image and could potentially retard character development. In the closing paragraph the Justices concluded "that in the field of public education the doctrine of 'separate but equal' has no place. Separate educational facilities are inherently unequal." Essentially, the Supreme Court ruled that segregated education violated the black citizens' constitutional right to equal protection of the laws under the Fourteenth Amendment.

By overturning the constitutionality of segregated schools, the Court had radically altered the foundation of school systems in twenty-seven states and the District of Columbia. At the time of the Supreme Court ruling, segregated schools were required by constitutional or statutory provision in seventeen states and Washington, D.C. Ten other states had permissive legislation allowing communities to operate a dual school system if they chose to do so. More than fifty-three million Americans lived in these twenty-seven states; thus about one-third of the nation's population could potentially be affected by the Court's decision. Missouri, and more specifically, the Kansas City school system, were among those affected.

Despite the magnitude and far ranging impact of the decision, the language of the Court's opinion was intentionally vague, non-technical, and short – only fourteen brief paragraphs. Chief Justice Warren had insisted the opinion be accessible and comprehensible to the layman whose life it would influence. In order to secure a unanimous decision, which Warren considered essential, the opinion was semantically bland enough to be acceptable to the conflicting personalities and differing constitutional perspectives represented on the bench. Three of the justices – Hugo Black, Tom Clark and Stanley Reed – were Southerners and may have balked at an opinion which pointed blame too severely at the South. Finally, the Court had no way of knowing what the future of school desegregation law would bring and thus sought to be decidedly non-committal on technical matters, thereby leaving its options open. The most immediate matter before the Court was the formulation of a decree for implementing the decision.

The implementation decree was handed down in May 1955 and bore a striking resemblance to the style and language of the original decision. The decree invested district courts with the authority to determine "whether the action of school authorities constitutes good faith implementation of the governing constitutional principles." Furthermore, it ordered segregated school districts to "make a prompt and reasonable start toward full compliance" with the 1954 decision, and concluded that it was "necessary and proper to admit to public schools on a racially non-discriminatory basis with all deliberate speed the parties to these cases." Again the language was exceedingly vague, and no definitive timeline was established. The Court recognized that local circumstances varied considerably and implementation at the "earliest practicable date" had to be a flexible standard. Having overturned the constitutional legitimacy of separate schools and established a rough set of parameters to govern desegregation, the Supreme Court fell silent on the issue of school desegregation for much of the next decade.

In one respect the 1954 and 1955 *Brown* decisions marked the culmination of more than two decades of NAACP litigation challenging the legitimacy of "separate but equal." On the other hand, the *Brown* decisions marked only the beginning of another protracted series of legal campaigns to define the standards of "all deliberate speed," "earliest practicable date," "good faith implementation," and "compliance." The *Brown* decisions ruled that segregated school systems must be dissolved; however, the Court established no definitive guidelines to assist districts in desegregating their schools. The method and pace of implementing desegregation were to be determined locally. The reactions of the states affected by the ruling ranged from immediate compliance and desegregation to complete intransigence.

Reaction to the *Brown* Decision

As one might have expected, in the Deep South, the *Brown* decision was roundly criticized. Louisiana's legislature reconvened to "take immediate steps to counteract this decision." In Virginia, spurred on by the state's Democratic leader, Senator Harry F. Byrd, Governor Thomas B. Stanley announced: "I shall use every legal means at my command to continue segregated schools," thus beginning that state's campaign of "massive resistance." Georgia Governor Herman Talmadge declared that the ruling "blatantly ignores all law and precedent and usurped from the Congress and the people the power to amend the Constitution, and from the Congress the authority to make the laws of the land." James F. Byrnes, Governor of South Carolina, had vowed prior to the decision: "South Carolina will not now, nor for some years to come, mix white and colored children in our schools." Following the decision Byrnes said he was "shocked that the Court had reversed itself." Such exclamations prompted Walter White of the NAACP, to label Talmadge and Byrnes as "the two most pathetic figures in American life today."

The response outside the Deep South was markedly different. States with permissive segregation codes and relatively small black populations, such as Kansas, rapidly moved to dissolve their dual systems. Indeed, each of these permissive states was engaged in desegregation even before the high court's decision. A few scattered districts in Oklahoma, west

Texas, and Arkansas with small black populations also initiated desegregation plans.

The most meaningful steps toward integration were taken in the border states, particularly in the cities which were hailed as "illuminating pilot operations for Southern cities." On June 3, scarcely two weeks after the initial *Brown* decision, Baltimore's Board of Education voted unanimously to desegregate its schools simply by removing the racial designation from the pupil assignment procedure allowing students to attend the school of their choice. Washington D.C., at the urging of President Eisenhower, launched a comprehensive plan of integration for its 60,000 black students. By November 1954, more than 100 schools in the nation's capital were operating on an integrated basis. Wilmington, Delaware unveiled a three-stage desegregation plan which commenced by integrating the city's elementary schools in September 1954.

"In the Midwestern states (Kansas and Missouri in particular) the decision was to a considerable extent *ex post facto*," one observer wrote, "expressing in terms of law what was already for the most part the general social conviction." Indeed, Missouri officials accepted the Supreme Court decision in a demeanor consistent with that of states having permissive segregation. Missouri Governor Phil M. Donnelly announced immediately after the decision that the state had every intention of complying with the ruling. Furthermore, Donnelly proclaimed he had no inclination to attend the conference of Southern governors, scheduled for June 7 in Richmond, which had been expressly called to discuss the Southern response to the *Brown* decision. Hubert Wheeler, Missouri Commissioner of Education, said that he "had been expecting the ruling for some time." Within one week of the first *Brown* decision, Wheeler was in consultation with Missouri's Attorney General, John M. Dalton, determining the legal status of the state's school system and the possibility of moving toward integrated schools.

The primary legal hurdles in disassembling the dual system in Missouri were the constitutional and statutory provisions requiring segregation in the public schools of the state. Article 9, Section 1 of the state constitution read:

> A general diffusion of knowledge and intelligence being essential to the preservation of the rights and liberties of the people, the general assembly shall establish and maintain free public schools for the gratuitous instruction of all persons in this state within ages not in excess of twenty-one years as prescribed by law. Separate schools shall be provided for white and colored children, except in cases otherwise provided for by law.

There is no record of any legislation enacted under the exception stated in the last sentence. The 1949 revised statutes of the state of Missouri declared, "It shall be unlawful for any colored child to attend any white school, or for any white child to attend a colored school."

While most Missouri school districts awaited word from the state Attorney General regarding the impact of the *Brown* decision, Sam C. Blair, a distinguished Jefferson City circuit court judge, offered his assessment of the ruling. Blair believed "the Missouri constitutional and statutory provisions setting up segregation become a mere shambles under the decision of the high court." State Attorney General Dalton contemplated the legal ramifications of the Supreme Court decision for better than one month before arriving at the same conclusion. On June 30, Dalton dispatched a ten page statement to each school district in the state documenting his assessment of the decision's implications. "It is the opinion of this office," Dalton wrote, "that provisions of the Missouri Constitution and Statutes relating to separate schools 'for white children and colored children' are superseded by the decision of the Supreme Court." He concluded that, "school districts may at the present time permit 'white and colored children' to attend the same school."

Most Missouri towns had small numbers of black students and therefore the decision did not involve any major realignment of the school system. Indeed, fully three-fourths of the state's black population was concentrated in two cities – St. Louis and Kansas City. For some towns maintaining a dual system was a tremendous financial liability. Compliance with the state constitution had required separate facilities, separate teaching staffs, and duplication of instructional materials and resources. In small towns such expenses bordered on prohibitive. For small communities with only a few black students, it had been unreasonable to maintain a separate school. In these circumstances, black students had been transported to nearby cities which maintained black schools. As an example, Grundy County, located in the north central section of the state, provided daily taxi service for its lone black student to attend school some fifty miles away. The county's cost was approximately $1,225 per year. For such towns the *Brown* decision, considered strictly from a financial perspective, was probably greeted with a sigh of relief. In addition, as these towns generally had very small black student populations, accommodating these students in the local schools was unlikely to incite mass anxiety throughout the community.

The St. Louis Board of Education did not wait for the approval of the state Attorney General, announcing its desegregation plan on June 22, 1954. Since more than one-half of the state's black students were enrolled in the St. Louis district, the bold leadership demonstrated by St. Louis was essential to the success of desegregation in Missouri. The St. Louis plan was a graduated scheme to integrate the special schools in September 1954, the high schools in January 1955, and the elementary schools in September 1955. It also provided for integration of the staff to coincide with integration of the student population. The racial composition of the staff was to reflect the racial composition of the student body at each integrated school. Furthermore, preliminary steps were taken to integrate gradually the administrative posts in the district. The prompt action in St. Louis was made possible by ten years of studying population trends and facility use in the district in preparation for an order to desegregate.

Virtually all other major cities in Missouri made plans to integrate their schools by September 1955. The solutions were typically to redraw attendance zones without racial bias or to adopt a plan which gave students the option to attend their school of choice. Within one year of the 1954 *Brown* decision, an observer wrote: "Integration in Missouri schools became an actuality with an attitude showing unanimity in thinking among school officials in accordance with the May 17 decision." Another source reported that "[I]ntegration in some form has begun on a voluntary basis in every section of the state." In *Time Magazine*'s September 1955 "Report Card" on school desegregation, Missouri was the only state to receive a grade of "A." Only in the southeast section of the state, the "Bootheel," did the practice of segregated schools persist as a rule. This rural section of the state bordered on Arkansas, Tennessee, and Kentucky, and was culturally much more akin to the old South than were of other sections of Missouri. Thus, it is not surprising that the "Bootheel" would resist desegregation.

The *Brown* Decisions and Kansas City

In Kansas City, the subject of school desegregation was not entirely foreign to district officials. In 1952, Harold Holliday, the leading African-American attorney in Kansas City, pleading for some relief from the gross overcrowding in the segregated black elementary schools, described segregated schools as "completely indefensible" and "in violation of the basic law of the land," and urged the school board to consider dissolving its dual school system. A year later, Anthony P. Nugent of the Kansas City Urban League came before the board to discuss half-day sessions at two black and three white elementary schools. He asked in the event of an emergency, such as a fire at an elementary school, "would it be within the discretion of the School Board to place Negro children in white schools in order to comply with the statutory requirements that educational facilities for Negroes should be substantially equal to those provided children in general?" Of course, the school board opted not to mix the schools, but on both occasions it did seek legal advice on the issue.

News of the initial *Brown* decision sparked more than casual interest in Kansas City. The afternoon edition of the *Kansas City Star* ran four front-page articles devoted to the high court's ruling on May 17, 1954. Like St. Louis, Kansas City had a substantial black population and the school district's response to the ruling would have significant impact on thousands of children. "We are very much gratified by the ruling," said Carl Johnson of the Kansas City NAACP. "We hope and believe the American people will accept the ruling in good faith." School board president Ray Joslyn, speaking in an unofficial capacity, told the *Star*: "Naturally we will abide by the law. We will do whatever the law says we should do."

The first official statement of the Kansas City school board came on May 20, just three days after the decision. After some general discussion, the board members moved to secure legal advice regarding the implications of the ruling. More importantly, the official position of the school board included a directive charging administrative officers of the school district "to start preparing plans for consideration by the Board of Directors to implement said decision." Kansas City would be in the vanguard of school desegregation, and the district's research department immediately began "to anticipate and evaluate the extensive array of changes that would have to be made to effect a desegregated school system."

On May 23, superintendents from five surrounding districts met in Kansas City to discuss the creation of integrated school systems. For the Kansas City schools, the meeting had a secondary purpose. The district sought to amend its long-standing policy of accepting tuition students from surrounding districts. The majority of the tuition students were black high school or junior high students not accommodated in their home district; fewer than a dozen were elementary age. The tuition students came from school districts near Kansas City which did not provide a secondary education for their African American students. In these school districts, the additional expenses commensurate with building and maintaining a segregated secondary school made it more economical to have the students educated in Kansas City's schools. Eight neighboring districts paid $750 for each student from their community matriculating in Kansas City. Although the policy could be considered mutually beneficial for all those involved, it had become burdensome in recent years. The rising enrollments at Kansas City's black high school, Lincoln, and its black junior high, R.T. Coles, were exacerbated by admitting tuition students. In February 1954, due to anticipated enrollment at Lincoln, Kansas City had been forced to deny all non-residents' requests for admission to the black schools.

As Kansas City prepared for desegregation, the status of non-resident tuition students had to be resolved. Although Superintendent Mark Bills did not terminate the policy of accepting tuition students, he explained that the district would no longer bear the responsibility of educating *all* of the black students in the surrounding communities. The neighboring districts were made accountable for educating their own black students.

As school officials in Kansas City contemplated the next steps, representatives from the black community came forward to offer assistance in formulating a policy for desegregation. At the June 3 board meeting, Lewis Clymer, representing the Education Committee of the Kansas City Urban League, offered "our experience and assistance in this important planning." Lee Reader, chairman of the Commission on Human Relations, appeared at the same meeting to discuss the results of a survey conducted by his office assessing attitudes toward integration. Reader concluded that, among students, those at the high school level were least receptive to the prospect of desegregated schools. His survey had also revealed some dissatisfaction among teachers at a few of the schools, especially those which would likely be receiving substantial numbers of black students. Reader further concluded that certain residential areas in the city were opposed to integration, particularly those neighborhoods which could potentially be affected by a change in school policy. He went on to make several suggestions which he maintained could be crucial in facilitating a smooth transition to integrated schools. Like Clymer, Reader offered the services of his office and staff in working with the school district on the transition policy for desegregation. Both men would ultimately be disappointed by the process through which the desegregation plans were formulated. Despite the offers of assistance, school officials would craft the plans for desegregation without consulting anyone outside of the district's central administration. This posture toward policy making, especially as it involved issues of race, became characteristic of the school district for the next twenty years.

In special session on June 11, 1954, the Kansas City school board approved a plan to desegregate summer school classes scheduled to begin the following Monday. For the first time in the district's history, black and white pupils would study together in Kansas City's public schools. Desegregating summer school classes was a small but symbolic act. Summer school classes were offered at only two high schools, Lincoln and Westport, and district officials were fully aware that the vast majority of the 101 black students enrolled would attend Lincoln because it was nearer their homes. Indeed, only three black students enrolled in summer school at Westport. The significance of the announcement lay in its indication of the board's commitment to move forward in dissolving one element of the dual system less than a month after the *Brown* decision.

Leaders in the black community, however, were not prepared to accept token gestures. Aware of the revolutionary steps taken in Baltimore, Washington D.C., and St. Louis, they sought an equally bold announcement from the Kansas City school board. On July 1, 1954, Lewis Clymer again appeared before the board members to present an outline of policy measures the Urban League believed were reasonable in any forthcoming plan for desegregation. He urged that attendance zones for schools be redrawn on the basis of geographic and building capacity criteria, and proposed integration of all school activities, reassignment of the teaching staff, and integration of the junior college. Clymer's comments revealed the growing impatience of the black community. He insisted, "I know the board is busy and this is a problem that requires a lot of thinking, but it is urgent that the board make some clear initial announcement soon." Although the school board took no action on the recommendations, one school board member assured Clymer that "Dr. Bills has this matter under consideration and I'm sure his staff is hard at work on it."

Lewis Clymer and others waited almost a month before the school district issued its next official announcement regarding desegregation. During the interim, the district's research department prepared its "Study of the Problems Involved in the Desegregation of the Public Schools of Kansas City, Missouri." The study presented the department's conclusions regarding five proposed plans for desegregation. The only significant differences among the five plans were the proposed timetables involved. The most radical plan provided for immediate desegregation at every level of the system, while the most conservative plan postponed any action on desegregation until the United States Supreme Court brought forth a directive delineating specific steps toward implementation of the decision. The bulk of the study was devoted to analyzing three plans of gradual desegregation – all of which provided for the completion of integration at each level of the school system by September 1955. The study grappled with considerations of enrollments, building capacities, and modifications to the existing attendance zones concomitant with desegregation.

The school board debated the merits of the proposed plans for two weeks before unveiling its decision to a small crowd of interested citizens at its July 29 meeting. The resolution set forth a two-stage process: the junior college and vocational schools would be integrated in September 1954, and the district's attendance zones would be redefined to facilitate desegregation of the elementary and secondary schools the following September. The plan was adopted by a vote of five to one. Mrs. Henry I. Eager cast the lone dissenting voice, arguing, "We should integrate first the high schools and then the elementary schools. It shouldn't be done all at one time and we shouldn't commit ourselves to certain dates." Carl Johnson, representing the Kansas City NAACP at the school board meeting, expressed precisely the opposite assessment of the timeline. Johnson felt desegregation should take place "as soon as possible" and the timetable would serve only to slow the process. In defense of the adopted timeline, Dr. Bills maintained that, "If integration were to become effective immediately, 47 percent of all Negro students would be in different schools from those they now attend." That, he argued, "means a lot of changes must be made in teaching assignments. If it just meant moving that many students, it would still be a terrific job."

The July 29 resolution established a clear timetable for the district's desegregation. The initial steps were simple enough. The faculties, resources, and records of black students at Lincoln Junior College were transferred to Kansas City Junior College during the summer. In August, each student received a letter from Miles G. Blim, dean of Kansas City Junior College, detailing enrollment procedures, curricular offerings, counseling, and other services. In the fall of 1954, about eighty black students who had previously attended Lincoln Junior College were integrated into the formerly all-white college.

The integration of the vocational school was accomplished with similar ease. Prior to integration, the vocational department for black students had been housed in R. T. Coles Junior High School; white students were served at Manual High School. The school district opted to combine the two departments at one of the schools. The logical choice was to use the facilities at Manual: it had adequate space to accommodate the 800 or so black vocational students. Conversely, R. T. Coles was already burdened with serious overcrowding and the addition of some 300 white vocational students would have aggravated the situation. A secondary advantage to integrating Manual was that a number of vacant classrooms would become available at Coles allowing the district to transfer seventh grade students from crowded black elementary schools to the junior high. Having weighed the advantages, the school district opted to integrate Manual, while R. T. Coles became strictly a junior high school. During the summer, the district transferred equipment, records, and faculty from Coles to Manual, and in September the vocational department opened with black students constituting just less than one-half of Manual's enrollment.

Developing a Desegregation Plan

Determining exactly how to achieve integration in the district as a whole presented a much more complex problem for school officials. The district's preliminary plan of July 29 indicated desegregation would be accomplished through dissolution of the two separate sets of lines defining attendance zones, one for black schools and one for whites, and the creation of a single set of zones based on the city's geography. The difficulty lay in the fact that the black attendance zones, being much larger, overlapped several of the white zones. Many blacks lived considerably closer to a white school, but in the segregated system they had been prohibited by law from attending white schools. For a significant number of white children the converse was true; they lived closer to a black school. In dissolving the separate attendance zones, thousands of children would find themselves living within the boundaries of schools other than the one they had previously attended.

The task of evaluating the massive volume of data to be considered in determining the new attendance zones fell to the research department. The enrollments and building capacities of the district's sixty-two white and fourteen black elementary schools had to be re-evaluated with the objective of operating each school at 85 percent of its capacity. Ideally, each school would be within walking distance for its students, defined as three-quarters of a mile radius around a school. In addition, district officials had to be cognizant of the staff and resources available at each building. For example, some schools served kindergarten through sixth grade; others went as high as the eighth grade, while still others had combination rooms which served children in different grade levels.

Major revisions of the secondary school attendance zones were also required. In 1954, all of the city's black students at the secondary level attended either Lincoln High School or R. T. Coles Junior High. White students were divided among seven high schools and three junior highs. The same considerations of enrollment, building capacity, staffing, and resources that influenced the redefinition of elementary school attendance zones applied to the secondary schools.

The research department compiled and analyzed its data throughout the summer and fall of 1954. Their task was simplified to some extent by the understanding that large sections of the city had few or no black residents. The student populations in those areas would be unaffected by desegregation and the attendance zones in those areas would not require alteration. According to the information compiled by the research department, thirty-three of the seventy-six elementary schools in Kansas City had no black students living within their attendance zones. In addition, sixteen schools had fewer than ten black students residing in their area, and the research department determined there was no reason to alter the feeder zones for these schools. Similarly, five of the thirteen secondary school zones required no significant change. Three high schools were projected to have no black students, while two others would have fewer than twenty-five.

The bulk of the research department's work focused on the remaining twenty-seven elementary schools and eight secondary schools whose racial composition would change with desegregation. In order to assist the research department in making its determinations regarding the attendance zones alterations, the district acquired large section maps of the city to plot student residences. As desegregation would have marginal impact in many areas of the city, it was not necessary to plot each student's residence, only those living in areas which would be affected by the plan. Using a system of color-coded dots, secretaries and additional clerical workers plotted the residences of some 25,000 students. Different colored dots were used to signify each student's race and grade level. By the time the research department was finished, the maps were both colorful and rather confusing.

Having the student residences plotted on maps, research department personnel set out to redraw the attendance zones bearing in mind the capacity of each school and other variables previously mentioned. The process was long and tedious, involving the counting of thousands of dots and penciling in boundaries which were likely to demand further alteration when the zones of adjacent schools were considered. The process of determining the new attendance zones and projecting the anticipated enrollments after desegregation consumed the research department for the remainder of 1954.

The last official word on desegregation in 1954 was the school board plan announced on July 29. From that point forward district officials were silent about any further developments regarding the evolving plan for integration. Although it was understood that the district's central administration was at work formulating a policy for transition, Kansas City's African-American community, and the city's civil right groups were growing impatient. More than six months passed without any word from the school board regarding a final, detailed plan for integration. Early in 1955, a coalition of black advocacy organizations led by Thomas Webster of the Kansas City Urban League contacted the school board requesting a meeting "to discuss the plans for desegregation of our schools."

As they had done in formulating the preliminary time line announced on July 29, school officials had not consulted any outside organization in developing the new attendance zones or the policy governing the transition. Indeed, the school board had consciously excluded outside organizations from the process. Technically, this was not improper. The school board alone was empowered by the state to "make all needful rules and regulations for the organization, grading and government of schools in the district." Nevertheless, civil rights groups which expected some consultation, or at least progress reports from the school board, held rather different views of the board's responsibility. Black community leaders fully expected their advice and expertise to be considered in a school board decision with such sweeping social ramifications. Lewis Clymer had made this clear as early as May 25, 1954, when he wrote to the school board: "We feel that you will need and deserve all the help that you can get from the leaders of the city in arriving at wise decisions." The school board, however, felt little compulsion to consult with any outside party in formulating district policy.

This fundamental difference would continually plague the school board for much of the first ten years of school desegregation in Kansas City. Clearly, school officials viewed these decisions as the domain of the district alone, and in February 1955 postponed meeting with the black advocacy groups "until the Board is further along in the development of plans." Judging from the school board's reply, one may have assumed that the plan was still in an embryonic state. This was not the case. Within one month the school board officially unveiled the transition plan in its final form.

By mid-February, the superintendent's office had completed the final version of the policy for integrating the schools. The one remaining step was to secure the approval of the school board. The 34-page proposed policy discussed the legal bases for the plan, described the new attendance zones based on the city's geography, included maps of the elementary and secondary zones, and set forth in detail the liberal transfer policy for those students who wished to attend a school other than the one serving their neighborhood. The school board met in an informal special session February 22 to examine the superintendent's proposed plan. The plan was received favorably and forwarded to the district's legal council. The following day, Robert Eastin, one of the district's attorneys, addressed his legal assessment to Superintendent Bills. Eastin's evaluation of the policy was generally favorable as well. Noting that the *Brown* decision only required that the dual system be dissolved, he concluded the district's plan clearly met the standard established by the Court. The attorney, however, expressed reservations regarding one part of the plan – the transfer policy.

The proposed plan for integration had retained the "long standing policy of granting requests for pupils to attend school outside the attendance area in which they live." The official language of the policy provided for "the liberal issue of District transfers when requested in good faith and when building facilities permit." The district had a three-tiered classification of schools in order to regulate the transfer policy. Schools that were at or above capacity were classified as "closed" and no transfers into these schools were to be issued. Those schools within one class unit (thirty-two students) of capacity were termed "critical" and specific reasons had to be verified in obtaining a transfer. All other schools were classified as "open" and a much less rigid standard of verification applied in securing a transfer. The acceptable reasons for requesting transfer included: to complete their final year at a school; to avoid hazardous traffic conditions; to accommodate families in situations where the child went to the parent's place of employment after school; and to afford convenience to parents whose children went to daycare after school. Reasons of health were also valid considerations for transfer.

In Eastin's estimation, "great care must be taken in handling transfers." He urged that, "it must not be used for the purpose of discrimination. Two things must be avoided: (a) forcing a pupil, resident in a district, to make a transfer, and (b) giving any preference to pupils of either race in connection with transfers." He had no objection to a transfer policy administered with equity. His primary concern focused on assuring that no student of either race received preferential treatment when applying for transfer. To this end, the school district opted not to request the student's race on the application for transfer form, each request would be judged on its own merit.

In a certain sense, Eastin's reservations regarding the awarding of transfers proved to be prophetic. Nevertheless, the school district's difficulties concerning transfers would not evolve from either of the problem areas identified by Eastin; indeed, the policy would be applied in an equitable fashion. Transfers would, however, be used as the primary vehicle by which the white population eluded integration.

The transition policy became official at the school board meeting of March 3, 1955. The board's unanimous approval of the policy garnered front-page attention in the *Kansas City Star* under the headline "Board of Education Takes Final Steps to End Segregation Here." A lengthy column described the policy in detail and the *Star* ran full page maps of the new elementary and secondary school zones. School board member John Gregory applauded the "outstanding job" done by the superintendent's office in working out the plan, and commented, "I don't see how it could have been any fairer."

The school administrators understood that in order to be effective the policy had to gain the acceptance of the school district's patrons. In order to promote this end, the superintendent and board members took several different tacks. The policy "is not a mandate," proclaimed Superintendent Bills. "It is an invitation and a challenge to people of good will, high moral purpose and dedicated religious motivations." School board president Homer Wadsworth put it in slightly different terms: "This is really a matter which gives all of us as citizens an opportunity to apply democracy all through the school system. The business of democracy comes down to being a good neighbor." Mrs. Ellsworth Haas, another school board member, reassured parents that children make adjustments "readily" and likely would be comfortable with the transition more quickly than parents or teachers. These overtures to the parents provide some insight into the nature of race relations in Kansas City in 1955.

Anticipating some resistance to change, the school board and superintendent justified the policy on higher moral, ethical, and legal grounds. If parents were not convinced by Mrs. Haas's reassuring comments or Mr. Gregory's statement concerning the fairness of the policy, then perhaps they would respond to moral or democratic appeals. District officials apparently expected some opposition, but none materialized and the school district commenced preparations for integration in the fall.

During the spring and summer, copies of the transition plan were distributed across the city informing the district's patrons of the new policies. Anticipated enrollments at four elementary schools necessitated the adoption of half-day schedules pending the completion of additions or new construction in those zones. The school board authorized the assignment of additional teaching personnel and temporary clerical help at twenty-two schools in expectation of some confusion at these schools "due to changed boundary lines and other problems incident to the elimination of segregation." In addition, school principals were asked to review the new boundaries for their schools and report on whether the lines were reasonable and functional. It became apparent that, in its zeal to match enrollments to building capacities, the research department had made a few ill-advised decisions. In two instances, the new lines violated the principle that, whenever possible, elementary school attendance zones should not cross a major thoroughfare which could pose a hazard for children walking to school. In another, more humorous case, the research department drew the line separating the attendance zones of E. F. Swinney School and E. C. White School down the middle of a hallway in an apartment building. Students living on one side of the hall were to attend Swinney, while children living on the opposite side were assigned to White. Obviously, there would have been considerable confusion in that particular building when school opened in September 1955. Fortunately, in each case school principals brought these errors to the attention of the superintendent and the zones were amended to rectify the problems.

One final, major obstacle remained for the school district during the summer of 1955: appointing a new superintendent to replace Dr. Bills, whose contract was not renewed by the school board. Although Bills was undeniably popular with the district's faculty, staff and patrons, a rift between the school board and the superintendent had developed. In February 1954, with more than a year remaining on his contract, Bills had resigned unexpectedly arguing that members of the school board were undermining his authority. The superintendent was persuaded to withdraw his resignation, but his relationship with the board remained strained, and when the time came to renew his contract in May 1955, three board members refused to approve Bills.

The school board debated its options for more than a month before deciding on James A. Hazlett as Dr. Bills's successor. Hazlett was a logical choice for the position. During his seventeen years of service in the Kansas City school district, Hazlett had served as a teacher, principal, and most recently as director of the research department. His work in the research department had uniquely qualified Hazlett to oversee the critical early stages of desegregation. He was arguably the most informed expert on the district's plan for integration, and at this critical juncture in the process, Hazlett's understanding of the situation was a paramount consideration in his appointment as superintendent. Two weeks after Hazlett accepted the post of superintendent, integrated schools became a reality in the city.

Impact of the 1955 Desegregation Plan

For the first time in the district's 88-year history, Kansas City's public schools opened on an integrated basis on September 7, 1955. The editor of the *Kansas City Call*, a widely circulated black weekly, wrote that not a "ripple of difficulty" accompanied the transition. One week later, Superintendent Hazlett delivered the first of what would become annual progress reports on desegregation. "There has been a smooth and effective transition into an integrated school system," the superintendent said, and he proudly announced, "Out of 78 elementary schools, 33 are integrated; and out of 14 secondary schools, 11 are integrated." Two high schools, one junior high, and forty elementary schools remained exclusively white. Five elementary schools were 100% African-American.

On the surface, Hazlett's announcement was impressive: black and white students were studying together in nearly one-half of the district's schools. Those figures, however, were misleading and belied the notion that mass integration was occurring in Kansas City. Several of the schools Hazlett described as "integrated" might more accurately be described as having only token integration. Ten schools which were predominantly white and five schools that were majority black enrolled fewer than a dozen students of the other race. A total of twelve schools, eight majority white and four majority black, had enrolled fewer than five students of the other race. Six of the schools Hazlett listed as integrated had enrolled exactly one student of the minority race. Of Kansas City's ninety-two schools, sixty-five remained 90% or more white and thirteen remained 90% or more black. Indeed, fully 70% of the district's 11,625 black students remained in schools which were 90% or more black. Moreover, 3,335 of those students, or about 28%, were enrolled in schools which remained all-black.

In short, Kansas City schools remained largely segregated. It is important to bear in mind, however, that in order to satisfy the legal standard defined in the *Brown* decisions, a school district was required merely to dissolve the former system of segregation and provide for assignment of students on a non-discriminatory basis. Thus, Kansas City was in full compliance with the Supreme Court's directive. Above all, the plan demonstrated the limitations of geographically defined attendance zones in a city with rigidly segregated residential areas. Moreover, this segregated residential pattern was not unique to Kansas City. Virtually every major city in the country demonstrated similar patterns of residential segregation. Furthermore, if each of these cities used geographically determined attendance zones, which was the common practice, then all would demonstrate common patterns of school segregation as well.

The residential pattern in Kansas City assured that regardless of how the attendance zones were drawn, several areas of the city would retain their exclusive racial quality. With the exception of three small black enclaves, the entire southern half of Kansas City remained virtually all white. The same was true of the large areas to the north and east of the primary black neighborhood. The overwhelming majority of the black population was concentrated in the area east of downtown and the new geographically determined attendance areas had very little impact on the racial composition of the schools which served this area. In 1955, there were 8,354 black elementary students in the Kansas City school district; of that number, 5,673 attended nine former black schools which served the central black area. Blacks comprised 98% of the total enrollment for these nine central schools. Four of the elementary schools which remained exclusively black in 1955 – Attucks, Phillips, Booker T. Washington, and Yates – were located in the heart of this neighborhood. Not only did geographically determined zones have no impact on these schools in 1955, the racial composition of these schools remained unchanged for the next twenty years. Attucks and Yates remained between 99% and 100% black until the mid-seventies, Phillips enrolled its first white student in 1974, and only four white students enrolled in Booker T. Washington before the school was closed in 1976.

Dunbar, the other school which remained all black in 1955, served a small black enclave on the eastern rim of the city. At a glance, the situation at Dunbar appears to be a clear example of the school district gerrymandering the attendance zone to perpetuate the segregation of black students in that neighborhood. Indeed, the research department had projected Dunbar to be 100% black. Moreover, while Dunbar remained exclusively black, the four schools whose zones bordered on Dunbar enrolled just twelve black students among nearly 2,000 white children.

It is unlikely, however, that the district intentionally organized Dunbar as an all-black school. First, Dunbar was a small school enrolling only 265 students, thus requiring that the area it served would necessarily be one of the smaller zones. In addition, Dunbar School was located almost precisely in the center of a rigidly segregated black residential section comprised of about thirty city blocks. Furthermore, the streets which formed the boundary of Dunbar's attendance zone were major thoroughfares, and whenever possible the district preferred not to create zones which crossed heavily traveled roads. These factors considered, it was not unreasonable for the district to assign the students in that neighborhood to Dunbar.

Due to the rigid patterns of residential segregation existing in Kansas City, meaningful desegregation was achieved only in those schools where attendance zones included isolated black neighborhoods with surrounding whites, or incorporated the transitional areas which separated black neighborhoods from white sections. Residential patterns, above any other single factor, determined whether Kansas City's plan for integration actually desegregated the schools.

By the 1950s, the black population in Kansas City had been growing steadily for more than four decades, and by 1955 numbered almost 60,000. More than three-fourths of those residents lived in the large black neighborhood east of the downtown area, and it was in this area that growth had been most accelerated and population pressures were most severe in the 1950s. In this exclusively black neighborhood crowding was a chronic problem, both in terms of housing and in the schools serving the area.

As the black population in the central neighborhood grew, it tended to expand into white residential areas bordering the predominantly black areas. The initial foothold was typically established by a small group of black home buyers who moved into the white neighborhood. Such a move was possible because the restrictive covenants many residential areas had previously relied upon to retain the all-white character of their neighborhood were ruled unconstitutional by the Supreme Court in the 1948 case, *Shelley v. Kraemer*. Prior to 1948 it was common for white homeowners and their neighbors to sign a restrictive covenant, prohibiting the sale of property in that neighborhood to blacks. Filed with the County Clerk or Registrar of Deeds, the document was legally binding, typically for a term of twenty-five to ninety-nine years, as specified in the agreement. Of course, the Court's decision in *Shelley v. Kraemer* did not end residential segregation; however, binding legal agreements were no longer constitutionally acceptable. The decision forced any such agreement to be an informal arrangement among neighbors, precisely the type of agreement that neighbors violated if they experienced difficulty attracting white home buyers. Thus, it was possible for blacks to gain a foothold in some of the white neighborhoods surrounding the concentrated black area.

The initial movement prompted some white home owners in the area to sell their property fearing that the presence of black residents in the neighborhood would devaluate the property. The process then often accelerated. More vacated homes were then sold to black families for two reasons: some blacks were anxious to move into the neighborhood and, fewer prospective white buyers emerged because of the popular perception that the neighborhood was destined to become mostly black. For a time, the neighborhood would be substantially integrated; however, it was generally far from stable. The typical pattern exhibited a steady exodus of white residents culminating in a new, largely black neighborhood.

In 1955 and in the years that followed, residential turnover continued at varying speeds in the areas bordering the central black neighborhood. To the north, residential patterns had stabilized by 1955 and, for the most part, remained relatively stable throughout the 1960s. In this area, three schools – Karnes, Humboldt, and Woodland – received substantial numbers of black students following the reorganization of the district's attendance zones while two other schools, Garrison and Garfield, received smaller percentages. The 1950 census revealed almost 7,000 black residents lived in the area served by these five schools; however, rigid residential segregation concentrated 86% of that black population within the new boundaries for Karnes, Humboldt, and Woodland. In 1955, the enrollment at Karnes was 18% black, Humboldt was 20% black, and Woodland was 23% black.

Judging from previous trends in neighborhood transition, one might have expected these three schools to transform rapidly into predominantly black institutions. But this simply did not occur. At Karnes, the black student population steadily declined and by 1960 stood at only 7%. The black enrollment at Woodland demonstrated a slow growth pattern rising from 23% in 1955 to 34% in 1960. Enrollment at Humboldt fluctuated yearly, but the percentage of black students never rose higher than 28%, nor fell below 12% until the school was converted to serve special education students in 1967.

It is impossible to determine exactly what forces produced the high degree of residential stability in the area north of the central black district. Residents certainly considered a myriad of factors prior to making a decision to move or remain. However, one major characteristic appears most prominently: median incomes for the census tracts in this area were between $2,050 and $2,450 lower than the average income of $5,799 for the city as a whole. In other words, it seems likely that residents remained in this section of the city because they lacked the means to move elsewhere. During the 1960s, however, one dramatic change did occur in this area, as the relative stability in the Woodland area collapsed and the percentage of black students grew markedly. A major catalyst in this turnover was the completion of the Wayne Minor public housing project within the Woodland zone during the 1962-63 school year. By 1965, Woodland's enrollment was 90% black.

In the area to the west of the large central black neighborhood the desegregation plan had a similarly minimal effect. The process of residential transition was reasonably static, allowing meaningful, stable integration to occur in five of the area's schools from 1955-1965. The black population on Kansas City's west side was largely confined to three segregated neighborhoods near the Kansas-Missouri state line. Each of these areas was small, fewer than twenty predominantly black blocks, and was isolated from the central black area.

Prior to integration, black elementary students on the west side were educated at Penn and Douglass schools. Penn served a very small black neighborhood of about a dozen city blocks and in 1954 enrolled only eighty-seven students. Penn was closed in the district's desegregation plan, and its enrollment was absorbed into a nearby formerly white school, Allen. The enrollment percentages at Allen testify to the stability of the residential pattern in this area. In 1955, Allen's enrollment was 24% black, and for the next six years remained between 25% and 30% black. Although the African-American enrollment at Allen grew during the 1960s, it never became a majority black school.

The stable residential quality of the Douglass attendance zone also facilitated meaningful, long-term integration. Prior to integration in 1955, Douglass had served the majority of the black elementary school population on the west side, enrolling almost 400 students. The desegregation plan provided for Douglass and Lowell, a former segregated white school, to share an attendance zone and gave students the option to attend the school of their choice.

The school district's decision to create an option zone was based on several considerations. The schools were only two blocks apart, and both were needed to accommodate the anticipated enrollment; furthermore, the Douglass-Lowell zone could serve as a test case of sorts for future combinations. The facilities at the two schools were comparable; thus, there was no reason for the research department to predict that one school would attract whites, while the other might appeal to black students. Given the racial composition of the area, enrollment at both schools was projected to be about 36% black.

During the first two years of its operation, the option plan could scarcely have been more disappointing. In 1955, Douglass enrolled only one white student, while only thirteen black students opted to enter Lowell. The two schools remained highly segregated in 1956: Douglass was 98.7% black, Lowell 98.8% white. The school district abandoned the plan in 1957 and closed Lowell, leaving Douglass to serve the area. Significant integration began immediately. From 1957 to 1967, black students comprised 32% to 39% of Douglass's enrollment each year.

The residential stability on the west side of the city is probably best illustrated by the racial characteristics of West Junior High. Being a secondary school, West Junior High drew from several elementary schools on the upper west side of Kansas City and thus provided insight to the residential stability of a much larger area. During the first ten years of integration, black students comprised no less than 12% and no more than 18% of the student population at West in any given year.

The degree of stability in the area west of the central black neighborhood may be attributed to two factors. First, as was true in the area north of downtown, the residents on the west side were among the poorest in the city. The median income for Kansas City as a whole was more than $1,000 above the median income for west side residents. Thus, a significant number of residents may have been financially unable to move. A second factor might well have been that the black neighborhoods in this area were relatively small and to a large degree isolated. A major population surge among blacks, creating pressures which spurred residential transition in other sections of the city, never materialized in these small black enclaves.

The situation in the area east of downtown was, however, a different matter. The process of residential transition was nearly complete in the Yeager and Greenwood areas, both of which had been largely absorbed into the growing, central African-American residential area prior to integration. The 1950 census indicated that the Greenwood neighborhood was less than 10% black, while the Yeager area was about 25% black. At that time, the white population had been sufficient to justify retaining the two schools for white occupancy only; however, the white enrollment in both areas was declining prior to desegregation.

In 1952, there were six vacant classrooms at Greenwood, while Yeager was operating at less than half capacity. More importantly, white residents accounted for only 56% of the population in the Yeager neighborhood. Two years later, even after absorbing white students displaced by the conversion of Benton School to black occupancy, both Yeager and Greenwood were operating at more than 200 students below capacity. By the time that the district desegregated in 1955, the process of residential transition was very nearly complete. Both schools opened in September 1955 with enrollments of more than 70% black. Four years later, only six whites enrolled at Greenwood while nearly 900 black students attended the school. The situation at Yeager was similar; by 1959; the school was more than 90% black and averaged an enrollment of 97% black until closing in 1972.

At the time of desegregation, residential turnover was just beginning in the areas served by the next tier of schools further to the east: Ashland, Kensington and Moore. The 1950 census revealed that these neighborhoods were virtually all white and the racial composition had changed little by 1955. The research department projected Ashland would receive no black students in the first year of integration while Moore was projected to be 2% black, and Kensington about 10% black. Following the shift to integrated schools in 1955, Kensington demonstrated the greatest degree of residential stability. The black enrollment there hovered within three percentage points of 10% for the first fifteen years of desegregation. Initially, the Ashland zone appeared to be a neighborhood destined for residential transition. The black enrollment steadily grew, rising to more than 20% by 1959. In the early 1960s, however, the rate of turnover stabilized and Ashland's black enrollment fluctuated between 21% and 27% for the remainder of the decade. By the mid-sixties, Kensington and Ashland were stable, integrated schools. Moore, in contrast, underwent a complete turnover.

In 1955, 98% of Moore's 518 students were white but the residential stability of the area was beginning to fracture. The black enrollment at Moore grew steadily over the first ten years of desegregation, generally adding between twenty and fifty black students and losing a comparable number of white students each year. By 1958, Moore was one-quarter black. It became a black majority school in 1961, and was nearly 80% black by 1966. Situated between the all-black Dunbar district to the southeast and the rapidly transforming Greenwood district to the northwest, the Moore district was a crossroads of gradual residential change over the first ten years of integrated schooling.

The largest path of migration from the central black district was to the south, and the Moore area was at the eastern edge of that migratory corridor. Although the residential transition occurring in the Moore zone was certainly part of the larger southern migration, the slow, even pace of transition in the Moore area stood in stark contrast to the rapid pace of residential turnover occurring directly south of the central black neighborhood.

Desegregation and Residential Transition

In 1950, Linwood Boulevard was the line which separated the predominantly black section to the north from the white area to the south. According to the census, just over one percent of the population south of Linwood Boulevard in 1950 was black. Of the fifty census tract areas located to the south of the boulevard, blacks comprised ten percent or more of the population in only three tracts; and none of those three tracts were as much as 25% black. During the fifties, however, the rigid line of residential segregation which had confined blacks to areas north of Linwood Boulevard faded, and the process of residential turnover steadily accelerated in the years following desegregation, eventually assuming dimensions that bordered on panic.

In the decade separating the 1950 and 1960 censuses, the black population south of Linwood Boulevard grew by almost 25,000 residents. The 1960 census revealed that more than 12% of the population south of Linwood was black. Eleven census tracts were ten percent or more black; five tracts were majority black. As might be expected, the tract areas undergoing transition were those nearest to the central black neighborhood. The seven tracts directly to the south of the large black area were 64% black by the 1960 census count.

The research department's projections for school enrollments indicate that as late as 1955, Linwood Boulevard had remained a rigid barrier to residential transition. For example, the boundary separating the attendance zones for Sanford B. Ladd School and D. A. Holmes School was Linwood Boulevard. Students living north of the boulevard were to attend D.A. Holmes, while those living to the south of the boulevard were assigned to Ladd. The research department projected the enrollment at Holmes to be 84% black, while Ladd was expected to remain exclusively white. In the nine-month interim between the research department's projections and the opening of integrated schools in September, the process of residential transition began in the Ladd area. Ladd's enrollment was 5% black in 1955 and it increased rapidly over the next four years. In 1956, Ladd was 29% black. The following year the percentage climbed to 59% black, then 81% in 1958, 97% in 1959, and 99% by 1960.

Ladd was the first, but not the only school south of the central black neighborhood to undergo such a rapid and near total transformation. In 1956, Horace Mann School welcomed its first black students, thirteen in all. Five years later, there were 982 black students at Mann, comprising 92% of the enrollment. Like Mann, Seven Oaks Elementary also received its first black students in 1956. That year eleven blacks enrolled at Seven Oaks. Five years later there were 543 black students at the school.

As the black population continued to move south, the pattern of residential turnover repeated itself with equal rapidity and thoroughness in one neighborhood after another. Within eleven years of the decision to desegregate, about 8.25 square miles to the south of the central black neighborhood were transformed from predominantly white to majority black. Fourteen schools to the south of the large central black neighborhood were majority black by 1966; nine of which had enrollments of greater than 85% black. Of these fourteen schools, seven had enrolled no black students in 1955.

By the mid-1960s it was apparent that, owing to the residential patterns in Kansas City, a substantial number of schools would rapidly complete a cycle of segregation-integration-resegregation. This cycle of turnover was especially apparent along the corridor of black migration to the south, and the process of residential transition showed no sign of slowing during the sixties. The 1970 census indicated the black population south of Linwood Boulevard had grown by more than 42,000 residents during the 1960s, while the white population had declined by about 18,000. A total of seventeen census tracts were majority black, six were more than 90% black.

Conclusions

District officials had never envisioned integration at all of Kansas City's schools. The research department's studies based on residential information had projected mixed enrollments at only forty of the district's ninety-two schools. The accuracy of these projections was apparent in the nearly flawless prediction of enrollments for those areas of the city that were affected little by residential integration. However, the margin of error was fairly substantial in those areas closest to residential transition neighborhoods. In those areas, the fallibility of the projections revealed the research department's inability to account for transfers or changes in residence between the time of the projection and the opening of school. Nowhere was this more apparent than in those schools which were formerly all-black.

A significant number of white students lived closer to schools that had previously been segregated for blacks than to the nearest white school. Thus, when the district's attendance zones were redefined, hundreds of whites were assigned to schools which had previously been all black. The research department's projections based on students' places of residence in January 1955 indicated five formerly segregated black schools would have enrollments that were 10% or more white. However, when school opened in September 1955, only one of the former black schools had a white enrollment greater than 10%. That school, Garrison Elementary, was exceptional because it was located in a predominantly white, specifically Italian neighborhood. Garrison had been converted to black occupancy in 1930 to relieve crowding in those schools which served the black district east of downtown. However, unlike other areas, the neighborhood around Garrison had remained virtually all white. Thus, when the attendance zones were redrawn Garrison's zone was 95% white, and when school opened in September 1955, white students comprised 93.4% of the enrollment.

With the exception of the unique situation at Garrison, it appears that the white population attached a stigma to assignments in a formerly black school and either moved or applied for transfers to schools with higher percentages of white students. For example, 154 white students lived in the attendance zone for Sumner School, a formerly black school, but when school opened in September only six whites enrolled. Similarly, seventy-four whites were assigned to Carver, but only two enrolled; 132 white students lived in the Wheatley zone, but only twenty-nine were enrolled there in September. Almost 300 white students lived in the zone served by the two formerly black secondary schools, Lincoln High School and Coles Junior High. When school opened, only two whites were enrolled at Lincoln and four at Coles. The situation was much the same at other black schools. Overall, more than 1,200 white students lived within the attendance zones of formerly black schools, but only 372 of them enrolled at these schools. When Garrison is removed from that equation, the figures are even more telling. A total of 854 whites were assigned to formerly all black schools, but only 12.5% of that number enrolled at those schools. In other words, 747 white students had either moved or transferred from those areas in the nine months since the research department's study. It seems likely that many of these white families initially took advantage of the district's transfer policy and perhaps moved from the area at some subsequent date.

The stigma did not apply exclusively to the formerly segregated black schools. It was also apparent Greenwood and Yeager, which were located in predominantly black neighborhoods. Prior to desegregation, the number of white students served at the two schools justified maintaining them as white schools, but when the attendance zones were redefined, the research department projected the enrollments at Greenwood and Yeager would be about 60% black. In September 1955, 78% of the students at Greenwood were black: almost eighty white students had moved or transferred. A year later, Greenwood was 94% black, a situation that prompted Mrs. William E. Holmes, the president of the school's PTA, to approach the school board protesting "free transfers and the district's attendance zones." The school board assured Mrs. Holmes that the transfers had been granted in accordance with district policy and nothing could be done to arrest the transformation occurring at the school. A similar situation existed at Yeager. In 1955, 73% of the school's 683 students were black: ninety-three whites had moved or transferred since the research department's residence count. Two years later Yeager was 90% black. The rapid turnover at these schools, as well as the situation at the formerly segregated black schools, demonstrated the reluctance of the white population to send their children to schools that they categorized as "black schools."

Substantial numbers of whites also took advantage of the district's liberal transfer policy when they perceived that the school their children attended was rapidly becoming a majority black school. The best example of this trend was the transformation of Ladd School. In 1960, Ladd was 99% black; of more than 1,600 students, only seventeen were white. Yet, the 1960 census indicated the Ladd neighborhood was only about 75% black, nearly 200 white elementary school age children still resided in the area. Again, it seems reasonable to conclude that whites initially utilized the transfer policy to elude integration and later moved from the area.

The combination of the transfer policy and the city's residential patterns insured that the desegregation plan based on geographic redefinition of the attendance zones would have limited impact. When they had the financial resources to move from areas undergoing transition, it appears that many whites did just that. In those cases where they were unable to move away from neighborhoods in transition, large numbers of whites utilized the transfer policy. J. Glenn Travis, the administrative assistant to the superintendent during the first decade of desegregation, estimated that, in some years, the district granted as many as 5,000 transfers.

Of course, avoiding integration was not considered a justifiable reason for requesting a transfer. Nevertheless, there is little doubt that those whites who sought transfers in order to elude integration found ways of obtaining them. The transfer application used by the school district throughout the 1950s and 1960s was a simple form which requested the student's name, age, grade, address, phone number, date of birth, the school the child currently attended, the school to which they sought transfer, and the reason for requesting reassignment. Arguably, the district should have been less accommodating in issuing transfers, but the policy was historically quite liberal and there was no simple way for administrators to determine which applications stated legitimate reasons and which did not. Furthermore, as the district had made public the acceptable grounds for requesting transfer in the transition policy, many Kansas Citians were certainly familiar with those reasons which would insure favorable action on their application.

Clearly, the district could have altered the attendance zones in some areas of the city and declined to grant transfers from some schools to promote a much greater degree of racial mixing. It is most important to bear in mind, however, that the Supreme Court did not require school districts to maximize integration until the mid-1960s, and then with many exceptions. Kansas City's plan based on geographic attendance zones completely satisfied the standards established in the *Brown* decisions. Furthermore, as the Supreme Court had made not addressed the issue of restricting transfers, Kansas City was not violating the ruling by granting them. More to the point, the district transfer policy was designed and promoted as a matter of convenience for parents and students, not as a means of evasion. Thus, when Superintendent Hazlett proudly announced that "Kansas City is now along with Washington, Baltimore, and St. Louis, identified as one of the big four among large cities with separate schools who have moved ahead in carrying out the directive of the United States Supreme Court," he could do so without doubting the district's compliance with the *Brown* decisions. Kansas City remained a highly segregated city with a highly segregated school system. Nevertheless, according to law, Kansas City's schools were satisfactorily integrated. Moreover, compared to the intransigence of the Deep South, the ugly episodes which accompanied token desegregation in Little Rock, and the closure of the public school system in Prince Edward County, Virginia, Kansas City had been a model of compliance.

CHAPTER 2

Crowding, Boundaries, and Busing

Civil Rights Protests, 1963-1965

Following the 1955 implementation of the integration plan, the Kansas City school district closely monitored its impact, tracking the shifting racial composition in neighborhoods and schools. The massive migration of Kansas City's black population from the central area toward the south had major implications for the administration of the school district and the desegregation program. For example, not only had the population shift transformed Ladd School from segregated white in 1954 to 99% black in 1960, but the school had also become overcrowded during the course of that transition, creating additional difficulties for district administrators. The school district was forced to address similar problems in other schools at both the elementary and secondary school levels. Typically, the district responded to population shifts by altering attendance zones.

Each summer, school enrollments were reviewed and attendance zones adjusted in an attempt to insure that schools would not exceed capacity when they opened in September. In addition to the modifications made necessary by population shifts, the school district carved out attendance zones for new schools built after the 1956 bond issue, and it redefined the zones of those schools where capacities increased with the construction of additions. Still further changes were required each time a school closed or as additional neighborhoods were annexed into Kansas City. Thus, minor alterations to the attendance zones were commonplace during the first ten years of integration. Generally, these modifications were fairly unobtrusive, inconveniencing only small numbers of residents, and they were well received by the public. In 1963, however, a parents' group took issue with what they perceived to be a pattern developing regarding the changing attendance zones.

In the first week of June 1963, Superintendent Hazlett presented his recommended changes in the district's attendance zones for the 1963-64 school year. The recommendations were made in light of the completion of a large addition at Southwest High School and the escalating enrollment at Central High School accompanying the black population's migration into that area. Basically, the modified zones reassigned students living in what was formerly part of the Central zone to Paseo High School and adjusted the lines of seven other junior highs and high schools to meet expected enrollments. As a result of these modifications, Southwest High School would remain virtually all white, while Central would remain 99% black and the racial composition at Paseo would climb from 23% to about 40% black. As was typical, the recommendations were approved without discussion.

Two weeks later, a racially mixed delegation of about thirty-five parents, representing the Paseo, Central, Manual, and Southeast areas appeared before the board to protest the changes and implicitly question the board's motivations. Their spokesperson, Mrs. Lee Hopfinger, unleashed what the *Kansas City Times* described as a "barrage of accusations." She argued that "the school board must consider the community problems when changing school boundaries." Hopfinger charged that the modifications, specifically those changes affecting the Paseo attendance zone were "an attempt to not only resegregate the schools but the neighborhoods as well." The group found "the unwritten law that Troost [Avenue] be the boundary separating the white population and Negro population" particularly objectionable. In her opinion, the addition at Southwest High School, an all-white school, afforded the school district an "opportunity to follow the unwritten law of the Troost line policy." Thus, Hopfinger's logic went, the school district could retain Troost as the eastern boundary for the Southwest zone and all of the white students living in that area could be accommodated at Southwest High School. None would be required to attend the neighboring, integrated high schools – Central, Paseo and Southeast.

The parents' group believed "the real need was at Central," not Southwest. Hopfinger charged that Central represented an "impossible situation due to unrealistic planning on the part of the school board or perhaps their deliberate plan to produce this very situation in order to resegregate our schools." For Hopfinger and the group she represented, the source of their frustration was clear. They pointedly noted that "a group of board members from the Southwest area of Kansas City do not understand the real problems of all the school district."

Following her litany of grievances, Hopfinger outlined recommendations proposed by the parents' group to ameliorate the alleged problems. The group urged that the new boundaries be repealed and better use be made of available classroom space in "the listed segregated schools." In other words, the board should redefine the attendance zones to promote integration as well as to utilize vacant classrooms. In addition, "to alleviate the overcrowded conditions at

Central," the group urged that "the school district must bear the expense of transporting the Central School overflow to schools where rooms are available," and she included the caveat that "Lincoln and Manual are not acceptable as this would only extend segregation." The group further recommended that the school district terminate "the liberal policy for white Central students [transferring] to Southwest and Southeast." Finally, the group proposed an "advisory committee be made up of citizens representing every school zone to study and acquaint the board with the feelings and needs of each area."

Mrs. Hopfinger closed her address with both a hint of optimism and a veiled threat of possible repercussions if the school board did not act in their favor. "We," she stated, "still have faith in the school board to take immediate action on our proposal thus preventing further unrest and dissatisfaction." The group pledged "there will be no rest or vacations for the parents in these districts until just school placements are decided."

Following Hopfinger, a number of other members of the delegation addressed the school board. Bernie Thomas, representing the Southeast Junior High P.T.A., objected to the new attendance zones due to the pejorative effect previous alterations had in that area. Noting increasing enrollments and the shifting racial composition of the area, Thomas protested, "We are fighting a two-way battle – resegregation and crowded schools." Other members of the delegation representing different sections of the city also complained of the feeder patterns. Harold Thornton, from the Paseo area, concluded, "In four or five years, we will have a Negro school."

The Manual Neighborhood Council spokesman, Fred Mancuso, argued the situation at Central should have been foreseen by district officials. Superintendent Hazlett shot back: "I doubt if one Negro child lived south of Linwood [Boulevard] at that time. If you were endowed with the ability to predict population shifts at the time, we could have used your help." Patience and courtesy evaporated on both sides and the meeting dissolved into an exchange of heated accusations and rebuttals.

"The Board of Education and its superintendent," Reverend Willis Tabor surmised, "are dedicated to a policy of containment of Negro children in segregated neighborhood schools, containment of Negro teachers in schools which are all or predominantly Negro, and dedicated to refusing to promote qualified Negro personnel to administrative positions." Cleo Muller, president of the St. Therese-Pershing Neighborhood Council, agreed with Reverend Tabor, and implied that the school board collaborated with real estate agencies to promote further resegregation. Board member Mrs. James A. Reed retorted, "If you think we have any deal with the Real Estate Board you are mistaken."

Eventually, the delegation began to insist on total integration of the entire school district. The group apparently concluded that the only solution to such divergent grievances regarding the district's desegregation policy and the residential composition of the city was integration on a district-wide basis. In essence, the group was demanding that the school district take action to counter the existing patterns of *de facto* residential segregation in the city. By 1963 standards, such proposals were generally regarded as excessive and unreasonable. "Go ahead and integrate the whole Kansas City area. Then you won't have demonstrations," urged a representative from the Southeast Homeowners Association. "Because of having a desegregated area at Central," Mrs. Milton Clark of the Central P.T.A. agreed, "we are in favor of total desegregation of the schools."

Although it was difficult to assess accurately how many parents and students were represented by the thirty-five person delegation, the school board filed the group's statement in the minutes of the meeting and agreed to investigate the charges made and the proposed reforms. School board president Homer Wadsworth stated his belief that, "this is a problem that affects every community in America today," and politely acknowledged that the Board of Education appreciated the group's input. He encouraged the delegation to present other concerns to the school board in the future.

Less than one week after the school board meeting, the district issued its response to the parents' group. "The board recognizes," the statement opened, "that the discussion of solving overcrowded conditions at Central High School is occurring at a time when racial tensions are increasing across the country." The district defended itself by contending that "Kansas City schools have a respectable record of integration." Nevertheless, the school board acceded to some of the parents' demands. The board restored the old attendance zones but implied that in the future other alterations might be necessary. "Changing boundary lines," the district argued, "is a widely used and legitimate method of adjusting school enrollments if changes are made without regard to race." The school board also pledged to expand the academic offerings at Lincoln and Manual high schools, if the enrollment justified such courses. Plans to form a human relations committee of three district administrators to work with parents, faculties, and students to "ease tensions and promote understanding," were also incorporated in the statement. Furthermore, the board announced that the number of schools having integrated teaching staffs would more than double to thirty-one in the upcoming year. Finally, the board members insisted that the district was engaged in an ongoing campaign to hire qualified applicants from all races. Despite the announcement, the controversy was not yet resolved.

One week after the school board meeting and only two days after the district's response to the parent group, a powerful new challenger materialized: the Kansas City branch of the Congress of Racial Equality (CORE). CORE's entry into the controversy assured that the number of persons protesting the school board's action would multiply and that their bargaining strength would increase. CORE also immediately broadened the stated goals of the protest. Although the Central and Paseo areas remained the primary focus, CORE also adopted the ultimate goal of the parents' group – integration on a district-wide basis. CORE's goals squarely challenged the existing patterns of *de facto* segregation in Kansas City.

CORE's first action was to organize a rally at the St. Stephen's Baptist Church on June 28, 1963. At the meeting, CORE discussed legal developments relevant to desegregation and formulated an agenda of reforms promoting integration to present to the school board. In order to instill their demands with a sense of legitimacy, the civil rights group sought to remind the school district of recent court decisions regarding desegregation. They were not, however, concerned solely with the law as defined by the *Brown* decision. New standards applied in school desegregation, and the decision which most strongly supported CORE's far ranging objectives had come from New Rochelle, New York.

CORE and the *Taylor* Decision

During the 1950s, the landmark school segregation decisions of the United States Supreme Court involved the constitutionality of state laws mandating the organization and operation of segregated school systems. The *Brown* decisions had abolished the practice of *de jure* school segregation that required segregation by law. The preeminent school integration issue of the 1960s involved the constitutionality of operating a school district which was largely segregated due to a city's demographics. The term *de facto* segregation was applied to those situations where the separation of the races in schools was causally related to the residential patterns prevailing in a city. Due to the high degree of residential segregation present in most American cities and the common practice of organizing school attendance zones on the basis of neighborhood schools, *de facto* school segregation was apparent in most major cities during the 1960s. The New Rochelle case was the first legal challenge to this situational segregation.

Styled as *Taylor v. Board of Education of the City School District of New Rochelle*, the suit was filed in 1960 by eleven black children and their parents. The plaintiffs disputed the school district's practice of gerrymandering attendance zone lines and granting transfers in such a fashion that one school serving a predominantly black neighborhood, Lincoln Elementary, retained a segregated character. The United States District Court and the Federal Court of Appeals both held that the practices were discriminatory and ordered the district to adopt a desegregation plan dictated by the court. The court order was notable for its moderation, requiring the district to grant transfers to all Lincoln

Elementary School students who applied. The parents were responsible for providing transportation to their child's new school and all transfers were subject to availability in receiving schools. The United States Supreme Court refused to hear the appeal and thereby silently upheld the decision of the Court of Appeals.

The Kansas City branch of CORE interpreted the *Taylor* ruling as a directive that decisions concerning the organization and administration of a school district must actively promote integration. This may have been a liberal interpretation of the ruling, but CORE was determined to win such a commitment from the school district. The *Taylor* ruling applied to school districts which gerrymandered attendance zones to minimize racial mixing in the schools. It was in this respect that CORE believed the New York ruling applied to the controversy brewing in Kansas City.

Two days after the rally at the St. Stephen's Baptist Church, CORE leaders in Kansas City finalized plans for a more public demonstration of their dissatisfaction with the school board. Following the lead of the national civil rights organizations, Kansas City's CORE members planned a march on the Board of Education building and a series of sit-ins at school board meetings beginning in early July and continuing until the controversy was resolved to the civil rights advocates' satisfaction. Reverend A. Cecil Williams, pastor of the St. James Methodist Church and a local CORE leader, defiantly announced: "We will sit-in until they know us by name. If that doesn't work, we will begin in September and sit-in with our children." To muster mass support for the march and sit-ins, Reverend Williams injected an appeal to black Kansas Citians' understanding of history. "The real tragedy," he proclaimed, "is that the people sitting here tonight believe that we have integration. We have been used, tricked, manipulated, harassed, and abused ever since we were brought to America."

The announcement of CORE's intention to march on the Board of Education building sparked a minor division within the ranks of the school board and the district administration. There was no consensus among district officials as to whether they should or should not be present when the demonstrators arrived at the doors of the building. School board president Homer Wadsworth, the primary liberal advocate of the black community on the school board, said that he would be there "against the advice of other board members." Even so, Wadsworth clearly did not approve of CORE's tactics. "Normally in such matters," Wadsworth told the *Kansas City Times*, "parades and demonstrations follow a breakdown of public discussion. This is a situation in which no meeting has been requested of us. The school board is willing to meet with the leaders of CORE, as with any group, to explore the matters involved." Board member James Kemper agreed to join Wadworth; the other four members declined. One day before the planned march it was unclear whether any other district official, aside from the two board members, would be present to meet the CORE demonstrators.

In the early afternoon of July 2, 1963, some 230 marchers bearing banners proclaiming "Color is only Skin Deep," "Integrate the School Board," and "Biracial Committee, Equal Rights Now," began their silent march through the streets of downtown Kansas City toward the Board of Education building at Twelfth and McGee. The procession was led by Reverend Williams and Dr. Robert Farnsworth, an English professor at the University of Kansas City. Wadsworth, Kemper, school board secretary Amos Burks, and Superintendent Hazlett were on hand to meet the marchers. Hazlett was attending the National Education Association convention in Detroit but had flown back for the day to meet with the civil rights leaders.

"We are here," Reverend Williams announced on the steps of the Board of Education building, "to dramatize by our marching, that there are real problems of segregation and re-segregation in the Kansas City public school system. . . . [and] that these problems affect the total community." The purpose of the march, he asserted, was to urge school officials "to take positive action" to promote more extensive integration in the public school system. Following Reverend Williams' remarks, which were punctuated by rounds of applause, the crowd was led in singing "We Shall Overcome."

At the invitation of Mr. Wadsworth, the meeting was continued in the board of education auditorium to escape the July heat. Dr. Farnsworth spoke first for the CORE delegation and most of his comments dealt with the application of the New Rochelle ruling in Kansas City's public schools. Dr. Farnsworth argued the *Taylor* decision could "be used as an authoritative statement of the meaning of the *Brown* decision." In Dr. Farnsworth's opinion, and indeed the opinion of CORE, the Kansas City school district "has failed to comply with the Supreme Court decision of 1954." His rationale was that the "school board of Kansas City has not actively attempted to undo a historic wrong committed against the Negro citizens of the community. The school board has not actively planned to provide integrated educational experiences wherever possible." To illustrate his point, Dr. Farnsworth argued that the transfer policy permitted whites to elude integration, new school sites had been planned without consideration of the possible implications for integration, boundary changes which perpetuated segregation had been adopted, only token integration of school faculties had been realized, and no blacks held posts in the district's central administration. In Dr. Farnsworth's assessment, each indicated how Kansas City had circumvented the intent of the *Brown* ruling.

Dr. Farnsworth emphasized that CORE had "not come in anger or bitterness," nor did they "accuse any members of the school board or any of the administrators of the public school system with malicious intentions." He acknowledged that, "the responsibilities of the school board are great and complex," but asserted, "We are not satisfied with the progress of integration in the Kansas City school system in the nine years since the Supreme Court decision." Having expressed the black community's grievances, Farnsworth deferred to Reverend Williams who presented CORE's recommendations for change in the district.

CORE proposed a comprehensive series of measures to remedy the perceived lack of sufficient progress toward integration. Williams argued the New Rochelle case "warrants a subsequent revision of [the district's] guiding policies," and he had come prepared, announcing, "We are making a number of suggestions." In all, CORE's recommendations numbered nine and addressed a wide range of district policies. The proposed reforms were presented with varying degrees of specificity. Some were articulated in great detail, while others were so vague as to require only token gestures of good faith on the part of the school district.

Essentially, all of CORE's recommendations could be reduced to a single sentence: "The school board should plan boundaries, transfer policies, proposed building sites and bussing [sic] policies, faculty selection and placement in a way that avoids placing any group of children at a disadvantage because of racial distinction." The guiding principle that propelled CORE's suggestions was the notion that in order to comply with the ruling in the New Rochelle case, district policies must be measured in terms of advancing the cause of integrated schools in Kansas City. To impress this point on the school officials, Williams emphatically enjoined, "It is the responsibility of the school board in every city to comply fully with the law of the land." To this end, he urged "that the school board state its belief that it must keep constantly before itself the goal of integration in all decisions effecting [sic] school organization and educational practice."

The school district officials listened attentively to the local civil rights leaders and assured CORE that the issues raised in the meeting would be brought to the attention of the school board and the district's central administration. Nearly a month passed before the school district responded to CORE's grievances and proposed reforms. Meanwhile, CORE continued to pressure the school district for change.

Reverend Williams and Dr. Farnsworth articulated another CORE demand at the July 25 school board meeting. They proposed that the school district provide transportation to predominantly white high schools for 195 black students living in the optional zone for Central and Paseo High Schools. Williams felt it would be advantageous to "spread black students around to white schools." Farnsworth agreed arguing that segregated public education "is a crime for which the entire community is responsible."

There was a dual purpose in CORE's suggestion: they believed the proposal would significantly reduce crowding at the two high schools, and ideally, the move would be the first step toward stable integration in all the district's secondary schools. Due to the southerly migration of the black community, Central had already completed the transition from segregated to integrated to resegregated. In 1955, Central had opened with black students comprising just over 11% of the enrollment; by 1963, Central was 99% black. Similarly, Paseo appeared to be accelerating toward resegregation. Paseo was less than 2% black in 1955. By 1963, the percentage had climbed to almost 25% with the trend showing no indication of stabilizing. The school board again refused to take immediate action on the proposal but reassured CORE that each of the recommendations would be evaluated and a response would be issued before August 15.

The issues presented by the parents' group and CORE marked the first serious challenge to the district's integration plan since its adoption in 1955. In formulating the original desegregation plan, school officials had not actively sought the advice of civic groups on matters of policy. What remained to be seen in the summer of 1963 was whether the district could be receptive to recommendations and criticisms from civil rights groups after nearly a decade of desegregation. Quite obviously, CORE's priorities and those of the school board were not entirely complementary, and in the end only the Board of Education had the authority to make policy. The school district's response to CORE's demands furnished a barometer of sorts by which the school board's perception of its duty to the community could be measured against the expectations of Kansas City's civil rights advocates.

CORE leaders were not seeking usurp the authority of the school district. Rather, Reverend Williams perceived CORE's role to be "bringing public concerns to the attention of the board so that they can make the necessary changes." Clearly, the civil rights leaders envisioned themselves in an advisory position and assumed that the district would seriously consider their proposals. Indeed, CORE fully expected some of their recommendations to be adopted although the school board was not obliged to do so.

There was nothing especially radical in the CORE demands. Several of the recommendations were already a matter of district policy, others required minor revisions, and only the demands for "maximum integration" in all future policy decisions and the formation of a biracial committee to advise school officials marked major departures from the district's existing integration plan. Despite the relatively innocuous nature of most of the CORE demands, the school board summarily rejected each of the recommendations. In doing so, the school board members signaled emphatically that they alone made district policy. Furthermore, the district's action again indicated its resistance to being pressured into assuming a position in the vanguard of social change in the city.

Superintendent Hazlett read the district's official statement at the August 1 school board meeting. The Board of Education understood, he said, "that the Negro presses vigorously for improvement of his condition and for training equivalent to that provided to any other person. No thoughtful person will deny the legitimacy of the Negro's aspirations." In promoting equity, the school board acknowledged and accepted its role in assisting the "integration of the Negro into full participation in the life of this community." However, the school board was clearly not yet prepared to accept CORE's proposal that all subsequent district policies be formulated in light of fostering "maximum integration." Rather, the school board's position had come no more than half the distance to that goal: "integration is a factor to be taken into account within the school system whenever it is possible to do so without destroying the fundamental principle of the school as a major service unit to the neighborhood of which it is a part."

The school board's refusal to accept "maximum integration" was underscored by the rejection of other CORE recommendations. The board objected to the proposed revisions to the transfer policy, reasoning that the district had "maintained an open enrollment policy for many years that permits transfers of pupils from one school to another, where room permits, for good and valid reasons." The board reiterated its pledge that "no transfer shall be given a white student solely because he seeks to avoid going to a school in which Negro children are enrolled."

In similar fashion, the school board dismissed CORE's request that 195 black students be bused from the Central-Paseo option zone to predominantly white high schools. "In our judgment," the statement read, "efforts made to force integration in schools, through bus transportation and the like, have failed to provide the quality of education needed by children, and is by its nature an artificial arrangement calculated to produce new and frequently insoluble difficulties … (including) resegregation." According to the district's pre-enrollment information, neither Central nor Paseo was projected to exceed capacity during the 1963-64 school year; conversely, East, Lincoln, Southeast, and Van Horn high schools were all projected to be overcrowded. From the school board's vantage point, Central and Paseo appeared to be in a much better position in terms of accommodating their enrollments than did several other schools in the district.

The school board's statement to CORE revealed several indications of a growing awareness of racial issues among school district officials. "The Board of Education," the statement read, "is well aware of the serious nature of the current problems in the civil rights field. It recognizes its obligations to take a position of leadership in dealing with those phases of the problem that are primarily related to education." Moreover, the school board pledged to "counsel all our people to take a constructive view of these questions and to develop an understanding of the aspirations of the Negro community for improvement of its circumstances." Why, then, had the school board treated CORE's moderate suggestions in such a cursory fashion? A number of possible answers are apparent.

First, it is quite likely that the school board perceived CORE's emphasis on the New Rochelle case to be a misinterpretation of the ruling. Judge Irving Kaufman's decision in the *Taylor* case was the first case to address school segregation resulting from residential patterns present in cities across the country, not only in the South. In the New Rochelle case, Kaufman ruled for the plaintiffs due to the preponderance of evidence indicating the school district had intentionally gerrymandered attendance zones to relegate the black population in one section of the city to an all-black elementary school. Kaufman found, "The neighborhood school policy certainly is not sacrosanct. It is valid only insofar as it is operated within the confines established by the Constitution. It cannot be used to confine Negroes within an area artificially delineated in the first instance by official acts."

With Kaufman's ruling in mind, CORE argued the school district in Kansas City was retaining the Troost line as a barrier to integration. There is, however, no evidence to support the allegation that the school district capriciously discriminated against the black population by defining the Southwest attendance zone as it had. The official enrollment figures indicate that the school was operating at or above capacity during the period in question and that extending the boundary to integrate black students living in the Central and Paseo zones would clearly have aggravated already cramped facilities at Southwest. Furthermore, using Troost as a defining line for the Southwest zone was consistent with the district practice of using major arteries as boundaries. In New Rochelle, Judge Kaufman stated the neighborhood school concept was not "sacrosanct," but this did not necessarily mean that organizing schools around a neighborhood principle was unconstitutional. Provided that the district acted in a non-discriminatory fashion, neighborhood schools were still entirely legal.

The facts involved in the New Rochelle case were appreciably different from the situation in Kansas City, and Farnsworth's assessment of the meaning of the ruling was arguable. To be sure, the interpretation professed by the Kansas City branch of CORE had some basis in Judge Kaufman's opinion in the *Taylor* case; however, the conclusion that it mandated all future policy decisions be evaluated with respect to maximizing integration was hotly debated. Kaufman had reasoned the *Brown* decision "imposed a legal and moral obligation upon officials who have created or maintained segregated schools to undo the damage they had fostered." Moreover, he recognized, "This obligation requires good faith and action with dispatch."

Members of the Kansas City school board believed that the district had acted promptly and in good faith to reverse the damage of segregation. More to the point, the school board argued its efforts to improve the educational benefits available to black students constituted an ongoing campaign. The school district had attracted over one million dollars in private funding and had appropriated a substantial sum of school district money to develop and expand "compensatory education" programs available to students living in "depressed areas," the majority of whom were black. One program provided nearly $500,000 in college scholarships "designed to identify and motivate deprived pupils." Other efforts focused on improving achievement among disadvantaged students. These programs included an intensive literacy track for functionally illiterate students, expanded special education services for emotionally disturbed students, an extensive network of work-study programs, an expanded staff of social workers to act as liaisons between school and the home to promote achievement, among other projects.

Those services already in place were to be supplemented by additional programs the school board was in the process of developing. The school district was completing plans for faculty exchanges, visiting teacher and administrator programs, and increased interaction between parents and teachers in order to apprise personnel of the needs and interests of minority groups in public education. Biracial committees were being formed to study the treatment of diversity and racial issues in the district's textbooks, materials and curriculum. From the school board's perspective, Kansas City's schools promoted racial awareness and understanding, and adequately accommodated the needs of their black students.

Another possible reason for the school board's rejection of CORE's demands is the inaccuracy of the civil rights group's facts. Both the original group of parents and CORE claimed Central and Paseo were grossly overcrowded; yet, the district's official figures indicated otherwise. In the five year period, 1958-1963, Central was one of only two Kansas City high schools which had not operated above capacity. Furthermore, Paseo had been at or above capacity only two of the five years. The district's data documented that every other high school in the city, with the exception of Manual, had experienced overcrowding in some or all of the five preceding years. Southwest High School, for example, had operated above capacity four of the five years. The situation at Southwest was of particular importance in light of the claim that the need for an addition at Central was greater than at Southwest.

The school board's statement refuted each of the contentions made by CORE and had supported its position with an array of statistical data which seemed to demonstrate that the district had acted responsibly. More to the point, the twenty-page response to CORE's proposed reforms reaffirmed that the school board would not be pressured into committing itself to changes it did not deem to be necessary. District policy making still resided firmly in the hands of the school board.

Surprisingly, CORE did not interpret the school board's response as a rejection of its demands. On the contrary, Gwendolyn Wells, representing CORE at the August 15 school board meeting, proclaimed "another milestone in the history of educational progress in this city" had been secured. "A responsible civil rights organization," Wells stated, "does not hesitate to applaud when applause is indicated. The board's forthright statement regarding integration demonstrates to us a philosophy, an awareness of democratic ideals that must be commended. CORE feels that based on the statement made by the board, Kansas City public school education can move into a new progressive era."

CORE opted not to contest the school district's decision to integrate within the neighborhood school concept but felt compelled to voice its negative assessment of other elements of the plan for the 1963-64 school year. CORE continued to push for a black school board member and a biracial advisory committee arguing: "The board is greatly handicapped in dealing with the problems of integration by the fact that the Negro citizenry is not represented on the board. It is the feeling of CORE that a biracial committee could partially alleviate this handicap and enhance the image of the board in the eyes of this segment of our community." Regarding the school board's decision not to provide transportation for 195 students in the Central-Paseo option zone, Wells stated, "It appears the problem that existed at Central has been resolved by relocating the problem at Lincoln." Indeed, with the adjustments to the attendance zones, Lincoln High School was projected to be 183 students above capacity but the school board intended to address this problem by assigning ninth grade students to adjacent junior highs.

CORE leaders believed the district's statement demonstrated "a high degree of consensus between ourselves and the school board regarding its basic responsibilities to all children of this city." In light of that "consensus," Wells envisioned changes accomplished within the neighborhood school system. The board's statement, she concluded, indicated that "in the future special efforts will be made to prevent the creation of two 'segregated' schools, side by side." Her idealism proved ill-founded, however, as the school district announced no further reforms during the 1963-64 school year.

Crowding and the Segregated Busing Program

Kansas City's schools continued to function in very much the same manner as they had in preceding years. However, to the chagrin of school officials, another, potentially more serious challenge developed during the 1963-64 school year. The district's busing program, undertaken to relieve crowding in the elementary schools, attracted the attention of Kansas City's civil rights organizations and another confrontation loomed. Gwendolyn Wells, who a year earlier had praised the "milestone" policy changes of the school board, would become a fixture at school board meetings in the fall of 1964. She represented a powerful alliance of civil rights advocates committed to substantive change in the Kansas City schools.

The launching of the busing program was necessitated by the migration of black families from the large central neighborhood to the south. In the late 1950s, Kansas City's population in general was highly mobile. More than one quarter of the city's residents moved to different places of residence within the city between 1955 and 1960. No group was more mobile than the black population: fully 60% of Kansas City's blacks moved in the five years preceding the 1960 census. Of nearly 45,000 black Kansas Citians who moved during that five-year period, about one-third moved into neighborhoods south of Linwood Boulevard. The overcrowding which developed in the schools serving these neighborhoods during the 1960s resulted from this southerly black migration.

Two distinct patterns of mobility were apparent among the black population in Kansas City. First, and of only marginal importance to the management of the school district, was the constant shifting of the population within the large central black neighborhood. African-Americans who resided in this area in 1960 were as likely as other blacks to change residences and they did so in astonishing numbers. It appears, however, that most of these moves were lateral and did not represent any significant change in social or economic status. The average income for blacks residing in the central area was about one-half the median income for the city and property values lagged well below the median value for Kansas City. The vast majority of blacks living in this large section were apartment dwellers who paid rents that were one-third to one-half the city median. In other words, the central area remained one of the poorest sections of Kansas City. Its black population was also appreciably older. The median age among blacks living in the census tracts that comprised the central area ranged from two to nine years older than the median age for blacks in Kansas City as a whole. Finally, blacks living in the central neighborhood tended to have fewer individuals residing in the home. These factors set the black population in this area apart from those residents who were moving to the south.

Blacks migrating to the southern half of Kansas City were quite different from the residents they left behind. Property values in the neighborhoods to the south were higher than those in the central area, but they were still between one and two thousand dollars lower than the city median. Moving to the south represented a small upward step in social and economic status. As might be expected, blacks migrating to the south were more secure financially than those who remained in the central neighborhood. The median incomes for black families moving south were about 20% greater than families who remained in the central area. The migrating blacks were also generally better educated, averaging between one and two more years of formal schooling. In addition, the blacks who moved south were remarkably young. The median age for the migrant group was around twenty-three years of age; whereas the median age for Kansas City as a whole was about ten years older. Finally, of the black population migrating to the south had slightly larger families. The median number of persons residing in Kansas City households was 2.93; among the black migrant group it was 3.25.

In the neighborhoods to the south, residential transition occurred at an astounding pace. The area around Ladd Elementary was transformed completely from virtually all white to virtually all black within five years and several other neighborhoods soon followed. In transitional neighborhoods, the whites who moved out were quickly replaced by black families. Stable integration was impossible as young families were the segment of the white population most likely to move away. For example, in one census tract nearing the completion of residential transition at the time of the 1960 census, the median age for whites was forty-eight years of age, while the black median was twenty-three. Previously, the white population residing in the neighborhood was well distributed in terms of age and, therefore, the enrollments tended to be fairly stable. However, the preponderance of youth among the migrating black families who were replacing the exiting white population upset the balance of enrollment and school capacity. As the composition of the neighborhood became increasingly younger, the schools were unable to accommodate the rising enrollments. The result was gross overcrowding in the elementary schools serving the neighborhoods swept up in transition.

The busing program that came under fire in 1964 had originated as an attempt to meet the challenge of overcrowding. In January 1960, the school district announced that 240 students would be bused from Ladd Elementary to Humboldt in an effort to relieve crowding at Ladd. Black students comprised 99% of Ladd's enrollment in 1960, thus the vast majority of the students on the buses were black. The receiving school, Humboldt, was 19% black. The decision was historic because it marked the humble beginning of a busing program which, although adopted as a temporary expedient, eventually grew into a massive yearly commitment.

In 1960, Ladd was the only school which bused children to other schools with vacancy; however, the ongoing black migration dictated an expansion of the busing program in order to relieve crowding at neighboring schools as well. Three schools adjacent to the Ladd zone were operated on half-day schedules in 1960 to accommodate the increasing enrollments. The school district had been unable to secure buses to serve these schools in 1960 but all three schools would subsequently be added to the busing program. The district's alterations to the attendance zones were ineffective in relieving crowding due to the scope of the migratory corridor which stretched over an area about two and one-half miles wide. Furthermore, the pace of transition was so rapid that the school district could not accurately project enrollment increases and take measures to ameliorate the condition. At Ladd, the enrollment had increased by more than 700 students in four years between 1957 and 1960. Similarly, the enrollment at Horace Mann increased by more than 500 students between 1957 and 1962.

Kansas City's busing program was unusual in that it removed entire classes of students from one building and placed them in schools having vacant classrooms. The students were not identified as a part of the school that received them but remained associated with the sending school. Essentially, the students who were transported to schools with vacancies were consigned to self-contained units at the receiving schools. They retained the same teacher and the same classmates and they mixed with the other students at the receiving schools only during recess, lunch, assemblies, and other all-school functions. Because the busing plan transported black students primarily and several of the receiving schools were predominantly white, this quarantined treatment at the receiving sites did nothing to advance integration in the school system. In 1964, Kansas City's civil rights community contested the blatant discrimination incorporated into this unconventional busing scheme.

Although it is difficult to conclude precisely what factors motivated the school district to adopt this particular busing format, a few considerations seem to take precedence. First, several schools in the district had vacant classrooms, so busing entire classrooms from one school to another made optimum use of the available facilities. Second, by busing classrooms of children at the same grade level, the school district only needed vacant classrooms at the receiving schools to accommodate the students. An area busing format – transporting *all* of the students who lived on certain blocks in a crowded area – would have entailed finding empty desks for children at all grade levels. While the receiving schools had vacant classrooms, these schools did not necessarily have empty desks in the classrooms that were already occupied. By busing entire classrooms of students, the school district circumvented this problem. Third, it appears that this particular busing scheme was guided in part by financial considerations. The district had selected the receiving schools carefully in an attempt to minimize the expenditures concomitant with providing transportation. Schools having vacant rooms to receive students were determined by the distance from the sending schools and the number of trips the buses could make between the schools on a given morning. By selecting receiving schools which were near to the sending schools, the district could manage the transportation scheme on a minimal number of buses. Finally, it should be emphasized that the decision to continue to identify the students as part of the sending school was not made by the school district alone. Parents accepted the initial busing plan as a temporary solution while insisting that the students continue to be identified as part of the enrollment in the sending schools. The parents reasoned that so long as the students were technically part of the sending schools, the district would remain cognizant of the need for additional construction in the crowded schools serving these neighborhoods.

The original plan to bus 240 fifth and sixth grade students from Ladd to Humboldt steadily escalated after 1960. In 1962-63, twelve classes from Ladd, ten classes from Horace Mann, and six classes from Linwood were bused to other schools. The following year, a class from Seven Oaks and two classes from Kumpf were added to the fraternity of schools transporting students to relieve crowding. By September 1964, the number of students riding buses had risen to just over 1,200.

The school district hoped to eliminate the need for busing through new school construction in those areas where enrollments had swollen above capacity. The proposed May 26, 1964 bond issue was positively crucial to the district's building program and formed the central component of long range plans to relieve the increasing enrollments that accompanied the process of residential transition to the south. The proposed bond issue provided more than seventeen million dollars to be used for new construction, renovation, and rehabilitation of existing school structures. Among the most pressing needs in the mid-sixties were additional schools in the areas undergoing residential transition. Nearly one-half of the bond issue money was earmarked for five new schools; three in the neighborhoods affected by the black migration to the south, and two in the Rock Creek area, the fastest growing white residential section, located on the eastern rim of the city. Unfortunately, only 54% of Kansas City voters supported the 1964 bond issue, which required 67% for passage. A dejected Superintendent Hazlett grimly predicted at least ten more classrooms of students would be bused in the following school year.

All told, forty-one classes of children boarded buses in September 1964 destined for one of the nine receiving schools in the city. The students were bused from seven schools located in the path of the black migration to the south. Each of the seven neighborhoods and schools had undergone complete transition since the decision to desegregate the schools. Six of the sending schools were more than 95% black in September 1964; consequently, the vast majority of the children on the buses were African-American. Furthermore, as the black southerly migration showed no signs of abating, it appeared likely that a massive expansion of the busing program would be necessary within the next few years. Ballooning enrollments at six other schools along the migratory corridor portended much more busing to come.

In 1964, the bused students were received at nine different elementary schools. Seven of the receiving schools were located to the west and north of the central black neighborhood. These areas were among the oldest and poorest in the city, and were deteriorating rapidly. The population in these neighborhoods declined steadily throughout the 1960s. Consequently, school enrollments dropped and several vacant classrooms were available at each of the schools. The receiving schools to the north – Carver, Attucks, and Humboldt – had large numbers of resident black students. Indeed, Carver and Attucks had been black schools in the segregated system and remained virtually all-black. One of the receiving schools to the west, Douglass Elementary, had a mixed student population. It was a majority Hispanic school with a black enrollment of about 25%. Other receiving schools to the west – Norman, Allen, and Volker – were predominantly white. The remaining receiving schools, Pinkerton and Nicholls, were located to the south and were virtually all white.

A Challenge from the Citizens' Coordinating Committee

The civil rights organizations in Kansas City unanimously agreed the segregated busing program was unfair, discriminated against black students, and had to be amended. They objected to the fact that virtually all of the students riding the buses were black, but they were most concerned about the segregated treatment those students experienced at the receiving schools. During the summer of 1964, the leaders of several prominent Kansas City civil rights groups, including the Urban League, NAACP, and CORE, formed a coalition calling itself the Citizens' Coordinating Committee (CCC) to present their grievances to the school board. Their primary objective was to have the children on the buses placed in integrated classrooms at the receiving schools rather than consigned to self-contained black classrooms. The coalition also embraced a number of other reform measures in order to promote integration at all levels of the school system. On September 3, 1964, Gwendolyn Wells presented the coalition's agenda for change to the Kansas City school board.

CCC's demands bore a striking resemblance to the recommendations CORE had proposed a year earlier. Above all, the Committee urged that the busing program integrate students at the receiving schools. They also sought reform of the transfer policy so that white students could not transfer from schools that were 65% or more black. The group also proposed the same 65% standard be applied to black students attending majority white schools. In addition to those measures, the CCC sought the redefinition of attendance zones in order to alleviate crowding and to promote increased integration. A final priority of the group was the integration of district personnel at all levels, including placing an African American on the school board.

The key difference between the reforms proposed by CORE and those of the Citizens' Coordinating Committee was not so much the substance of the issues but rather that the Committee managed to frame some of its objectives in concrete terms. CORE had pressed for assurances from the school district that policy decisions would promote integration. During the 1963-64 school year it became clear that CORE and the school district did not share the same perspective regarding what was meant by promoting integration. Having learned from the disappointment of a year before, the CCC proposed actual remedies for the busing situation and the transfer problem. It was unlikely the school board would be able to dismiss the suggestions casually.

The CCC, like other groups before them, recognized the importance of generating publicity for their proposals. Organized picketing began during the first week of September 1964 at the Board of Education building and at six of the receiving schools. Blacks and whites marched together carrying banners demanding, "Tear Down the Iron Curtain," and "Integrate the School Board." In a more radical move, CORE members planned to block the buses during the second week of September, preventing them from making their rounds. As tensions mounted, both major newspapers, as well as the *Call*, Kansas City's black weekly, followed the controversy with growing interest.

Seeking to defuse the situation before it evolved into a major controversy, the school district responded to the CCC on September 10, only one week after Wells had addressed the school board. The statement was exceedingly vague and did not address the transfer problem or the busing situation in a forthright manner. Essentially, the Board of Education restated its vow to "encourage integration of school services in every possible way," within the neighborhood school concept. The statement skirted any discussion of how the students on buses figured into the neighborhood concept. Rather, the district emphasized the shifting population and the problem of crowding in general, noting that the CCC "fails to point out that until the total community sees the need for a bond issue, busing of students will increase." Despite its non-committal tone, the statement provided an opportunity for negotiations, proposing a series of meetings with the CCC.

Some members of the Committee perceived the statement as an affront to the legitimate demands of the civil rights coalition. The CCC's reply to the district stated: "Much of the wording of the seven points included in Mr. Hazlett's letter is of such a general nature as to be meaningless in any operational sense." The Committee further alleged that the statement revealed the Superintendent's "adverse attitudes about Negroes." Nevertheless, the coalition agreed to meet with school district officials on September 15 in order to discuss the busing situation.

Kumpf Elementary was mutually agreed upon as an appropriate site for the first meeting. Kumpf was deeply involved in the busing program. About 200 students were bused from the school to relieve crowding. Furthermore, because many parents at Kumpf were undecided on the issue of whether their children should be integrated at the receiving schools, the school promised to provide a forum receptive to an exchange of opinions on the subject. Some 300 parents attended the meeting to hear the different perspectives offered by Gwendolyn Wells and others representing the CCC, and Superintendent Hazlett for the school district.

Wells created a stir in the meeting when she claimed to have figures from the school district indicating there were 8,000 empty desks in Kansas City schools. Specifically, Wells charged the district had in fact avoided genuine desegregation across the district. "Integration," she said, "must be a problem with the school board because they have only bussed [sic] in two directions, west and north." This allegation was particularly damning because the neighborhoods to the west and north were among the oldest and poorest in the city and declining rapidly, but due to population shifts, schools serving these sections of the city were among those having vacant classroom space. Fully 95% of the bus students rode to schools in the west and north. Wells believed if the students were to be bused away from their neighborhood schools, they deserved to be educated in better facilities than those available in the west and north. She alluded to space for 300 additional students at Marlborough, stating, "I don't know what's wrong with the Southwest area because there are plenty of classrooms available there. Yet, you call for more schools and say that's the answer." Two schools in the southwest area were receiving bused students; however, four other schools in that area were operating more than 100 students below capacity. Arguably, the district was sheltering certain white neighborhoods from involvement in the busing format. Speaking directly to Hazlett, Wells condemned the busing plan's discriminatory flavor, "After the last school bond issue failed, you predicted 'schools on wheels.' Well, now only the Negroes are on wheels."

After Wells's statement the audience grew increasingly hostile toward Superintendent Hazlett. The meeting's moderator, Reverend LeMoyne Whitlock, remarked: "I think she has given us an avenue for relieving the situation somewhat." Curious about the validity of the allegations, Whitlock asked if Wells's report was accurate. The superintendent replied that as far as he knew the information was correct.

At that point the majority of the 300 parents in attendance turned against the superintendent. One man charged that Hazlett could relieve half of the parents' complaints "at any time with a phone call." The superintendent maintained, "We hope to get rid of the whole busing operation, but it cannot be done in one day with a phone call." Even the moderator's impartiality evaporated as Whitlock proclaimed: "We should not stop with Mr. Hazlett. We should call for a confrontation with the board of education which hired him." He argued, "As long as the board members can send a superintendent to cushion themselves from you there will continue to be meetings like this that get nowhere. We must make it clear we do not want this temporary busing of students to continue until our children are grown up." If the first public meeting between the CCC and district officials was any indication, there appeared to be little potential for cooperation between the two sides.

Following the public meeting, the Coordinating Committee shaped its demands in more concrete terms. Nine objectives were defined by the coalition and presented to the school board on September 17. Eight of the objectives addressed the busing controversy specifically. The coalition demanded above all that the bused students be "regularly enrolled" at the receiving schools. In addition, the CCC urged that the teachers of bused students be assigned to the receiving schools and no longer required to ride the bus with their classes. Other proposals urged a reduction in the number of students on each bus and that the size of the classes being bused be reduced to twenty-five students. A feasibility study to investigate the possibility of area busing, as opposed to transporting class units, was recommended. The Committee also argued that some means of transporting students who missed their buses should be provided. The lone objective not specifically related to busing demanded a joint study of the district's attendance zones by school officials and representatives of the coalition.

Several heated exchanges erupted as Gwendolyn Wells presented the coalition's proposed reforms to the school board. At one point in the meeting, Wells alleged that the Board of Education demonstrated "an arbitrary indifference" to the needs of black students and "callously ignores" the concerns of black parents. When the school board proposed the formation of a biracial committee to resolve the situation Wells retorted, "We cannot but feel at this time that such a committee would serve little purpose but to offer this board a continuing excuse for its failure to take action to implement its own stated policy." During Wells's discussion of the coalition's proposals to resolve the busing situation, school board president Homer Wadsworth interjected, "If you are asking this board to use busing to force integration, the answer is 'No.'" It was clear in late September that, for both parties, compromise would be difficult.

In order to further pressure the school district to integrate the busing students, the CCC brought June Shagaloff, an education specialist from NAACP's national offices, to Kansas City. The *Call* emphasized the need for a spirit of cooperation in the talks. "It is time to stop making charges and countercharges," an editorial stated, "and to sit down, carefully review the facts, determine what is feasible and desirable and then work out a plan to achieve what is best for our children." Shagaloff provided another voice of reason. She posited that, "when white parents are assured there will be stability in their schools and that their schools are good schools, they will remain in their old neighborhoods."

On September 23, Shagaloff and ten members of the CCC met with Hazlett and other district officials to discuss the busing dilemma. The Coordinating Committee's statement, drafted after the meeting, indicated the two sides were still at loggerheads. "First, we made crystal clear our firm opposition to the establishment of self-contained Negro classes in receiving white schools," the statement began. "We await the response of the superintendent on this." The Coordinating Committee asserted it "was not proposing the mass busing of Negro or white pupils, helter-skelter, from one end of the city to the other." Rather, they proposed, "meaningful plans to alleviate the segregation so harmful educationally to all children." The meeting marked a minor breakthrough as the coalition "suggested that these discussions be continued." However, the fact that the two sides remained at an impasse was apparent in the statement's closing sentence. The Committee warned that, "unless the Kansas City school system meets these problems squarely and directly, we will have no alternative but to consider appropriate actions, including litigation."

Integrating Busing

The threat of litigation produced immediate results. At the school board meeting the following week, Superintendent Hazlett announced: "By October 15, 1964, all children being transported, except for the eleven classes at Ladd transported to Humboldt, will become part of the receiving school." Parents in the Ladd area specifically requested their children not be integrated. In addition, the school board ordered that, "teachers of the transported children will become a part of the faculty of the receiving school and adult bus riders will be hired to replace the supervision of teachers." The school board's recalcitrant defense of the busing program had collapsed under the threat of litigation. However, the acceptance of the new policy by the city's white population remained uncertain for the moment.

The school board did not need to wait long for the reaction of the white population. One week after announcing that the bus students would be integrated, Hazlett postponed implementation indefinitely. The Parent-Teacher Associations at four schools of the receiving schools requested opportunities to address the school board. The P.T.A. groups represented schools affected by the change in policy and sought to voice their opposition to integrated busing. Each of the organizations was granted a place on the school board agenda for October 21.

Mrs. Howard Murray, president of the Norman School P.T.A., told the school board: "We do believe in the neighborhood school system and are strongly opposed to busing except in emergencies of overcrowding." As the present arrangement had been necessitated by crowding, the Norman P.T.A. did not object to receiving three classes of seventh grade students from Kumpf, as long as they remained separate. "The classes of both schools," Mrs. Murray believed, "would be disrupted by mixing them together at this point in the year. At Norman, this would be a three to one ratio (black to white) in the seventh grade, which is a difficult enough age group without the added turmoil of mixing." She also objected to separating children from their classmates and justified this point by stressing the harm especially to "the children who are bussed [sic], since they are already being taken away from their own school and neighborhood."

The president of the Swinney P.T.A., Mrs. William Lutz, agreed with Murray. "This is not the proper time in the school year to make such a change," she argued, "just to please a minority group." Despite their displeasure with the announcement to integrate transported students, the Swinney P.T.A. pledged to abide by the school board's decision provided that adequate staff and equipment were made available to the school.

Mrs. Betty Hayes, of the Allen P.T.A., revealed just how deep seated the opposition was in certain areas of the white community. She claimed that the "board is being pressured into this by a few minority groups," maintaining that, "the majority of the people have not been heard." Hayes asserted, "Adults are pushing this thing just to mix the Negroes and whites, at the expense of all children." Integrating the students, in her opinion, "cannot further the education of either of them, but only cause confusion, rebellion, and emotional instability." She asked the school board, "Is forced integration of classrooms on a short term basis worth it?"

The P.T.A. presidents from Norman, Swinney, and Allen who spoke to the board were white and represented receiving schools. The perspective of these schools generated one set of reasons for opposing integrated busing. Mrs. Donald Stevenson, the president of the Linwood P.T.A., also opposed the policy but for different reasons. In 1964, Linwood Elementary was 97.3% black and sent six classes of students to Douglass School, located on the west side of the city. The Linwood P.T.A. objected to the integrated busing scheme not as a matter of principle, but because they did not want their children to be too closely associated with the neighborhoods on the west side. The Douglass area was among the poorest in the city and had been in decline for a number of years. The black and white populations in the Douglass area had begun to vacate the neighborhood during the 1950s and the remaining population was largely Hispanic. Apparently, the Linwood parents, having been successful enough to move away from deteriorating areas, perceived the Douglass as a step down socially and economically, and objected to their children interacting with the students at that school. "Culturally," Stevenson argued, "our children will not benefit from being reassigned to the Douglass community. As we have stated before we were dissatisfied with that section of Kansas City long ago. We feel the north and west areas will not be suitable." Furthermore, Stevenson insisted, "We were never satisfied with the transporting system from the beginning. We have accepted this arrangement because we were told that it was a temporary arrangement." The Linwood P.T.A. urged the school board to reassign their children to "good schools," rather than Douglass.

One school board member, after having listened to the P.T.A. groups, asked the superintendent to offer his assessment of the legality of maintaining segregated classes for bused students. Hazlett speculated that the "school district would be in the vulnerable position of maintaining segregation." It appeared the school district was legally and ethically obliged to integrate the classes, particularly in light of the plan to do so announced three weeks earlier. Hazlett requested a special meeting of the school board "to consider the various problems in connection with the transportation of pupils." The Board of Education agreed to meet on October 28.

Resolution

Hazlett arrived at the meeting with a proposal in hand addressing the busing situation. From a legal standpoint, the superintendent believed that if "transported students are sent to schools of predominantly another race, then integration is necessary to avoid what in fact is a segregated condition." Yet, he contended, there were other factors to consider in any plan to integrate the students. He emphasized that "time for preparation of parents, teachers and pupils is very important." Furthermore, "if racial integration is to provide constructive educational results," Hazlett argued, "the integrated situation must not cause a 'threat' in the receiving school and neighborhood." Ideally, "a degree of racial balance must be sought." In Hazlett's reasoning, "the 'principle of wide distribution' is indicated. More schools must share in providing integrated situations." The plan would integrate the bused students, but it would spread them around as thinly as possible in hopes of averting panic among white residents. This decision marked a turning point of sorts in the district's approach to integration. In one respect, the school district began to use busing to promote integration, but it attempted to do so in such a way that the city might retain its white population.

Hazlett's plan involved a two-stage process. Fourteen classes were to be integrated in November at ten different schools, some of which had never before enrolled black students or received students in the district busing plan. The second phase provided for the integration of students bused from Ladd and Linwood schools the following school year. Both of these schools had objected to having their pupils identified as part of the receiving schools and Hazlett had honored their request. In September 1965, the students from Ladd and Linwood were to be integrated at more than a dozen different schools around the city. The school board members debated Hazlett's proposal for almost two hours before approving the plan.

The Citizens' Coordinating Committee's campaign against segregated busing ended on November 30, 1964, as the first classes were fully integrated at the receiving schools without incident. Additional classes were integrated during the second half of the school year. In September 1965, four additional elementary schools – Faxon, Meservey, Graceland and Melcher – joined the fraternity of schools busing to relieve crowding and the number of children on the buses climbed to 1,750. Again, the vast majority of the bused students were black, reflecting the enrollment of the sending schools, which were 86% black on the average. In all, nine elementary schools in the black migratory corridor to the south were busing students to twenty-two different schools around the city. Hazlett's insistence on a policy of "wide distribution" was in place. In addition, the 1965 plan provided for area busing, transporting all the children living on certain blocks to new schools. This was significant because it permitted children from the same family to be bused to the same receiving school. Previously, the busing plan had split siblings who were in different grades. "All of us were pleased with their total understanding of the problem," Hazlett told the *Kansas City Times*. He proudly announced: "No one approved of transporting students as a permanent solution, but people showed a willingness to exploit the educational values that could come out of this temporary situation."

Fletcher Daniels, chairman of the CCC agreed. "It appears to be a step in the right direction. . . . We do not advocate busing for integration purposes alone, but if children are to be bussed [sic] to relieve overcrowding, we want them to go to good schools." Similarly, several other members of the Committee voiced their approval of the school district's new busing plan.

Conclusions

The school district elected, for several reasons, to deal with the Coordinating Committee in a much different manner than they had with CORE during the summer of 1963. Certainly, the fact that the CCC represented a coalition of the most powerful civil rights organizations in the city had some impact on the district's decision to treat their concerns more seriously. In addition, it appears that a turning point was reached when the Committee called on June Shagaloff, a national civil rights leader, to assist in the negotiations. The preliminary announcement to end segregated busing was presented less than ten days after Hazlett and other school officials met with Shagaloff and the CCC. Perhaps the prospect of national civil rights organizations injecting their resources into the Kansas City controversy persuaded school officials that it would be preferable to resolve the situation before it attracted the full attention of the NAACP, Urban League, or CORE.

The largest factor, however, would seem to have been the legal issues involved in retaining segregated busing. Kansas City's integration program, although it had its flaws, had consistently complied with prevailing legal standards. The busing program, however, was clearly a situation where the district defied the law, and the preliminary announcement of plans to terminate the practice of busing self-contained classes of blacks was made only after the CCC threatened litigation. Still, when the white community responded unfavorably to the announcement, the district suspended implementation and considered reneging on the plan. The final decision hinged on the superintendent's conclusion that the continuation of segregated busing would place the district "in the vulnerable position of maintaining segregation." One week after Hazlett reminded the school board of the possible legal ramifications involved in retaining the onerous segregated busing scheme; the final plan for integrating the classes was adopted.

The school board had been well aware of the precarious legal standing of the segregated busing plan since its genesis in 1960. But, the district refused to integrate the classes until the civil rights coalition raised the specter of litigation. In nearly ten years of desegregation, the school district had gained insight to the manner in which white schools and neighborhoods reacted to the introduction of black students. In many cases, whites applied for transfers or moved away. Neighborhoods resegregated, defeating the purpose of integration. This phenomenon was most acute in schools that received large numbers of black students over a relatively short period of time, as was true of the neighborhoods in the path of the black migration.

The initial busing plan assigned large numbers of black students to a limited number of receiving schools. It is likely the school district decided upon self-contained classrooms for the bused students to forestall a white exodus from those schools. It is not surprising that the parent-teacher organizations from Allen and Norman sent delegates to the school board meeting to oppose integrated busing, inasmuch as both schools received more than 100 African-American students. In 1964, Humboldt was receiving eleven classes of predominantly black students from Ladd. To have integrated at that point would have shifted the racial composition of Humboldt from 15.5% black to more than 50% black. Previous experience had taught the school district that schools which approached 50% black rapidly became virtually all-black. Thus, Superintendent Hazlett's reasons for insisting that more schools become involved in accommodating the busing students becomes apparent. The superintendent recognized the "onus" borne by the few schools receiving the majority of the busing volume had to be relieved. Given the district's history, the alternative appeared to be resignation to the probability that those schools would become predominantly African-American schools. Consequently, the eleven classes of students from Ladd were not integrated in November 1964 at Humboldt. The following year, in an application of Hazlett's principle of "wide distribution," Ladd students were integrated at five different sites. Although none dared say it, school officials recognized that too much integration too quickly had failed in some sections of the city. Therefore, they delayed a decision on integrated busing as long as possible, and then diluted the volume so that the number of students integrated at a particular school would not prompt whites to seek transfers or move.

Despite the smooth transition to integrated busing, school officials clearly did not perceive busing as a long term solution. The district remained committed to the neighborhood school concept and repeatedly told patrons that "transportation will be discontinued as rapidly as funds become available and new facilities can be constructed." In February, 1965, the school district reintroduced a bond issue nearly identical to the one that had been defeated in 1964. The 1965 bond issue was approved by a margin of three to one, easily securing the two-thirds majority necessary for passage. The heaviest approval came from the black wards in the central area and to the south, as well as the exclusively white neighborhoods in the southwest. It is not surprising that support for the bond issue came from these wards. The black neighborhoods were desperately in need of more schools to relieve crowding, while the white wards in the southwest were among the most affluent in Kansas City and had a long history of supporting bond issues.

The school district now had the funds to relieve the crowding through new school construction; however, selection of building sites would prove to be another source of controversy for the school district. By the mid-1960s, Kansas City had made some progress toward creating an integrated school system. But there remained a clear divide between the school officials' assessment of their duty to manage the system in the interest of all its patrons and the black community's expectations that the school district craft policies that which would promote more extensive racial integration in the city's schools.

CHAPTER 3

Missed Opportunities

The Havighurst Study and Hazlett's "Concepts for Changing Times," 1965-1969

Population change, particularly the expansion of the large central black neighborhood toward the southeast, created numerous challenges for school administrators in Kansas City during the 1960s. In the schools serving the neighborhoods within the black migratory corridor, the immediate problem was overcrowded classrooms. But the massive population shifts associated with the expansion of the corridor also raised the specter of resegregation. These associated problems first became prominent in the area served by Central High School. The enrollment at Central rose by more than 500 students between 1955 and 1963, and the racial composition of the school shifted from 11.2% black in 1955 to 99.1% black in 1963. Moreover, the pattern at Central was certain to continue. Over the same period, the number of students in enrolled in just eight of the elementary schools that fed Central grew by more than 3,300. These schools were all located in the black migratory corridor and rapidly progressed toward resegregation. By 1963, five of the eight schools were more than 95% black and all of the schools were grossly overcrowded.

In the short term, the crowding situation was addressed by the school district's agreement on the busing program reached in 1964 with the civil rights organizations arrayed in the Citizens' Coordinating Committee (CCC). Busing thousands of black children, however, was not a long term solution to the problems created by population shifts and residential transition in the Central area. A lasting solution, district officials hoped, would be forged through the construction of new schools to serve the growing population and possibly promote greater integration in this area.

Kansas City school officials were acutely aware of the population shifts in the Central area and began planning for relief in 1963. That fall, plans were developed for three new elementary schools and a new junior high school in the Central area, with hopes that the buildings would be completed by September 1966. Construction was necessarily postponed, however, pending approval of a bond issue to finance the projects.

On May 26, 1964 the school district presented voters with a $17 million bond issue to renovate and rehabilitate existing schools as well as to build several new schools. Nearly one-half of the bond issue funds were earmarked for six new schools, the three elementary schools and a junior high school in the crowded Central area, and two elementary schools for the Rock Creek area, a rapidly growing white residential section on the eastern rim of the city. However, the 1964 bond issue won the support of only 54% of Kansas City voters, well short of the necessary 67%. Thus, the proposed construction stalled for nine months until the bond issue was resubmitted and passed in February 1965.

Voting patterns on the bond issues reveal much about how residents in different areas of the city viewed the school district and by extension the school district's integration programs. It is important to remember that one major focus of the bond issue was the Central area. Many white Kansas City voters associated the Central area with "blockbusting," racial turnover, and declining real estate values. When the bond issue was first proposed to Kansas City voters in May 1964, the measure won the required 67% approval in just four of the city's twenty-four wards, the overwhelmingly black Second and Fourteenth Wards, the largely black Seventeenth Ward, and the Eighth Ward in the affluent southwestern section of the city. Although the bond issue received majority support in eleven more wards, it fell several thousand votes short of the necessary two-thirds approval rate. The bond issue was soundly defeated in the white working class areas north and east of downtown. In those four wards, fewer than 40% of the voters approved the bond issue.

When the bond issue was put to the voters again in February 1965, three-fourths of those who cast ballots approved of the measure. The 1965 bond issue won more than two-thirds majorities in 17 of the city's twenty-four wards, and was supported by a simple majority of the voters in the remaining wards. The approval of the 1965 bond issue was a dramatic reversal of the result from the preceding May. In part, the shift in the voting patterns was attributable to school district efforts to publicize the bond issue and persuade concerned patrons to vote. The publicity effort resulted in 12,000 more votes cast in the 1965 bond election than in the previous year's vote. Second, the reversal among voters in the 1965 bond vote may be in part attributable to the shift in school district policy concerning those black students bused to relieve crowding in the Central area. At the time of the 1964 vote, entire classrooms of black students were bused to vacant classrooms in nine other schools. By 1965, the school district had amended the intact busing program. The 1965 busing scheme integrated black busing students at the receiving schools, and increased the number of schools receiving busing students to twenty-two. Superintendent Hazlett's policy of "wide distribution" of the busing students meant that schools in all sections of the city were involved in the busing program. It seems reasonable to conclude that the shift in the busing program helped to acquaint a larger part of the city's voters with the problem of crowding in the elementary schools serving the black residential corridor around Central. Indeed, it is likely that some voters concluded that the sooner the new schools were completed, the sooner the integrated busing program would end.

With the approval of the February 1965 bond issue, the school district had funding for its construction and renovation projects, and the district's central administrative staff immediately delved into the task of evaluating sites for the new schools. Because of the need to relieve crowding and the desire to reduce busing, acquiring sites for the new schools in the Central area was a top priority. In their initial evaluations of possible building sites in the Central area, school officials concerned themselves primarily with the availability of the site, the cost of acquisition, and the cost of developing the site. They neglected to consider how site selection might influence the school district's integration plan. The city's civil rights organizations recognized, however, that site selection and school construction could be an instrument that either promoted or inhibited school integration, and in 1965 the CCC made its concerns known to the Board of Education.

In early June 1965, Superintendent James Hazlett and Assistant Superintendent for Buildings and Grounds, Dr. Dewey Smith, reported on site selection for three new elementary schools and a new junior high school to relieve crowding and reduce busing in the Central area. The school board approved the sites and began the process of acquiring these properties at a cost of over $1.1 million. The school board's actions, however, met with opposition. In mid-July, Fletcher Daniels of the CCC expressed "serious reservations" about these sites in light of "the challenges of a rapidly increasing and shifting school population and *de facto* segregation." Essentially, the CCC's position was that building new schools on these sites would do nothing to advance integration. The sites were located in predominantly black neighborhoods and would likely perpetuate *de facto* segregation in these areas. The CCC urged the district to delay acquisition of the sites and recommended that a panel of experts be hired to consult on issues of "racial segregation and their relationship to school boundaries [and] site selection of new schools."

Following the meeting with the CCC, a stalemate developed as the school board divided evenly over the issue of employing consultants to study residential patterns and site selection for the new schools. One bloc was led by Henry Poindexter, a conservative businessman who lived in the exclusive southwest section of the city. These board members were somewhat less concerned with the overall impact that school board decisions might have on integration and generally less sympathetic to the interests of the black patrons in issues of school management. These board members tended to favor action, in this case supporting measures to acquire the sites and build the schools as quickly as possible in order to relieve the problem of crowding, regardless of whatever interests the black community professed over the location of the buildings and the effect that the schools might have on integration. Dr. John Ramos, a radiologist and the school board's lone black member, and school board president Homer Wadsworth, the director of the Kansas City Association of Trusts and Foundations, a philanthropic organization, led the other bloc. These board members tended to be more mindful of integration issues and were more likely to favor building sites that promoted additional desegregation. They also tended to have somewhat greater respect for the concerns raised by the black community and its representative organizations.

The divide between these camps was clearly illustrated at the July 30 special board meeting. Poindexter moved that the sites be acquired without the services of a consultant but was unable to secure a majority among the board members. Similarly, a motion by Dr. Ramos to employ a consultant failed to win approval. Meanwhile the CCC adhered to its original position that consultants be employed. The deadlock was broken when Superintendent Hazlett spoke in favor of hiring a consultant. Hazlett reaffirmed his approval of the current sites but also welcomed a review by a consultant and recommended that a panel be consulted for future site selection studies. Hazlett's confidence in the appropriateness of the sites already approved persuaded board members to assent to hiring a consultant with instructions to report to the board in three weeks, on August 20.

The Havighurst Study

Dr. Robert J. Havighurst, a professor of education and the director of the Center for the Study of Metropolitan Problems in Education at the University of Missouri-Kansas City, was tabbed as the chairman of the consulting group brought in by the school district. Havighurst was assisted by William L. Cobb, the Assistant Superintendent for Human Relations in the San Francisco Public Schools, and Norman Drachler, the Detroit Public Schools' Assistant Superintendent for School-Community Relations. The consultants were charged with examining the district's building needs, site selection procedures, and policies regarding integration.

The greatest immediate difficulty facing Havighurst and his associates was the three week timeline in which they were to report on the sites. Havighurst informed Hazlett that meeting the deadline was impossible; nevertheless, at its August 20 meeting, the Board of Education moved forward with the acquisition of the sites. Hazlett again recommended that the sites be purchased stating that he could not "in good conscience with funds made available by the voters to construct new schools to reduce bussing [sic], approve of further delay in acquiring the approved sites." Hazlett's sense of urgency was heightened by his understanding of population trends in the Central area. He foresaw the number of school children bused out of the area steadily rising from 1,700 in 1965-66, to 2,750 in 1966-67, and over 3,800 in 1967-68. Hazlett argued, "If site acquisition started tomorrow it would be optimistic to consider the buildings being ready by September 1967." On Hazlett's recommendation the school board voted 4-2 to purchase the three sites. Curiously, the school board also approved Hazlett's recommendation that Havighurst's consulting team continue their study and report to the board in December.

The school board's action to purchase the sites touched off a storm of protest from Kansas City's black community. Having hired the consultants to study school sites, members of the black community were understandably outraged when the school board moved to acquire building sites without having seen the consulting team's recommendations. Indeed, the school board's action gave the impression that the consultants had been hired merely to placate the CCC, while the district moved forward in acquiring sites that they had already decided upon. Displeasure with the school board mounted when the largest of the three sites was purchased. Sixty ministers signed a petition urging the school district to postpone acquiring the other sites until Havighurst had concluded his study. The city's NAACP and CORE offices announced that they were considering legal action to prevent the school district from developing the sites.

Under pressure from the CCC, the board suspended efforts to acquire the other two properties until Havighurst completed his study. Henry Poindexter lambasted his colleagues for bowing to "a few self-styled leaders of various Civil Rights [sic] groups." The interlude while the school board awaited Dr. Havighurst's report clearly illustrated the racial polarization within Kansas City. The decision to postpone acquiring the other two sites undoubtedly pleased many blacks, but it also enraged a significant number of the district's white patrons. While awaiting the consultant's report the school board was bombarded with some 400 letters expressing opposition to the delay in constructing the new schools.

Havighurst's interim report was presented in early November and the final draft of the study unveiled at the December 2 school board meeting. Havighurst first addressed population trends in the Kansas City metropolitan area and the issue of where to build the new schools to relieve crowding in "the Seven-School area," referring to the elementary schools in the Central area that were involved in the busing program – Faxon, Kumpf, Ladd, Linwood, Mann, Meservey, and Seven Oaks.

Havighurst recommended that schools be built on two of the sites that the board had approved despite acknowledging that they "would probably be *de facto* Negro schools." Indeed the consultants saw no "practicable way of getting integrated schooling for the entire group of Negro children in the Seven-School Area, as long as the present pattern of residential segregation persists." Although Havighurst concluded that integration for all black students in the area was impossible he suggested several measures that would foster increased integration. The report proposed building a middle school for fifth through eighth grades in the area of Brush Creek and Paseo with attendance zones drawn such that the school could "maintain a racial balance of approximately equal numbers of Negro and white children." The consultants also recommended building a new integrated high school in the Northwest area, converting the Metropolitan Junior College building into a junior high school, and the construction of a new junior high school on the eastern fringe of the black corridor to relieve crowding at Central Junior High and promote integration.

Beyond the issues of facilities and site selection the consulting team urged the school district to reevaluate the busing program, modify the transfer policy in order to "prevent re-segregation," and promote staff integration "so as to achieve a balance between Negro and white teachers," while also taking into account factors such as experience, age, and gender. Finally, the consultants advised that the district expand its compensatory education programs in schools serving low income areas, as well as create a new administrative position for a Director of Public Relations to work in "areas where there are integration problems."

Following the overview of the report, Hazlett commented, "All of the suggestions have merit and should be carefully considered." Particular attention, he said, "should be given to financing the various recommendations." The superintendent pledged to examine the study more thoroughly and report back to the board. None of the school board members commented although the majority had been highly critical of the interim report, particularly the proposed middle school.

When Hazlett presented his report seven weeks later, he noted that several of Havighurst's suggestions were already incorporated in the district's plans, including the construction of the elementary schools and junior high school in the Central area, and the conversion of the junior college building into a junior high school in the Westport area. Hazlett suggested that other recommendations could be handled administratively, such as the formation of a busing advisory committee comprised of patrons living in the areas that sent or received bus students. The superintendent maintained that still other recommendations, such as the proposal for a new junior high east of the Central area, should be considered in future planning sessions. At Hazlett's urging, the board approved two items, the creation of a position titled Community Development Officer, and the appointment of two school community agents to work in neighborhoods undergoing residential transition, specifically the Paseo and Southeast areas. Hazlett did not address the most controversial proposals included in Havighurst's report: the new integrated high school in the Northwest area, teacher integration, reforming the transfer policy, and the new middle school.

In early 1966 the process of acquiring the sites, razing the structures currently occupying the sites, developing architectural plans, and breaking ground for the three new schools in the Central area began. Each of the schools was slated to open in the 1968-69 school term. In the two years between the school board's approval for these schools and the completion of construction the problems of crowding and resegregation in the Central area intensified. In 1966 Central Junior High enrolled 1,900 students, all but thirteen of whom were black. Ninety-one classes at Central Junior High had enrollments of more than forty students. Additional teachers were added to the faculty and the teaching load for others was increased, including offering some classes that met after the regular school day had ended. For part of the year classes were held in the hallways with students sharing textbooks. The situation in the elementary schools was similar. Eight elementary schools in the Central area were overcrowded and more than 1,500 students rode the buses. In spite of the busing, the situation remained acute in these schools. All had pupil-teacher ratios of better than thirty students per teacher. At Kumpf the enrollment ran as high as forty-one students in a class, while one class at Meservey had fifty-two.

With the school construction projects underway in the Central area, Hazlett and the school board considered the remaining elements of the Havighurst report. They first focused on the recommendation that a new integrated high school be built in the northwest area. School district studies indicated that "the over-all pupil population base in this area is stable," and according to 1965 enrollment figures, the racial composition in the schools that would feed the proposed high school was 56% black and 44% white. Although these figures made the new high school an attractive proposition, other considerations rendered its construction unlikely. The best available site for the proposed school was located within the Manual urban renewal project area and many students would have to "walk over a mile ... through declining business neighborhoods, [and] areas of extremely heavy traffic." These conditions implied that the school district would need to provide transportation for some students or build a second school. Several school board members voiced objections to both of those prospects. More significantly, fiscal realities intruded on the plans. No allocation for a new high school had been included in the 1964 bond program, and in spite of efforts to divert money from other projects, the district was more than $1.7 million short of the funding necessary to build the school. Nevertheless, the prospect of an integrated high school in the northwest area sparked the imagination of district administrators and garnered support from school district officials for the next decade.

Among the more challenging of Havighurst's recommendations was that steps be taken toward greater teacher integration and achieving balance among the teaching staffs in terms of racial composition, age, gender, and experience. With respect to racial composition, Havighurst noted that segregated faculties were most evident in the elementary schools. In 1965, forty-two of the district's eighty elementary schools had single race faculties. Of those schools, nine had all black faculties and thirty-three were exclusively white. Twenty-three other elementary schools had only one or two teachers of the minority race on staffs which were otherwise single race. For instance, at Richardson one white teacher worked with thirty-two black colleagues, while at Whittier the teacher corps of twenty-two included a single black. Thus, of the city's eighty elementary schools, sixty-five had teaching staffs that were either single race or possessed only token integration. At the secondary level, only Lincoln Junior High had a single race teaching staff in 1965. Tokenism, however, was apparent at eleven of the district's seventeen other junior highs and high schools. The type of "balance" that Havighurst endorsed clearly did not exist in the Kansas City public schools in 1965.

Superintendent Hazlett assigned the task of developing plans for teacher integration to Herb Sang, an assistant superintendent for personnel. Sang produced a rough plan of action, but the district did not adopt a formal policy regarding teacher integration during the mid-1960s other than attempting to persuade teachers that they would benefit from "varied experience." Despite this encouragement few teachers sought transfers to positions that would have increased the amount of integration among the faculty at a particular school and very few teachers were forcibly transferred. Ultimately, when the school board adopted a formal policy statement on teacher integration in 1969, it was more a vague pledge "to work affirmatively in implementing its objective of effective integration of faculties" than a serious plan of action.

Nevertheless, teacher integration made some progress, principally through the hiring of new teachers. The number of schools possessing single race faculties was trimmed to twenty-eight in 1967, and to twenty-three by 1972. Similarly, the number of schools with token staff integration was reduced to twenty-two schools by 1972. Much work remained to be done, however. Almost 50% of the city's schools still had single race or predominantly single race teaching staffs in 1972. A preponderance of the city's black students, particularly in the elementary schools, continued to be taught by predominantly African-American teaching staffs, while a majority of the city's white students continued to receive instruction from faculties that were disproportionately white. In 1968, Carver Elementary closed without ever having employed a white teacher. Conversely, in 1972 twelve schools, located primarily on the exclusively white eastern edge of the city, had never employed a single black teacher.

In accord with Havighurst's recommendation, teacher integration was among the school district's goals in the late 1960s and early 1970s. But progress toward that objective proceeded in a haphazard fashion and varied widely from one building to the next. Integrating faculties on a district-wide basis did not become an urgent priority until 1973 when the school district was faced with the suspension of federal funding by the U.S. Department of Health, Education and Welfare.

Havighurst had also suggested that the school district revise its long standing, liberal transfer policy "whenever it is not working in the best interest of maintaining racially balanced schools." He recognized correctly that "the numbers of transfers have been relatively large" and had undermined desegregation in the district. School district records supported Havighurst's conclusions. More than 3,000 requests for transfer had been granted each year since the district began integration, and in some years nearly 5,000 transfers were approved. School district administrators also confirmed that granting transfers had "reduced the potential number of white pupils at some schools," notably in the areas served by Central, Paseo, and Manual high schools. Moreover, school officials agreed that although transfers were denied when the stated reason for the request was "to avoid integration," there was "no real doubt that this is the underlying reason" for numerous requests. District policymakers were reluctant, however, to tamper with the transfer policy arguing that the ability of parents to obtain transfers for their children "has been an important factor in delaying the change of some neighborhoods . . . from white to Negro." Buttressed by this line of reasoning, school district officials were not inclined to consider revising the transfer policy. Even so, it was clear that school officials were familiar with how the transfer policy was used to avoid integration and the argument that the policy slowed "white flight" from the district was specious in that, either through a transfer or by moving away, white students evaded school integration. By retaining the transfer policy, school officials subtly bowed to the interests of whites and compounded the problem of racial separation in the schools.

Paseo High School was identified by Havighurst as an opportune site for testing changes to the transfer policy. When integration began in 1955, Paseo enrolled just twenty-seven black students in a school of 1,665. Black students comprised less than 10% of the enrollment at Paseo for each of the first six years of integration. Between 1961 and 1965, however, the black enrollment at Paseo steadily increased from

16% to more than 60%, and the school appeared to be destined for complete resegregation. In his 1965 report to the school board, Havighurst observed: "The neighborhoods around Paseo are confronted with all the tensions that exist in large cities when neighborhoods are going through a change." Yet, he argued, "Many citizens in these areas, white and Negro, are committed to the idea of integration." What was necessary to maintain integration in the Paseo area, Havighurst suggested, was for the school district to "demonstrate in every way possible that quality education and integration are inseparable." The consultant urged the school board to "initiate special programs and features within Paseo High School." Moreover, he urged the transfer policy be restricted somewhat for Paseo and "aimed at maintaining a better racial balance" at the school.

Until the mid-1960s, school officials viewed transfers almost exclusively in terms of space available in the schools, with no consideration of the impact transfers had on integration. For several years the district maintained no record of the racial breakdown among transfers, and thereby was incapable of measuring the effects of the transfer policy on integration. Nevertheless, school administrators were aware of how the policy was exploited by whites to transfer out of schools undergoing racial transition, and acknowledged in 1965 that this was occurring "presently at Paseo." Indeed, between 1961 and 1965, 197 white students transferred from Paseo to all-white Southwest High School, and an additional 220 students had transferred to 91% white Westport High School. Even so, for the time being, district administrators chose not to modify the transfer policy generally, or for Paseo specifically.

The school district may not yet have been alarmed by the use of the transfer policy to evade integration or by Paseo's progress toward resegregation, but residents around the school were. In March 1966, a delegation of parents, led by Thomas Vleisides, expressed to the school board their concern that "Paseo be maintained as a truly integrated high school." They asserted that "Paseo High School offers the Kansas City Board of Education a unique opportunity" to promote integration, "make Paseo a better school," and "make possible the continuation of the racially integrated residential pattern in the area around the school."

The Paseo delegation urged that the school board close the routes of evasion to Southwest and Westport high schools by prohibiting transfers into or out of Paseo and maintaining the attendance zone boundaries to the south and west. Moreover, the parents suggested that the district add advanced placement and academically talented courses at Paseo, and that the school environment be made safer through the hiring of additional supervisory personnel and better coordination of police patrols.

The parents stated it was important that area residents feel that "they can trust the school board" to act in the interest of preserving integration at Paseo. The delegation emphasized that Paseo residents were "engaged in a struggle to maintain integrated housing patterns" and that "this summer looks to be a crucial time" as pressures mounted in the real estate market. Prompt action was requested, and the group's recommendations carried significant weight. The proposals were endorsed by six Paseo area PTAs, four neighborhood councils, and the Paseo community council.

Under pressure from Paseo residents, the first significant modifications to the transfer policy came at the next school board meeting. Hazlett unveiled ten points of action designed to address the various concerns raised by the parents. The superintendent assured Paseo patrons that the school's high academic standards would be preserved and that an advanced placement center would be opened at Paseo offering introductory college level courses. Additional personnel were hired to address the safety and security concerns, and the board approved "human relations" in-service training for Paseo's staff. Most significantly, Hazlett assured Paseo area residents that no further transfers would be granted for the remainder of the 1966-67 school year and alluded to the possibility that transfers into or out of Paseo could be prohibited for the entire 1967-68 school year. In this way the transfer policy, or more accurately the district's refusal to grant transfers, was finally envisioned as a pro-active instrument for maintaining integrated schools. Attempting to restore the residents' confidence in the district, Hazlett's ten points were mailed to every household in the Paseo area.

Paseo area residents, exercising their new found clout with the school board, continued to exert pressure on school district administrators during the spring and summer of 1966. Delegations from the Paseo area appeared at several school board meetings making small requests, such as various maintenance projects to improve the general appearance of the building. In August, however, the Paseo group overestimated their influence and asked for the impossible – that all transfers in the school district be denied for a trial period of two years. Although school board members were fully aware of how the transfer policy had been routinely used to avoid integration, they considered it to be a necessary concession in order to retain the white student enrollment. Without the transfer policy, many school officials feared that "white flight" from the district would increase dramatically. School board members balked at the request to deny all transfers and instead deferred to Hazlett's recommendation that a two year moratorium on transfers be applied to Paseo only. Hazlett also proposed that at Central, Lincoln, Southeast, Southwest, and Van Horn high schools, and the junior high schools that fed those schools, transfers be denied in 1966-67 due to crowding. The measures left four high schools, two junior highs, and all elementary schools which were not crowded open to transfers.

Over the next two years, school district administrators closely monitored developments at Paseo. The results were rather discouraging. In spite of the prohibition on transfers, the addition of advanced placement courses, the human relations in-service training, improved security at the school, and completion of various maintenance projects to make the school more attractive, Paseo moved toward resegregation. Over the two year period, the white enrollment at Paseo fell by 73 students, while the black enrollment grew by 338. One year later, when the restriction on transfers was lifted, the white enrollment fell by 240 and the school was 88% black. By 1969, black students accounted for 98% of the school's enrollment. Moreover, as Paseo resegregated, the school district diluted the curriculum, moving its physics course to Southwest High School, which then had two such courses. In its place Paseo began offering "industrial sanitation," a course in janitorial science.

The school district's measures at Paseo had temporarily held much of the school's white enrollment. School district policies, however, were no match for the momentum of the real estate market. Regardless of the assurances from residents that prompt action by the school district could preserve the racially integrated character of the Paseo area, the neighborhoods served by the high school began to resegregate during the late 1960s. Census figures indicate that in 1960 the area served by Paseo was 86% white, but as blacks migrated out of the large central neighborhood during the 1960s, the racial composition of the area changed dramatically. During the sixties, almost 16,000 blacks moved into the Paseo area while the white population declined by more than 17,000. Troost Avenue again appears to be the dividing line between black and white occupancy. About 80% of the Paseo attendance zone was located east of Troost and these neighborhoods made the transition from white to black residency with startling speed during the 1960s. Of the more than 15,000 black residents who moved into the Paseo area during the 1960s, 99% settled in the neighborhoods east of Troost, while the number of blacks living in the Paseo zone west of Troost remained unchanged. Once the restriction on transfers was lifted, white students in the western part of the Paseo attendance zone sought placements elsewhere, and Paseo became a virtually all-black school.

The middle school proposal in the Havighurst report was the focus of the most bitter debate. To a large degree, discussion of the report and its numerous recommendations crystallized around the middle school proposal. School board members and district patrons who favored the middle school were also those who favored a more aggressive and creative approaches to integration. Those who disapproved of

Havighurst's middle school tended to rally around the cause of neighborhood schools and a more parochial perspective of the challenges that race and demographic change posed for school district administration.

Havighurst suggested that the middle school be built near the intersection of Paseo and Brush Creek where it would "go far toward relieving the overcrowding" in the Central area schools. Moreover, he argued that the school could "serve an area wide enough to include Negro and white residential neighborhoods and can maintain the kind of racial balance that is desired by parents." Because of this site's proximity to the University of Missouri-Kansas City, Havighurst envisioned "a close working relationship" with the university that ultimately could lead to the middle school becoming "the major center for innovation and demonstration for the intermediate grades in the Kansas City area." Finally, he argued that the middle school could be "a key element in the maintenance of a prosperous integrated neighborhood."

Havighurst proposed that the middle school draw students from the Faxon, Bancroft, Mann, Kumpf, Willard and Nelson attendance zones, and that the district aim to maintain "approximately equal numbers of Negro and white children" at the school. The racial composition of these schools ranged from 97.9% black at Mann and 96.8% black at Kumpf to just 1.1% black at Nelson. To achieve racial balance Havighurst suggested that the middle school's attendance zone be drawn "so as to include only part of Kumpf and Mann." Finally, he recommended that the school board appoint an advisory council comprised of area residents and school staff to assist with the planning for the building and its educational program.

The middle school proposal appeared to be a reasonable solution to a few of the school district's most vexing problems. The school could relieve crowding, promote integration, and possibly combat resegregation. The middle school proposal, however, was met with a chorus of negative reaction. A few befuddled parents, apparently unsure of the geographic area from which the middle school would draw its enrollment, questioned whether it was intention of the school district to begin busing white children. Some school board members attacked the choice of the busy intersection at Paseo and Brush Creek as the site for the middle school. Other board members questioned whether the consultants had spent enough time in Kansas City to formulate an expert opinion on the city's schools. Accordingly, on January 31, 1966, Superintendent Hazlett asked the school board to form a committee to study the middle school proposal. The committee submitted its report one week later.

The committee was made up of five district administrators who oversaw elementary and secondary education, instructional services, and buildings and grounds. Generally, the committee members were critical of Havighurst's suggestions and pointed out "certain fallacies" in his study. They argued that yearly adjustments would be necessary to maintain the racial balance of the school and that based on current enrollments in the feeder schools, the middle school would rapidly become overcrowded. They also asserted that the middle school's attendance zone would "overlap considerably" with the zones of the new junior high being built in the Central area and with Westport Junior High School, which the district planned to open in the Metropolitan Junior College building. The committee report was a quickly produced preliminary study and offered no solid recommendations for action. Additional progress reports were to be forthcoming and the school board laid over discussion of the middle school proposal. Meanwhile, the attacks on Havighurst and his report continued.

In April 1966, the consultant's reputation and his middle school proposal were the focus of a curious smear campaign orchestrated by school board member Henry Poindexter and Alpha K. Brown, a local newspaper editor. Brown initiated the fireworks by publishing excerpts from a study prepared by the U.S. Senate subcommittee on internal security titled, "The Anti-Vietnam Agitation and the Teach-In Movement: The Problem of Communist Infiltration and Exploitation." The subcommittee was chaired by Senator James O. Eastland, a Mississippi Democrat and a rabid opponent of civil rights and integration. The report questioned Havighurst's loyalty because he favored a negotiated peace in Vietnam and because he had been a member of the education committee of the National Council of Soviet-American Friendship, which was later declared to be a "Communist-front organization." Furthermore, the report charged that Havighurst was a member of the National Committee to Oppose the McCarran Internal Security Act of 1950. At the April 8 school board meeting, Poindexter read into the record five telegrams he had received which cast doubt on Havighurst's loyalty and his qualifications as a consultant. He also attacked the middle school stating, "The F.B.I. has issued an official Communist party blueprint for subversion of the school system in New York City. Part of that plan was the development of middle schools." By endorsing the middle school concept, Poindexter argued, Havighurst was "a willing dupe" in a communist plot.

Havighurst vigorously defended his reputation. He clarified that he had served on the National Council of Soviet-American Friendship while the United States and Soviet Union were allies during World War II, but that the education committee had disbanded in 1947, two years before the organization was declared subversive. Moreover, a statement from the loyalty board of Civil Service commission confirmed that "there was no reasonable doubt as to his loyalty." Havighurst dismissed the allegation that middle schools were a communist inspired notion as "just plain silly," and FBI officials confirmed that the Bureau had "issued no such statement at any time." Moreover, some of Havighurst's supporters attacked Poindexter for his reckless allegations. A letter from CORE charged that Poindexter's ability "to distinguish fact from fancy" was "woefully limited." With respect to the remainder of Poindexter's term on the board, CORE's letter stated: "while we endure its continuation, we look hopefully to the voters of the Kansas City school district at the next election."

Havighurst and his supporters also continued to lobby for the middle school. Additional studies of the city's residential patterns and projections of black population growth were circulated as was a second report analyzing the feasibility of maintaining integration at the middle school. In mid-1966, the middle school proposal emerged as an acid test of sorts regarding the school district's duty to promote integration, and thereby laid bare the racial divide in Kansas City. All of the major civil rights organizations in the city – NAACP, CORE, the Urban League, and the CCC – supported for the middle school, while substantial numbers of whites opposed any movement toward racial balancing in the schools.

In this charged atmosphere, delay became the school district's strategy of choice. Progress reports and school board discussion of the middle school were put over from one meeting to the next for more than a year. By the time the school board received the committee's last report, final architectural plans had already been approved and construction started on the two elementary schools and the junior high school in the Central area.

The school board's day of reckoning on the middle school finally came in June 1967. At the June 14 school board meeting Hazlett presented his recommendation on the middle school. He acknowledged that the middle school had become a "symbol" that encapsulated the different perspectives on integration in Kansas City. "On the one hand," Hazlett stated, "it is a symbol of Board indifference to integration; and, on the other, it is a symbol of unrealistic demands by certain civil rights leaders." Hazlett weighed the integration benefits of the middle school against the fiscal state of the district and concluded that "prudent management of funds," dictated that the school not be built. He speculated that the site that Havighurst had selected as the most suitable for the school "would cost at least $1,000,000," and construction costs perhaps another $1,500,000. With these figures in mind, Hazlett argued that "from a practical standpoint" it was "academic" that the district could not afford to build the facility. Furthermore, Hazlett asserted that, although integration was desirable, "the notion that only integrated education can make for quality education is a myth that needs to be exploded." He labeled the proposed middle school "one of those mechanical arrangements which pays temporary homage to integration," arguing that lasting integration at the school was unlikely, and flatly stating, "balance in the same area [is] no longer possible." Following Hazlett's address, the school board voted three to two against building the middle school.

The middle school vote split the board along the same lines that it had divided two years earlier in considering whether to hire Havighurst. Homer Wadsworth and Dr. Ramos cast the two votes in favor of the middle school, while Poindexter, Mrs. Thomas Stubbs, and Mrs. James Reed voted against the proposal. Reaction from civil rights groups was swift and fierce. One group demanded that the district build the middle school and that Hazlett be removed from the post of superintendent. The CCC angrily responded that they would seek a federal investigation of segregation in the Kansas City schools. One week later, an official from the U.S. Office of Education began an inquiry to determine whether the school district was in compliance with the provisions of 1964 Civil Rights Act. However, the federal investigator insisted that he had not come at the behest of Kansas City's civil rights organizations.

In the end the integrated middle school was defeated by budgetary concerns, red baiting and allegations that such a facility was "the beginning of the end of the neighborhood school." On another level the middle school was a victim of the impulse to "do something about this immense and unpardonable delay" in building schools to relieve crowding and reduce the need for busing in the Central area. In short, the school board chose to "build schools where the children are" in spite of the evidence that those buildings would open with enrollments that were virtually all black. For a majority of the school board the objective of promoting integration in the area between Paseo and Central ranked beneath the need to relieve crowding in the Central area schools. Clearly there was an overwhelming need to address the crowding issue. However, the decision to build three additional *de facto* segregated black schools to go along with seven virtually all black schools already serving the Central area would later be interpreted as evidence that school district actions that perpetuated and abetted continued segregation in Kansas City's public schools.

During the 1968-69 school term the three new schools approved for the Central area – Martin Luther King Junior High, Weeks Elementary, and C.A. Franklin Elementary – opened their doors. Each enrolled more than 1,000 students, and each was 98% or more black. The decision to build these schools while rejecting the proposal for an integrated middle school would haunt the school district in the 1970s and 1980s.

"Concepts for Changing Times"

The Havighurst report exposed the community's deep divisions over issues of integration. Following the middle school controversy,

Superintendent Hazlett, at the urging of several civil rights organizations, proposed that the school district develop a "master plan" that would guide the district's integration efforts. In March 1968, Hazlett offered suggestions for a master plan in a pamphlet titled, "Concepts for Changing Times." His proposals were organized under five broad headings: pupil integration, faculty integration, curriculum materials, human relations activities, and related responsibilities. The bulk of the document focused on the rationale behind the master plan and on relatively mild initiatives, many of which were already adopted as district policy and incorporated into the district's operational budget. On the other hand, the sections on pupil integration and related responsibilities challenged much of the conventional thinking about neighborhood schools and integration in light of the changing demography of the metropolitan area.

In the introductory sections to "Concepts for Changing Times," Hazlett put forth the rationale behind the proposed master plan. He addressed the legal mandates to integrate, and alluded to sociological studies which had concluded that integration promoted higher achievement by disadvantaged students. Hazlett also argued that historically the public schools had played a significant role in "the constructive amalgamation of people of various nationalities, religions, and ethnic backgrounds into an American type without destroying values found in differences." For these reasons Hazlett believed that the district should seek to "maximize integrated enrollments" in the Kansas City public schools. Before considering specific proposals, however, Hazlett reviewed the criteria which should guide the district's efforts toward increased integration. He emphasized that all proposals had to be educationally sound, and fiscally attainable, contain provisions "which would prevent the acceleration of resegregation," and win the support of Kansas City residents at the polls.

Having laid out the rationale and guidelines behind the plans, Hazlett turned to discussion of specific proposals. As was noted earlier, many of these suggestions were relatively benign. In faculty integration, Hazlett pointed to the district's success in reducing the number of the single-race faculties, and emphasized that the school district would continue its efforts to build diversified staffs at all Kansas City schools. To facilitate additional faculty integration, he suggested a "rotation system" in which teachers could be reassigned to different schools every seven years.

Hazlett also proposed that the district become more sensitive to ethnic diversity in the selection of instructional materials. He advocated the elimination of all "racially and ethnically biased material" and urged the adoption of "multi-ethnic" books and support materials. Furthermore, the superintendent suggested that the district's curriculum reflect the diverse student population in the Kansas City schools. In particular, he noted the need to develop courses in African-American history, as well as greater emphasis given to the contributions of Hispanics in American history and culture. Some of this work was already underway, and in 1969 the Kansas City schools adopted a new multi-ethnic reading series developed by Scott Foresman. In the late 1960s and early 1970s multicultural materials were adopted for other subject areas and new courses were developed in order to meet the interests of the district's ethnically diverse student population.

The human relations component in "Concepts for Changing Times" basically summarized programs already in operation. The district's human relations personnel oversaw the in-service training in cultural awareness for new employees, worked to develop better school-community relations, and acted as liaisons between the school district's central administration and the various parent associations, civic organizations, and community groups. Hazlett recommended that the human relations staff be expanded and that they consult in the selection of ethnically sensitive curriculum materials.

The section titled, "Related Responsibilities" reflected Hazlett's position that the issue of integration was a metropolitan concern. He noted that the Kansas City public school district "is the only district in the Missouri part of the metropolitan area that has important problems of integration." For Hazlett, the district's difficulties in addressing issues of race were symptomatic of the changing demography of the metropolitan area. Since 1956, the black enrollment in the Kansas City public schools had grown by more than 21,000 students while the white enrollment had fallen by more than 8,000, and those trends showed no signs of slowing. Hazlett observed that as the black enrollment grew at a rate of about 2% each year, "white residents move to suburban school systems."

The superintendent appealed to "all persons in the metropolitan area" to assist in the development of an "open community" where "racial isolation in all aspects of life can be reduced." He urged citizens of the metropolitan area to embrace measures which were in the interest of the "social health of the total community." Residential integration, Hazlett argued, was a crucial to promoting racial acceptance in the metropolitan area. "A spirit of acceptance and cooperation," he said, "must supplant a feeling of segregation and hostility." Specifically, he called upon religious leaders, community leaders, organized labor, and the business and industrial community to "give vigorous support to integration," and work toward promoting racial acceptance. His appeals fell largely on deaf ears. Although numerous religious, civic and business leaders endorsed Hazlett's vision of racial cooperation and acceptance, there was no groundswell of support for his proposals in the suburbs, where residential segregation remained rigid.

Hazlett's most controversial proposals came under the heading of pupil integration. He challenged the district's allegiance to traditional school organization concepts, flatly stating that, "the neighborhood school does not lend itself to significant integration." Hazlett asserted that the time had come for the Kansas City public schools to begin experimenting with innovative organizational structures which would promote greater integration, and he presented several possibilities for consideration.

On the elementary school level, Hazlett suggested that four "cluster" plans be implemented in various sections of the city. Under these arrangements, the attendance zones of three adjacent schools are fused into a single zone in which all of the primary grade students are assigned to one school, the intermediate grades to another school, and the upper grades to the third school. For example, one proposed cluster involved Ashland, Askew and Moore elementary schools. Ashland's enrollment was 26% black, while Moore was 81% black, and Askew enrolled no blacks. Combining the attendance zones of these three schools was projected to result in a racial mix of about 33% black at each school. He also suggested the "pairing" of Dunbar and Leeds elementary schools. Pairing is similar to a clustering but only involves two schools. The Dunbar-Leeds pair was projected to produce a 52% black enrollment at each school, which would have been a significant change for both buildings. To this point, Dunbar had never enrolled a single white and Leeds had never enrolled a single black. Hazlett's proposed cluster and pairing arrangements were all located on the periphery of the black residential district and drew together schools on both sides of the rigid lines of residential segregation. Finally, he suggested that consideration be given to developing an elementary school campus, a large school complex which would bring together all of the elementary schools students from several schools at a single site. Like the cluster plans, the attendance zone for an elementary campus could surmount residential segregation patterns by serving a much larger area than a traditional neighborhood school.

In the secondary schools Hazlett recommended the creation of three magnet high schools – the School of Science, the School for Performing and Fine Arts, and the Vocational-Technical School. Enrollment in the magnet programs would be open to high school students from throughout the district with the expectation that each theme would attract roughly equal numbers of white and black students. Each of the proposed magnet schools would have a specialized faculty and facilities, and would offer a high-quality curriculum centered on the school's theme.

Hazlett closed "Concepts for Changing Times" with a discussion of steps that should be taken before the plans were implemented. He asked the citizens of the metropolitan area to read the pamphlet with "thoughtfulness and the recognition that unanimous endorsement of so complicated a set of ideas and principles cannot be fully achieved." He recommended that the school district form a task force to "assess resources and costs" inherent in the plan. To provide for maximum "citizen participation," Hazlett suggested the formation of a "Council of Thirty," with representatives drawn from civil rights groups, PTAs, organized labor, teacher organizations, local government, and business and real estate interests. The Council would "serve as the sounding-board during various stages of public scrutiny, evaluation, and improvement of this plan," and was charged with reviewing the plan thoroughly, coordinating a series of public forums, and reporting back to the school board. The public forums were scheduled to be held in each of the ten secondary school areas, and were designed to provide school district patrons with opportunities to offer criticism of the plan, suggest alternatives, and build greater community understanding of the proposed concepts.

The importance of giving Hazlett's proposals a fair hearing became all the more pressing when the U.S. Supreme Court handed down its decision in *Green v. County School Board.* Following the 1955 implementation decree in *Brown v. Board of Education*, school districts were required to dissolve segregated school systems, but that order had been ambiguous about how quickly change had to take place and how much integration was required. Resolving these difficult issues fell largely to the lower federal courts. In the mid-1960s, the federal courts of the Fifth Circuit began to fashion firmer standards for school districts regarding the pace and scope of integration. Fifth Circuit judges struck at tokenism and school district delay tactics, and moved toward adopting statistical measures in evaluating the effectiveness of southern integration plans. In the *Green* decision the Supreme Court endorsed the approach of the lower courts, ruling that school districts had an "affirmative duty to take whatever steps might be necessary to convert to a unitary system in which racial discrimination would be eliminated root and branch." Moreover, the Court ruled that the days of tokenism and delay were over. "The burden on a school board today," the Court ruled, "is to come forward with a plan that promises realistically to work, and promises realistically to work *now*." The *Green* decision was aimed at the evasive school districts of the South, but it clearly held serious implications for districts such as Kansas City, where remnants of the former segregated system still lingered.

In the wake of the *Green* decision and its directives, the Council of Thirty and the school district task force began the process of evaluating the proposals suggested in "Concepts for Changing Times." The task force reported in August 1968 that Hazlett's recommendations would cost about $21 million, the bulk of which was earmarked for the construction of six new schools and the remodeling of other buildings. Meanwhile, the series of public meetings on the various proposals was underway. It would be more than a year before the Council of Thirty presented its conclusions and report to the school board. During the course of that year, the racial divide in Kansas City and the strong differences over the direction of the school district's integration policy were apparent at the public forums and in the conflicting reports the Council of Thirty.

Public meetings held to discuss an elementary cluster proposed for the Paseo area were typical of the reaction to Hazlett's recommendations and plainly demonstrate the manner in which these proposals polarized the races. The proposed cluster involved Troost, Nelson, and Willard elementary schools. In 1968, the enrollment at Troost was 11% black, Nelson was 17% black and Willard was 66% black. At Willard the cluster plan was well received, while at the two majority white schools, hundreds of residents protested at the public meetings and signed petitions opposing the cluster. Apparently some of the resolve to promote integrated schools and residential patterns in the Paseo area had waned since 1965 when residents requested that the school district act in order to preserve integration at Paseo High School and in the surrounding neighborhoods. "The opposition is ferocious," school board member Henry Poindexter observed after one of the cluster proposal public forums. He concluded that a cluster was "not a concept this community is prepared to accept."

After a year of sampling public opinion, conducting interviews, and moderating public forums such as those held in the Paseo area, the Council of Thirty presented two reports to the Board of Education. A majority report was submitted by nineteen members of the council. The representatives from the civil rights organizations, the majority black schools, the clergy, and the city government all signed their names to the majority report. Arguing that "an integrated school experience is an important aspect of a good education," the majority report enthusiastically endorsed most of Hazlett's proposals. Indeed, the majority urged that several of Hazlett's recommendations be adopted on a broader scale than had been suggested in "Concepts." The majority report announced that "the committee is strongly in favor of the Cluster Plan," and pleaded that "consideration be given to the implementation of master elementary districts, where feasible, on a wider basis." The majority also supported the creation of large elementary school campuses, arguing that such facilities could "help stabilize communities," provide more comprehensive services, and be built at lower cost per pupil. Furthermore, the majority endorsed the proposed magnet schools at the high school level and urged the school district to consider magnet schools which would focus upon Human Relations, Communications Media, and Labor-Management, in addition to those discussed in "Concepts." Plans to pair Dunbar and Leeds were the lone element of Hazlett's proposals which the majority report rejected, citing minimal educational advantages in such an arrangement.

A minority report was also submitted to the school board in July 1969. Written by Robert Lund and Mrs. Charles Tyler, the two representatives from the largely white Van Horn and East High School areas, the minority report was diametrically opposed to the conclusions of the majority. Lund and Tyler implied that a generally favorable report from the majority had been assured by virtue of the composition of the Council. They contended that many of the representatives were "very strongly in favor of increased integration" and only a few "could be considered as completely open minded." The minority report went on to strike at most of Hazlett's proposals while regularly singing the mantra of neighborhood schools and preying upon two of the greatest fears of school district officials – that the measures would stimulate white flight or that the taxpayers would refuse to fund the initiatives. "Many patrons," the minority report held, "would be compelled to sell their homes if they are *forced* into a situation such as the Campus or Cluster Plan. (emphasis in original)" Moreover, "the vast majority of taxpayers and parents," the dissenters argued, "are opposed to any type of educational plan that will take their child out of the neighborhood school." The minority report asserted that these statements held true for both races. "The overwhelming majority of parents, black and white, still want their school close to home with a minimum of bussing [sic] for their children." The minority found that the general trend among patrons of both races was "definitely opposed," and concluded that "it is abundantly evident that the community is not ready to accept this plan." The minority supported just one of Hazlett's proposals, the magnet schools, because enrollment in such schools "would be on a *voluntary* rather than a compulsory basis.(emphasis in original)"

Faced with the two conflicting reports, the school board was again paralyzed with indecision, and refrained from seriously addressing the issue of implementing the superintendent's recommendations. The school board never took a vote on the proposals raised in "Concepts for Changing Times," and the initiatives were quietly dropped from the district's agenda. As Hazlett's proposals died of atrophy, school board consideration of "master plans" for integration faded as well. Indeed, the school board would not adopt a district-wide plan for integration until 1977.

Conclusions

On August 9, 1969 Superintendent Hazlett left his office for the last time. Having risen from the position of classroom teacher to superintendent, he had devoted thirty-one years of service to the Kansas City public schools, and he had overseen the first fourteen years of integrated education in Kansas City. Although his record is somewhat mixed, Hazlett was generally regarded as a very capable administrator who was genuinely concerned with promoting greater integration. Nevertheless, he left Kansas City a disappointed man, discouraged that his final initiatives designed to produce integration on a grand scale in the city's schools had been defeated by a conservative, largely white school board supported by a conservative, largely white populace. With Hazlett's exit, a chronic problem emerged in the Kansas City public schools – a revolving door of new superintendents, and, consequently, a lack of consistent leadership. Between 1969 and 1999, eighteen different men would hold the position of superintendent in Kansas City. Before leaving the Kansas City schools to take a position with the U.S. Department of Education, Hazlett offered a grim prophecy for his successors. "We are hemmed in by boundary lines, we occupy only one-fourth of the city, and we are facing an ever-increasing exodus of white people whose movement is accelerated by integration attempts," he argued. "There is no possible way," he concluded, "for the Kansas City school district to achieve a balanced integrated situation."

During the middle and late 1960s, a number of innovative recommendations with the potential of producing significantly more integration in the Kansas City schools were presented to school district policymakers. It is lamentable that so few of these recommendations were vigorously pursued. Some progress was made in terms of teacher integration, and in creating a more culturally sensitive curriculum. Generally, however, school district policymakers proved reluctant to abandon the concept of neighborhood schools in the face of overwhelming evidence from the expanding black residential areas that a neighborhood schools approach did not result in effective integration. Stable integration simply did not occur in those schools which served neighborhoods undergoing racial transition. Moreover, the tendency toward resegregation in these schools was generally accelerated by the continuation of the liberal transfer policy which allowed whites to evade integration in the neighborhood school once the racial composition of that school began to turn over. Fiscal limitations also played a significant role in the school district's reluctance to adopt innovative approaches to integrating the schools. Funding projects which would maximize integration, such as those discussed in Hazlett's pamphlet, required the approval of the voters. Although the school district became majority black in 1970, the city's electorate remained majority white, and some Kansas City residents expressed their frustration with the school district's management of integration by casting votes to defeat bond issues and levy increases. When Kansas City voters approved a tax levy increase in 1969, it was the last time that they sanctioned a levy increase or bond issue.

For a variety of reasons, the Kansas City public schools made little headway toward greater integration during the 1960s. The extremely difficult position that the school board occupied was revealed during the debates over the Havighurst and Hazlett proposals. Pressure from civil rights organizations and the black community to adopt measures that would promote increased integration were countered by, and typically overwhelmed by, pressures to preserve neighborhood schools and resist initiatives that traversed the lines of residential segregation. The school board consistently eschewed innovative concepts for integration and deferred to the established policies and practices of the district. From the perspective of the majority of the school board, apathy appeared to be the way to retain the support of the city's white majority. The pitfalls of inaction, however, were that as neighborhoods and schools resegregated the polarization of the city's population became all the more obvious. The school board's neglect, moreover, began to establish a clear pattern that the district was derelict in carrying out the "affirmative duty" to fully integrate the black student population as required by the 1968 *Green* decision.

District officials would later regret having passed on these opportunities. In the early 1970s, the Kansas City public school system became embroiled in legal actions that ultimately would last two decades and produce sweeping change for the district. In the late 1960s, however, few school district officials in Kansas City recognized the grave consequences that accompanied the district's failure to take positive steps toward greater inclusion for black students. Henry Poindexter would later acknowledge that at least one person in the district could foresee the coming difficulties. "Hazlett," he said, "saw more clearly than some of the board members that the laws were going to cause change, whether or not they were resisted by conservative school board members."

CHAPTER 4

Mounting Problems

Racial Discord and Fiscal Difficulties, 1968-1974

In April 1968, Dr. Martin Luther King Jr. arrived in Memphis, Tennessee to lend his support to striking sanitation workers and to lay plans for a "Poor People's Campaign," which he envisioned as a means of exposing the nation to the multitude of problems associated with black poverty. However, Reverend King did not live to see the resolution of the sanitation strike in Memphis or to lead the Poor People's Campaign. In the early evening hours of April 4, 1968, while he spoke with friends on the balcony of the Lorraine Motel, Dr. King was struck down by an assassin's bullet. As news of the assassination reached the public, riots erupted in Memphis, Chicago, Washington D.C., Harlem, and other cities. Over the course of the next week, more than one hundred cities were racked by riots. Nationwide, more than 50,000 federal troops and National Guardsmen were called out to quell the riots, but not before forty-six people were killed, another 3,000 injured, some 27,000 arrested, and more than $45 million of property were lost. In most cities, the rioting of April 1968 was far less intense than the bloody and awesomely destructive disorders in Detroit and Newark the previous year. Cumulatively, however, the breadth of the rioting in 1968 marked the single greatest manifestation of racial unrest in the nation's history.

Initially, it appeared that Kansas City might be spared from the wave of civil disorder which swept through America's cities in 1968. For four days after Dr. King's assassination, an uneasy calm prevailed in Kansas City. On the evening of April 9, however, rioting erupted in the black neighborhoods of the central city and raged there over the course of the next three nights. For the first time in Kansas City's history, an emergency curfew was imposed in the city, but thousands of residents violated the order and took to the streets. Hundreds of businesses were looted and more than 200 fires were set in the black neighborhoods. A state of emergency was declared and some 2,900 national guardsmen were deployed in Kansas City to assist the police. For the next three nights, looting and arson continued unabated. Snipers exchanged gunfire with police and national guardsmen, and shot at fire fighters battling blazes. Order was restored on Good Friday, April 12. All told, rioting in Kansas City left seven blacks dead and at least seventy more were treated for injuries at city hospitals, including dozens of gunshot victims. More than 500 suspected arsonists, looters, and snipers were arrested, and property damage in the city was estimated at about $4 million.

Kansas City's public schools were not immune from the rioting that rocked the city in April 1968. Indeed, events in the schools provided the spark that ignited the city-wide rioting. Racial tension in the schools had been building, particularly at Paseo and Southeast. Both of these high schools served areas of the city undergoing racial transition, and racially-oriented conflicts were not infrequent during the late 1960s. On Friday, April 5, the day after Dr. King was killed; building principals in Kansas City's predominantly black high schools and junior highs reported that classes were "unusually quiet." The following week, however, tension increased in the inner city high schools. Police clashed with students from Lincoln, Central, and Manual on several occasions, using tear gas to disperse student demonstrations and break up large groups of students. Dozens of windows were smashed at schools, the cafeteria at Paseo was ransacked, scores of racially-oriented fights broke out, and in a few schools, teachers were assaulted. At Central, cars were overturned, windows broken, and a student attempted to set fire to the library with a Molotov cocktail. Thousands of parents refused to send their children to the disorderly schools, and several schools reported absentee rates of more than 50% during the week. School officials dismissed classes before lunch on Tuesday and Wednesday, and canceled school on Thursday. Each evening, after the police clashed with students during the day, looters, arsonists, and snipers took to the streets. On Friday, April 12, Kansas City students were dismissed for the Easter holiday. Discord in the schools and on the streets waned. The following week, building administrators reported that classes resumed in normal fashion. Damage to school district property was estimated at less than $5,000.

It is difficult to determine whether the students at the inner city high schools and junior highs protested, destroyed property, and clashed with police in order to express their dissatisfaction with the state of race relations and racial equality in the city or simply because civil disorder in the city provided opportunities for students to act out deviant behavior. Certainly, it is likely that at least some of the students participated in the general disorder at the inner city schools for the thrill of challenging authority. But students also harbored genuine grievances concerning the school district's handling of racial issues. The schools they attended were racially isolated, overcrowded, desperately in need of repair, and, at times, dangerous. Two years after the rioting, fights, gang activity, and students bringing weapons to school were such serious problems at Central that the school's five security guards refused to return to work until they were allowed to carry side arms.

Kansas City's blacks had serious concerns regarding the general decline in the quality of education and in the adequacy of the facilities serving the inner city. Furthermore, to many black patrons and students it seemed as though the school district was often deaf to their complaints. There was no ignoring the events of April 1968, however. The Task Force on Civil Disorder assembled by the Kansas City Commission on Human Relations described the rioting as "undeniably the most spectacular display up to that time of frustration and anger on the part of black residents in Kansas City." According to the Task Force report, the disorder of April 1968 was the "culmination of many hints" of dissatisfaction on behalf of the city's blacks, and the Task Force urged "positive action in response to the many current symptoms of social turmoil ... [as well as] resolution of problems that precipitate such disorders." In searching for the causes of the riot, the Mayor's Commission on Civil Disorder identified a broad spectrum of issues which demanded attention. Among the Commission's recommendations were improvements in health clinics and hospital facilities, demolition of dangerous buildings and the construction of more low income housing, expanded recreation and community services for minority youth, and steps to improve relations between the police department and the black community.

The Mayor's Commission also found that lingering problems in the school district had contributed to the frustration of the black community and, consequently, the 1968 riot. In order to improve the school district's relationship with the black community, twelve courses of action were suggested. A few of the proposals, such as staggering the dismissal times for Central High School and Central Junior High, involved simple adjustments. Other recommendations involved expanding the existing programs for compensatory education, vocational and technical education, and summer school. The Commission also advised that the district expand its human relations in-service training for teachers and administrators throughout the district. Still other suggestions, such as the directive to "integrate the faculties and student bodies of all schools to the fullest extent consistent with educational objectives," demanded extensive research and a district-wide effort replete with familiar hazards. Indeed, one point, which endorsed Superintendent Hazlett's comments with respect to metropolitan integration, proposed that "the boundaries of the existing Kansas City school district should be expanded to include all of Jackson County," and required an act of the state legislature. The Commission's final recommendation urged the district to reconsider the Havighurst Plan and give serious thought to implementing some of the integration strategies in Hazlett's "Concepts for Changing Times," which had been released just one month before the riot. Commission members asserted that by adopting these measures it was possible for the school district to "stabilize neighborhoods, relieve the serious overcrowded conditions, and achieve maximum integration."

All told, the Mayor's Commission on Civil Disorder made recommendations for sweeping changes in order to address the causes of racial discord in the city. At least to some degree, Commission members recognized the breadth and gravity of the city's racial difficulties and attempted to suggest remedies which affected numerous city agencies and services. What remained to be seen was whether the various departments of city government and the school district would become more responsive to the concerns of the black community in the wake of the riot.

Within the school district's central administration, the findings and recommendations of the Mayor's Commission met with mixed reactions. Hazlett and other administrators agreed that several of the recommendations could be instituted without great difficulty. He vowed to continue the district's efforts with respect to compensatory education, summer school, and vocational education, and to expand those programs as funds became available. Moreover, the district would expand its human relations in-service program and Hazlett pledged to continue the effort to integrate the faculties, although the district's success in this regard had been modest.

The Superintendent's response to the recommendations which touched upon "maximum integration" of students was more guarded. He noted that the existing school district policy was "to maximize integration within the neighborhood concept." He also recognized, however, that the extent of residential segregation in Kansas City imposed severe limits upon the amount of racial mixing that took place within the neighborhood schools. Nevertheless, the Superintendent envisioned more integration in the coming years. Clearly, he entertained hopes that the integration measures proposed in his "Concepts for Changing Times" would be adopted, but he could not presume that any of those plans would become policy. With regard to the Havighurst report, Hazlett was among those who were pleased to see the middle school proposal defeated, but he was also among those who hoped to see the integrated high school proposed for the northwest area built.

Northwest High School: Manual and the West Side

It is rather curious that the new high school proposed for the northwest area should have drawn so much attention in the late 1960s. Dr. Havighurst's comments on the proposal amount to only two brief paragraphs in his study. Nevertheless, the prospect of creating an integrated high school in this section of the city had won widespread support among school policy makers and the Northwest High School proposal did not die along with the rest of the Havighurst report in 1967. On its face, the Northwest proposal did not appear to promise much integration as the school was conceived to serve black students from Manual and part of the Lincoln area. A school district study indicated, however, that it was possible to create a stable, integrated enrollment at the high school by drawing off non-minority students from the west side of the city and the Northeast High School zone. Even so, the school district study warned that an integrated enrollment at the school could be maintained "only if reassignments [transfers] from this district are prohibited and if a certain number of Negro pupils are assigned to some other school." Nevertheless, school district analysts concluded that the proposed Northwest High School was both "feasible and desirable," and by mid-1966, the proposal to build the high school had acquired substantial momentum in school district circles. The most significant remaining questions about the project involved site selection and how to finance construction of the school.

Funds for the construction of a new high school had not been allocated in the $17.5 million building bond issues approved by the voters in 1965. Those funds were earmarked for two new elementary schools in the Rock Creek area, and two new elementary schools and a junior high school to relieve crowding in the Central area. Moreover, the school district was already committed to building the new Kansas City Technical Education Center, a magnet school for vocational and technical education programs. For a time, members of the central administration staff tinkered with possibilities of shifting funds from other projects to the Northwest project. On each occasion, however, these attempts at creative accounting resulted in shortfalls of at least $1.7 million for the proposed high school. Building the high school demanded another bond issue, and securing the passage of bond issues was becoming increasingly difficult in Kansas City.

Site selection for the high school presented additional problems. The site that could be acquired most easily and at the least expense was the existing site of Manual High School, which had been designated as an urban renewal area. The school district planned to build the new Technical Education Center on this site, and district planners argued that by enlarging the site, the new Northwest High School could be built on adjacent property. However, as preliminary site selection plans for the new high school were made public, community groups began to appear before the school board expressing their dissatisfaction with the location.

A handful of the city's civil rights organizations comprised one faction that opposed the Manual urban renewal site for the new high school. In August 1966, Fletcher Daniels, Chairman of the Community Committee for Social Action, addressed the school board concerning the organization's reservations regarding the Manual site. He argued that the site was too close Lincoln High School and "not close enough to the area where it will – or should – draw most of its students." A site further north and west of the Manual site, Daniels maintained, would be preferable in "furthering the integration process." Above all, the Committee for Social Action was concerned that the Manual site would not draw an integrated enrollment. Daniels urged that "no new school should be erected in this district without a commitment from this [school] board that it will exert maximum effort and authority to achieve maximum integration in that school." To this end, he was encouraged by statements in the school district's studies which implied that white students who had transferred out of Manual would be compelled to attend the new high school. Daniels's comments on the Manual site were endorsed by Charles Curry, the Co-Chairman of the Education Committee of Kansas City's chapter of the Congress of Racial Equality. Reverend James Blair, representing another civil rights organization, the Council for United Action, echoed Daniels's objections to the Manual site and informed the board that the Council would not support the Northwest High School proposal until the school district adopted a "program for integrating education throughout the school system."

Representatives from Kansas City's Hispanic community also opposed the Manual site. In 1960, the bulk of the city's Mexican-American population lived on what residents called the "West Side," a large neighborhood situated on a bluff in the northwest part of the city. The West Side was somewhat isolated from the rest of Kansas City, cut off by a combination of the area's geography and the massive highway construction projects of the 1950s and 1960s. To the west of the neighborhood lay the steep slope of the bluff, rail yards, and the Kansas state line. The neighborhood was hemmed in on east and south by the Southwest Trafficway and Interstate 35, and to the north by Ninth Street, the Central Avenue viaduct and Interstate 70. Aside from its isolation from the rest of the city, the West Side had significant social and economic ills. Almost 60% of the neighborhood's residents had fewer than eight years of formal education, unemployment rates on the West Side were roughly double that of the city as a whole, and almost 35% of the area's families lived below poverty level. Moreover, the population of the West Side declined by almost 5,000 residents between 1960 and 1968 due to land clearance for Interstate 35 and the construction of the interstate loop around Kansas City's central business district. Most of the residents who remained lived in deteriorating low rent housing or the area's two public housing projects, West Bluff and Pennway Plaza. Given the West Side's serious socio-economic problems, many residents of the area embraced better education as the means of breaking the cycle of underachievement, unemployment, dilapidated housing, and poverty.

In hopes of promoting better education on the West Side, area residents were increasingly active in school district affairs during the mid-1960s.

The school district had created an unusual feeder system for students on the West Side. Switzer, Douglass, and Benjamin Franklin elementary schools served students in kindergarten through sixth grade. West Junior High served grades seven through ten, and West Side students completed their education at Manual High School. West was the only junior high school in the district that included tenth grade. Critics of this arrangement alleged that West Junior High included tenth grade as a convenience of sorts for potential dropouts. By offering tenth grade at West, a student could reach the legal age to dropout of school without having to attend a high school outside of the neighborhood. Indeed, West had the district's highest dropout rate among junior high schools. During the 1966-67 school year, 9% of the students enrolled at West dropped out. In addition to the dropout problem, achievement levels lagged in all West Side schools, and absenteeism rates at West Side schools ranked among the highest in the district.

In February 1966, Agapito Maya, a representative for the Mexican-American Organization for Progress, addressed the school board concerning the proposed Northwest High School. Maya argued the Hispanic residents living on the West Side were "forgotten orphans of an ever-expanding and enlightened city," and that in the city's policy-making circles, no one had "ever spoken a good word for us." The Mexican-American Organization for Progress aimed to rectify that situation by pressuring the school board on the proposed new high school. The Manual urban renewal site, Maya argued, was too far from the West Side and left the neighborhood without a high school. Moreover, he argued that in part the high dropout rate among West Side students could be attributed to their present assignment to Manual. He maintained that transportation to the Manual area imposed a financial burden which West Side families could not afford, and that even if the school district provided busing, transporting West Side high school students "from one depressed area to another will not solve the problem." The solution that Maya and the Mexican-American Organization for Progress favored was building the new high school either at the present site of West Junior High or another location on the West Side.

Dr. Dewey Smith, Assistant Superintendent for Buildings and Grounds, evaluated building sites in the West Side area, including two sites recommended by the Mexican-American Organization for Progress. Dr. Smith's reports discouraged West Side residents. He informed the school board that due to the rugged topography of the area, the available sites on the West Side would be extremely difficult and expensive to develop. Undeterred, West Side activists continued to press the school board to build the new school in their area. Moreover, they sought to enlist the aid of a powerful ally in their cause – the federal government.

In 1967, members of the Hispanic community reported to the United States Department of Health, Education, and Welfare (HEW) that students in the West Side area were denied of equal educational opportunity because the neighborhood had no high school. It is true that there was no high school on the West Side area, but Latino students were able to complete their high school education at Manual. Nevertheless, Richard Parra, a West Side resident, alluded to the curious feeder pattern and irregular grade structure at West Junior High in asserting that school officials reasoned that "Mexican-Americans are not capable of achieving anything more than a tenth grade education." In July 1967, officials from HEW conducted a brief investigation of the allegations that Hispanic students were denied equal educational opportunities. HEW suggested that the junior high curriculum be expanded and that free transportation be provided for high school students living on the West Side. HEW did not go so far as to recommend that the school district build the proposed high school on the West Side.

Plans for Northwest High School stalled in 1968 as school district officials turned their attention to the completion of the elementary and junior high school projects approved in the 1965 bond issue. Numerous questions remained unresolved regarding the proposed high school and how to accommodate the students currently attending Manual High School and West Junior High. High school students in the northwest section of the city continued to attend Manual High School even as the ground adjacent to the school was cleared and construction commenced on the Kansas City Technical Education Center in the fall of 1968. If construction at the site progressed as scheduled, Manual High School was to be razed the following summer. On the West Side, students in grades seven through ten continued to attend West Junior High, and the Hispanic community continued to push for a high school. By mid-1968, the persistence of the West Side activists began to reap benefits.

Over the course of several months of meetings, Hispanic community organizations had managed to persuade the Assistant Superintendent for Human Relations, Robert MacNeven, of the need for changes in school district policy regarding the West Side. In a lengthy memo, MacNeven shared his concerns with Superintendent Hazlett. MacNeven asserted that the time had come for the school district to recognize "the Mexican-American group as an ethnic minority meriting special consideration." Among his recommendations, MacNeven urged that the administration of the schools serving the West Side be reorganized in order to provide for greater input from the community. He suggested that a Community-School Committee be selected by West side residents to consult with administrators regarding the educational program for the area. He further recommended that counseling services should be expanded and the number of home-school coordinators increased in order to improve achievement levels and reduce the number of dropouts in West Side schools. Moreover, MacNeven urged modifications to the curriculum in the area's schools in order to better reflect the needs and interests of Hispanic students. He suggested offering courses on Mexican History and Hispanic culture at the secondary school level and implementing bilingual instruction at the elementary level. In addition, MacNeven proposed that the school district improve its relationship with the community through the expansion of "extended services" such as tutoring, GED preparation, adult literacy courses, and arts and crafts offerings at the schools. Finally, MacNeven speculated that the school district might employ an ombudsman for the West Side to investigate patrons' complaints concerning school district policies, the curriculum, and personnel.

Members of the West Side Educational Planning Board enthusiastically endorsed MacNeven's suggestions. On the other hand, Superintendent Hazlett was not prepared to accept all of MacNeven's recommendations, but he was convinced the situation on the West Side merited additional attention. Within central administration, however, questions abounded over what exactly the school district could do to better serve the West Side. A school district study of enrollment trends on the West Side indicated that, due to the relatively small number of high school age students living in the area, a high school located there would only be able to offer a "very limited program" or a full high school curriculum "at extreme cost" to the district. Clyde Baer, the director of the school district's research department, speculated that perhaps other motivations were at work in the Hispanic community's pushing for a high school on the West Side. He concluded that West Side residents felt threatened by "encroachment by other societal developments on established cultural and community traditions." He believed that the Hispanic community sought greater control over the neighborhood's institutions, including the schools, in order to shape the "personal value systems" of the area's youth. If the new high school were established elsewhere in the city, Baer believed that West Side Hispanics would perceive that a measure of the community's influence in the lives of the area's children would be lost. Beyond the motives at work, Baer was unconvinced that pupil achievement would improve significantly, despite the "sincere concern" of the community, and questioned whether achievement could accurately be measured if the curriculum offered on the West Side differed radically from that of other district schools.

In spite of the reservations of some administrators, Hazlett had not ruled out the possibility of creating a high school on the West Side and taking other steps to accommodate the area's students. In July, at the superintendent's request, the school board authorized a study to explore the feasibility of converting West Junior High into a four-year high school. After consulting with Charles Lona of the West Side Planning

Board, the school district contracted the architectural firm of Runnells, Winholtz, and Associates to conduct the study. The school board also addressed West Side complaints regarding the assignment of eleventh and twelfth grade students to Manual. Between 1966 and 1968, numerous West Side residents had appeared before the school board arguing that their children, in short, "deserve more than to be sent from one poor school [West Junior High] to another [Manual]." In August, the board agreed to provide transportation for West Side high school students to attend Westport High School for the 1968-69 school year.

In early December 1968, David Runnells presented the feasibility study to the school board. The study recapitulated the familiar litany of problems facing West Side residents and students and the objections of West Side patrons to the Manual urban renewal site as the location of the proposed Northwest High School. Runnells asserted that a new high school at the Manual site was "likely to carry with it the old stigmas," and that "it is apparent that by the time a Northwest High School was built, it would be a *de facto* segregated school." Conversely, the West Side, Runnells argued, was "characterized by a population almost equally divided among Negroes, Mexican-Americans, and residents of Anglo ancestry." He concluded that a high school on the West Side "would be integrated in a most natural way."

Following the sections on population trends, enrollment projections, and the condition of existing school facilities on the West Side, the feasibility study presented several proposals for the school board to consider. Among the "interim" recommendations, the architects suggested that the district reassign seventh grade students attending West Junior High to vacant classrooms at Douglass Elementary. In addition, the consultants proposed that West Junior High be remodeled over the course of the coming summer so that by September 1969, "a small but comprehensive high school as well as a community resource center" could be established at the building. Runnells recommended that West High School serve only those students living on the West Side, meaning that the school would have a projected enrollment of fewer than 550 students. The study's long-term "optimum" recommendations for the West Side alluded to the possibility of building as many as five new schools, including a new high school just west of Penn Valley Park on the lower West Side.

Administration and shaping the educational program for schools on the West Side presented additional challenges. Runnells asserted that in order for the West Side schools to be successful, it was imperative to involve the community in these decisions. The study proposed initiating an experiment of sorts in "participant democracy." West Side schools, it was suggested, would be under the direction of an area superintendent, who would work in consultation with a decision-making board. That board would be comprised of members representing the district's central administration, the faculty and staff of the West Side schools, concerned faculty members from Kansas City colleges and universities, and West Side community organizations. Ideally, Runnells speculated, the policy-making board would arrive at decisions by consensus and direct the area superintendent to implement changes. Runnells argued that this unique administrative scheme would place Kansas City "in the vanguard of the nation in the use of participant democracy for the solution of inner-city educational problems."

School board members took no action on the recommendations but directed Hazlett to study the proposals further and report back to the board. The district had reached a critical juncture regarding the proposed Northwest High School. The feasibility study suggested abandoning or modifying the plans for a high school at the Manual site. If the decision were made to abandon that project, the district lost little since no funding had yet been approved for Northwest. However, the dilemma of finding space for the present Manual students remained. According to the recommendations in the West Side Study, Manual students could not be accommodated at that site. Nevertheless, space had to be found for those students because the existing Manual building was slated to be demolished over the summer to make room for a wing of the Technical Education Center. With these considerations in mind, Hazlett reported to the school board in January.

The superintendent was something less than thoroughly enamored with the recommendations offered in the West Side Study. In his January 7 report to the school board, Hazlett criticized the "poor research" methods employed in the feasibility study and challenged several of the conclusions reached by the architects. Moreover, Hazlett reiterated his concerns that the small enrollment on the West Side did not justify the creation of a high school to serve the area. Nevertheless, under continued pressure from the city's Hispanics, the central administration staff was directed to prepare an organizational model for a high school program at West.

At the next school board meeting, Dr. Richard Ball, Director of Secondary Education, presented a model for upgrading the educational program at the school. Five new teachers and one half-time counselor were to join the staff so that additional courses and credits could be added to the school's curriculum. Under Ball's plan, the educational program at West would offer a total of forty-eight credits, enough to satisfy state requirements for a comprehensive high school, but only about one-half of the credits and course options available to students at other Kansas City high schools. The curriculum at West was necessarily limited because of the paucity of students projected to attend the high school. The enrollment was projected at 386, assuming that forty-six eleventh grade students attending other high schools returned to West.

Every high school in the district, with the exception of Manual, enrolled at least 1,000 more students than were projected to attend West. Southwest High School enrolled fully 2,000 more students. However, considering the limited curricular program at West, the expense of the project was not unreasonable. Ball estimated the cost of converting the junior high into West High School at roughly $73,000.

West High School was approved on an "interim" basis by the school board on January 16, 1969. For West Side residents it was an encouraging sign that the school district might implement additional recommendations from the West Side Study, including the new high school in the Penn Valley Park area. The school board had something else in mind, however. Plans to build the proposed Northwest High School at the Manual site had not yet been abandoned altogether. Moreover, because Manual High School was scheduled for demolition over the summer, school district planners still had to solve the problem of finding a school for students currently attending Manual. Over the course of the next five months, the school board turned its attention to resolving both issues.

Superintendent Hazlett and members of the school board remained committed to building the new high school in the northwest area. Their intention was to place the students from Manual elsewhere temporarily while the district secured passage of a building bond issue and the new high school could be built in the Manual urban renewal zone. In February 1969, Hazlett recommended busing the Manual students to the former Metropolitan Junior College building, one block from Westport High School. The plan mirrored the district's busing program to relieve crowding in the black elementary schools in the early 1960s in which classrooms of black students were bused intact to vacant classrooms at predominantly white schools. Just as the black elementary students initially were not integrated at the receiving schools, school officials expressed no intention of integrating the 95% black student body from Manual with students at 73% white Westport. Essentially, the district would maintain two separate high schools, one overwhelmingly black and the other predominantly white, one block apart.

School board members delayed action on Hazlett's plans to use the junior college building for the upcoming year, and for the next two months a steady parade of delegations from the Manual and Westport areas expressed their concerns over such an arrangement to the board. For different reasons, parents and community groups in both the Manual and Westport areas opposed the relocation scheme. In discussions with school district administrators, Westport patrons expressed the conviction that two high schools located in such close proximity to one another would create discipline problems, and that the use of the Westport area for "temporary crisis-solving . . . will create a mass exodus to the suburbs and destroy any hope we have had for at least one successfully integrated high school in Kansas City." A number of Manual patrons and the Council for United Action also vigorously opposed the school district plan. Some of these parents expressed great anxiety over sending their students to an area "where they are 'not wanted' and where they might come under personal attack by whites." Others resented how the busing scheme took advantage of blacks. Still others expressed doubts as to whether the school board was genuinely committed to building the proposed Northwest High School. Without a new high school in the Manual area, some patrons feared that the busing of Manual students would continue indefinitely.

The school district's options with respect to the Manual students were rather narrow. It was not possible for the students to be divided up and bused to other high schools in the city. Manual students opposed such a solution and there were simply not enough empty seats in the high schools. School officials considered building temporary classrooms at Manual, but the expense of nearly $700,000 outweighed the benefits of that option. Another possibility involved relocating the students to vacant elementary schools. In this scenario, Manual's ninth and tenth grade students would be assigned to Humboldt, while the eleventh and twelfth graders were to attend Carver. Among the drawbacks to this option were that the majority of Manual students would require busing, and, again, the students insisted that they would not accept splitting the student body between buildings. Finally, the school district could halt construction on the Technical Education Center and allow Manual High School to remain at its present site. This alternative was as unsavory as the others. Manual was an older facility and in dire need of repair; moreover, if the district stopped construction of the Tech Center it stood to forfeit $2.5 million in federal funds for the project.

Given these options, school board president Homer Wadsworth maintained that busing the Manual students to the junior college building was the best of "several bad alternatives." In agreement with Wadsworth's assessment of the situation, the school board approved a measure closing Manual High School at its existing site and transporting those students to the former junior college.

The decision pleased no one. Manual patrons argued that the school board had again demonstrated little regard for the concerns of the city's blacks and that the busing scheme smacked of discrimination. The curious arrangement of two high schools virtually side-by-side was compounded by the school board's awkward decision to extend a policy approved in 1968 which afforded about 250 students from the Manual area the option of transferring to Northeast High School rather than boarding the buses. The area designated as an optional zone was located on the northern fringe of the Manual attendance zone above Independence Avenue, and included two public housing projects,

Riverview and Guinotte Manor, both of which were virtually all white. In 1968, of the 680 families residing in the Riverview and Guinotte Manor housing projects, 677 were white. Not surprisingly, when given the choice of attending Northeast or riding the buses for Manual, the great majority of the students living in the optional zone chose to attend Northeast, which was 96% white in 1969. The decision to continue the optional zone in 1969 was plainly at odds with a resolution approved by the school board just three months earlier. In March 1969, the school board vowed to "continue to work affirmatively in implementing the objective of effective integration of faculties and student bodies in all Kansas City schools." In the case of the optional zone, however, the school board had clearly created another vehicle by which whites could avoid integration.

Despite all of the difficulties in relocating the Manual students, school board members took some solace in the conviction that the arrangement would be only temporary. What remained to be done in order to serve the Manual students in a facility nearer their homes was to secure passage of a bond issue and begin construction on the proposed Northwest High School. The school district's 1969 bond proposal included some $5 million for the construction of the new high school at the Manual urban renewal site. On three occasions that year the district presented the bond issue to the electorate, and each time the proposal was defeated.

Voting patterns on the 1969 bond issues provide an indication of which sections of the city generally favored the direction of school district policy and specifically the proposal to build a new high school in the northwest area. The first bond election was held on April 1 and secured just 44% approval, well short of the required two-thirds. In just seven of the city's twenty-four wards had a simple majority of voters approved the measure. The proposal received majority support in each of the predominantly black wards and in three exclusively white wards located in the affluent southwestern section of the city around Country Club Plaza and Southwest High School. In only one ward, the heavily black Second Ward which included much of the Manual High School area, did the proposal win two-thirds approval. Conversely, the bond issue was rejected by overwhelming majorities in the predominantly white working class wards in the eastern and northeastern sections of the city. In these areas, fewer than 40% of the voters approved of the proposal, and in four of those wards barely one-fourth of the ballots cast favored the bond issue. Voters on the West Side also rejected the bond measure by a margin of three to two, as did the electorate in the area served by Westport High School. Voting was evenly split in the southeastern wards which were undergoing racial transition.

The bond proposal was resubmitted to the voters in May and July and twice more failed. In May, the bond issue received 50% approval, securing majority support in nine of the city's twenty-four wards, and won two-thirds approval in two wards. The bond issue fared even better in the July vote, capturing 57% approval city-wide. Simple majorities in nineteen wards approved the measure and in four of those wards more than two-thirds of the votes cast favored the proposal. Nevertheless, the district came up short of the necessary two-thirds approval city-wide. In each of the elections, the white wards in the southwest area and the predominantly black wards solidly supported the measure. But in each case, these wards were unable to off-set the staunch opposition of white voters in the northeast and east, and only tepid support for the measure elsewhere in the city.

Manual, Westport, and the West Side were the areas most directly affected by the bond issue and the construction of the proposed high school. In the ward enveloping much of the Manual area, voters overwhelmingly approved of the bond issue at each election. Approval rates for the Second Ward tallied 70%, 77%, and 79% for the April, May, and July elections respectively. The lopsided margin by which Manual area voters approved of the bond issue indicates that, although opponents of the proposed high school were quite vocal in that neighborhood, those individuals did not represent the majority of the area's patrons. A healthy majority of the voters in the Manual area sought a new high school for their children.

On the West Side, just 40% of the voters favored the bond issue in April, although the approval rate rose to 48% in May, and 52% in July. The reluctance of West Side voters to solidly support the bond issue may be interpreted as expression of that area's satisfaction with developments earlier in the year. In January, the school board had agreed to establish a high school on the West Side and patrons in that section of the city were opposed to the construction of a new high school which would likely result in the closure of West High School and the resumption of West Side high school students being bused to the inner city.

The rejection of the bond proposal by voters in the Westport area is curious because the passage of the measure would have worked in their favor. Approval of the bond issue would have signaled that Manual students would be bused to the Westport area for only a few years while the new high school was built. Nevertheless, a majority of Westport voters, perhaps expressing their general disapproval for recent school district policy choices, rejected the measure in April and May, and were evenly split in July.

With the defeat of the bond proposal, plans for Northwest High School were crushed. The school board dropped serious consideration of the project and fell back on the contingency plans involving West and Manual. In September 1969, Manual became what Assistant

Superintendent Edward Fields called "a school on wheels," and remained so for the next eight years. Over those eight years, the arrangement grew increasingly onerous as the Manual students being bused to the former junior college building became almost exclusively black. In 1969, over one hundred Hispanic and white students boarded the buses along with more than one thousand black students bound for the new Manual location. The following year, sixty-eight whites and Hispanics remained enrolled at Manual. For the last six years of Manual's history the school's enrollment was 99% black. Moreover, the number of black students enrolled at Manual increased significantly in the early 1970s to the point where, in 1972, the district was compelled to open an annex for Manual students at Yeager, an elementary school which had been closed the previous year. The busing arrangement for Manual area students finally ended in 1977 with the adoption of a new district-wide desegregation program entitled Plan 6-C. Under the plan, the former junior college building became Westport Junior High and the majority of the high school students living in the Manual attendance area were assigned to Northeast High School.

West High School served the West Side for the next eleven years. It remained a racially balanced school, enrolling roughly equal numbers of black, Hispanic, and white students. Throughout its eleven year existence, the enrollment at West remained the lowest among Kansas City high schools, never rising above 500 students. Consequently, the educational program remained quite limited despite the fact that the district spent more money per pupil at West than at any other high school. Moreover, the area continued to struggle with the problems of low achievement and high rates of truancy and absenteeism, and the dropout rate at West remained among the highest in the district fluctuating between 20% and 34% annually.

In short, West High School was a disappointment to both school district administrators and West Side patrons. Despite infusions of additional funding and staff through federal Title I funds, the significant problems with underachievement and the dropout rate eluded a simple solution. West Side patrons maintained that an earnest commitment by the district to make West High School successful never materialized. During its eleven years of operation, West Side residents complained that the learning environment at the building remained "psychologically demoralizing" due to the deterioration of the physical plant, and that the school's staff and administration remained somewhat insensitive to the needs and cultural diversity of the area's students. In particular, Hispanic residents lamented what they perceived as deficiencies in the district's bilingual education program in the West Side schools which were not addressed until 1980.

When results on the West Side failed to improve, school officials argued that it was too costly to operate a large school for so small an enrollment, and that the students could be better served by attending Westport High School. Over the course of the school's eleven year history, the topic of closing West High School was discussed periodically by the board, but in each instance the Hispanic community vigorously opposed the measure and the school remained open. In 1978, the school district changed course and established a business and management magnet program at West. The magnet theme, however, did not solve the school's problems. Two years later, school board member Karen Lewis found that West "as a high school program, is extremely deficient," and that "in good conscience, I could not recommend anyone participate in it." Her fellow board members agreed and voted to close the school. Once more residents of the West Side rallied to preserve the school. A group of about two dozen Hispanic activists led by Nacho and Don Pecina seized control of the building and occupied it for more than a week. Ultimately, the school district acquiesced to the Hispanic activists' demands and agreed to create a community school at West. Establishing the community school was contingent upon receiving federal funding for the project and when those funds were not approved, West High School closed its doors for good in 1980.

In many respects the unfolding conundrum involving the proposed Northwest High School, the difficulties in accommodating students on the West Side, and the problem of finding satisfactory arrangements for students in the Manual area illustrates the essence of a serious dilemma for school district officials in the late 1960s and the 1970s. The school district's difficulties stemmed largely from the interplay of two factors. First, the 1960s and 1970s witnessed increased activism on the part of community groups seeking greater influence in school district affairs. A plethora of different organizations representing constituencies of the white, black, and Hispanic communities constantly pressured the school board for various changes in the schools serving their particular areas of the city. Second, during the same period, the school district experienced desperate financial difficulties which placed severe limits upon the district's capacity to implement changes which would mollify the critics. In short, the district's dilemma was that various community groups sought greater influence in school district decisions, but the demands of those groups were rarely tempered by an appreciation of the school district's fiscal situation. Consequently, distrust and hostility characterized the outlook of many patrons and community groups with respect to the school district, and the district's relationship with its patrons in general suffered irreparable damage.

Clearly one aspect of the school district's deteriorating relationship with its patrons in the late 1960s and 1970s involved the three-way struggle for influence in the formulation of school district policy. The

1960s not only witnessed the continued activism of the city's African-American population and white community groups, but also marked the emergence of Hispanic activism in Kansas City. Each group pressured the school district for change in the use of facilities, the programs offered in the curriculum, alterations to the district's attendance zones, modifications to the busing program, and a host of other issues. The interests of these different constituencies, however, often clashed and placed the school district in the difficult position of seeking solutions without disaffecting those groups most interested in the outcome.

For their part, school district officials attempted to placate community groups when feasible but often found it impossible to reconcile the wildly divergent points of view represented by the different community groups. Thus, in many cases the school board adopted policies which to some degree alienated different segments of the city. Such was the case in the placement of Manual High School students. Although a number of possibilities were considered for accommodating the Manual students, all had significant drawbacks and when the school board agreed that busing the students to the former junior college building was the best of several bad alternatives, the decision was supported by very few patrons in either the Manual area or the Westport area. Moreover, when the school district satisfied the immediate interests of one group, such as the creation of West High School, limits as to the amount of money and personnel that could be committed to a project left patrons feeling betrayed. Often, then, regardless of the course of action taken by the school board, the district's relationship with its patrons suffered.

Reforming the School Board

One area of school district policy which demanded reform, and held potential for improving relations with the public, involved the school board. A source of frustration for all of the groups vying for influence in the school district was the composition of the school board, which many Kansas Citians viewed as a grossly unrepresentative body. Throughout the 1960s, the school board was comprised almost entirely of upper class white members from the southwestern section of the city. In short, blacks and Hispanics, as well as much of the city's white population had no advocate on the school board who represented their section of the city. Although school board members were elected, the elections generally were nothing more than a formality. The Jackson County Democratic and Republican committees each selected three candidates and those nominees ran unopposed for the six school board seats. There was no campaigning, and all of the candidates were endorsed by both parties. Few school board members had political experience or ambition, but rather were generally leaders in the business community, philanthropic organizations, women's associations, and civic groups. As a result, for the first ninety years of the school district's operation, the school board was comprised of civic minded individuals from upper class and upper middle class neighborhoods who shared little in common with the city's blacks, Hispanics, or working class whites.

By the late 1960s, the traditional process by which school board members were chosen and the resultant composition of the board year after year had become a rather grievous public relations problem for the school district. For a great many school district patrons the perception was that board members who resided in the isolated upper class enclaves "could not understand the needs and interests of the city's minority population." The imbalance of the school board grew all the more apparent in the late 1960s as the district's enrollment neared 50% black. Indeed, only one black, Dr. John Ramos, had ever served on the school board, and he had not been elected but rather was tabbed to fill vacant seat. Dr. Ramos served on the school board from 1964 to 1970. During that period, all of his fellow board members resided in the exclusively white southwestern part of the city.

Reforming the composition of the school board was an attractive proposal because it could be accomplished at minimal cost and promised to win the support of thousands of district patrons, minorities in particular. In 1967, the state legislature passed a measure reforming the process by which Kansas City school board members were elected. The new law provided for the school district to be divided into six geographic sub-districts, each of which would elect one school board member. Three additional board members were to be elected at-large from the entire district. The task of drawing the lines for the six sub-districts fell to the Kansas City and Jackson County Board of Election Commissioners. In late 1967, the election commissioners settled on boundaries for the sub-districts. Essentially, they followed existing precinct and ward lines, and used 1960 census data in order to ensure that each district included between 71,000 and 72,000 voters. School officials hoped that the new format would be implemented in time for the 1968 elections, but due to legal challenges, the first election under the sub-district plan was not conducted until January 1970.

The adoption of the sub-district format assured that minorities would be better represented. Sub-districts IV and V, which encompassed much of the central black corridor and contained the Lincoln, Central, Paseo, and Southeast High School areas, were almost sure to elect black representatives, and the election of another black was possible in the at-large races. The election of a Hispanic school board member was less certain. Sub-district I included the West Side, but Hispanics did not constitute a majority of the voting population for the sub-district. Even so, the sub-district format promised far greater opportunity for minorities to win representation on the school board than had been true previously. Moreover, the new format provided that school board members would be elected from across the city, rather than chosen almost exclusively from southwestern Kansas City.

In 1970, Kansas City voters elected eight new school board members; the ninth seat, occupied by Henry Poindexter, was not up for election that year. Black candidates won the seats in sub-districts IV and V, and one of the at-large seats. The remaining five seats were won by whites. 1970 marked the first year in which more than one black served on the school board and was also the first year in which a majority of the enrollment in the Kansas City schools was black. Accordingly, one may have expected that black candidates would win more than just three of the school board's nine seats. Although the schools were majority black, Kansas City's population remained almost 75% white and two-thirds of the school board was white. Nevertheless, the 1970 elections helped to defuse complaints that the district's minority patrons were denied representation at the highest levels of school district policy making. Redistricting, however, did little to persuade district patrons to address the district's other major problem – financing.

Fiscal Problems

For much of its history, Kansas City's school district had enjoyed budget surpluses and presented bond issues and tax levy measures to the public in full confidence that these proposals would be approved. Indeed, of the seventeen bond issues presented to voters between the founding of the district and 1956, only one had failed. However, beginning in the late 1960s, the school district's financial base became less secure. Voters had approved the 1965 bond issue providing $17.5 million to build two elementary schools in the Rock Creek area and two elementary schools and a junior high school in the Central area. Tax levy increases were also approved in 1964, 1967, and 1969. The 1969 tax levy proposal, however, marked the last time that the public assented to a school district fiscal measure. Between 1969 and 1987, nineteen consecutive bond issue and tax levy initiatives were defeated by Kansas City voters.

With the failure of these financial measures, the school district began its slow descent toward insolvency. To be sure, the school district benefited significantly from massive infusions of federal funds available under the Great Society's educational programs, particularly the Elementary and Secondary Education Act. But these programs amounted to just 10% of the school district budget. The bulk of the district's operating funds came from property taxes and the state's education foundation program, and by the late 1960s and early 1970s, these revenue sources were insufficient to permit the school district to continue operating as it previously had. The budget simply did not grow at a rate commensurate with the rising cost of education. In 1969, the cost of providing public education in Kansas City was about $720 per pupil. Six years later the cost was nearly $1,300 per pupil and rising. Inflation and rising energy prices in the late 1960s and early 1970s, coupled with the relatively meager growth of the operating budget, insured that the school district would experience great difficulty in maintaining its schools, retaining many of the district's educational programs, and offering competitive salaries which would satisfy staff members. Moreover, the dismal fiscal status of the Kansas City schools in the late 1960s and 1970s guaranteed that the district would not undertake any new desegregation initiatives. Maintaining the schools as they were was challenge enough.

Property taxes accounted for the majority of the school district's operating budget, and that revenue was based upon the prevailing tax levy rate for the district. In 1969, the district secured approval for its last successful tax increase which raised the levy to $3.75 per $100 of assessed valuation. The $3.75 levy remained in effect for the next sixteen years. By 1974, the tax levy rate for the Kansas City school district was the lowest in Jackson County, Missouri and, the Kansas City schools operated with a budget deficit of nearly $3 million.

Although the quality of education in Kansas City was clearly spiraling downward due, at least in part, to the district's financial difficulties, the public proved most reluctant to authorize any increase. In April 1974, Dr. Robert Medcalf, Superintendent of the Kansas City schools, lamented "the bankrupt condition of the district," and a school district statement released to the *Kansas City Star* asserted that "the Board of Education is faced with the impossible task of running the School District with an operating levy which has remained the same since 1967." As school officials desperately pleaded with the district's patrons to "merge their various interests into a cooperative program to enable the Board of Education to finance adequately all of the requirements for quality education," little relief was forthcoming. In June 1974, voters rejected a tax levy increase. Indeed, seven times between 1969 and 1986, voters were presented with measures to increase the tax levy, and on each occasion the proposed increase was defeated.

In part, the failure of the school district's tax levy increases stemmed from the general objection to tax increases during the inflationary early 1970s; however, an undercurrent of racial hostility was also at work. It seems more than mere coincidence that 1969 marked the last year in which the school district secured approval for a levy increase and it was also the last year in which white students comprised a majority of the district's enrollment. Although the public school enrollment in Kansas City was majority African-American from 1970 forward, the city's voting population remained majority white. In some parts of the city, voters proved exceedingly reluctant to approve fiscal measures that benefited a majority black school district.

With the failure to secure approval for tax levy increases, the school district was compelled to trim the budget by eliminating staff positions and cutting educational programs. Major reductions in staff were initiated in 1969 and 1971. In July 1969, the school board authorized the elimination of 256 staff positions, including 150 classroom teachers. In addition, the board terminated the industrial arts, homemaking, Spanish, and academically talented programs in the elementary schools, and trimmed the number of personnel assigned to the district's art, music, physical education, and special education programs. Staff reductions two years later were equally devastating. In 1971, more teaching positions were eliminated, all schools lost nursing service, the music and physical education programs were radically reduced to the point where one vocal music consultant worked with 303 elementary school teachers, and physical education classes in the elementary schools were reduced to one thirty-minute session every three weeks. Cuts to the library, counseling, physical education, and music programs came at a high price. The Missouri Department of Education downgraded the Kansas City schools from AAA, the state's highest rating, to AA. Moreover, with the radical reductions in staff and the elimination of various programs, the quality of education in the Kansas City schools declined and the dissatisfaction of thousands of patrons grew.

Not only did the district's cost cutting measures adversely effect the quality of education in Kansas City, some of the budget reductions sparked allegations of racial discrimination. In particular, Superintendent Medcalf's reorganization of central administration in 1974 drew the ire of civil rights organizations. Since the early 1970s, the Kansas City NAACP had engaged in a constant assault on what the civil rights group perceived as "racist practices in hiring and promotion" within the district. NAACP maintained that the district had systematically discriminated against black employees for years, denying them pay and advancement opportunities equal to those offered to whites. The civil rights group argued that this pattern of discrimination pervaded all levels of the school district from administration down to maintenance personnel and common laborers. Although the school district convincingly rebutted NAACP's allegations, civil rights activists remained dissatisfied, especially with the relatively small number of blacks working in the offices of central administration and the slovenly pace of the district in adopting an official affirmative action policy, which was not implemented until 1974. That year, enrollment in the Kansas City public schools was 58% black, yet blacks comprised just 35% of the central administration staff. Fully aware of these figures, Superintendent Medcalf announced plans to reorganize central administration and demote certain administrators as a cost cutting measure.

Superintendent Medcalf unveiled his plan to reorganize the school district's central administration in July 1974. The plan was conceived of as a budget cutting measure which would save some $578,000 while rendering the administration more efficient by streamlining the chain of command. However, the plan was unpopular within certain administrative circles, and no sooner was it announced than the plan was assailed by administrators and the NAACP. Reorganization was delayed for almost one year. After refining the plan, the savings were expected to amount to $131,000 and only thirteen administrators were to be demoted. However, nine of the thirteen administrators slated for demotion were black, including Julia Hill, the president of Kansas City's branch of NAACP, who was to be removed from her position of supervising paraprofessionals in the Title I program and placed in a classroom teaching position. Again the NAACP protested and two of the demoted administrators filed lawsuits seeking reinstatement in their former positions and $200,000 in damages. By September 1975, a majority of the school board reached the conclusion that cutting $131,000 from the budget at the expense of lawsuits and the increasing hostility of the NAACP was insensible. Moreover, Medcalf, the plan's architect, had resigned and the plan was abandoned. Individuals who were demoted in April 1975 were restored to their previous positions in September, and district officials explored other avenues for cutting the budget.

The fiasco surrounding the aborted reorganization of central administration is illustrative of the great difficulty the district experienced in attempting to adjust to the new realities of the budget. Despite the budget reductions accomplished through eliminating staff positions and cutting programs, the district's financial woes continued during the 1970s. In particular, the school district experienced increasing difficulty in meeting the salary and benefit demands of the district's teachers. In 1974, when negotiations failed to result in satisfactory agreements, the teachers went on strike. The strike was settled in mid-April after teachers had been off the job for about six weeks. The settlement offered teachers a 5.7% increase in salary, which pushed the district's projected deficit for the following year to more than $5 million. The teachers were also promised an additional 2.5% raise contingent upon passage of a tax levy increase slated for June 11. Teachers returned to work but only received the 5.7% increase, as just 54% of the voters approved the June levy measure.

The disruption of the school year caused by the strike was troubling enough, but was especially devastating when coupled with the abundant evidence elsewhere that the district was spiraling downward. For several years buildings across the district went without repairs, old equipment was not replaced, and purchases of new materials and supplies were greatly reduced. By the mid-1970s, the district was more than a year behind in paying some of its bills and even had difficulty keeping the grass around schools cut.

The district's dire financial straits were relieved somewhat in 1974 with the passage of one-half cent county sales tax to support educational programs in Kansas City and twelve surrounding districts. In 1975, the Kansas City schools received 59% of the revenue generated by the sales tax, an additional $5.3 million. With the voters' approval, the one-half cent sales tax was extended in 1975 and again in 1977. A few of the educational programs that had been cut in the early 1970s were restored with funds from the sales tax. Even so, the district remained deeply troubled financially. None of the funds generated by the sales tax were allocated to teachers' salaries, and consequently, Kansas City teachers again went on strike in 1977. Thousands of the school district's patrons responded by removing their students from the public school system and placing them in the city's parochial and private schools or in schools outside the district.

The decline of quality education associated with the elimination of numerous programs, reductions in the teaching staff, and the loss of the school district's AAA rating from the state, coupled with the disruptions of the teachers' strikes persuaded thousands of Kansas City parents to abandon the public school system. School officials admitted during the 1974 strike that in recent years the school district had been "going backward" in many respects and that "the Kansas City schools are not meeting the standards expected of good schools in Missouri." The teachers' strikes were what seemed to signal for many district patrons that the public schools were deeply troubled. Enrollment in the Kansas City public schools declined each year after 1967, typically at a rate of about 2,000 students per year. Following the two teachers' strikes, the rate at which students left the district more than doubled. During the six-week strike in 1974, school officials estimated that 600 students were removed from the district. A great many more left the district over the summer. When schools opened for the 1974-75 school year, some 6,000 fewer students were enrolled in the Kansas City public schools than had been the previous year. A similar pattern followed the 1977 strike; approximately 5,400 fewer students attended the Kansas City public schools in September 1977.

Parents who removed their students from the Kansas City public schools had several options for continuing their child's education readily available in the metropolitan area. As was true for numerous other urban school districts experiencing tight budgets and racial discord in the 1960s and 1970s, parochial and private schools were often the beneficiaries of the public school system's misfortune. Parochial and private schools in the Kansas City area steadily drew in students from families which had grown disenchanted with the public schools. In 1977, Catholic schools in the Kansas City area enrolled almost 15,000 students. Most of the Catholic schools were filled to capacity and several had waiting lists. Moreover, these schools were no longer filled with Catholic students. Catholic schools near the inner city, such as St. Therese and St. Martin De Porres, tended to be between 60% and 70% non-Catholic, and the majority of students were black. Although the standing policy at the city's Catholic schools was not to admit students whose parents said they were trying to avoid busing or escape desegregation, there is no question that some families sought enrollment in the parochial schools as an avenue to escape conditions in the public schools. Indeed, according to Sister Jean Best, the principal at St. Therese, "The parents told us they were thoroughly disgusted with the public school system." When asked what parents liked about the Catholic schools, Sister Jean said that "they listed religion, discipline, and the academic standards – not necessarily in that order." Most of the city's private schools also operated at full capacity during the 1970s, and private schools proved to be a growth industry of sorts as dozens of new private schools were founded in the Kansas City area during the 1970s.

To be sure, a majority of those parents who removed their children from the Kansas City public schools did so because the family was moving. Thousands of families relocated to the growing suburban ring each year and the enrollments at suburban schools rose accordingly. According to school district figures, about 75% of the students removed from the Kansas City public schools during the 1974 teachers' strike enrolled in public schools outside the district. Similarly, a *Kansas City Star* survey revealed that 68% of students who left the city's public schools during March 1977 were attending suburban schools. Although the great majority of these families had moved to the suburbs, the *Star* found that in some cases, families had enrolled their children in suburban public school systems by using the addresses of friends or relatives living in the suburbs.

Declining enrollment in the Kansas City schools completed the vicious cycle which characterized the school district's financial troubles in the 1970s. State aid for education was, in large part, allocated on the basis of enrollment, and as the number of students attending the Kansas City public schools declined, the district's share of the state funds fell commensurately. Moreover, in some years the legislature demonstrated no inclination to boost the level of state aid despite the fact that the cost of education was steadily rising. In fact, in 1970, the state cut aid to the schools by about 40% due to shortfalls in the expected volume of sales tax revenue collected.

State funding for education was a source of considerable frustration for Kansas City administrators. During the 1974 teacher strike, Superintendent Medcalf complained bitterly that the school district was faced with "a state legislature that has shown little understanding of the problem facing the Kansas City district and other major urban districts in the state." From the perspective of school officials in Kansas City, it was bad enough that the state seemed to be unable to adequately finance the schools, but many also believed that the legislature made it unreasonably difficult for the school district itself to raise funds. They argued that Kansas City could solve its own fiscal problems if the state legislature amended the law requiring two-thirds public approval for tax levy increases and bond issues. Kansas City administrators favored proposals requiring only a simple majority. The legislature, however, resisted pleas from Kansas City and the law continued to require two-thirds approval until it was reduced to four-sevenths for bond issues in 1988.

The school district's desperate financial situation and the declining quality of education in Kansas City were troubling to many of the school district's patrons, be they white, black, or Hispanic. While some patrons expressed their dissatisfaction by voting against bond issues and tax levy increases, others simply removed their children from the Kansas City public schools. The frustration felt by black patrons was compounded by the lack of a meaningful desegregation plan in the district. In the early 1970s, the amount of student integration that was occurring in the district was confined to that which could be accomplished through a neighborhood schools system coupled with a relatively modest busing program. Given the residential patterns in Kansas City, the neighborhood schools concept virtually assured that the great majority of the district's schools would remain racially segregated. By the early 1970s, a strong argument could be made that the original integration plan based on neighborhood schools and implemented in 1955 had failed miserably. Moreover, it could be argued that school district officials had consistently resisted adopting additional plans for integration, such as those found in the Havighurst proposals and Hazlett's "Concepts for Changing Times." In short, it was possible to conclude that as integration had pushed forward elsewhere, Kansas City had fallen out of step and was no longer in compliance with legal standards. By the early 1970s, the Kansas City public schools were clearly vulnerable to a legal challenge seeking a district-wide integration plan, and in 1973, the Kansas City chapter of the Southern Christian Leadership Conference (SCLC) filed a desegregation lawsuit in federal district court.

The *Scott* Desegregation Lawsuit

In 1973, African-American students accounted for about 55% of the enrollment in the Kansas City public schools. Relatively few of these students, however, attended schools which were integrated to any meaningful degree. More than three-fourths of the district's roughly

35,000 black students attended schools which were more than 95% black. Eleven Kansas City schools remained all black, and several more enrolled just a handful of whites. Another twelve schools remained all white and thirteen more enrolled fewer than a dozen African-American students. In short, the schools serving the neighborhoods in the roughly seven-mile long black corridor stretching from the Manual area near downtown to the Southeast High School area were virtually exclusively black, while schools located in the eastern section of the city remained all white. Integration was largely confined to schools where the attendance zones straddled the prevailing lines of residential segregation.

Profoundly concerned with the school district's statistical record on integration, Kansas City's SCLC filed a lawsuit in January 1973 seeking integration of the district's secondary schools. The suit, styled as *Scott, et al v. Kansas City, Missouri School District, et al*, was filed as a class action on behalf of all black students in Kansas City and was initiated by the mothers of two black high school students with the support of SCLC. SCLC's suit claimed that greater integration was both possible and desirable in the city's junior highs and high schools, and attacked the manner in which the school district's attendance zones channeled thousands of black students into "racially segregated or racially imbalanced" secondary schools. Because junior high schools and high schools drew enrollments from much larger geographic areas than elementary schools, one could argue that significantly more integration could be accomplished by merely redrawing the secondary school attendance zones. Although the arguments presented in SCLC's complaint were sound, the organization's pursuit of the case was troubled from the beginning by virtue of the way in which the suit was crafted.

School district attorneys asserted that the SCLC complaint failed to define the terms "racially segregated and racially imbalanced," and therefore the school district had no idea as to how large or how small the class of black students affected by the case might be. Moreover, the district's legal counsel argued that two black high school students were not sufficient to represent the entire class of all black students in the Kansas City public schools, and maintained that SCLC should be dismissed as a plaintiff because the organization was not a part of the class it purported to represent. Finally, the school district argued that, should the case proceed, at least four suburban districts – North Kansas City, Center, Raytown, and Independence – should be named as defendants in order for the court to consider the question of integration on a metropolitan basis.

The district court refused to consider metropolitan desegregation in 1973. Nevertheless, SCLC's legal challenge stalled. On February 5, 1974 the district court dismissed the *Scott* suit because SCLC's counsel had withdrawn from the case and the organization was unable to raise the funds necessary to pursue the suit. Of course, the dismissal of the SCLC suit was a great relief to school officials but by no means was there cause for celebration. The school district continued to be assailed by dissatisfied patrons and there appeared to be few desirable solutions to the familiar litany of fiscal problems. The district had staved off its latest challenge, but the quality of education in Kansas City remained suspect and relatively few of the district's 57,000 students received their education in integrated schools. Although the school district enjoyed a temporary reprieve with the dismissal of the *Scott* case, the deep-seated dissatisfaction of many of the district's patrons in the early 1970s virtually assured that the school officials would face additional challenges regarding desegregation, finance, and the educational program in Kansas City.

Conclusions

The late 1960s and early 1970s witnessed a dizzying array of problems for the Kansas City public schools. Activism on the part of minority groups, civil rights organizations, and neighborhood associations continued unabated and the school district experienced increasing difficulty in satisfying its patrons. Due to the dismal financial standing of the district, schools fell into disrepair, curricular programs were dropped, faculty and staff positions were cut, teachers went on strike, and to the great displeasure of the black community, no new desegregation program was developed. With each budget cut, the quality of education in the Kansas City public schools suffered and the dissatisfaction of the district's patrons grew proportionately. Families which had grown weary of the constant paring away at the district's educational program, the continued racial discord, and the teachers' strikes expressed their frustrations in various ways. Some patrons protested to the school board, while others wrote angry letters to the superintendent or to the city's newspapers. Still other disaffected residents voted against school district bond issues and tax levy increases, and a great many removed their children from the Kansas City public schools.

Most damaging to the school district was the loss of students, particularly white students. Between 1968 and 1975, while the number of black students enrolled in the Kansas City public schools remained nearly constant, the school district lost more than 20,000 white students. The effect of these losses on school district planners was profound. First, the declining enrollment compounded the school district's financial woes as a smaller percentage of state funding flowed into the district. Second, the loss of so many white students influenced the manner in which school board members and district administrators thought about desegregation. Considering the large number of white families who were leaving the district, school planners were wary of launching any new plan to promote greater integration. Some school policy makers concluded that if whites were already withdrawing from the district at a rate of 2,000 students or more each year, a new desegregation initiative would only spur further white flight. Thus, the polarization of the races in Kansas City persisted into the early 1970s with little affirmative effort by school officials to reverse the trend. The school district escaped litigation in 1974 when the SCLC case was dismissed, but the sighs of relief among school board members and administrators were somewhat restrained. Just as the district was extricating itself from the *Scott* case, new inquiries into the progress of integration in the Kansas City schools were undertaken by an agency with far greater resources than SCLC. In 1973, an in-depth probe of school integration in Kansas City was launched by the United States Department of Health, Education, and Welfare.

CHAPTER 5

The Federal Connection

Disadvantaged Students, H.E.W., and the Kansas City Public Schools 1964-1978

In January 1963 representatives from the Kansas City and St. Louis school boards and the superintendents of those districts traveled to Jefferson City to plead for additional funds from the state legislature to be used in the schools serving impoverished areas of the inner cities. The school officials argued that problems unique to inner cities, such as low income, substandard housing, and rapid population change, "create educational and social problems not faced in other communities." At the time, administrators in Kansas City estimated that the district included some 31,000 "culturally disadvantaged" students. Homer Wadsworth, president of the Kansas City Board of Education, asserted that providing these students with expanded services and educational programs required "imagination, experimentation, and increased expenditures." The school officials left Jefferson City disappointed: no additional funds were forthcoming from the legislature. Even so, the trip to the capital marked an important turning point for the Kansas City schools. For the first time, school officials had committed themselves to addressing the difficult problems of lower academic achievement among "under-privileged" students.

During the 1960s, school administrators in Kansas City and elsewhere grew increasingly concerned with the educational plight of inner city, largely minority, students. Significant differences among schools were observed in terms of academic achievement, graduation rates, retention rates, absenteeism, and truancy. These disparities often occurred along racial and socioeconomic lines. Because race and socioeconomic status influence housing patterns, the result in large cities like Kansas City was often a significant disparity between achievement levels in those schools which served the more affluent, and virtually all white, neighborhoods and those schools which served the poorer, virtually all minority neighborhoods. Indeed, several studies documented the differences in achievement, truancy, and graduation rates. The reasoning went that the quality of educational opportunity was generally significantly higher in schools that served the more affluent, majority white neighborhoods than in those schools which served the poorer, largely minority sections of a city. Reformers speculated that these disparities were caused by a wide variety of socioeconomic and environmental disadvantages apparent in poorer sections of cities, and that these disadvantaged students were not adequately served by local and state education programs. In order to address, and, it was hoped, to overcome these disadvantages, special programs were implemented for target groups that shared certain characteristics deemed to indicate educational disadvantage. Typically socioeconomic status and race served as proxy indicators for students in need of compensatory educational programs.

The first initiatives in the area of compensatory education in Kansas City came in the early 1960s. Administrators in the central offices and school principals generally agreed that the problems of underachievement were most acute in the largely black and Hispanic schools that fed West Junior High, Manual High School and Lincoln High School. Analysis of standardized test scores indicated that the lowest achieving schools were clustered in these areas. With these results in mind, building principals from the district's largely minority inner city schools formed the Educators' Study Club and began "to consider educational programs which might be especially helpful to under-privileged children." After visiting St. Louis to observe that district's compensatory education program, the Banneker Plan, in operation, the Study Club convinced Superintendent Hazlett of the need for similar programs in Kansas City. In August 1963, Kansas City's school board allocated $75,000 for compensatory education programs.

Five elementary schools and one junior high school were selected for the Lincoln Plus Project, Kansas City's initial compensatory education program. All six of the schools were located in the Lincoln High School attendance area and were at least 97% black. The project's objectives were to raise students' achievement levels, build self-esteem and the motivation to learn, and develop stronger ties between home and school. Four reading specialists and two home-school coordinators were appointed to the project. Intensive small group reading sessions, reading discussion groups, after school recreation and study programs, a breakfast program, and remedial math and reading summer school were among the new programs initiated in the Lincoln Plus Project. The project's success during the 1963-64 school year prompted Hazlett to recommend that compensatory education programs be extended to four more elementary schools in the largely black Manual High School attendance area for the 1964-65 school year.

After two years of operation the Lincoln Plus and Manual Plus project director reported that students at the nine pilot elementary schools made above average gains in vocabulary and reading comprehension on the Metropolitan Reading Test and that absenteeism had declined at the target schools. Kansas City's compensatory education efforts, however, remained limited to the schools in the Lincoln and Manual attendance areas due to the fact that the programs were funded entirely by the school district alone. A more comprehensive effort to reach all of the 31,000 educationally disadvantaged students in the district was necessarily postponed until additional funds became available through the massive infusions of federal money in the mid-1960s.

The Federal Government and Public Education

Until the middle decades of the twentieth century the federal government played a limited role in public education, that responsibility falling almost exclusively to state and local governments. Following World War II, however, federal funding for education rose dramatically. There were a number of reasons for this shift in federal education policy. The growth of the school age population alone placed enormous demands on local school systems. Due to increases in the birth rate and in the number of students remaining in school through high school, the nation's school population nearly doubled between 1946 and 1965. The need to build and maintain new schools, enlarge existing facilities, expand faculties, and provide equipment and supplies to serve the booming school population placed extreme pressures on the local school finances. Aside from the sheer increases in the school age population, numerous other considerations pointed toward increased federal funding for education. Economists emphasized that investment in education was the single most important element in sustaining and promoting national productivity and economic prosperity. The desire to promote science and mathematics education as Cold War imperatives further implied the need for federal assistance to schools. Growing concerns for children's health and nutrition led policymakers to urge that schools operate lunch and milk programs. Finally, the Supreme Court's 1954 *Brown v. Board of Education* decision foreshadowed subsequent legislation to provide all students with equal educational opportunities. The Court's finding that segregated schooling was "inherently unequal" implied that an effort must be undertaken to provide equal educational opportunity to all children. If merely dismantling segregated school systems failed to result in equal educational opportunities the implication was that additional funding, resources, and programs must be committed to the task of providing such opportunity.

Meeting any one of these needs would have severely strained the resources of local districts. Together these diverse concerns constituted a ringing demand for additional federal funding. Congress responded with several pieces of legislation, and federal funding for education steadily rose. Federal assistance to the nation's public schools roughly doubled between 1957 and 1964, and doubled again in 1965 with the passage of the Elementary and Secondary Education Act. By the mid-1970s, the federal government was providing more than $4 billion in annual assistance to the nation's elementary and secondary schools.

Kansas City benefited significantly from the increases in federal funding during the post-World War II period. The district received substantial amounts of federal assistance for vocational education programs and through the National Defense Education Act during the late fifties and early sixties. These funds, however, were not so critical to the operation of the school district as was the federal assistance made available through the Johnson administration's War on Poverty. The Great Society education programs initiated in mid-1960s in order to address the needs of the impoverished and educationally disadvantaged school population had significant impact in Kansas City, and carried serious consequences for the school district.

The War on Poverty and its education components were initiated with the passage of the 1964 Civil Rights Act. Title VII of the 1964 Act provided for technical assistance to school districts in the process of integrating. Passage of the Economic Opportunity Act in 1964 made additional federal funding available to school districts, primarily through the Head Start program. In Head Start programs, school districts often acted in partnership with local agencies to provide disadvantaged preschool children with educational and health services designed to prevent developmental deficits and prepare children for successful entry into the school system. Still more federal funding was made available to school districts through programs such as Follow Through, Upward Bound, Neighborhood Youth Corps, and the educational components of the Model Cities program. Much of the federal money available under these programs was earmarked for the impoverished and educationally disadvantaged. Administrators in Kansas City, conscious of the educational needs of the city's impoverished and largely minority school population, eagerly pursued federal funding. Their efforts were consistently rewarded as Kansas City was among the first cities to receive federal funding through these programs during the 1960s.

The capstone to the Great Society's War on Poverty education programs and the federal government's commitment to provide for equal educational opportunity was the Elementary and Secondary Education Act (ESEA) signed by President Johnson on April 11, 1965, in a one-room schoolhouse he once attended. ESEA provided more than $1.2 billion in assistance to the nation's schools, the bulk of which was earmarked for "meeting the special educational needs of educationally deprived children" under Title I of the act. Eligibility for federal education funds under ESEA was contingent upon a school district's compliance with Title VI of the 1964 Civil Rights Act prohibiting discrimination on the basis of race, color or national origin in any program receiving federal financial assistance. School officials in Kansas City confidently signed the compliance forms and the federal money began flowing into the district. The initial ESEA grant awarded to the Kansas City schools in 1966 amounted to more than $2.1 million and raised the federally funded portion of the school district's operating budget from just over 1% the previous year to more than 6% for the 1966-67 school year. Federal assistance to Kansas City under ESEA eventually rose to more than $4 million in 1968-69, accounting for more than 10% of the school district's operating budget. As the volume of federal assistance rose and the importance of federal funding to the functioning of the school district increased, the central administration of the Kansas City public schools was reorganized. A new administrative branch, the Division of Urban Education, was created in 1966 to manage the numerous programs receiving federal assistance aimed at the educationally disadvantaged of the inner city. Robert Wheeler, an African-American graduate of the Kansas City public schools, was appointed Assistant Superintendent for Urban Education.

With federal funding came a degree of federal oversight and a somewhat more active federal presence in monitoring race related issues in the school district. Among the consequences of accepting ESEA funding in the late 1960s was that Kansas City was twice investigated by federal officials for possible violations of Title VI. The first federal probe of the school district's compliance with the Civil Rights Act came in June 1967, in the immediate aftermath of the Havighurst middle school controversy. The preliminary investigation by Dr. Benjamin Hunton revealed that "a full review of the integration policies of the Kansas City school district" was in order, and in mid-July an eight-member investigative team arrived in Kansas City.

The federal officials were principally concerned with the district's policies and practices regarding teacher assignment and student integration. With respect to integration of students, the federal agents sought to determine whether the site selection process for new schools, the school district's adjustments of attendance zones, and the transfer policy functioned in a manner that discriminated against black students. With respect to school faculties, investigators examined the possibility that the school district assigned teachers to schools such that teaching staffs were racially isolated in a way similar to the racial isolation of much of the student population.

The investigative team concluded their probe in one week and returned to Washington. Hinting that HEW could request certain changes made in the school district, Hunton told the *Kansas City Star*: "We have some very imaginative experts in Washington that we would be delighted to send out here to work with the Board of Education." Those "imaginative experts" were never sent; in fact HEW did not communicate with school officials in Kansas City until September. Even then, correspondence from HEW in Washington only suggested that Kansas City make a more concerted effort at teacher integration, and that the district consider offering free transportation for Hispanic high school students living on the West Side. No citations resulted from HEW's 1967 investigation, nor was the district cited after a similar probe conducted by the Justice Department in 1968.

Federal investigations in the late 1960s were a source of some anxiety and inconvenience for school officials in Kansas City. Administrators conceded that the school district had not yet solved its racial problems and that the integration program in Kansas City had its failings, but few felt that the district had failed to comply with Title VI. Moreover, most agreed that when compared to the delay tactics and evasion in states such as Alabama and Mississippi, Kansas City remained a model of compliance.

School officials cooperated with the investigations and various federal requests for statistical information in part because they were confident that the district was fully in compliance with federal requirements and the most recent court orders on desegregation. In part, however, they cooperated because ESEA funding was critical to the functioning of the Kansas City schools in the late 1960s and early 1970s. In spite of millions of dollars in federal assistance and despite of numerous program cuts and staff reductions, the school district teetered on the verge of insolvency. It is not surprising then, that when additional federal funds became available in 1972 under the Emergency School Aid Act (ESAA), Kansas City was among the first school districts to develop a grant proposal.

Kansas City's 1973 ESAA Grant

ESAA funds were allocated in order to assist school districts in developing and implementing desegregation plans. In particular, ESAA funds were intended for three purposes: to plan voluntary desegregation programs between school districts, to assist school children in overcoming the educational disadvantages of racial isolation in schools, and to eliminate, reduce or prevent racial isolation. The Office of Education defined racial isolation as a condition in which the enrollment at a school was more than 50% minority.

School officials in Kansas City began making preparations for an ESAA grant application in January 1973. The administrators determined at the first meeting that it was not feasible for the district to eliminate racial isolation in the Kansas City schools. In 1972-73, there were thirty-four elementary schools, four junior high schools, and six high schools in Kansas City which met the Office of Education's definition of racial isolation. In other words, 90% of Kansas City's 35,000 black students attended racially isolated schools. Moreover, by 1972 the student population in the Kansas City schools was 54% black which made the elimination of racial isolation throughout the district impossible. With these considerations in mind, the Board of Education favored the more attainable goal of reducing racial isolation for some minority students.

In accord with ESAA regulations a racially balanced Citizens' Advisory Committee was named in February to work in collaboration with school district officials in formulating desegregation plans. The eighty-four member citizens' committee was comprised of equal numbers of whites, blacks and Hispanics. The committee included representatives from all sections of the city, different community groups, civil rights organizations, parents, students, and school administration. Over the course of the next two months this diverse group collected statistics, conducted public forums, and met on numerous occasions to evaluate thirteen different desegregation options for the district's ESAA grant application.

In the course of the committee's meetings it became clear that a majority of the group favored relatively narrow measures aimed at relieving racial isolation in schools on the periphery of the large black residential area. Indeed, the Citizens' Advisory Committee recommended that only one of the thirteen proposals originally under consideration be incorporated into the district's ESAA application. That proposal involved a small pilot program at Blenheim Elementary to improve achievement, reduce absenteeism, and relieve racial isolation. Beyond the Blenheim proposal, the panel favored minor reductions in racial isolation in the West and Westport high school areas accomplished by altering attendance zones and curtailing transfers. Finally, the committee recommended that a single seventh grade center be organized at Leeds-Dunbar to serve all of the seventh grade students living in the racially mixed East High School attendance zone.

Fearing that the district's ESAA plans would not result in meaningful integration on a broad scale, persons critical of the ESAA committee's work regularly voiced their concerns to central administration and the school board. Among the more vocal critics was one of the highest ranking African-Americans in central administration, Dr. Edward Fields, the Assistant Superintendent for Urban Education. He characterized the proposal for the West High School area as "sawdust filler," and suggested that plan for Westport "does absolutely nothing as far as ESAA objectives are concerned." Dr. Fields argued that by bowing to pressure from certain sections of the city to "preserve their neighborhood school," the district was "preserving the white majority attitude" which he argued had produced "a great deal of the difficulty in the first place." He maintained that the committee's ESAA proposals, "take full advantage of the less vocal parents," by placing the burdens of busing and reorganization upon those schools, neighborhoods and parents which were not sufficiently well organized to protest loudly. Moreover, Fields was disgusted by the suggestion made at a committee meeting in April that "for any white school receiving black kids there would be a guarantee of '$20 per head' following such children into these schools." He concluded, "it is obvious . . . that the million plus dollars are more important than the actual attack on racial isolation." Dozens of parents, community leaders, and civil rights activists echoed Dr. Field's concerns at the March and April school board meetings.

In spite of rising opposition and the recognition that the ESAA plans had stirred "feelings of frustration, anger, and anxiety," the school board approved the ESAA grant proposal on April 11, 1973. The ESAA package which the school board members endorsed bore slight resemblance to the proposals recommended by the advisory committee. Although the school board approved the committee's recommendations for a pilot program at Blenheim and the Leeds-Dunbar seventh grade center for the East High School area, board members rejected the proposed boundary changes and reorganization of the West and Westport high school areas. To fill out Kansas City's ESAA grant proposal, school board members resurrected several of the original thirteen proposals which the citizens' committee had rejected. The board members approved five different measures to bus a total of 661 minority students out of racially isolated schools to majority white schools. All told, Kansas City's ESAA proposal promised to relieve racial isolation for some 1,300 black students. Considering that there were more than 31,000 black students attending racially isolated schools in Kansas City, the school district's ESAA plans were certain to make little difference to the great majority of Kansas City's African-American students.

Before Kansas City's ESAA grant could be considered by the Office of Education, the district had several issues to resolve with HEW officials. A pre-grant review of the school district raised serious questions regarding the district's compliance with Title VI and its eligibility for ESAA funds. Based on previous experiences with HEW investigations, school officials in Kansas City assumed that another inquiry would be a minor inconvenience. The 1973 probe, however, proved quite different from earlier investigations. Whereas HEW's 1967 investigation had lasted one week, the probe initiated late in 1973 continued for eighteen months. The standards for school integration required by HEW had changed dramatically since the mid-1960s and the Kansas City public schools were clearly not in compliance by the early 1970s. Moreover, the school district faced a federal department tested by hundreds of legal battles for school integration in the Deep South, and more determined to hold Kansas City to a higher standard on integration.

HEW and School Integration

By the early 1970s, federal officials were fully committed to securing complete compliance with Title VI and district-wide school integration, and HEW had an arsenal of tools to use as leverage against recalcitrant districts. Compliance guidelines, initially developed by HEW in 1965, grew increasingly stringent. The 1966 guidelines called for all school districts to integrate their faculties, and included provisions to measure the effectiveness of integration plans by establishing standards based upon the percentage of black students attending predominantly white schools. The guidelines required that a school district at least double the percentage of black students attending integrated schools the following year, and indicated that future compliance would be measured by the progress made in increasing the percentage of minority students attending majority white schools. Moreover, organizational reforms that centralized the enforcement of HEW guidelines and Title VI compliance in the Office of Civil Rights (OCR) allowed HEW to process more efficiently its staggering workload of thousands of cases. School districts which failed to comply with HEW guidelines were subject to termination of their federal funding and those which persisted in resisting faced Justice Department lawsuits. Most importantly, HEW's statistically based compliance formulas were consistently endorsed by the nation's courts. Indeed, the HEW guidelines had their greatest impact as they were incorporated into court decrees which held school districts to increasingly specific standards for integration.

In the late 1960s, HEW focused most of its attention on the school districts of the Deep South. One decade after the *Brown* decision, only 2% of the black student population in the eleven states of the Old Confederacy attended integrated schools. During the late 1960s and early 1970s, however, HEW's compliance guidelines, designed to compel integration in the South, had the intended effect. Confronted with HEW's standards, Justice Department lawsuits, and federal courts unsympathetic to pleas for delay and tokenism, massive integration came to the South. In relatively short order the school systems of the South capitulated and became the most integrated in the nation. By 1970, 39% of southern black students attended majority white schools, and in 1972 that figure had risen to 46%.

While HEW secured greater integration in the South, school districts elsewhere made little progress toward increased integration. In 1972, only 28% of black students in the North and West were enrolled in majority white schools. The shortcomings of integration outside the South were attributable in large part to the distinction drawn by HEW and the nation's courts between *de jure* and *de facto* segregation. During the 1960s, HEW tended to deal with the school districts of the North much differently than southern districts. Northern states had not required segregated schools by law and some question existed as to whether HEW could hold northern school districts to specific standards on integration. The difficulties HEW encountered in its 1967 attempt to secure greater integration in the Chicago schools discouraged the department from launching similar actions against northern cities with no history of *de jure* segregation. The border states, too, presented a situation different from the entrenched resistance of the Deep South in the 1960s. Although the border states had by law required segregation, many border state school districts, such as Kansas City, had taken steps to dismantle their segregated systems shortly after the *Brown* decision. Such districts had clearly made a "good faith start" toward integration and, were generally considered to be more amenable to adopting additional integration measures.

In the late 1960s, HEW's unwritten policy for northern and border state school districts was to move those districts along gently toward greater integration through consultation, negotiation, and compromises without resorting to the ultimate sanction of withholding federal funds. During the 1967 investigation of the Kansas City schools, Benjamin Hunton conceded that HEW officials "don't believe in cutting off aid if we can possibly help it, that's inflicting punishment upon innocent students." Rather, he said that HEW's practice in the North had been "to point out violations of the Civil Rights Act or the Fourteenth Amendment." Hunton's experience had been that the "districts have generally been receptive" to this approach.

Consistent with Hunton's comment, some $14.25 million in federal ESEA assistance flowed into the Kansas City schools between 1968 and 1973 even while the district's compliance with Title VI and HEW guidelines remained questionable at best. A report issued in 1971 by Kansas City's Human Relations Task Force concluded that school integration in the city had actually regressed since 1968. Indeed, by 1973, 84% of the city's black students attended schools which were more than 90% black, whereas 69.5% had attended such schools in 1968. In light of these statistics, officials in the Kansas City regional offices of HEW's Office for Civil Rights moved to resume investigations of the school district's integration policies.

The 1973 *Adams* Letter

Beginning in 1973, HEW's posture in dealing with Kansas City changed dramatically. In some respects the renewed interest in the problems of integrating the Kansas City public schools was forced upon HEW by the federal courts. In February 1973, John Pratt, a federal district court judge in Washington D.C., announced his decision in *Adams v. Richardson*, a case in which the defendant was the Secretary of HEW, Elliot Richardson. Pratt ruled that HEW had failed to exercise its ultimate sanction, termination of federal education funds, against numerous states and school districts which HEW had determined were not in compliance with Title VI of the 1964 Civil Rights Act. Pratt found that HEW continued to provide financial assistance to 127 school districts in fifteen states despite the fact that the districts were not in compliance with Title VI or the most recent Supreme Court decisions regarding desegregation. Pratt noted that, contrary to the Supreme Court's 1969 ruling in *Alexander v. Holmes County Board of Education* requiring that desegregation begin "at once," HEW approved desegregation plans for eighty-seven school districts that postponed integration until 1970.

Moreover, Pratt found that HEW had neglected to enforce the Supreme Court's 1971 milestone ruling in *Swann v. Charlotte-Mecklenburg Board of Education.* "The objective today," the Court declared in *Swann*, was "to eliminate from the public schools all vestiges of state-imposed segregation." In attacking those "vestiges," the Court announced a "presumption against schools that are substantially disproportionate in their racial composition." The Court defined disproportionate racial composition as the existence of one or more schools in which the racial composition of that school deviated by more than 20% from the racial composition of the school district as a whole. The Court did not prohibit the existence of a small number of racially disproportionate or even one-race schools, but held that school districts provide adequate documentation and reasonable justification for retaining such schools. In short, the Court ordered federal agencies and the federal courts to hold districts having one or more racially disproportionate schools to a higher level of scrutiny. Judge Pratt found that HEW continued to provide federal funds to at least eighty-five school districts possessing racially disproportionate schools without having required those districts to provide any justification for retaining such schools.

Kansas City was among those school districts listed by Pratt as not in compliance with the *Swann* decision. In 1973, the Kansas City public schools were 57% black and therefore, according to the standard announced in *Swann*, the acceptable range for racial composition of individual schools was between 37% and 77% black. Only six of Kansas City's ninety-eight schools fell within the acceptable range.

Judge Pratt condemned HEW's "administrative inaction." He insisted that the time for "securing voluntary compliance for these districts ... has long since passed," and ruled that HEW had a duty to begin termination proceedings. He ordered HEW to communicate with each of the non-complying school districts within sixty days, "putting them on notice to rebut or explain the substantial racial disproportion" existing within those districts. Pratt further ordered HEW to commence termination proceedings within 120 days against those school districts which remained in non-compliance.

Kansas City received its "Adams letter" from HEW on April 17, 1973. Acting Superintendent J. Glenn Travis initially responded by submitting various documents relative to the *Scott* case, SCLC's pending desegregation suit against the district, as well as statistical data documenting the racial composition of the Kansas City schools, maps depicting the school district's attendance zones, and copies of school district policies regarding integration. Essentially, the documentation submitted by Travis defended the position that the school district operated a racially neutral system of neighborhood schools and that racial imbalance was a product of segregated residential patterns which the school district was impotent to change. Although officials from Kansas City's Regional Office for Civil Rights (OCR) later determined that the information submitted by Travis was "not sufficient to rebut the presumption against the district's one-race schools," no letter of non-compliance was sent to the district. Rather, OCR officials in Kansas City informed the school district that an investigation would begin later in 1973.

The investigation of the Kansas City schools launched by OCR in 1973 would not be concluded until April 1975. During that period, the Kansas City public schools received two federal grants under the Emergency School Aid Act, but in both instances the money came with strings attached. Before funding the district's 1973 grant, HEW required one major change in the Kansas City schools. ESAA regulations stipulated that participating school districts maintain racially balanced faculties at all schools. Fulfilling this precondition would demand massive reassignments of teachers.

Teacher Integration

Previous efforts at racially balancing school faculties through voluntary teacher transfers had been dismally disappointing. In 1972-73 the Kansas City public schools employed more than 2,000 teachers. That year only fourteen teachers submitted voluntary requests for transfers which promoted faculty integration. The district enjoyed greater success in placing newly hired teachers in positions that advanced faculty integration. School officials estimated that by assigning new teachers to positions that promoted racial balance, the district would be in compliance with ESAA regulations by the 1975-76 school year. However, the district's legal counsel concluded that requesting a three-year waiver on the ESAA requirement for racially balanced faculties would be rather awkward and advised instead that the district comply before the opening of the 1973-74 school year.

The task of racially balancing the faculties fell to the assistant superintendents in central administration and to newly hired superintendent Dr. Robert L. Medcalf, formerly of the Hammond, Indiana, public schools. In 1973, 42% of the district's teachers were minorities, and these teachers tended to be concentrated in schools which were predominantly black, rendering such schools racially identifiable by both their enrollments and the composition of their faculties. Achieving a rough balance where minorities comprised between 30% and 50% of the faculty at each school necessitated transferring almost 600 teachers, about one-fourth of the district's teachers, during the summer. Guidelines were developed in early August allowing principals to "freeze" 40% of their faculty in order to retain exceptional teachers or faculty members who were essential to the continuation of certain curriculum programs at a school. Some teachers were exempt for medical reasons and other "hardships." All other teachers were subject to transfer.

Letters informing teachers of their school assignment for the 1973-74 school year were mailed in mid-August, less than three weeks before school opened. Ninety voluntary requests for transfer were honored, while more than 500 teachers were reassigned involuntarily. Expecting some resistance, district administrators established procedures for hearing grievances, and by the end of August more than 150 teachers had filed appeals for reinstatement in their former assignments. Some teachers protested that colleagues with less experience were not required to transfer; indeed the district had forcibly reassigned eighteen teachers who were older than sixty-five years of age and had in excess of twenty-five years of service to the district. Others argued that they had been placed in the transfer pool despite medical conditions which should have exempted them from transfer. Still others argued that they were not treated with respect or felt threatened by the students in their new assignment. A few teachers put off the inevitable by simply refusing to report to their new assignment. The grievance process dragged on for weeks, but the district managed to remain in compliance.

Balancing the faculties demanded an "effort almost beyond comprehension," but the district was rewarded with an ESAA grant of $1.1 million for the 1973-74 school year. Having secured the initial grant, school administrators in Kansas City set out to develop additional ESAA proposals for the following year, and in December 1973, submitted applications requesting more than $1.6 million for the 1974-75 school year.

The district's 1974-75 basic grant application proposed expanding the services provided to the students bused out of racially isolated black schools and at the Leeds-Dunbar seventh grade center funded by the initial ESAA grant. The district sought to reduce pupil-teacher ratios, provide innovative reading and math instruction, and expand the remedial services offered at those schools. The district's pilot grant application called for continuation of the Blenheim project, but also focused upon the different needs of minority students in the areas served by Southeast and Central High School. Both Southeast and Central were studies in residential transition and how rapidly enrollments could turn over from virtually all-white to virtually all-black. The schools in the Central area had undergone complete transition from white to black during the early 1960s, and as the large black neighborhood continued to expand toward the southeast in the late 1960s and early 1970s, the schools in the Southeast area had turned over as well. Most troubling to Kansas City school administrators were the significant lags in achievement that students in the central and southeastern sections of the city demonstrated on standardized tests. At Central the problems of underachievement and maladjustment to school translated to a drop-out rate of 26% in 1972. The district's ESAA pilot grant application aimed "to overcome the negative impact of minority group isolation" through intensive, individualized reading and math instruction for all students at Southeast Junior High, and for "educationally disadvantaged" students at Central High School.

Negotiations with OCR

As Kansas City administrators developed the grant proposals in the last months of 1973, the district's relationship with HEW in general, and the Kansas City branch of OCR in particular, began to sour. The investigation, which OCR had warned the district about in June 1973, began in November of that year. From the start it was clear that OCR would require the district to adopt additional measures to bring Kansas City into compliance with the HEW guidelines and the prevailing judicial standards. The massive faculty reassignments of the previous summer were but the first condition which HEW placed on Kansas City's ESAA funding.

The investigation that commenced in November 1973 was spearheaded by Jerold Ward, Elementary and Secondary Education Branch Chief of OCR's Region VII offices in Kansas City, and Taylor August, Director of OCR Region VII. Ward was a University of Michigan graduate with seven years experience as a civil rights advisory specialist and Title VI compliance officer. August was a graduate of Tuskegee Institute and a former teacher and administrator in Selma, Alabama. Before his appointment to OCR, August was employed by the Office of Economic Opportunity and oversaw Title VI compliance for community action programs.

Due to staff limitations in OCR's Kansas City offices, the investigation began slowly with a series of informal discussions with district administrators. The HEW officials' initial concerns hinged on whether the school district's long standing liberal transfer policy functioned in a manner that discriminated against minority students and provided whites with a vehicle to evade integration. By the early 1970s there was no longer any question that Kansas City's transfer policy had inhibited integration. School district studies clearly illustrated the manner in which both races had used transfers to avoid integration. In 1970, 662 black elementary students were granted transfers, the overwhelming majority of whom obtained transfers to predominantly black schools. More than 80% of the black elementary transfer students had requested and been granted transfers to schools which were more than 85% black. Of the five elementary schools receiving the largest numbers of black transfer students, four of those schools were more than 98% black, and the fifth school, Moore Elementary, was 89% black. White transfers followed a similar pattern. More than 900 transfers were granted to white elementary students, 40% of whom secured transfers to just five predominantly white schools. Of the five schools receiving the largest numbers of white elementary transfers, four were more than 95% white, and the fifth, Kensington Elementary, was 89% white. Hundreds of students at the secondary level also evaded integration through the transfer policy. August noted that in 1973, more than 100 white students had obtained transfers to Northeast High School, which was 97% white. Another sixty-one white students had secured transfers to Southwest High School, a school which was 93% white. The pattern for black students was similar. In 1970, almost 200 black students had secured transfers to Manual, Central, Lincoln, and Paseo high schools, all of which were more than 90% black.

August concluded that, "these transfers do not appear to be supported by sound educational reasons," and he was undoubtedly correct. The primary determinant considered in granting a transfer had merely been the availability of space at the receiving school. Once a transfer had been granted, even space ceased to be a concern inasmuch as the district allowed transfers to be carried over from one year to the next without a re-application. In April 1974, the school board finally reformed this system. A school board resolution passed on April 11 required all transfer students to reapply for transfers during the 1974-75 school year. Moreover, the resolution prohibited transferring a student from a school in which the child was part of the minority race at the building to a school where the student would be part of the majority race. The intent of the new policy was to review each transfer granted, determine the impact that transfers had on integration, and revoke those transfers which had an adverse effect on integration. Exceptions were made for special education students, and to allow high school seniors to graduate from the school that they had been attending. Severe economic hardship could also justify a transfer provided that the hardship was "documented and corroborated... [and] that the transfer can be shown to alleviate the economic hardship and benefit the student educationally."

Reforming the transfer policy was an important step toward compliance with HEW. The change, however, was not well received by some parents' organizations and neighborhood groups. Parents accustomed to securing transfers for their children were outraged by the new policy. As may have been expected, the most rabid objections to the new transfer policy came from neighborhoods caught up in racial transition. Each year numerous requests for transfer came from the transitional neighborhoods where parents sought reassignments for their children from schools where the racial composition was changing or where their children were part of the minority race at the school.

In the early 1970s one such neighborhood was the area between Paseo and Southwest high schools served by Nelson and Troost elementary schools. In 1973, the Troost's enrollment was almost 90% black, and blacks comprised 31% of the enrollment at Nelson. Residents living in this area organized the 49-63 Neighborhood Coalition, named for the streets that formed the northern and southern boundaries of the neighborhood. In August 1974, the 49-63 Coalition filed a lawsuit in federal court against the school district and HEW seeking an injunction to block the district's cancellation of transfers granted the previous year. The neighborhood group also made clear, however, that it would drop the lawsuit if the school district adjusted the attendance zones so that all of the neighborhood would be included within the Southwest High School area. Without transfers or an adjustment to the attendance zones, students living in the eastern part of the Troost and Nelson area would be assigned to Paseo High School, which by 1973 was 99.8% black. For the parents in the 49-63 Coalition, Southwest High School was preferable to Paseo not only because Southwest was only 6.6% black but also because it had long been considered the premier high school in Kansas City. Nevertheless, the school district refused to bow to pressure from the 49-63 Coalition and the lawsuit was later dismissed.

Having made some progress on the transfer issue, Kansas City school administrators made additional assurances to OCR. Specifically, Taylor August had expressed concern that the district assigned principals and counselors such that individual schools were racially identifiable by virtue of the race of the administrators. OCR officials concluded that the district's organizational structure divided schools into two groups. Majority white schools, OCR argued, were administered by the School Management Division. The seventy-three schools included in the School Management Division had a total enrollment which was 47% black and were under the direction of a white assistant superintendent. Conversely, the thirty-one schools included in the Urban Education Division were under the direction of a black assistant superintendent and had a total enrollment which was almost 97% black. August further noted that minorities comprised just 29% of the building administrators and counselors in the School Management Division schools but filled 66% of those positions in the Urban Education Division.

August also questioned whether the district had made a faithful attempt to identify gifted black students and provide them with educational opportunities equal to those provided for gifted white students. He pointed to the fact that while minorities made up 59% of the district's enrollment, they comprised just 9% of the enrollment in the Academically Talented program. Moreover, five of the six Academically Talented centers were located at schools having "overwhelmingly non-minority enrollments."

Superintendent Medcalf informed OCR that the district would address these issues before beginning the 1974-75 school term. The superintendent vowed to maintain the racially balanced faculty assignments and extend that policy to building principals and counselors. He further assured OCR that the district would review the records of every student currently placed in the gifted program, and redouble its efforts to identify, screen, and assign students to the program in a way that insured equal opportunity. Once again the district's progress toward compliance with Title VI was rewarded with ESAA grants totaling more than $1.6 million. Now the school district now had to find a way to keep the promises it had made to OCR in March. The task proved difficult.

In order to achieve a racially balanced administrative staff, the school board began in April 1974 by taking the ungraceful step of firing every administrator in the district from the assistant building principals up to the assistant superintendents. Although Medcalf had advised the school board against the mass dismissal of administrators, board members reasoned that such action would provide the flexibility to reassign administrators to positions that would satisfy OCR's requirements. Administrators were understandably confused and outraged by the board's action, and found little comfort in the cavalier assurance from school board president, Mrs. Robbie Tyler, that they would be in limbo for "such a short time [that] it should not be a problem." However, like the faculty reassignments the previous year, the administrative reorganization was not finalized until mid-August.

Reassigning the counselors and elementary school principals proceeded smoothly. Twelve counselors and twenty-nine elementary principals were given new assignments for the 1974-75 school year. At the secondary level, however, reassigning principals in a manner that was satisfactory to OCR proved to be more difficult. The district's high school and junior high school principals made it clear that they were unanimously opposed to the transfer of any principals. Reluctant to transfer principals at the secondary level, the school board attempted to satisfy OCR by shifting vice principals and administrative assistants. OCR insisted, however, that additional reassignments were necessary. Specifically, OCR instructed the district that the black building principals at Paseo High School and King Junior High, two schools which were 99.8% black, needed to be switched with the white principals at Northeast High School and Nowlin Junior High, schools which were

96% and 99% white respectively. The school board refused to make additional reassignments arguing that to do so less than two weeks before school opened would be "educationally unsound, and disruptive." Rather, the school board instructed Medcalf to meet with August and Ward in an attempt "to resolve differences with the HEW officials on staff integration without transferring additional secondary school principals."

Talks with OCR officials in late August failed to resolve the differences between the school district and OCR. Ward and August continued to insist that the school district fulfill the assurances made in March and April. Specifically, OCR demanded that the district reassign additional principals and provide documentation verifying the changes made to the transfer policy and Academically Talented program. Medcalf, conveying the school board decision, argued that reassigning more principals was "not administratively desirable" and that those reassignments already effected were sufficient to meet HEW requirements. The superintendent also assured OCR that documentation confirming the reform of the gifted program and transfer policy was forthcoming. With respect to the Academically Talented program, however, the superintendent stretched the truth to the point of falsehood. The official decision had been made to discontinue the program, although it would continue to operate on an informal basis at some schools.

Clearly, OCR was not pleased. August alluded to the possibility of an HEW administrative hearing to terminate Kansas City's grant should the district fail to make the necessary reassignments. Medcalf's understanding of the meeting was that the district would receive written notification if OCR concluded that the district was not in compliance. Five months passed without any notice from OCR, and the superintendent incorrectly assumed that OCR had determined that the Kansas City public schools were in compliance with ESAA requirements. The district's ESAA programs were allowed to proceed. Much to the chagrin of district administrators, the superintendent was informed in January 1975 by Herman Goldberg, HEW's Associate Commissioner for Equal Educational Opportunity Programs, that Kansas City was not in compliance with ESAA regulations.

HEW's notice to Kansas City addressed the same three areas about which Ward and August had expressed concern about nine months earlier. The district's refusal to reassign four principals at the secondary level, the continued operation of the gifted program on an informal basis, and a "large number" of questionable non-minority transfers were cited as evidence of the district's failure to comply with the assurances made to OCR officials the previous Spring. Based upon these findings, HEW officials in Washington D.C. determined "that there are grounds to terminate [Kansas City's] ESAA assistance," and Goldberg's letter closed with a detailed explanation of the administrative hearing procedures. Effective January 30, the district's ESAA funds were suspended and the termination hearing was scheduled for February 19, 1975.

The prospect of losing the district's ESAA funding presented a crisis for school administrators in Kansas City. Medcalf's staff estimated that to continue the ESAA programs without federal assistance would require a minimum of $500,000, which the district did not have. District officials chose to seek a settlement with HEW in which Kansas City could retain its ESAA funds, and preserve its eligibility for additional grants.

After four weeks negotiation, the school district grudgingly acquiesced to HEW's demands. School board members favored transferring the four principals in August but agreed to carry out the reassignments on March 1. Board members preferred to reform the Academically Talented program over the summer but agreed to identify and place all students who qualified for the program by March 1. Moreover, the district agreed to open five new gifted centers, four of which were to be located at schools possessing enrollments which were more than 90% black. Finally, and with profound reservations, school district officials agreed to revoke 199 student transfers which HEW maintained violated the district's policy prohibiting transfers having an adverse effect on integration.

In a matter of days after signing the settlement agreement, the school district began to encounter difficulties in fulfilling its terms. To begin with, the timetables for implementing the provisions were extremely tight. For the gifted program alone, the records of thousands of students were reviewed, eight new teachers hired, and transportation arranged for newly identified gifted students. The cost of the program rose by more than $10,000. More difficult still was the obligation to review and revoke the questionable transfers granted the previous September.

On February 25, letters were mailed to the parents of the 199 students whose transfers HEW had challenged, and shortly thereafter a review board began hearing individual cases. Following the hearing, students whose transfers were revoked were immediately reassigned to the school in their proper attendance zone. The review board's work, however, came to an abrupt halt in early March. The parents of several students whose transfers had been revoked brought suit in state court arguing that rescinding transfers constituted a breech of contract on behalf of the school district, and Judge Richard Sprinkle issued an injunction preventing the school district from revoking student transfers. Sprinkle's blistering order berated the school district for becoming "addicted to that insidious and popular Federal drug called 'financing,'" and scolded the district for playing "musical schools." He found the school district failed to provide parents with reasonable time to respond to the retransfer notice and prepare for the hearing. Sprinkle also objected to the manner in which the district placed the burden on the student to justify their present assignment. Finally, the judge concluded that in revoking transfers the school district violated the implicit understanding that a transfer once granted would be in effect for the entire school year.

The injunction made it impossible to meet the settlement's timetable for re-transferring students, and the school district's legal counsel sought to renegotiate, but Herman Goldberg of HEW declined. Although Goldberg recognized the "legal necessity" of abiding by a state court order, he asserted that the injunction did not relieve the school district of its obligations under the settlement agreement. Goldberg "reluctantly concluded" that "in light of recent events, I have no choice but to resume proceedings to terminate your district's grants." ESAA payments were suspended effective April 1 and Goldberg informed the district that the termination hearing was scheduled for April 15. Superintendent Medcalf labeled HEW's actions "entirely deplorable" and lamented that the Department's determination to pursue termination had prevailed over "valid considerations of what is educationally reasonable for the children of the district."

At the April termination hearing, arguments revolved largely around the 199 questionable transfers that the school district was instructed to revoke. The school district's attorneys, Dave West and Shirley Ward Keeler, argued that much of Kansas City's difficulty concerning transfers could be attributed to the delay, from September 1974 to January 1975, before HEW served notice that the 199 transfers should be reviewed. It was during this period that the school district, unaware of HEW's objections, approved the transfers in question. HEW's legal counsel, Frank Smith and Paul Cacioppo, maintained that the crux of the dispute lay in correspondence between HEW and the school district more than a year earlier. HEW's attorneys pointed to the superintendent's letter to Taylor August dated March 26, 1974 in which Medcalf had assured OCR that the school board had resolved to reassign principals at the secondary level, reform the Academically Talented program, and revoke transfers which had an adverse effect on integration – all before the start of the 1974-75 school year. Smith and Cacioppo asserted that since the school district had failed to fulfill those assurances, the four month delay in notification was of no consequence.

HEW's Administrative Hearing Officer, Judge Bryan Samuelson from St. Louis, ruled in favor of the school district. Samuelson found that, with regard to administrative reassignments and the Academically Talented program, the district had complied with the remedial action requested by HEW. On the transfer issue, Samuelson ruled somewhat curiously that there had been no non-compliance on the part of the district since the original transfers had been properly granted. The regional office appealed the ruling, but the Assistant Secretary of HEW affirmed hearing officer's findings.

Samuelson's ruling insured that Kansas City's ESAA funds were secure and district administrators no longer had to contemplate the awful prospect of repaying more than $1.6 million to the federal government. Fresh from their victory in the termination hearing, Kansas City school officials busied themselves assembling the final draft of the district's 1975-76 ESAA grant proposal. The termination hearing convinced school district officials to seek waivers for the three alleged areas of non-compliance: student transfers, administrative assignments, and the Academically Talented program. Even so, before the grant proposal could be submitted, a new hurdle had arisen. During the April termination hearing, the school district received notice that Judge John Pratt had entered another order in the *Adams* case.

The 1975 *Adams* Letter

Two years had passed since Judge Pratt entered his first order in *Adams v. Richardson* and some of the circumstances of the case had changed in the interim. The Department of Health, Education and Welfare had a new secretary and the 1975 case was styled *Adams v. Casper Weinberger et. al.* More importantly, Judge Pratt recognized that "substantial progress has been made in this difficult and complex area" over the two years. Indeed, of the 127 school districts named in the original order as being in violation of Title VI and the most recent Supreme Court rulings, eighty-nine had come into compliance or had been subject to HEW enforcement activity.

Despite this apparent progress, Pratt agreed with the conclusion of the United States Commission on Civil Rights that "there appears to be an over-reliance by HEW on the use of voluntary negotiations over protracted time periods and a 'reluctance in recent years to use the administrative sanction process where school districts are known to be in non-compliance.'" As he had in his 1973 order, Judge Pratt found that the time for negotiation had expired. "Where efforts to obtain voluntary compliance do not succeed within a reasonable period," Pratt wrote, "HEW has a duty to commence prompt enforcement activity." He ordered HEW to notify an expanded list of 170 school districts in sixteen states that those districts had 60 days to achieve compliance with Title VI and ESAA regulations. Fifty-six Texas school districts were named in the order, twenty-two others, including Kansas City, were in Missouri.

Virtually all 170 districts named in the order, including Kansas City, operated schools that violated the Supreme Court's stricture in *Swann* prohibiting one-race schools or schools "substantially disproportionate in their racial composition." In 1975, Kansas City's public schools were 58% black, and according to *Swann*, the acceptable range for each school was between 38% and 78% black. Just six of Kansas City's ninety-six schools possessed enrollments within that range. Seventeen Kansas City schools were 99% or more white while another thirty-three schools were 95% or more African-American.

Plan E

A copy of Judge Pratt's order arrived at Superintendent Medcalf's office on April 16, 1975. Enclosed with the copy of the *Adams* order was a cover letter from the Region VII Director of OCR, Taylor August, which stated more clearly the nature of Kansas City's non-compliance. The findings presented in August's letter were drawn largely from OCR's recently concluded eighteen month investigation of the Kansas City public schools. The probe, which had progressed in fits and starts since November 1973, expanded dramatically in mid-1974, and culminated in an intensive, full scale review of the district's integration efforts since 1954.

Borrowing language from the Supreme Court's 1971 *Swann* decision, August maintained that Kansas City had "failed to eliminate vestiges of the former dual [segregated] school system." In support of this allegation, he pointed to the enrollments of the fourteen formerly segregated black elementary schools since the district began desegregation in 1955. He found that six of those schools remained virtually all black throughout the period 1955-1975. Six others were closed since 1955 but had been virtually all black throughout their existence. Of the two remaining schools August found that one was largely occupied by Hispanic students and in 1975 was 88% minority. Furthermore, fewer than ten white students had attended Lincoln High School, the formerly segregated black secondary school, in the twenty years since desegregation began in the Kansas City schools.

In addition to the vestiges of the former dual system, the OCR director alleged that the district's policies and practices governing the assignment of students to schools consistently perpetuated segregation. Specifically, August argued that site selection for new schools, alterations to attendance zones, and the liberal transfer policy had stymied desegregation in the Kansas City schools. He also lambasted the school district for having summarily rejected the recommendations presented in the Havighurst report and Hazlett's "Concepts for Changing Times." Finally, August maintained that "the discriminatory treatment of minority children is further aggravated by the failure of the School District to provide them with educational services and opportunities equal to those provided non-minority children." He alleged that the curriculum in Kansas City's five virtually all black high schools was "significantly limited in breadth and depth when compared to that offered at the high schools with low minority enrollments."

August concluded that "further desegregation of the schools is necessary and feasible," and instructed school officials to submit a desegregation plan remedying these violations to the regional OCR office by May 13. Requiring an approved desegregation plan within roughly 30 days was consistent with the time frame established in Judge Pratt's order and deemed by OCR to be within the "normal range of time" needed to develop a plan. According to OCR's Jerold Ward, in most cases, school districts anticipated a finding of non-compliance after a lengthy investigation and therefore already had plans under consideration. In Kansas City, school officials had been working on new desegregation proposals since October 1974.

To term the Kansas City proposals "desegregation plans" is, however, both misleading and generous. In each of the four plans, the objective of racial mixing was clearly subordinated to larger concerns of attendance zone boundaries, grade structure, and maximum utilization of existing school facilities. None had been drawn with racial integration as the primary focus. Rather, each was essentially a study of attendance zone boundaries which district officials attempted to pass off as an integration plan. Nevertheless, in April 1975 these plans represented the district's best hope for a desegregation plan which would be acceptable to OCR.

The likelihood that OCR would approve any of the four plans without drastic modifications was slim. Kansas City had been named in the *Adams* order for maintaining racially disproportionate schools and none of the proposals promised to remedy that problem. According to the district's analysis, regardless of which plan was adopted, no less than 80% of the district's schools remained racially isolated according to the *Swann* standard. Paul Holmes in the district's Desegregation Advisory Office, conveyed the grim outlook to Superintendent Medcalf. After having studied the projections of each school's racial composition, Holmes flatly concluded, "None of these plans would be acceptable to the Office of Civil Rights."

In late April, school officials met with Jerold Ward to discuss OCR's criteria for desegregation plans. Ward reviewed the standard announced in the 1971 *Swann* decision and reiterated the requirement to dismantle the lingering vestiges of the segregated system, especially racially identifiable and one-race schools. In addition, Ward emphasized that the burdens of desegregation, typically busing, had to be borne equally by white and black students. Each of these criteria presented significant problems for school officials inasmuch as none of the plans had been developed exclusively as a desegregation plan. Because the primary focus had been on redrawing school attendance zones to maximize use of existing schools, the district's principal concern had been the number of students residing within each attendance zone. No one had bothered to count how many of those students were black or white. Consequently, because the neighborhoods around schools tended to be largely segregated, the schools that served the neighborhoods remained racially imbalanced. Where busing was mentioned in the plans it tended to be strictly in the context of busing black students out of overcrowded schools. The use of busing, then, as contemplated in the district's plans, constituted an unequal burden on black students. Although the district's busing proposals often promoted integration at the receiving schools, it was unlikely that OCR would validate a scheme in which the vast majority of the students being bused for purposes of integration were African-American.

Faced with these rather significant difficulties, the school district failed to submit a plan to OCR by the May 13 deadline. In lieu of a desegregation plan, the school board offered a broad resolution pledging that minority students would comprise a minimum of 30% of the enrollment at every school in the district. OCR did not accept the resolution as a desegregation plan but granted the district a sixty day extension to develop a plan.

By early June the Kansas City Board of Education was seriously considering adoption of Plan E, an amalgam of the four plans previously under consideration. True to its roots, Plan E was founded largely on attendance zone modifications with boundaries extended "as far into the core of minority population density as possible." In order to meet the school board resolution's objective of 30% minority enrollments at every school, the plan also called for busing more than 2,600 minority students out of overcrowded core area schools to the largely white fringes.

Twenty years after the school district adopted the initial desegregation plan based on neighborhood schools, the school board reaffirmed its allegiance to this model of school organization, and in doing so, bowed to the interests of the city's white majority. Clearly, modifications to the existing attendance zones could not bring integration to those virtually all-black schools which served the heart of the black residential area. Although Plan E promised to promote integration at the predominantly white schools, it completely neglected the black corridor area. Under the plan, twenty-five schools serving black neighborhoods remained more than 90% black. Almost 20,000 black students, or two out of every three black students in Kansas City, attended these twenty-five schools. For these students Plan E promised little change in their situation. Yet, the school board was loathe to consider busing schemes in which white students from the fringes of the city might be compelled to attend an overwhelmingly black school in the inner city. Black students could be bused for integration, but the vast majority of white students in the district would continue to attend schools in their own neighborhood. In spite of the fact that Plan E was not responsive to some of OCR's stipulations, school board members were not prepared to endorse options that would have placed a greater share of the burden of integration on whites. To do so, would be to risk the possibility of more white students withdrawing from the district. In 1975, the school district was losing roughly 2,000 white students per year, and the school board was intensely wary of further alienating the white population.

The school board approved Plan E on June 16 by a vote of eight to one, and copies of the plan were then transmitted to the OCR regional office for consideration. As OCR reviewed Plan E, the school district began preparations to implement the plan for the coming school year. It was rather telling that as Plan E was approved, the review board was in the process of evaluating more than 750 student requests for transfer.

Four weeks later, Taylor August informed Superintendent Medcalf that Plan E was unacceptable. Among OCR's chief objections to the Kansas City plan were that more than twenty schools remained more than 90% black and that the burden of busing for integration fell almost entirely upon black students. Furthermore, August and the OCR staff concluded that in some areas, particularly between Southwest and Paseo high schools, the new attendance zones appeared to be "superimposed on a pattern of marked residential segregation," thereby inhibiting desegregation in that part of the city. Still further, Plan E clearly failed to satisfy the prevailing legal standards for school integration. The *Swann* decision directed school districts to produce racial mixes at each school which deviated by no more than 20% higher or lower than the racial composition of the district as a whole. In Kansas City, the district as a whole was 63% black which made the acceptable range according to the *Swann* standard to be 43-83% black at each school. Plan E promised to produce racial mixes that satisfied the *Swann* standard at nine of the district's eighteen secondary schools and eleven of the city's seventy-two elementary schools. Considering that during the 1974-75 school year just four elementary and three secondary schools satisfied the standard, Plan E represented some progress. Even so, bringing just twenty schools into compliance fell well short of the *Swann* standard. Finally, August noted that "vestiges of state-imposed segregation" remained in the district, the most onerous being the all-black student body at Lincoln High School, the city's segregated black high school prior to 1955.

Taylor August acknowledged Plan E as an important "first step toward achieving voluntary compliance," but the school board proved unwilling to take a second step before the beginning of the 1975-76 school term. Over the summer, the district failed to produce a revised desegregation plan and scrapped plans to implement Plan E in September. Essentially, the school board announced its intention to allow the existing structure of racially polarized neighborhood schools to remain intact for at least one more year. The district's intransigence infuriated August and others at OCR. Kansas City's 1975 ESAA application was rejected in July and proceedings to terminate the school district's federal funding were initiated in August.

In hopes of salvaging its relationship with HEW, in September the school board approved the formation of a Desegregation Task Force comprised of some sixty members and charged with developing a desegregation plan for the following year. The fallout from the rejection of Plan E produced two other school board decisions that had profound long-term implications for the Kansas City schools. First, the school board directed district administrators to begin developing plans for a district-wide magnet schools system. Using magnet schools to promote integration had been suggested in the 1968 pamphlet "Concepts for Changing Times," and the 1973 opening of the Kansas City Technical Education Center was one manifestation of the magnet concept in operation in the district. Moreover, some members of the school district's central administration were long-time adherents of magnet schools and were eager to develop programs which could draw enrollments from across the city. The school board endorsed the magnet concept and sent administrators around the country to study magnet schools in 1975. It would be two years before the district experimented with additional magnet schools, but by the mid-1980s, Kansas City thoroughly embraced the magnet and organized magnet schools on a scale inconceivable to school planners in 1975.

Second, in a step that most clearly illustrates the mind-set of school board members and much of the district's administration, the board directed the school district's legal counsel to begin making preparations for a metropolitan lawsuit which would compel the suburbs to cooperate with and participate in Kansas City's integration plans. A widely held belief among school board members and officials in the district's central administration was that those parents and students who sought to evade integration within Kansas City often found refuge in suburban districts. The reasoning went that as neighborhoods and schools changed from white to black and with each new integration measure that the school district announced, greater numbers of disaffected whites left the district and enrolled in suburban schools or parochial schools in the city. The Kansas City public schools were losing white students at a rate of about 2,000 students per year. In 1960 more than 51,000 white students were enrolled in the Kansas City public schools; fifteen years later that figure had fallen to less that 20,000. Consequently, whereas white students comprised 71% of the district's enrollment in 1960, they accounted for less than 40% of the enrollment in 1975. Over the same period, the suburban population grew dramatically and remained almost exclusively white. The conclusion reached by many district planners mirrored that of school board president, Robbie Tyler, who argued in August 1975 that "a final solution to integration of this district can occur only as part of an overall metropolitan plan." Preparation for the metropolitan suit consumed almost two years. When it was ultimately filed in May 1977, the suit named five Kansas school districts, thirteen Missouri school districts, the states of Missouri and Kansas, public officials in both states, and three federal agencies as defendants.

Before the metropolitan suit could be launched, however, the school district had more immediate problems to address, the most pressing being the search for a new chief administrator. In the wake of the summer's discouraging developments regarding Plan E, Superintendent Medcalf stepped down in early September. Given the school district's precarious funding situation and legal status, filling the position promised to be challenging. The Associate Superintendent, Edward Fields, was elevated to the post on an interim basis while the search for a new superintendent commenced. Dr. Fields held the position for the next seventeen months.

The 1975 HEW Termination Hearing

As Dr. Fields assumed the responsibilities of the superintendency, the school district prepared for the hearing in which HEW sought to terminate the district's federal funding. Pre-hearing conferences were held in August and October, and the formal hearing opened on December 8, 1975, lasting more than one month. The Honorable Rollie Thedford, serving as Administrative Law Judge, presided over the hearing. Thedford was a hearing officer from the Social Security Administration in Wichita, and had little background in civil rights matters.

In the termination hearing HEW's attorneys, Frank V. Smith III and Daniel J. Flanigan, built their case around three broad arguments – that in the period since 1955, Kansas City had not eliminated the vestiges of the former segregated school system, that the district had taken actions and instituted policies which had segregative effects, and that minority students in the Kansas City public schools were denied equal educational services. Over the course of the next month, Smith and Flanigan offered a dizzying array of documentary, statistical, and anecdotal evidence for Judge Thedford's consideration. Evidence substantiating each of the allegations was presented by HEW's star witness, Jerold Ward, who had spearheaded the investigation of the Kansas City schools since the inquiry began in 1973. With respect to the charge that vestiges of the segregated system remained in Kansas City, Smith referred to the virtually all-black composition of Lincoln High School in the twenty years since Kansas City began desegregating. The HEW attorneys also cited Banneker, Sumner, Wheatley, Holmes, and Carver as examples of elementary schools which were segregated black schools prior to 1955 and had enrolled only a handful of white since. As examples of school district actions that had discriminated against African-American children, Ward's testimony cited the school district's operation of the segregated busing program to relieve crowded black elementary schools in the early 1960s and the busing of Manual high school students in the late 1960s, the transfer policy and the district's decisions to build new schools at sites with little potential to promote integration. On the point of equal educational opportunities, HEW argued that the curriculum at majority black schools, particularly at the high school level, was inferior to that offered at majority white schools. For example, OCR investigation revealed that while twenty-seven different English courses were offered at predominantly white Southwest High School, just seven were offered at 100% black Lincoln High School, and just six at the majority Hispanic West High School.

The school district's attorneys, James Borthwick and Shirley Ward Keeler, opened their case with a motion to have the termination proceeding removed to federal court and prosecuted by the Justice Department. Such a move, Borthwick argued, would allow the court to consider integration on a metropolitan scale. Coincidentally, the Justice Department was already involved in a desegregation case just across the state line in Kansas City, Kansas. Moreover, in that case the Kansas City, Kansas, school district had sought to merge with school districts in Wyandotte and Johnson counties in a more modest version of the metropolitan plan that Kansas City, Missouri school district would later pursue. At any rate, Judge Thedford denied the district's motion to remove the hearing to federal court reasoning that issues such as "white flight" and the possibility of metropolitan integration were beyond the scope of the termination proceeding.

Failing to have the case removed to federal court, the school district's counsel settled into a much more conventional defense. Borthwick and Keeler argued that the district had pursued a policy of racially neutral school assignments for twenty years and that demographic factors beyond the school district's control had produced a system of *de facto* segregated neighborhood schools. Moreover, witnesses called for the school district maintained that white flight was already a significant problem in Kansas City and that a massive busing plan would only lead to greater racial isolation as more whites would leave the district. With respect to HEW's allegations regarding site selection for new schools, the district's legal counsel maintained that the schools were built where they needed to be in order to absorb growing enrollments, not to perpetuate the segregation of the black children who attended them. The district's attorneys further argued that the regulations articulated in the transfer policy had consistently been applied to all applicants, black and white, and that placements reflected the personal choices of individual applicants, not the preference of school officials. The district also disputed the irregularities in curricular offerings at different schools, insisting that the number and variety of courses available to students was generally proportional to the school's enrollment, not the racial composition of the student body. Judge Thedford closed the hearing proceedings in mid-January 1976 and did not offer his ruling on termination for almost a year.

Busing and Plan 6-C

While the district awaited Thedford's ruling, school district attorneys continued their preparations for the metropolitan case and pursued a new line of negotiations in order to resolve the conflict with HEW. The district's attorneys believed that recent developments regarding opposition to busing gave the district greater leverage in reaching a settlement with HEW. Opposition to forced busing for integration purposes had steadily increased in the early 1970s, and had emerged as a pressing national issue by 1974. That year and the next, the nation was shocked by the violence which accompanied a federal court order busing black students to schools in the working class Irish enclaves of South Boston and Charlestown, Massachusetts. In response to the swell of anti-busing sentiment, the United States Congress in September 1975 approved the Byrd Amendment to the 1976 Labor-HEW appropriations bill. Introduced by Senator Robert Byrd from West Virginia, the measure prohibited HEW from using any funds to require "the transportation of any student to a school other than the school which is nearest the student's home, and which offers courses of study pursued by such student, in order to comply with Title VI of the Civil Rights Act of 1964."

School district attorneys met with Taylor August and Jerold Ward of OCR's regional offices in an attempt to formulate guidelines for an acceptable desegregation plan in light of the Byrd Amendment's busing limitations. At the meeting August was unable to offer an official OCR interpretation of the amendment and maintained that OCR would only discuss a completed plan which had been approved by the school board. Not until April 1977 did the school district receive an official OCR interpretation of the Byrd Amendment, nevertheless, work on developing an acceptable desegregation plan proceeded throughout 1976.

The Community Desegregation Task Force, formed in August 1975, met regularly over the course of 1975-76 in an attempt to fulfill its daunting task of developing an integration plan which would meet with the satisfaction of both the school board and OCR. In August 1976, the Task Force presented the board of education with two proposed integration plans. Plan A was an ambitious scheme to provide for statistical balancing by race at all district schools. Busing, clustering, pairing, and student exchanges were all elements of Plan A. Although Plan A was not rejected out of hand by the school board, it was never seriously considered for adoption. School board members tended to favor the second plan, titled Plan 6, which was presented with three options labeled A, B, and C. Ultimately, the majority of the school board settled upon Plan 6-C as the option with the greatest likelihood of gaining public acceptance and the approval of OCR.

Like Plan E, developed the previous year, Plan 6-C set as its goal a minimum of 30% minority student enrollment at all schools, and proposed to accomplish that goal in part through methods similar to those recommended in the previous plan. Attendance zones were shifted for a number of schools and thousands of students were to be bused out of the crowded schools in the black residential core area to predominantly white schools on the fringes. However, unlike Plan E, the Desegregation Task Force's proposal called for busing large numbers of white children as well. In pairing and clustering arrangements, Plan 6-C proposed busing more than 2,200 students from predominantly white schools to predominantly minority schools. For example, one cluster proposed in Plan 6-C involved three elementary schools in the East High School attendance zone – McCoy, Manchester, and Greenwood. In 1975-76, McCoy's enrollment was 16% black, Manchester 21% black, and Greenwood 97% black. Under Plan 6-C, Greenwood would serve grades 4-6 exclusively and McCoy and Manchester would both serve only grades 1-3. Students in grades 4-6 at McCoy and Manchester would be bused to Greenwood, while students in grades 1-3 at Greenwood would be bused to McCoy and Manchester. The Task Force projected that the resulting enrollments at McCoy, Manchester, and Greenwood would be 40% minority, 42% minority, and 42% minority, respectively. Clusters and pairs proposed for schools in other parts of the city were projected to have similar impact in terms of racial balance.

For those schools within the core black residential area, however, Plan 6-C promised no more than its predecessor. Twenty-one elementary schools, four junior high schools – Central, King, Lincoln, and Southeast – and four high schools – Central, Paseo, Lincoln, and Southeast – would remain more than 90% black. Thus, for more than 17,000 black students Plan 6-C offered little immediate change. The Task Force suggested that integration at the four high schools could be promoted through the establishment of magnet schools, but such schools were presented merely as possibilities for future consideration, not as firmly recommended elements of the plan.

Generally, the public response to Plan 6-C was favorable. The majority of the plan's critics came from the largely white residential areas served by Northeast and Van Horn High Schools. The revised boundaries defining the attendance zones for Northeast and Van Horn incorporated largely black neighborhoods which previously had been assigned to high schools in the black core area. These shifts profoundly changed the racial composition of both schools. The black enrollment at Northeast High School was projected to increase by 300 students, while at Van Horn the black student population would grow by more than 500. Under Plan 6-C, elementary schools in both areas were projected to undergo similar transformations as schools which previously had enrolled but a handful of black students were paired with schools which were virtually all black. Critics from the Van Horn and Northeast areas sang the praises of neighborhood schools and railed against the plan's forced busing components, but the Task Force and school board demonstrated little inclination to mollify these patrons by altering the plan.

By December the school board was clearly moving toward adoption of Plan 6-C, despite the fact that there had been no communication with OCR regarding the plan and no indication that the federal agency would approve it. Moreover, Judge Thedford had not yet rendered his decision in the termination hearing. A favorable decision in that case, although unlikely, would relieve the district of the necessity of implementing a new plan. One uncertainty was resolved on December 22, 1976 when Judge Thedford ruled in the termination case.

The judge's decision stung school district officials. In a lengthy opinion of seventy-nine pages, Thedford ruled in favor of HEW on virtually every point. Citing the transfer policy, the manipulation of attendance zones, the organization of the school district around neighborhood schools, and the large number of one-race schools, Thedford found it indisputable that the Kansas City schools remained "in a segregated condition." In the opinion, Thedford acknowledged that Kansas City was perhaps "not conducive to total desegregation," and recognized that the "concentrated residential pattern of the minority population dictates that some minority schools must remain." Nevertheless, the judge characterized the school district's efforts to date "an extremely poor record," and ordered HEW to terminate the Kansas City school district's federal funds. School officials estimated that the district stood to lose more than $10 million in federal assistance.

In response to Thedford's ruling, the school district pursued three courses of action. First, the school board instructed the district's legal counsel to appeal the decision to the Civil Rights Reviewing Authority. The district's attorneys believed several points in Thedford's ruling could be overturned. Moreover, although HEW could continue to defer funding, the department was prohibited from terminating federal funds while an appeal was pending. Second, the school board directed the district's legal counsel to file the metropolitan suit in federal court as soon as possible. Third, and most importantly, school officials reopened negotiations with OCR in order to gain approval for Plan 6-C and restore the district's federal funding. In his ruling, Thedford had suggested that in an acceptable plan "at least fifty percent of the minority students must be assigned to schools with less than eighty percent minority enrollment and that no school shall have less than thirty percent minority enrollment." Although it did not meet the requirement that 50% of all minority students attend schools with enrollments of less than 80% minority, Plan 6-C, came tantalizingly close to satisfying Thedford's standards.

The man charged with spearheading the negotiations with OCR was the district's new superintendent, Robert Wheeler, a graduate of the Kansas City public schools. Dr. Wheeler had previously served as a teacher, building principal, and Assistant Superintendent for the Urban Education Division in the Kansas City schools. At the time of his appointment to the superintendency, Dr. Wheeler held the post of Deputy United States Commissioner of Education, and was the highest ranking African-American at HEW.

On March 20, 1977 the school board approved Plan 6-C for the upcoming school year by a vote of seven to two. The two dissenting votes were cast by James Bonadonna and Maurice Dwyer, members elected from the Northeast and Van Horn subdistricts, respectively. A copy of the plan was then submitted to OCR and the deferral on federal funding to the district was lifted while Plan 6-C was reviewed. Over the course of the next three months, school board members and district administrators met with OCR officials in Kansas City and Washington D.C. on several occasions to discuss the plan. Missouri's United States Senators, Thomas Eagleton and John Danforth, attempted to aid the school district's cause by appealing to HEW Secretary, Joseph Califano, to accept the Kansas City plan. Despite these efforts, OCR rejected the plan in early July.

Essentially, OCR officials found Plan 6-C unacceptable because the district would continue to operate twenty-nine schools with minority enrollments in excess of 90%. In his letter rejecting the plan, David S. Tatel, Director of OCR in Washington D.C., suggested the district consider additional pairs or clusters of elementary schools, and pairing schools at the secondary level. In taking these steps, Tatel argued that the number of racially isolated schools in the district could be reduced to eleven.

Instituting the changes suggested in Tatel's letter would greatly increase the number of students bused for desegregation and the distances that those buses would travel. Not only would increased busing for desegregation likely trigger a new round of protests from district patrons, it violated the latest anti-busing amendment passed by the United States Congress. In 1977, Congress strengthened the language in the Byrd Amendment and placed additional limits on busing for desegregation. The 1977 amendment to the HEW Appropriations Act was co-sponsored by Missouri Senator Thomas Eagleton and Delaware Senator Joe Biden, both of whom had compelling interests in seeing limits imposed on HEW's authority to order busing. Eagleton was concerned principally with the difficulties that the Kansas City and St. Louis school district were experiencing with integration and forced busing. Biden sought to provide protection for the Wilmington, Delaware, schools, which also were embroiled in a protracted desegregation dispute with HEW. Borrowing language from the Byrd Amendment, the Eagleton-Biden Amendment provided that no HEW funds could be used to require busing of any student beyond the school nearest to the student's home, except for purposes of special education. The 1977 amendment clarified that this prohibition applied to plans which involved pairing or clustering of schools. The anti-busing measure did not apply to magnet schools. The pairs and clusters suggested by Tatel, some of which involved busing students more than ten miles, clearly violated the amendment's stricture against busing students beyond the school nearest the student's home.

In his response to Tatel's letter, Superintendent Wheeler indicated that he believed HEW's authority to require additional pairs or clusters of schools was prohibited by Congress, and argued that Plan 6-C adequately addressed the violations found by Judge Thedford. Wheeler argued that it was "unreasonable to incur excessive financial and social costs in order to change percentages the slight degree which remains theoretically possible above that presently contained in the plan." He asserted that in Plan 6-C, "the reduction of racial isolation is significant" and that OCR's decision to reject the plan and withhold federal funding "cannot be justified." Wheeler closed by informing OCR that Kansas City would implement the plan in September and that the district sought additional meetings to resolve OCR's remaining objections.

Plan 6-C was implemented on September 7, 1977, with more than 5,000 school children boarding the buses. The students were joined by city council members, the mayor, the superintendent, and numerous school district employees in a show of support for the "peaceful implementation of the plan." Despite the smooth transition to Plan 6-C, negotiations with OCR continued to drag on unsatisfactorily. The school district's position remained that Plan 6-C adequately addressed the issue of past discrimination. Moreover, district officials continued to emphasize to OCR that more forced busing was not acceptable, and that such measures would "undermine the progress the district has made in recent years." Nevertheless, OCR expressed no intention of accepting Plan 6-C without revisions.

An agreement acceptable to OCR was eventually negotiated in January 1978. Discussions with OCR Director Tatel in Washington D.C. yielded six points which OCR demanded be met before lifting the deferral on federal funding and finding the district in compliance with Title VI regulations. Four of Tatel's demands were already district policy. These items concerned racially balanced faculties, non-discriminatory optional attendance zones, and strict scrutiny of transfer requests. The two remaining points required action on the part of the school district to promote additional integration. The first involved Lincoln High School. Lincoln had long been a source of concern to officials at OCR, its enrollment figures confirming that the district had not dismantled its segregated system, and under Plan 6-C the school remained 99% black. To reverse the pattern of virtually all black enrollments at Lincoln and convert it to an integrated building, OCR required that by September of the 1978-79 school year the enrollment at Lincoln be between 15% and 30% non-minority. OCR Director Tatel suggested that this might be accomplished by creating a magnet school.

The second point required additional desegregation at twenty-one virtually all black elementary schools. OCR demanded that beginning in September 1978, all new educational programs at the elementary level be initiated at schools where they would promote integration.

Kansas City's school board readily agreed to the conditions of the settlement with OCR, passing a resolution that incorporated each of the six provisions into district policy. OCR then accepted Kansas City's Plan 6-C, and the district and OCR jointly moved to have the appeal of Thedford's decision in the termination proceeding dismissed from the Reviewing Authority. In April, HEW released $266,000 to the Kansas City schools for magnet school planning. Preparations began immediately for establishing Lincoln Academy for Accelerated Study, a magnet school offering advanced courses and more individualized instruction. The district also undertook plans for a business management magnet at West High School, and all-day kindergarten magnets at Pinkerton, C.A. Franklin, Weeks, and Wheatley, four virtually all black elementary schools. During April and May recruiters visited each of the district's junior highs and high schools in an effort to persuade students, particularly white students, to consider enrollment at Lincoln or West the following year. In addition, the district created a magnet schools office and established a hotline to provide patrons with information.

The school district had little difficulty in attracting integrated enrollments to the all day kindergarten magnets and the business magnet at West. Each of these programs attracted between 25% and 50% non-minority enrollments. The situation at Lincoln was different. Initially it appeared that the district would be able to meet the 15% non-minority requirement at Lincoln. By mid-August, 183 white students had enrolled at Lincoln Academy for the upcoming year, accounting for 12% of the school's projected enrollment. At that point, however, some non-minority students began to retract their enrollment at Lincoln. Because HEW had not yet approved Kansas City's latest ESAA grant application, there was some question as to whether the Academy would be able to deliver the high quality academic program as promised. The district's 1978 grant requested $5.3 million for the magnet schools, of which $4.2 million was earmarked for Lincoln. HEW approved the funds in late August, but non-minority parents and students continued to have doubts. When school opened on September 7, 1978 just eighty-five white students were enrolled at Lincoln.

The school district's inability to attract a 15% non-minority enrollment at Lincoln violated the terms of the agreement reached with OCR in February. OCR Director Tatel urged Superintendent Wheeler to develop an aggressive plan for attracting additional white students, and extended the deadline for meeting the 15% requirement to February 8, 1979. Between October 1978 and January 1979, the school district's recruitment efforts for Lincoln intensified and slowly the white enrollment at the high school grew. By late November, the non-minority enrollment at the academy reached 10%, and stood at 14.47% one week before the deadline. One final recruiting surge in late January and early February, attracted twenty-eight new white students, raising the white enrollment at Lincoln to 240, lifting the non-minority enrollment at the academy to 15.58% on February 8.

In meeting the goal, the district was aided by twenty-six blacks at Lincoln who graduated when the semester ended on January 22. Moreover, some forty blacks transferred from Lincoln to other high schools during the last two weeks of January. At least one-half of these black transfers were involuntary, leading the *Kansas City Star* to term them "the Lincoln purge." The school district justified the reassignments arguing that the students had given false addresses so that they could attend Lincoln. District officials denied that the black students had been reassigned in order to raise the white percentage at Lincoln. Nevertheless, to some patrons it seemed that the district had chosen a peculiar, albeit fortuitous time to address the problem of high school students falsifying enrollment information.

In achieving the goal of a 15% non-minority enrollment at Lincoln Academy the school district's lengthy, occasionally bitter struggle with OCR and HEW came to an end. Although the federal departments continued to monitor the state of desegregation in the Kansas City schools, the district's compliance with Title VI was secure. Moreover, after more than four years of uncertainty regarding federal funding, those funds now seemed secure as well, and the school district wasted little time in filing new grant applications for additional funds. In 1979, ESAA grants totaling more than $6 million were awarded to the Kansas City public schools, bringing the total amount of federal money flowing into the district to nearly $20 million for the 1979-80 school year. Given the district's tenuous financial state, these federal funds were absolutely critical to the operation of the city's schools.

Conclusions

Kansas City's relationship with HEW during the 1960s and 1970s is a fascinating case study of the manner in which the federal government used a "carrot and stick" approach to bring about reforms in school district policy and promote additional desegregation. Federal funds rarely amounted to more than 10% of any school district's operating budget, and Kansas City was no exception. However, in the Kansas City public schools and many other urban districts, federal funding was crucial to the operation of numerous programs. The programs in Kansas City which depended almost exclusively upon federal funds were those designed to serve "disadvantaged" students in the majority black schools. Thus, when HEW sought to terminate federal funding because of the school district's alleged discrimination against minority students, the students who stood to suffer most gravely from the loss of those funds and programs were the very same minority students whom the funds benefited. As a consequence HEW generally attempted to resolve difficulties with school districts such as Kansas City through negotiation without resorting to termination proceedings.

Pressure from OCR resulted in several changes in the Kansas City schools. The district's tendency to assign teachers and administrators to schools in a manner which rendered schools racially identifiable was reformed at the behest of OCR. Grudgingly the district scrutinized student transfers and reformed the onerous liberal transfer policy. What previously had been the simplest, most commonly used and most readily available vehicle for evading integration was transformed into a policy which could be used only to promote integration. Under pressure from OCR the school district was compelled to study the boundaries of attendance zones and refashion them with the foremost objective being to increase the scope of desegregation in the district. Moreover, in Plan 6-C, the district adopted school pairs and clusters, and instituted a busing program which bused equal numbers of African-American and white students for purposes of integration. Finally, through negotiations with OCR, the school district implemented magnet programs at predominantly minority schools as a means of eliminating the vestiges of the district's former segregated system. Each of these measures significantly altered the course of desegregation in the Kansas City schools, and each of these changes came about in part due to the prodding of OCR. Indeed, it is not unreasonable to argue that, without the intervention of OCR and HEW, and the possibility of forfeiting the district's federal funding, several of these reforms would not have been initiated.

The district's turbulent relationship with OCR is also indicative of how important statistical data had become to evaluating school integration. HEW's desegregation guidelines, initially developed in 1965, revolved around statistical measures of compliance in terms of student and faculty integration, and since the Supreme Court's 1968 decision in *Green v. County School Board*, the federal courts had moved increasingly toward using statistical data to evaluate desegregation plans. With respect to Kansas City, OCR relied heavily upon statistical measures to evaluate the extent of faculty and student integration, the burden of busing plans, and the equity of the curriculum offered to students at different schools. What is curious is the manner in which at some point in the evaluation process, statistics came to supercede other educational considerations. In monitoring the business magnet at West High School, OCR was clearly more concerned with the racial composition than with the quality of the program. When the district announced that the business magnet had met its goal of a 50% non-minority enrollment, OCR extended warm congratulations and confirmed that the district was fully in compliance with Title VI. Although the business magnet had achieved its goal for racial composition, the program was deeply troubled. The great preponderance of the school district's funding and energies were committed to developing the centerpiece of the magnet program, Lincoln Academy, while West struggled by on a limited budget. Indeed, a 1979 study of West High revealed that magnet program was poorly coordinated and did not offer numerous courses as advertised. Moreover, considering that West was the business magnet school, its library holdings included but a handful of business journals, two salesmanship books, one economic geography book, and one general business book, all of which were copyrighted before 1958. The library's lone marketing book was copyrighted 1916.

Despite the problems with the magnet program at West, it is undeniable that the Kansas City schools became much more integrated as a consequence of the relationship with OCR and HEW. Aside from the reforms effected through pressure from the federal agencies and the broader scope of integration in the Kansas City schools accomplished in Plan 6-C, the school district's relationship with OCR and HEW brought forth two additional legacies. First, the district's struggles in formulating a desegregation plan acceptable to OCR convinced a growing number of school administrators and school board members that only a plan which was metropolitan in scope could bring a lasting solution to the district's racial imbalance. In 1979, the Kansas City schools were 67.5% black, while the surrounding suburban districts remained overwhelmingly white. Proponents of metropolitan desegregation argued that a plan providing for two-way busing between the suburbs and the central city could overcome the gross racial disparity, promote stable integration, and eliminate the suburbs as a refuge for whites who sought to escape integration. The school board's decision to press forward with the metropolitan desegregation suit is attributable in part to the frustration experienced by district policymakers in seeking an agreement with OCR in the mid-1970s. In May 1977, while school officials negotiated Plan 6-C with OCR, the metropolitan suit was filed in federal court.

The second legacy of the district's relationship with the federal government during the 1960s and 1970s was the adoption of magnet schools to promote integration. With the success of Lincoln Academy and the all day kindergarten programs, a growing number of school board members and administrators became adherents of magnet schools to promote integration. Over the course of the next fifteen years, Kansas City would create a system of magnet schools which dwarfed those of other cities. When the attempt to create a metropolitan school system by judicial order failed, the Kansas City public schools fully embraced magnet schools as the next best solution. Superintendent Wheeler foreshadowed this possibility in 1978 when he speculated that once the district could "crystallize the design" of its magnet programs, "the attractiveness to students in the metropolitan area ought to increase proportionately."

CHAPTER 6

A Changing Metropolis

Demographic Patterns and the Launching of the Metropolitan Suit, 1950-1980

On March 6, 1967 the boys basketball team from Kansas City's Central High School squared off against Truman High School from Independence, a Kansas City suburb, in the Missouri state tournament. Some 2,800 fans jammed Kansas City's Interscholastic League Fieldhouse to watch what promised to be a thrilling first round match-up. Central, the defending state champion, entered the game with a perfect 21-0 record. Truman, making its first appearance in the state tournament, boasted an 18-8 record and was riding an eleven game winning streak. Some of the finest athletes in the Kansas City metropolitan area were on the playing floor that March evening. Of the ten young men who started the game, five went on to play basketball at the collegiate level, two others played college football, and another played organized baseball in the New York Yankees minor league system.

The game was characterized by physical play under the basket and much of the scoring fell to the guards. Both teams started slowly, and Central struggled throughout the game with sloppy floor play and turnovers against the scrappy Truman defense. After the first period the score was tied 10-10, and for much of the second quarter the teams battled evenly with Central going to the locker room holding a slim 30-27 advantage. Central may well have trailed at halftime had it not been for their rebounding advantage and the play of point guard Herman Sykes, who scored ten points in the closing three minutes of the half. In the second half, Central's taller frontcourt wore down their opponents, and the Truman guards tired of chasing their lightening quick Central counterparts. Central built a sixteen point lead during the third quarter and held off a late Truman surge to win 68-56. Central's Sykes led all scorers with thirty-three points. Central went on to defeat De LaSalle in the state quarterfinals and Beaumont in the semifinals to reach the state championship game. The Eagles' quest for a second consecutive state title ended on March 11 when Central fell to Joplin, 58-53 in overtime.

Occasionally athletic contests capture the essence of social change in a striking and dramatic manner. Jackie Robinson's breaking of major league baseball's color line in 1948 is one rather obvious example, but basketball, too, has furnished its share of moments filled with social drama. One such episode came in 1966 when Don Haskins coached Texas Western to the NCAA basketball title. Texas Western's all black starting five defeated an all white Kentucky team coached by segregationist Adolph Rupp, thereby symbolically chipping another piece out of the wall of segregation. A year later, the Central-Truman playoff game spoke volumes about social change and shifting demographics in the Kansas City metropolitan area.

In 1967, Central High School was one hundred years old and had occupied the same piece of real estate in Kansas City for fifty years. For much of its history, Central, along with Southwest High School, was considered one of the premier public high schools in the city, having a fine reputation for academics and a rich athletic tradition. Counted among Central's more notable alumni were entertainment mogul Walt Disney, baseball manager Casey Stengel, actor William Powell, several Kansas City mayors, and some of the most successful members of the city's business community. For much of its history, Central had also been all white, but during the 1950s, the area around Central began to change. Black families began to move south and east out of the large core residential area and into the neighborhoods around Central. When integrated schooling began in Kansas City in 1955, Central welcomed its first black students. Of the 1,748 students attending Central that year, 196 were black. Racial transition proceeded with remarkable speed over the course of the next several years. In 1959, Central was 70% black, three years later the school was 99% black, and by the time of the game against Truman in 1967, just two whites were enrolled among the 2,350 students attending Central.

In contrast to Central, Truman High School had only opened in 1964, and was virtually all white in 1967. Truman was built along Noland Road to accommodate students in the rapidly growing southern section of Independence. Hap Graff, a member of the 1967 Truman basketball team, later recalled that as he was growing up, "Independence just stopped south of 23rd Street." By 1967, however, Independence stretched nearly two miles further south to Interstate 70. Indeed, during the 1960s, the population of Independence nearly doubled as the city added some 59,000 persons. Much of that growth occurred in the southern half of the city served by Truman High School. Moreover, Independence remained virtually exclusively white, with African-American residents accounting for less than 1% of the city's population.

The Central-Truman game provided a vivid snapshot of the Kansas City metropolitan area's demographic divide in 1967. Central, the inner city school, was essentially all black and the all black contingent of fans rooting for the Eagles that March evening occupied the bleachers on one side of the field house. Truman's all white basketball team was supported by an all white, suburban cheering section that sat opposite the Central fans. The only area where the races willingly mixed that evening was on the basketball floor; otherwise the field house was as segregated as the residential patterns in the metropolitan area.

The separation of the races which was so plain to the fans sitting in the Interscholastic Fieldhouse in March 1967 was in some respects due to population changes which had occurred in the area around Central High School in the late 1950s and early 1960s. As black families began to move south across Benton Boulevard and into the Central area in the middle and late 1950s, white families moved away. What chance there was of an integrated neighborhood developing rapidly evaporated as white families left the neighborhood in a panic. By 1960, more than 25,000 blacks had moved into the formerly all white area around Central and the neighborhood completely resegregated during the 1960s. Between the 1950 and 1970 censuses, 30,000 whites moved out of the Central High School area and were replaced by more than 35,000 blacks. Moreover, many whites who moved away from the transitional neighborhoods, such as the Central area, relocated elsewhere in the metropolitan area, and one of the fastest growing suburbs was Independence. John Duncan, a historian for the Kansas City public schools, once noted that, "In many ways, the integration of Central created Truman."

The forces which produced the population changes in the Central area and the suburban developments around Truman High School in the 1960s had been operating in Kansas City since the late 1940s. Very few stable, integrated neighborhoods existed in greater Kansas City, and residential patterns for the vast majority of the metropolitan area tended to be rather rigidly segregated along racial lines. In those sections of the city where residential patterns seemed to indicate integration, the population was exceptionally fluid. The clear tendency in transitional areas was for the entire neighborhood to resegregate in relatively short order after the arrival of the first black families. Of course these demographic trends were by no means unique to Kansas City. Scores of cities across the country witnessed similar population shifts in the decades following World War II as white families moved to the suburbs and the urban black population swelled. In Kansas City between 1950 and 1980, huge sections of the central city underwent a profound transformation from white occupancy to black, while the largely white suburbs experienced phenomenal growth.

African American Population Trends

Shifting demographics in the Kansas City area were a source of concern for school district administrators. On one hand, the growth of the black population in Kansas City and the concentration of most African-

Americans in a single sprawling neighborhood presented certain difficulties for the school district. In 1950, black residents in Kansas City numbered about 55,700 and accounted for just over 12% of the city's population. During the 1950s, the African-American population in Kansas City grew by more than 27,000 persons, an additional 28,900 were added during the 1960s, and still another 10,000 in the 1970s. By 1980, the black population in Kansas City numbered roughly 123,000 and accounted for more than one in four of the city's residents.

Since the 1950s, the vast majority of the growth in the black population occurred along the expanding corridor stretching from east of downtown toward the southeastern edge of the city. By 1960, the southern limit of the black corridor had reached 47th Street and the Swope Parkway, about four and one-half miles south of the original core black neighborhood. In 1960, just 1,300 blacks lived in neighborhoods south of the Swope Parkway and the great majority of those resided in a long established black enclave east of Prospect between 53rd and 55th Streets. During the 1960s, however, the black population below the Swope Parkway grew dramatically. More than 21,000 blacks moved into these southeastern neighborhoods during the 1960s and an additional 17,000 blacks were added the following decade. All told, by 1980 almost 40,000 blacks resided in the southeast section of Kansas City and accounted for 75% of the population in the area stretching from the Swope Parkway on the north, and Troost Avenue on the west to the eastern and southern limits of the city. Thus, by 1980 the southeasterly growth of the black residential area within Kansas City was nearly complete. The 1980 census counted more than 103,000 blacks, or about 85% of Kansas City's black population, living in and along a corridor ten miles long and three to four miles wide which ran from the former core neighborhood east of downtown to the southeastern fringe of the city.

As the black population expanded into neighborhoods in the southeastern section of the city, the schools serving these areas typically underwent a transformation from virtually all white enrollments to virtually all black. In a manner similar to the transformation of the area served by Central High School in the late 1950s and early 1960s, and the Paseo High School area in the late 1960s, the schools of southeastern Kansas City rapidly turned over during the late 1960s and early 1970s. In 1960, of the ten elementary schools located east of Troost and south of the Swope Parkway, just one had an enrollment that was more than 10% black. Five years later, five of those schools possessed black enrollments in excess of 30%. By 1970, eight of the elementary schools in southeastern Kansas City were majority black, and by 1975 all ten of these schools had black enrollments of more than 75%. Indeed, in 1975 nine of those elementary schools had black enrollments in excess of 90%. Southeast Junior High and Southeast High School witnessed similar transitions in the late 1960s and early 1970s. In 1965, although the number of black students in the southeast area was rising, blacks comprised less than 30% of the enrollment at either school. Just two years later, the black enrollment at Southeast Junior High stood at more than 40% while the area's high school was one-third black. By 1970, both schools were rapidly resegregating. That year Southeast High School was almost 80% black and black students accounted for 85% of the enrollment at the junior high. By 1975, of the roughly 3,400 students who attended Southeast High School and Southeast Junior High just seventy were white, the black enrollment at both schools stood at 98%.

White Population Trends

Coupled with the growth and concentration of the black population, school officials were forced to cope with disconcerting declines in the city's white population and the steady loss of white students. During the 1950s and 1960s, the white population in Kansas City declined by more than 75,000 and the number of white students enrolled in the school district fell by about 12,000. As damaging as those losses were, developments during the 1970s were worse as both the white population in the city and the white student enrollment plummeted. During the 1970s, the white population in the city dropped by more than 86,000 and the number of white students enrolled in the city's public schools fell by almost 25,000. At the same time suburban communities around Kansas City were experiencing unprecedented growth.

Between 1950 and 1980, the population of the suburban ring around Kansas City grew by 513,000 residents, the overwhelming majority of whom were white. In 1980, African-Americans accounted for less than 3% of the residents in the metropolitan area's suburban counties. In the first ring of suburbs, those immediately adjacent to Kansas City, blacks comprised a small fraction of the population. The Missouri communities of Lee's Summit, Independence, Raytown, Gladstone, and Belton all reported black populations of 1% or less in 1980, while Liberty and Grandview had 3% and 8% respectively. Across the state line in Kansas, black residents accounted for less than 3% of the population in each of the seven Johnson County suburbs included in the Kansas City metropolitan area in 1980. Thus, as the suburbs grew by more than one-half a million persons between 1950 and 1980, the vast majority of those residents were white. Part of that growth could be attributed to population lost from the central city.

Clearly, not every white family moving away from the central city relocated in Kansas City's suburban ring, but substantial numbers had and the loss of white students was viewed as one of the school district's most significant problems. Not only did the exodus of white families to suburbia render stable integration in the Kansas City schools untenable but the lurking fear of spurring additional white flight stymied plans that could have promoted further integration. Developments during the 1970s aggravated what was already a significant problem. As white families continued to move from the city, the school district's tax base shrunk dramatically and school officials confronted serious budgetary crises throughout the early 1970s. Furthermore, the HEW investigation, the uncertainty surrounding the availability of federal funding, the curtailment of numerous school district programs, the continued deterioration of school facilities, and two teacher strikes all signaled the precipitous decline of the public schools in Kansas City. Moreover, the continued migration of African-Americans to the city and the process of neighborhood transition occurring along the leading edges of the black residential area further fueled white migration out of the central city. Given these circumstances, school officials struggled to find some means of retaining the existing white student population and began to debate measures designed to draw in students from the suburbs.

Looking Toward the Suburbs

Notions of incorporating parts of the surrounding suburbs into the Kansas City school district had been discussed periodically since the mid-1960s. Former Superintendent James Hazlett first suggested in 1967 that a metropolitan approach to education and integration should be considered. He maintained that "school integration is a problem of the total metropolitan area," not merely Kansas City. Hazlett vaguely proposed "cooperative arrangements with suburban areas," but his interest in metropolitan school integration was not widely shared by his suburban counterparts. The superintendent's overtures were met with what has was described as "deafening silence" by suburban school administrators.

In 1968, another recommendation for consolidating school districts in the Kansas City area surfaced from a most unexpected source – a commission appointed by the state legislature. The nine-member group, chaired by James Spainhower, a state representative from Marshall and the chairman of the House Education Committee, was charged with reporting on the feasibility of reorganizing the state's school districts. Although the commission's primary interest was in consolidating rural school districts, the panel also explored school district reorganization as a means of promoting racial integration and advancing the educational opportunities available to students in the inner cities of Kansas City and St. Louis. Chairman Spainhower recognized that "the metropolitan area may be even more critical than the rest of the state and equitable solutions more difficult to attain." For Spainhower and the other members of the commission, the central problem in the organization of school districts in Missouri was that "taxable wealth and educational needs are distributed unevenly throughout the state." This problem clearly existed in poor rural districts but was also found in metropolitan areas where "the heavy concentration of disadvantaged children in cities contrasts with other large concentrations of children from high income families who have fled to the suburbs." The commission released its recommendations regarding rural school district consolidation in October 1968. Reorganization of the Kansas City and St. Louis metropolitan areas was the subject of second detailed report, titled "Equal Treatment to Equals," released in June 1969.

Central to the commission's reasoning on equal educational opportunity in the metropolitan areas was the assumption that educational opportunity and high quality education are directly tied to financing. In the report on the state's metropolitan areas, the commission argued that the existing system of financing school districts devoted "many more resources to educating suburban children than city children," and was "highly discriminatory against the poor." The result, commission members argued, was the creation of two "separate and unequal" societies in the cities and the suburbs where the population had been split "into distinct groups, the poor and the affluent, the well-educated and the poorly-educated, blacks and whites." Indeed, the commission found that in the Kansas City area, the virtually all white suburban communities spent more than twice as much per capita on education as did the inner city. To remedy these fiscal disparities, the commission endorsed an organizational scheme which clustered urban and suburban schools.

The commission proposed that four new local school units be established in which most Kansas City schools would be grouped with suburban school districts. Under this recommendation, the area served by Southeast High School would be paired with Raytown; the Paseo and Southwest areas were to be clustered with Center school district; and the Westport, Manual, Lincoln, and Northeast areas would be grouped with the school districts of Pleasant Valley and North Kansas City. The three remaining high school areas in Kansas City – East, Central, and Van Horn – would comprise the fourth local school unit in the city. Although the report made no overt mention of promoting integration, the possibilities for increased integration were readily apparent. Each of Kansas City's predominantly black high school areas – Southeast, Paseo, Central, Lincoln, and Manual – had been paired with one or more predominantly white areas. Moreover, vague references to the need for public schools to "redeem promises and ideals by opening [their] doors to cultural, racial, and economically deprived minority groups" seem to suggest that commission members had contemplated the potential of school district reorganization for furthering integrated education.

As might have been expected, reaction to the commission's reports spanned the entire spectrum. Not surprisingly, urban school administrators tended to be supportive of the proposal. However, while Kansas City school board member Homer Wadsworth called the proposal "eminently sound" and pledged to support the reorganization plan, the response from outside of Kansas City was decidedly less enthusiastic. Many rural communities were committed to resisting further pressure to consolidate, and suburbanites rallying around the principle of "local control" balked at proposals to cluster their schools with inner city schools. In the end, the Spainhower Report was doomed by protests from the suburbs, objections that reorganization interfered with local control, and the reluctance of lawmakers to adopt a structure that represented such a radical departure from traditional school district organization. The state legislature never seriously considered adopting the commission's recommendations.

Proposals at the state level to create metropolitan school districts that incorporated both city and suburb may have ended with the Spainhower Report, but the prospect of drawing in white suburban students continued to entice school administrators in Kansas City. In the mid-1970s, school officials in Kansas City, desperate for a lasting solution to the district's integration problems, again looked toward the suburbs. Faced with the increasing concentration of black residents in the central city, the continued loss of white students, and the fallout stemming from the protracted HEW investigation, school board members began in 1975 to seriously consider action that might be taken to recapture some of the white student base lost to suburban school districts. Although it is difficult to ascertain the feelings of school district patrons concerning the creation of a metropolitan school system, school board members grew increasingly enamored with the idea. Calls for a metropolitan solution to the city's school integration difficulties became more frequent during the early 1970s, particularly during the torturous negotiations with HEW.

Launching the Metropolitan Suit

In July 1975, shortly after HEW had rejected the school district's Plan E desegregation proposal, the school board took its first steps toward seriously pursuing a metropolitan solution. School district attorneys were directed to begin investigating the possibility of the school district filing a metropolitan desegregation suit. The investigative work was led by James Borthwick and Shirley Ward Keeler of the Blackwell Sanders firm. The attorneys were assisted in their research by Dr. Daniel Levine, a University of Missouri-Kansas City professor of education who had previously worked on the Havighurst Study, and Dr. Robert Frielich, a University of Missouri-Kansas City law professor with expertise in urban housing and land use issues.

Conducting the research necessary to launch the metropolitan suit consumed much of the next year, and Borthwick and Keeler encountered a considerable procedural dilemma. In desegregation cases of a metropolitan nature, the central city school district is more logically a defendant than a plaintiff. With this in mind, efforts were made throughout much of 1976 to solicit funding so that the suit might be filed on behalf of school children rather than the school district. The fund-raising effort was unsuccessful and by early 1977 the school district was prepared to file the suit as plaintiff on behalf of the district's students.

On March 20, 1977, the same day in which the school board approved Plan 6-C to meet the HEW's requirements for desegregation within the school district, the school board chose to seek a court ruling which would incorporate the suburbs into the city's desegregation efforts. By a vote of seven to two the school board directed its attorneys to file the suit seeking metropolitan desegregation. Borthwick and Keeler were tabbed as lead counsel in the suit, and they were assisted by Freilich, Levine, and Robert Manley, an Ohio attorney with experience in school desegregation cases. The school district also retained the assistance of attorneys from North, Colbert and Fields, one of the few black law firms in Kansas City. The school district's complaint was filed in Kansas City's federal district court on May 26, and was initially assigned to Judge John Oliver.

Styled as *School District of Kansas City, Missouri et al v. Missouri et al*, the case marked the first time in the nation's history that a school district had initiated a metropolitan desegregation suit. As might be expected in case involving an entire metropolitan area, the plaintiff group was large and defendant groups named in the suit were numerous. Plaintiffs in the suit were the Kansas City school district, Superintendent Robert Wheeler, the seven school board members who had voted in favor of initiating litigation, and the children of school board members Joyce Stark and Edward Skaggs who attended schools in the district. The school district's complaint named sixty-seven defendants, which could be loosely grouped as Missouri defendants, Kansas defendants, and federal agencies. Defendants from the state of Missouri included the governor, members of the state board of education, thirteen school districts in suburban Kansas City, and the superintendents of those districts. The Kansas defendants included the governor, members of the state board of education, five school districts in suburban Kansas City, and the superintendents of those districts. The metropolitan suit also named three federal agencies as defendants – Health, Education and Welfare (HEW), Housing and Urban Development (HUD), and the Department of Transportation (DOT). All together the sweep of the school district's complaint included almost 225,000 students in six Missouri and Kansas counties.

Kansas City's suit was founded upon eight counts of alleged constitutional violations which had produced the segregation of black students in the Kansas City public schools. Although the school district's complaint was rather vague, it alluded to numerous allegations of discriminatory conduct with respect to education, housing, employment, recreation, and transportation. The district's complaint reached decades into the past and implicated individuals and government agencies at the local, state, and federal levels. The legal reasoning of the complaint rested upon the elaboration of a complicated historical web of discriminatory actions and failures to act for which the defendant groups were allegedly liable. These actions, the attorneys argued, had cumulatively produced the racial isolation of blacks in the inner city and had therefore impeded the school district's ability to administer an integrated school system.

Two inter-related aspects of the suit were clearly the most crucial. Education and housing issues were at the heart of the school district's arguments. In part, the school district's case rested on the history of segregated schooling in Missouri and Kansas. The complaint maintained that the state-mandated operation of segregated schools in both states prior to 1954 had contributed to the concentration of blacks in the central city. The attorneys reasoned that black families had been drawn to Kansas City in part because they valued education for their children, and education for a black child through high school was only available in the state's larger cities. Numerous communities with few black residents provided no schools for blacks or only offered an elementary school education. Prior to 1954, a number of smaller communities in the Kansas City area, including those named in the school district's complaint, sent their black students to the Kansas City schools on a tuition basis. Such an arrangement allowed the surrounding communities and school districts to provide for the education of black children without having to operate their own segregated schools. Kansas City's attorneys concluded that in the field of public education, school districts were the preferred "tools" used by the states to maintain segregation in the public schools.

Kansas City's suit further alleged that after the 1954 *Brown v. Board of Education* decision, the state of Missouri had failed to take affirmative steps to remedy the racial isolation of black students in Kansas City. Indeed, the school district maintained that the state of Missouri's intentional neglect of the Kansas City schools had resulted in the district being branded with a "badge of inferiority" and denied the district's students of equal protection under the law. Furthermore, the state's negligence had promoted white flight to the suburbs and had robbed the school district of an important part of its tax base and taxing potential. The school district's complaint argued that the movement of middle class families away from Kansas City had generated a "progressively higher percentage enrollment of economically and socially disadvantaged minority race students." The rising number of minority students, the school district argued, had in turn resulted in increased operating expenses for the school district. "Disadvantaged children," the complaint read, "are in greater need of individual attention, compensatory education, counseling, and other educational services," which the school district was increasingly less able to provide due to the city's shrinking tax base. These circumstances, the school district maintained, demanded a remedy of metropolitan scope.

Housing and the extent of residential segregation in the metropolitan area were closely tied to the school district's educational problems. In the complaint, the Kansas City school district contended that two separate housing markets flourished in the metropolitan area, one for blacks and one for whites. These markets functioned in a manner which separated the races and produced the sharp lines of residential segregation in the metropolitan area. The school district argued that prior to the Supreme Court's 1949 *Shelley v. Kraemer* decision which struck down the enforceability of racially restrictive covenants, these legal agreements had been the primary instrument which maintained exclusively white residential areas and relegated black residents to the densely packed core neighborhood east of downtown. Before *Shelley*, restrictive covenants had drawn their enforcement power from the legal machinery of the state, and therefore the states were implicated in the creation of the segregated residential patterns of metropolitan Kansas City. Furthermore, complaint contended that restrictive covenants continued to be enforced in Missouri for a period of years after the Supreme Court's *Shelley* decision.

In addition to the alleged segregation stemming from the pervasive use of restrictive covenants, the school district complaint argued that racially discriminatory housing policies at the federal and state levels had reinforced the separation of the races in the city and spurred the growth of suburbia. The mass exodus of whites to the suburbs had in large part been abetted by the easy availability of FHA insured mortgages. Blacks, however, were most often excluded from the suburbs and were thereby compelled to buy homes in the city. Arranging a mortgage was still another hurdle blacks confronted in the housing market. Major lending institutions in the city, it was alleged, often refused to make home loans to blacks and the FHA frequently denied black applicants because the neighborhoods in which homes were available to African-American buyers had been "redlined" by the FHA and deemed to be deteriorating or unsatisfactory. Blacks then were typically consigned to making their own arrangements for home loans and generally paid considerably higher interest rates than whites.

Real estate brokers licensed by the state were also instrumental in concentrating the African-American population in the inner city. The complaint alleged that real estate interests in the city had frequently used "blockbusting" to destabilize neighborhoods and manipulate the market. In such instances, an unscrupulous real estate broker would move a black family into a white neighborhood thereby frequently touching off a panic among white residents that the area would soon be largely black and property values would plunge. In such a climate, thousands of whites sold their properties for the best price that was available and moved away. Still further, the school district alleged that the practice of "steering" blacks toward homes and apartments in black neighborhoods reinforced patterns of residential segregation. Indeed, it was common practice for many real estate brokers to refuse to show homes in white neighborhoods to potential African-American buyers. Rather, a steady stream of black buyers was steered toward the expanding corridor stretching toward the southeastern section of the city.

Steering African-Americans to predominantly black residential areas was not solely a tool of local real estate interests: the school district argued that it was also widely practiced by the federal government agencies operating in Kansas City. Urban renewal activity and the construction of the interstate highway system through Kansas City displaced thousands of residents, many of whom were black. Relocating residents displaced by these massive construction projects was among the duties of HUD and the Department of Transportation in cooperation with city and state housing authorities. The school district's complaint contended that the relocation programs were administered in a manner which reinforced existing patterns of residential segregation and contributed to the racial isolation of black students in the Kansas City schools. While displaced whites had been relocated throughout metropolitan Kansas City, the overwhelming number of displaced African-Americans had been relocated in the growing black corridor.

The suit also argued that site selections for public housing projects and other FHA programs aimed at benefiting the largely minority low income population further reinforced residential segregation in the metropolitan area. In Kansas City, thousands of public housing units had been built in areas which were largely or exclusively occupied by minorities. The Pennway Plaza and West Bluff housing projects were both built on the city's predominantly Latino west side, while Heritage House, Wayne Minor, T.B. Watkins, and Dunbar Gardens projects were all built in the black corridor. These housing projects, the suit maintained, underscored the separation of the races in Kansas City. Furthermore, initiatives such as the FHA 235 housing program designed to assist low income families in acquiring new or rehabilitated homes, channeled blacks into the southeast corridor. Between 1968 and 1972, while the FHA 235 program assisted almost 500 families moving into southeastern Kansas City, just thirty families used the program to move anywhere else in the metropolitan area. For the school district's attorneys, the construction of public housing and the allegedly discriminatory administration of other HUD housing programs had perpetuated and reinforced patterns of residential segregation in Kansas City. These federal activities had promoted separation of the races on a metropolitan basis, increased racial isolation within the Kansas City schools, and had inhibited integration efforts in the school district.

In order to remedy these alleged constitutional violations, the school district's complaint proposed an exchange of students on a metropolitan basis. Although the suit did not suggest the creation of a single school district for the entire metropolitan area, it did mark the first time that a school desegregation complaint pleaded for a remedy extending across state lines. By eschewing the creation of a metropolitan school district, the school district's lead attorneys, James Borthwick and Shirley Keeler, hoped to circumvent several sticky legal points. Without question, reconciling the differing educational funding formulas used in Missouri and Kansas would have generated protracted litigation, and would likely have taken years to resolve. Beyond the finance issues, scores of other difficulties would certainly have arisen concerning the metropolitan district's administrative hierarchy, record keeping, curriculum alignment, and so on. To be sure, Kansas City school officials anticipated numerous problems with the student exchange proposal alone, but by limiting the proposed remedy to the exchange of students it was hoped that many of the most serious pitfalls might be avoided.

The proposed exchange remedy was necessarily vague and rather short on details. The main thrust of the plan, however, was essentially a two-way busing program. Under such a plan, minority inner city students were to be placed in suburban school districts for a period of some years during their educational career, while white suburban students would be bused to the inner city schools also for an unspecified period of their school years. Of course, voluntary transfers which promoted integration would be encouraged and accommodated. It was clear to all, however, that voluntary transfers would not suffice. An element of forced busing was necessarily incorporated in the proposal. This type of remedy, the school district argued, would solve the problem of racial isolation in the Kansas City schools. Moreover, it would relieve part of the school district's financial burden for educating a disproportionate number of the metropolitan area's disadvantaged students, and would provide relief for the grievous economic harm which the school district contended had been caused by white flight and the loss of part of the district's tax base.

Six years passed before Kansas City's metropolitan suit proceeded to trial. Because of the breadth of the school district's complaint, numerous legal issues arose concerning the scope of the suit, and the proper alignment of the parties named in the suit. Furthermore, the school district's case was immediately assailed by various motions to dismiss the case. Pending the resolution of these issues, the suit remained in limbo and the court prohibited all sides from beginning the discovery process of investigating further through the use of court procedures.

The first issue which the court addressed concerned a motion to disqualify Judge John Oliver from hearing the case. Prior to his appointment to the federal bench, Judge Oliver had worked as a partner in the law firm of Blackwell Sanders and had represented the Kansas City school district. In October 1977, five months after the complaint was filed, Oliver disqualified himself and assigned the case to Judge Russell Clark. Raised in a family of educators, Clark was the junior federal judge in the Kansas City district court, having been appointed to the bench just months before being assigned the case. Oliver assigned the case to Clark because the junior judge was from Springfield, Missouri, and had no connection to the parties involved. Although his experience with school desegregation law was limited at the outset, Clark was destined for a long tutorial: he would preside over the Kansas City case for the next two decades.

A full year passed before another ruling was issued in the Kansas City metropolitan suit. Nevertheless, under Judge Clark the remaining legal issues began to progress toward resolution. By May 1978, all of the parties had filed arguments on the dismissal motions and the Kansas City school district had filed its statement of facts indicating what the district intended to prove with respect to the Kansas defendants. Five months later, Judge Clark issued the first important ruling in the metropolitan suit, and it was one that would profoundly reshape the school district's case.

Dismissals and Realignment

Judge Clark's October 6, 1978, opinion simultaneously addressed all of the motions to dismiss the case and ordered a momentous realignment of the parties. In essence, the October order resolved four major legal points. First, the judge refused to dismiss the case, concluding that a claim had been established upon which relief could be granted through further litigation. Second, Clark dismissed all of the Kansas defendants. Third, Clark denied all motions to dismiss the Missouri defendants and the three federal departments. Fourth, in a surprising twist, the judge ordered that the Kansas City school district be realigned as a defendant and that a new plaintiff group be named to the suit within sixty days.

In refusing to dismiss the case Judge Clark found that the allegations raised in the complaint and the school district's supporting briefs had sufficiently demonstrated that the Kansas City public schools were unconstitutionally segregated. Having made these allegations, Clark ruled that "the plaintiffs are entitled to the opportunity to present evidence on the issue at trial." Clearly Judge Clark was not convinced that all of the arguments presented in the school district's complaint merited further inquiry. He did, however, find some issues compelling and reasoned that the breadth of the unconstitutional condition in the Kansas City metropolitan area should properly be determined at trial.

The trial, however, would not include the Kansas defendants. In part, the school district's complaint argued that the segregated condition of the Kansas City schools resulted from constitutional violations which transcended school district boundaries, city limits, and state lines. In order to support this assertion, the judge reasoned that Kansas City's attorneys were saddled with the burden of conclusively demonstrating that racially discriminatory actions in the state of Kansas had contributed to or resulted in the racial isolation of black students in the Kansas City, Missouri, public schools. Judge Clark found that, for the period prior to 1954, the school district's attorneys had demonstrated that the various Kansas defendants promoted segregation in the metropolitan area by mandating segregated schools, enforcing restrictive covenants in housing, engaging in racially discriminatory employment practices, and operating segregated recreation and transportation facilities. Even so, Clark concluded that each of these instances of discrimination had "occurred entirely within the state of Kansas," and that "none of the Kansas defendants' authority extends beyond the territorial boundaries of Kansas." The immediate victims of discriminatory action in Kansas, Clark reasoned, were the "unidentified blacks" who allegedly relocated to Kansas City "due to the racial climate on the Kansas side of the state line." He ruled that those actions were not "legally related" to the school district's case. In short, Clark determined that the Kansas City's case sought solely "to rectify an unconstitutional condition of education," and not to redress "the collective harm experienced for sixty years by blacks in Kansas City, Missouri." Judge Clark summarily dismissed all of the Kansas defendants, but he did so with one caveat. He recognized that at some point in the subsequent litigation "it may very well become apparent that the Kansas defendants are indispensably necessary" to the adjudication of the suit and could be rejoined to the case later.

The Missouri and federal defendants were not so fortunate as the Kansas defendants in the judge's ruling. Both defendant groups had argued that the school district complaint was "so vague as to make a responsive pleading difficult if not impossible," and urged that the suit be dismissed. Clark denied both motions. With respect to the arguments presented by the Missouri defendants, he concluded that Kansas City's allegations concerning the drawing of school district lines, the operation of the state mandated segregated school system, the transfer of black students across district lines for purposes of segregation, the failure of the state to eliminate vestiges of segregation in the public schools, the enforcement of restrictive covenants in housing, and the discriminatory hiring practices employed by the state of Missouri and the suburban school districts were specific enough to have apprised the defendants of the nature of the claims against them. Similarly, with respect to the federal defendants, Clark found that the relocation of persons displaced by urban renewal and highway construction, the site selection for public housing projects, and the nature of HEW's relationship with the school district all merited that the federal departments be retained as defendants.

Perhaps the most unexpected aspect of Judge Clark's ruling was the realignment of the school district as a defendant. In reaching this conclusion the judge relied primarily upon considerations of acting in the best interest of the district's students. In particular, Clark questioned whether the school district could be an effective advocate for its students. He reasoned that in examining the extent of the constitutional violations in the metropolitan area, "it is elementary that the inquiry must begin with the students' own district," and Clark found that there existed "the distinct potential for the evidence to uncover acts of discrimination by the plaintiff School District itself." In such instances, the judge was concerned that the school district might "resist the introduction of incriminating evidence concerning its own past or present actions." Furthermore, Clark questioned the school district's commitment to "zealously argue for the rights of the aggrieved students," in litigation that was likely to drag on for years. Specifically, the judge was unconvinced that future school boards would support continued litigation, and he speculated that the suit might "be abandoned in midstream due to disgruntled taxpayers bringing pressure upon the elected school officials." Moreover, Clark suspected that if future litigation resulted in an order that relieved the school district of its economic hardships, the school district's determination to pursue additional litigation on behalf of its students might wane. These concerns, Clark concluded, raised grave doubts as to the appropriateness of the Kansas City school district acting as the primary advocate for its students. Indeed, Clark found that these considerations militated that the school district be realigned as a defendant in the suit.

Appeals to the Eighth Circuit Court

Judge Clark understood that his order fundamentally changed the nature of the school district's suit, and he conceded that with respect to each of the four major points "there are substantial grounds for difference of opinion." For these reasons he provided for the unusual step of permitting immediate appeals on each of the points despite the fact that a final order had not yet been entered in the suit. Indeed, appeals were almost certain to follow. School board members in Kansas City were shocked by the shift ordered in Judge Clark's opinion and began immediate discussions of what course to pursue. Although a majority of the Kansas City school board favored appealing Clark's ruling, the board's initial enthusiasm for the suit and confidence of a favorable result were flagging. Indeed, two board members, James Bonadonna and Mary Roberson, urged that the school district cut its losses and drop the suit. Nevertheless, in December 1978 the school district appealed the dismissal of the Kansas defendants and the realignment of the school district as a defendant in the suit. At the same time, the Missouri defendants petitioned the Eighth Circuit Court in St. Louis to have the suit dismissed, arguing that the school district's use of school children as plaintiffs was "a sham."

In their brief to the appellate court, Kansas City's attorneys argued that the school district, fiscally troubled as it was, constituted the only organization in the city which both had an interest in the suit and possessed the financial resources to pursue the case. The school district maintained that although civil rights groups had expressed some interest in the case, all were in agreement that they lacked the resources to prosecute the suit to its conclusion, which would likely take years. Given these circumstances, Borthwick and Keeler insisted that the school district remained the only effective advocate for the students and should be reinstalled as plaintiffs.

In February 1979, a three-judge panel of the Eighth Circuit Court of Appeals ruled on both the school district and Missouri petitions. In a brief opinion, the appellate judges denied both appeals, and remanded the case to the district court. Kansas City opted not to request a review by the United States Supreme Court, and the Missouri defendants renewed their motions to dismiss the suit. Thus, after almost two years the Kansas City metropolitan suit appeared to be finished before it had ever gone to trial. The school district could not act as the plaintiff, and it was uncertain whether another plaintiff group would come forth to pursue the complaint. Without new plaintiffs, the metropolitan suit stood to be dismissed.

Conclusions

The Kansas City school district's leading role in the metropolitan suit ended in 1979. Nevertheless, the decision to launch the lawsuit provides a fascinating snapshot of how school officials viewed the district's situation in the mid-1970s. In some respects, the metropolitan suit may be viewed as an act of desperation. By the mid-1970s, the Kansas City public schools were plagued by numerous problems, many of which stemmed from the school district's sorry financial state or the changing demographics of the city. Dozens of Kansas City schools were old and in dire need of repair but the school district had been unable to pass a bond issue or tax levy increase for a decade and lacked the funds to finance renovation or new construction. Maintenance of the schools had also been trimmed and a great many Kansas City schools simply were not pleasant environments for education. Understandably, many Kansas City families with the resources to finance a move to the suburbs or to enroll their children in parochial or private schools did just that. Infusions of federal education funds allowed the district to remain solvent, but did little to improve the negative image that most residents had of the Kansas City public schools. Nearly one-half of the parents responding to a *Kansas City Star* survey in 1977 described the city's schools as "poor" or "not very good." Moreover, the school district's participation in the federal programs had brought increased scrutiny from HEW, and some school officials questioned whether the district had profited at all from its relationship with HEW. Indeed, some administrators viewed HEW's treatment of the Kansas City schools as capricious and blamed HEW for accelerating white flight from the district.

The exodus of whites from the city's public schools continued unabated during the 1970s as the white enrollment in the district fell by nearly 25,000 during the decade. Although whites continued to comprise a majority of the city's population, the school district became majority black in 1970, and by 1979 two out of three students in the district were black. These demographic shifts were inexorably entwined with the school district's financial woes. The loss of the white population deprived the school district of some of its taxing potential. Furthermore, it seems safe to conclude that to some degree the white voting majority was reluctant to favor fiscal measures which benefited the majority black school district.

Financial difficulties and the shifting demographics of the Kansas City schools lay at the heart of the metropolitan suit, and in both respects Kansas City school officials eyed the suburbs as a solution. Student exchanges with the suburbs, it was argued, could solve the school district's integration problems. Moreover, cooperative agreements with the suburbs promised some relief for the district's financial straits. Under the exchange program the Kansas City schools would no longer be responsible for educating the great majority of disadvantaged students in the metropolitan area, students whose needs, it was argued, demanded larger investments than suburban students. In order to realize the advent of the metropolitan student exchange program, however, the school district had to demonstrate that the suburbs, the states of Kansas and Missouri, and the three federal departments had caused the isolation of black students in the Kansas City schools. Therein lay the most substantial obstacles to the school district's ambitious plans.

Kansas City's metropolitan suit was hindered by significant procedural and conceptual problems from the very start. By seeking to act as the primary advocate for its own students the school district opened itself to charges of a conflict of interest. It would be difficult to dispute Judge Clark's observation that a trial could reveal instances in which the school district had acted in a manner which discriminated against its black students and had perpetuated segregation in the Kansas City schools. However, because no other plaintiff group could be organized to pursue the suit in 1977, the school district was compelled to file the complaint. Seeking the inclusion of suburbs on the Kansas side of the state line further complicated the suit, and arguing that discrimination in Kansas had caused the isolation of blacks in the Kansas City, Missouri, schools proved to be a connection that Judge Clark was not inclined to make. Moreover, although Kansas City's attorneys could conclusively demonstrate that the Missouri suburbs had transferred black students to Kansas City's segregated schools prior to 1954, the allegations that those communities and school districts had acted in a manner which contributed to the isolation of black students in the Kansas City schools since the mid-1950s was less than thoroughly convincing in a legal sense. Perhaps the strongest elements of the school district's case involved allegations that the actions of the federal agencies had reinforced the patterns of residential segregation in the city, and that the state of Missouri had failed in its duty to assist in dismantling the remaining vestiges of segregation in the school district. Even so, the school district's claims were all overridden by Judge Clark's realignment of the case.

The school district's role as a plaintiff in the suit ended with the federal circuit court's denial of Kansas City's appeal in February 1979, and, for a time, the future course of the case was uncertain. Unless a new plaintiff group could be organized, Judge Clark appeared ready to dismiss the suit. Indeed, some of the parties involved in the litigation concluded that the case was all but finished. George Feldmiller, an attorney for the Missouri suburbs, interpreted the appellate court's decision as "a great victory" for the suburbs, but he spoke too soon in predicting that it marked "the death knell for the lawsuit." A new plaintiff group was already being organized and four years later, the attorneys for the state of Missouri, the suburbs, and the three federal departments would all find themselves back in court along with the latest defendant, the Kansas City, Missouri, public schools.

CHAPTER 7

From Metropolitan to Magnets

The Evolution of *Jenkins v. Missouri*, 1983-1990

During the autumn months of 1983, Kansas City attorney Arthur A. Benson II frequently woke up groggy and stiff from another fitful night's sleep on the cot in his office. Benson was the attorney for the new group of plaintiffs organized in 1979 to pursue Kansas City's metropolitan desegregation suit, and by September he was working around the clock preparing for the case. Six years had passed since the school district had filed its initial complaint, and four years since the Eighth Circuit Court of Appeals had denied Kansas City's petition to be reinstated as a plaintiff in the suit. Much had transpired in the four years since Benson took on the case, but by October 1983 the suit was finally ready to proceed to trial before Judge Russell Clark.

Arthur Benson represented a plaintiff group comprised of eight school age children in the Kansas City area. He had begun following the metropolitan desegregation suit while working in the Kansas City office of the American Civil Liberties Union, and was one of the few attorneys in the city that expressed an interest in pursuing the case for the city's school children after the school district had been realigned as a defendant. Most Kansas City lawyers, including Benson, recognized that the case was likely to drag on for years and few had confidence in their own or the plaintiffs' ability to shoulder the expenses that such a case would undoubtedly generate. Nevertheless, Benson accepted the challenge and worked zealously in building a case for the plaintiffs. In 1982, the NAACP's Legal Defense and Education Fund joined the litigation on behalf of plaintiff school children. Throughout the lengthy litigation NAACP attorneys assisted the Kansas City lawyer in preparing and arguing the case, and helped to defray some of the costs of pursuing the suit. Nevertheless, Benson remained the primary advocate for the city's school children in the suit for the next two decades.

In May 1979, Benson filed the plaintiffs' amended complaint. Similar to the Kansas City school district's original complaint presented two years earlier, the plaintiffs alleged that the Kansas City public schools were unconstitutionally segregated due to discriminatory actions and failures to act by many of the same parties specified in the school district's initial complaint. The state of Missouri, thirteen suburban school districts in the Kansas City area, the federal departments of Health, Education and Welfare (HEW), Housing and Urban Development (HUD), and Transportation, as well as the Kansas City school district were named as defendants. The suit was originally styled as *Black v. State of Missouri.*

Two months after Benson had filed the plaintiffs' complaint, attorneys for the Kansas City school district filed a cross-claim against the state of Missouri. In its motion, the school district argued that the state had failed to take affirmative steps to dismantle the segregated school system after the *Brown v. Board of Education* decision, and thereby was liable for the remaining vestiges of segregation of the Kansas City schools. The district's attorneys argued that the state should be required to participate in the development of a desegregation plan for the city's schools. More importantly, the district's cross-claim sought additional financing from the state in order to implement a plan for desegregation.

The prospect of securing increased funding from the state actually provided the school district and its attorneys with compelling reasons to assist the plaintiffs. Should the plaintiffs demonstrate that the extent of the segregation in the Kansas City schools stemmed from the discriminatory actions of the school district and the state, a remedy would be necessary to restore the plaintiffs to the position they would have occupied absent any unconstitutional discrimination. School district officials anticipated that such a remedial order would require massive spending in order to improve the educational program and upgrade the district's facilities. Thus, by filing the cross-claim, school district officials hoped to assure that the state would be required to provide the additional funds necessary for such improvements. Kansas City school board president, Dr. Edward Scaggs, summed up the rationale for the cross-claim, stating that the school district "could realize [its] goals quickly by going the state route." The cross-claim became a powerful motive governing the manner in which school district officials and their attorneys approached the plaintiffs' suit.

Not surprisingly, many Kansas City school officials were sympathetic to the plaintiffs. The suit had been originally filed by the school district and the new plaintiffs continued to seek a metropolitan solution to the city's school integration problems. The school district's attorneys, many members of the district's administration, and a majority of the school board continued to believe that a strong case could be made against the state of Missouri and the surrounding suburban districts. Now that the suit was properly aligned, many of those close to the Kansas City case believed that Judge Clark would order the creation of a metropolitan school district or the development of a student exchange program between the city and the suburbs.

After the filing of the plaintiffs' amended complaint and the school district's cross-claim against the state in 1979, Judge Clark considered several motions to dismiss the suit or disqualify the attorneys representing the plaintiffs and the school district. These motions delayed the start of the trial for more than three years. Ultimately, Clark refused to dismiss the case and rejected motions by the suburbs and the state of Missouri to disqualify the lead attorneys for the plaintiffs and the school district. Having resolved these issues, preparations for arguing the suit began in earnest in 1982.

The process of investigating and assembling evidence proceeded for more than a year. In preparing for the case, attorneys for the parties involved reviewed, cataloged, and summarized millions of pages of documents. By the time the trial began in October 1983, thousands of documents prepared by the various parties in the suit were filed with the court. More than 3,000 exhibits and 300 potential witnesses in the case were listed with the court, and depositions taken in the case consumed some seven feet of shelf space.

In preparing for the trial, Kansas City school district officials and their attorneys actively assisted Benson and the plaintiffs. Lawyers for the school district and the plaintiffs frequently held joint planning sessions in which the attorneys discussed strategy in the case, the evidence that each side would introduce at trial, and the testimony that witnesses would provide. Indeed, these meetings revealed one of the brilliant ironies of the suit. It became patently clear that the school district, although it was a defendant in the case, was firmly on the side of the plaintiffs and eager to assist in presenting the case against the suburbs, the state, and the school district itself. Judge Clark later called the school district and the plaintiffs "friendly adversaries," but the relationship was more than that. Cooperation between the two parties was complete and the two could hardly be termed "adversaries" at all.

Due to changes in the plaintiff group, by the time the suit reached trial, it had been renamed *Jenkins v. Missouri*, and Arthur Benson represented not only the eight named plaintiffs, but a certified class of all present and future Kansas City school children. Furthermore, the Department of Transportation and two of the suburban districts, Belton and Raymore-Peculiar, were dismissed from the suit at the request of the plaintiffs. Finally, the efforts made by a group of civic leaders to resolve the suit through a settlement agreement before the trial began had failed. The non-jury, metropolitan desegregation trial opened on October 31, 1983 in Judge Clark's courtroom.

The trial itself promised to be lengthy and extremely complicated. James Borthwick, one of the attorneys for the Kansas City school district, speculated that the trial might last three months. It dragged on more than twice that long. Essentially, the trial can be viewed as three separate cases – one against the suburban school districts, one against the state and the Kansas City school district, and one against the two federal departments. Indeed, Judge Clark treated the case in precisely this fashion. Although the plaintiffs' attorneys pursued a strategy designed to demonstrate how the actions of all of the defendants cumulatively produced segregated conditions in the Kansas City schools specifically and throughout the metropolitan area more generally, the judge drew sharp distinctions between the defendants. Over the course of the trial, Clark issued three separate opinions which plainly illustrate that he dealt with the defendant groups as separate cases. The first opinion, dated June 5, 1984, addressed the plaintiffs' allegations regarding the suburban school districts.

The Suburban School Districts Decision

From the beginning of the trial, the plaintiffs' attorneys experienced difficulty in presenting a conclusive case against the suburban districts. Before the trial began, Judge Clark characterized much of the plaintiffs' research as a "tremendous fishing expedition," and at trial, he continually questioned the relevance of the exhibits and much of the testimony offered by witnesses for the plaintiffs. During the trial's first four weeks, Benson and other attorneys for the plaintiffs attempted to demonstrate that prior to 1954 the lack of educational opportunities for blacks in the region around Kansas City had spurred black migration to the city. Judge Clark was not convinced. He characterized much of the testimony as "interesting history," but little more. The judge allowed the testimony but in doing so added, "I'm not saying I'm buying the theory." Similarly, Clark found that many of the documents submitted by the plaintiffs had no value in the suit and expressed his concern that he was being "buried" by exhibits. Clark claimed that he only accepted the documents into the record in the event that a higher court disagreed with his assessment and because, as he succinctly put it: "I don't want to have to come back and try the case again."

Judge Clark also tended to discount many of the plaintiffs' arguments that residential segregation in the metropolitan area implicated the suburban school districts. Expert witnesses in urban geography, economics, city planning, and sociology all testified that race was the most significant factor in determining the distribution of the population in metropolitan Kansas City. Attorneys for the suburban school districts challenged this conclusion arguing that residential patterns in the metropolitan area resulted from economic differences and personal preferences. The judge, tending to view the causes of residential segregation in a manner similar to the suburban attorneys, made it clear that he did not interpret the housing testimony as direct proof that suburban school districts had discriminated against African-Americans. Clark also struck from the record numerous statements offered by witnesses for the plaintiffs who alleged that a certain racial animus toward blacks existed in the suburbs. When witnesses failed to point to specific acts of discrimination, Clark had their testimony stricken.

Clearly what Judge Clark sought was evidence of specific acts of discrimination against blacks by the suburban school districts or public officials in the suburbs. That sort of evidence proved to be non-existent. Indeed, during the trial Benson was forced to concede that the plaintiffs lacked direct evidence of intent in the suburban districts to exclude or discriminate against blacks, stating at one point: "We don't have those kinds of smoking guns in this case." Without direct evidence of constitutional violations occurring in each of the suburban school districts, the judge concluded that he was obligated to dismiss the suburbs. Clark's June 5, 1984 order did that just that, the eleven suburban school districts were excused from the suit.

In dismissing the suburban school districts Judge Clark relied most heavily on the standards announced in the Supreme Court's 1974 *Milliken v. Bradley* opinion. In *Milliken*, the Court had considered a sweeping metropolitan desegregation plan involving schools in the Detroit, Michigan area. In 1971, Judge Stephen Roth, the federal district court judge who originally heard the case, found that the state of Michigan and the Detroit Board of Education, through a variety of actions, had obstructed integration and promoted the segregation of black students in the city's schools. In order to remedy these violations, Roth ordered the creation of a huge metropolitan school district consolidating the Detroit public schools and fifty-three surrounding suburban districts. The resulting school district encompassed much of three counties and contained some 780,000 students, of which 310,000 would be bused daily in the interest of integration. The Sixth Circuit Court of Appeals affirmed Roth's order a year later.

At the Supreme Court, however, the order establishing the massive metropolitan school district was overturned. By a vote of five to four the Justices determined that the suburbs had been wrongly included in Roth's order to desegregate the Detroit schools. Writing for the majority, Justice Lewis Powell concluded that, "Before the boundaries of separate and autonomous school districts may be set aside by consolidating the separate units for remedial purposes or by imposing a cross-district remedy, it must first be shown that there has been a constitutional violation within one district that produces a significant segregative effect in another district." In the case of the Detroit suburbs, the Court found no evidence of constitutional violations which justified the consolidation of fifty-four school districts. "Without an interdistrict violation and interdistrict effect," the Court found, "there is no constitutional wrong calling for an interdistrict remedy." In excusing the suburbs and ordering that the remedy for the effects of segregation be confined to the city of Detroit, the Court dealt African-Americans their first loss in a school desegregation case since integration began with the *Brown v. Board of Education* decision in 1954.

Relying on the standards set forth in *Milliken*, Judge Clark concluded that there was no justification for holding the suburbs. He characterized much of the plaintiffs' evidence as "speculative" and "weak," and found that "there is no credible or substantial evidence of a constitutional violation by these suburban school districts." Clark noted, "Witness after witness, including witnesses who had been actively involved in the promotion of civil rights, testified that they knew of *no* acts by the suburban school districts that were done with discriminatory intent." He rejected the plaintiffs' contention that racially discriminatory motives were evident in the manner in which school district boundaries had been established and maintained. Clark also dismissed as "insignificant" the number of black students who had transferred from suburban school districts to the Kansas City schools in the period before the *Brown* decision. He found that "jobs and economic opportunity were primary motivators" for blacks moving into Kansas City. Clark further ruled that although the suburbs and city had cooperated in providing special education services, lobbying the state legislature for educational funding, and in sharing revenue generated by the one-half cent sales tax, these associations did not bind the suburbs to assist the Kansas City schools in desegregating. Moreover, the judge found that no lingering vestiges of segregation were apparent in the suburban districts. Each of the suburban districts employed African-American teachers and enrolled African-American students.

Based upon these findings, Clark ruled "there is no *duty* on the part of any suburban school district to cooperate in the racial balancing of the metropolitan area." The judge also dismissed the plaintiffs' argument that the patterns of residential segregation in the metropolitan area implicated the suburban districts. He bluntly concluded that suburban school districts, "had no involvement in or influence on the manner in which blacks or whites made residential decisions." To the extent that other agencies or individuals had shaped the residential patterns of the metropolitan area, Clark refused to hold the school districts liable, finding that such practices are "totally beyond the control of any particular school district." Finally, the judge rejected the plaintiffs' argument that the suburban school districts were mere creations of the state of Missouri and could be reorganized in order to remedy the discriminatory actions of the state. Clark found that each school district was a "locally autonomous and independent entity," and that "none can be held vicariously liable for the acts of the state."

In essence, Judge Clark ruled that the plaintiffs' evidence did not establish a clear cause and effect relationship between the suburban school districts and the Kansas City schools. In order to justify an interdistrict remedy, Clark reasoned that the plaintiffs needed to prove conclusively that the suburban school districts had not only discriminated against blacks within their own districts but that those actions had caused substantial segregative effects in Kansas City. He found that the suburban districts had done neither. Clark characterized the plaintiffs' evidence of segregative acts by the suburban school districts as "anemic," and concluded that the districts had been administered in a manner fully consistent with the prevailing constitutional standards since 1954.

The HEW Decision

After the dismissal of the suburban districts, the trial proceeded for two more weeks before Clark granted HEW's motion to be dismissed from the suit. The plaintiffs' complaint against HEW claimed that the department had failed to enforce effectively the nondiscrimination provisions of Title VI in the 1964 Civil Rights Act. In short, Benson and the plaintiffs maintained that due to insufficient staff and mismanagement of funds, HEW failed in its duty to conduct a metropolitan investigation of Kansas City area schools in the late 1960s and early 1970s. Essentially, the plaintiffs' attorneys argued that the extensive HEW investigation of the Kansas City schools in the 1970s should have triggered a broader investigation of the suburbs as well.

Judge Clark flatly rejected the plaintiffs' allegations against HEW. He ruled that departmental decisions to assign a preponderance of HEW field staff to the states of the deep south in the late 1960s and early 1970s had been completely reasonable given the slow progress of school desegregation in that region. Even so, Clark found that HEW had responded to every formal complaint that the agency received concerning the Kansas City schools. Moreover, Clark concluded that, to some degree, the plaintiffs' arguments against HEW were based upon "pure speculation," and that the department had no duty to conduct a metropolitan-wide investigation. The judge noted that each of the suburban school districts filed the appropriate Title VI compliance forms with HEW and that none of the suburban school districts had ever received a so-called "Adams letter" from HEW informing the district of suspected non-compliance with Title VI. All told, Clark found that HEW's investigative efforts in the Kansas City area had been "diligent, reasonable, and timely." Indeed, he maintained that HEW's investigation of Kansas City's schools had been extremely aggressive and that the plaintiffs' allegations of lax enforcement were groundless. Clark concluded, "There is simply no proof that HEW officials acted with a racially discriminatory purpose," and the department was thereby dismissed from the suit.

Judge Clark's rulings dismissing the suburbs and HEW simplified the case and shortened the trial. Even so, Arthur Benson believed that the dismissal of these defendants did not fundamentally change the litigation or the interdistrict remedy that the plaintiffs sought. Benson maintained that should the state of Missouri be found liable for failing in its affirmative duty to eliminate the vestiges of the segregated system, an order compelling the suburbs to cooperate in an interdistrict remedy could still be won. Moreover, Benson did not lament the dismissal of HEW concluding that, "we'll just have to get the [federal] money from HUD."

Following the dismissal of the suburban defendants and HEW, Judge Clark's attention focused on the allegations against the three remaining defendants – HUD, the state of Missouri, and the Kansas City public schools. The trial continued for nearly two more months before the lawyers for all parties rested and the judge began drafting the final order of the trial. Clark's third order, which addressed the remaining defendants, was announced on September 17, 1984.

The HUD Decision

With respect to HUD, Benson and other attorneys for the plaintiffs had argued at trial that the federal agency had violated its obligations under Title VI of the 1964 Civil Rights Act and Title VIII of the 1968 Civil Rights Act, which prohibited discrimination in federal housing programs. The plaintiffs alleged that HUD's urban renewal and public housing programs contributed to the segregation of blacks in Kansas City, while FHA mortgage insurance programs facilitated the development of a virtually all white ring of suburbs around the city. In support of these allegations the plaintiffs called several Kansas City blacks to testify regarding their first hand experiences with public housing and urban renewal activity, as well as a number of expert witnesses. Much of this testimony focused on the site selection for public housing projects and the relocation of residents displaced by urban renewal. Witnesses contended that HUD authorized the construction of large public housing projects, such as the T.B. Watkins Homes and Wayne Minor Court, with the full understanding that these projects were to be built in black neighborhoods and would be filled with African-American tenants. Moreover, Benson alleged that HUD rejected proposals to build public housing projects in the suburbs, and made little effort to inform African-Americans of vacancies or to attract black residents to projects located in predominantly white areas of the city.

Aside from the allegations of discrimination in the site selection and occupancy of public housing projects, the plaintiffs maintained that HUD sanctioned discrimination against blacks in relocating residents displaced by urban renewal and highway construction. Specifically, the plaintiffs argued that HUD violated its Title VI and Title VIII obligations when it continued to fund the Kansas City Land Clearance for Redevelopment Authority (LCRA) after the federal department was aware that LCRA was following racially discriminatory practices in its relocation efforts. Yale Rabin, a professor and associate dean of the University of Virginia school of architecture, was the plaintiffs' star witness concerning relocation. Rabin testified that 756 black families were displaced by the construction of the South Midtown Freeway between 1968 and 1973. His research found that 87% of those families were relocated in predominantly black areas, most notably the southeast corridor, and that none had been relocated to the white areas of Independence, Lee's

Summit, or North Kansas City. Moreover, he found that the vast majority of the 668 white families displaced by the South Midtown Freeway project were relocated to areas outside the predominantly black residential zone. Rabin further testified that the pattern illustrated by the South Midtown Freeway study was no aberration. He mapped the moves of nearly 14,000 households displaced by urban renewal and highway construction between 1953 and 1973, and found obvious differences in the relocation of black and white families. Blue pins, representing the nearly 9,000 white households, were "all over the map," whereas the red pins, representing more than 5,000 black families, "all extended in a steady band southeast of downtown."

In defense of the department, HUD officials testified that the agency had consistently pursued a policy of balanced housing in the Kansas City metropolitan area. Refuting allegations of discriminatory site selection for public housing, federal witnesses testified that HUD thoroughly reviewed housing project proposals, including the racial characteristics of project areas, and had rejected some of the proposed projects because they were located in areas which were exclusively black. HUD officials produced exhibits which documented that projects insured or subsidized by HUD were scattered throughout the metropolitan area. According to HUD's statistics, nearly 6,900 multi-family units of federally assisted housing were located within the Kansas City school district area, while almost 9,900 such units were located in the suburbs. HUD officials provided additional evidence that the department carefully followed affirmative fair housing marketing regulations in filling vacancies, and that the existence of predominantly one-race occupancy within a project did not prove that HUD had acted in a discriminatory fashion. For example, Ruth Sechter testified that in the development of Parvin Estates, a housing project built in predominantly white North Kansas City, HUD had informed eligible blacks of vacancies and aggressively marketed the project to potential African-American residents. Even so, only 12% of Parvin Estates' residents were minorities.

HUD officials further testified that the department was not responsible for the relocation of residents displaced by urban renewal and highway construction projects. Thomas Kilbride, area manager of HUD's Kansas City offices from 1975 to 1983, insisted that those responsibilities lay with city officials in the Kansas City Housing Authority and the Land Clearance for Redevelopment Authority. Moreover, Kilbride testified that HUD had investigated Title VI complaints regarding the relocations and informed the city agencies in 1973 that the relocation program had to be reformed or HUD would begin withholding funds for neighborhood development. That year, the city authorities and HUD reached an agreement in which the city assumed all responsibility for the relocation program.

In his September 17, 1984 opinion, Judge Clark dismissed HUD from the suit. He concluded that HUD had consistently followed "a balanced housing policy," and had attempted to insure that "assisted housing located in the inner city area was balanced by assisted housing projects in the suburban areas." Clark also found that HUD had monitored closely its affirmative fair housing and marketing plans in Kansas City, and found no evidence of discriminatory intent in HUD's oversight of public housing projects in the city. The judge further noted that HUD's Section 8 program provided housing assistance payments for qualified applicants not only in Kansas City, but also in Independence, Liberty, and Lee's Summit. He dismissed allegations that public housing authorities steered blacks to locate in Kansas City, finding instead that Section 8 participants were instructed to locate housing of their own choosing within any of the four cities that honored the certificates. Clark further determined that there had been no discrimination in the distribution of FHA mortgage insurance and asserted that there was "no evidence whatsoever" to support the allegation that blacks were routinely denied approval by FHA. Finally, with regard to the relocation program, Clark laid blame squarely on the city authorities. He concluded that 1973 agreement between HUD and the city agencies, in which the city assumed full responsibility for managing the relocations, exonerated HUD and was a reasonable solution given that withholding federal funds would have penalized those low income families most in need of housing.

In essence, the September 17 ruling concerning HUD underscored Judge Clark's own personal beliefs about residential segregation. He ruled that the extensive segregation in the Kansas City metropolitan area was not attributable to the actions of the federal government. Clark was much more inclined to believe that income level, personal preferences, and the actions of individuals operating in the real estate market shaped residential patterns. He did not deny, however, that housing in the metropolitan area was segregated: that was patently clear to all involved in the suit. Moreover, he conceded that the discriminatory practices of blockbusting, racial steering, and red lining had contributed to the separation of the races. Clark, however, was loath to find that the defendants had engaged in such practices. By analyzing housing from the narrow perspective of overt actions on the part of the named defendants, and refusing to find that the metropolitan area's housing patterns were in part the result of the cumulative actions of the defendants, as well as hundreds of unnamed private offenders, Clark effectively eliminated issues of residential segregation from the suit. This is not to say that Clark acted improperly in interpreting the evidence as he did; his conclusions regarding housing and residential segregation were completely justifiable in a legal sense. However, a judge more inclined to view housing issues in broader terms may have produced a more favorable finding for the plaintiffs.

The Kansas City and State of Missouri Decisions

The dismissal of HUD left the suit with only two remaining defendants: the Kansas City public schools and the state of Missouri. Clark's September 17 order went on to analyze the plaintiffs' allegations against these defendants, and resolved Kansas City's cross-claim against the state. It was in ruling against these final two defendants that Judge Clark established liability for the segregation of black students in the Kansas City schools. After nearly eight months at trial, hundreds of witnesses, more than 2,000 exhibits, and a transcript of the suit consuming some 22,000 pages, the plaintiffs finally won their first favorable decision.

Presenting a convincing case against the Kansas City public schools was certainly the simplest aspect of the plaintiffs' suit. Not only was there evidence of discrimination, but the school district's attorneys gladly assisted Benson and the plaintiffs' attorneys in establishing the district's liability. During the course of the trial, school district personnel and patrons of the district testified to the district's failure to implement effective policies to promote integration and the inability to eradicate vestiges of the former segregated system. In short, the plaintiffs alleged that since the initial 1955 desegregation plan which dissolved the dual attendance zones and assigned students on the basis of a neighborhood schools concept, school district policies had thwarted meaningful integration, discriminated against blacks, and denied students of equal protection under the Fourteenth Amendment.

School officials freely admitted during the trial that the district had not thoroughly dismantled its segregated system until the 1977 implementation of Plan 6-C, the first district-wide desegregation plan adopted in Kansas City. Reams of exhibits and testimony were presented regarding the busing of intact classrooms of black elementary students during the early 1960s, the rejection of the integration proposals made in the Havighurst study and Hazlett's "Concepts for Changing Times," the use of the transfer policy to evade integration, the constant shifting of school attendance zones, the high number of one-race schools, the paucity of stably integrated schools, and the district's reluctance to integrate faculties and administration. All of these, the plaintiffs asserted and the school district generally concurred, demonstrated that the district had failed in its duty to integrate.

Not surprisingly, Judge Clark ruled that the Kansas City public schools "had not yet become integrated on a system-wide basis," and that "vestiges of [the] dual system still remain." He found that the 1955 adoption of a neighborhood schools approach to desegregation "did not substantially change the segregated school system." Moreover, the judge ruled that the liberal transfer policy coupled with the use of optional zones and adjustments to attendance zones "allowed attendance patterns to continue on a segregated basis." In determining that vestiges of segregation persisted in the Kansas City schools, Clark noted that in 1984, there remained twenty-four schools with enrollments in excess of 90% black. Further establishing the segregative intent of school district actions, the judge lambasted the intact classroom busing program. Harkening back to Chief Justice Earl Warren's conclusions in the 1954 *Brown v. Board of Education* decision that segregation "generates a feeling of inferiority," Judge Clark wrote of the busing scheme: "Certainly black children subjected to that experience well remember the feelings of isolation and inferiority obviously produced by the practice." Clark was less critical of other school district policies. Nevertheless he concluded that, with respect to many of the allegations, school district officials had acted with segregative intent and the policies adopted had served to perpetuate segregation in the Kansas City schools.

The lone remaining question, then, involved the extent to which the state of Missouri was accountable for the segregation of the Kansas City schools. Both the plaintiffs and the Kansas City school district, by virtue of its cross-claim, insisted that ultimately the state bore responsibility for the failure to integrate the city's schools. The plaintiffs and school district alleged that those vestiges of segregation which remained in Kansas City were a product of state mandated segregated schools, and that the state had failed to take the necessary remedial measures to eliminate segregation. The plaintiffs' attorneys maintained that since 1954 the state had "abdicated any responsibility for undoing the effects ... of its prior system of segregated education," and had provided school districts with "no directives, advice, or leadership in this regard." Moreover, it was alleged that the state's enforcement of restrictive covenants prior to 1950 and its tolerance of discriminatory housing practices since that time were the primary causes of the concentration of blacks in Kansas City and white flight from the city. Witnesses for the school district agreed that these demographic shifts were attributable to the actions and inactions of the state. Furthermore, school district attorneys argued that the shifting demographics had the dual effects of depriving the district of part of its tax base while increasing the number of economically and socially disadvantaged minority students in the Kansas City schools. Finally, the school district alleged that disparities in the state's educational funding formula contributed to the Kansas City schools' inability to desegregate or to provide adequate services for disadvantaged students.

In the September 17 order, Judge Clark ruled that, along with the Kansas City school district, the state of Missouri was liable for the segregation of students in the district. Essentially, Clark found that in mandating the creation of the state's segregated school system, the state also had "the constitutional obligation to affirmatively dismantle [the] system of *de jure* segregation, root and branch." Clark flatly dismissed the state's contention that, under its constitutional provisions regarding the autonomy of school districts, it was powerless to have done more to dismantle Kansas City's segregated school system. Clark went so far as to assert that there was nothing in the state constitution which would have prevented the General Assembly from enacting legislation to consolidate school districts in order to eliminate segregation. On the housing issues, Judge Clark found that the state of Missouri had "created an atmosphere in which private white individuals could justify their bias and prejudice against blacks." Moreover, Clark asserted that, in some respects, "The State has encouraged racial discrimination by private individuals in the real estate, banking and insurance industries." Even so, the judge concluded that although these private institutions were regulated by state agencies, their discriminatory conduct could not be construed as "state action" for which the state of Missouri could be held liable. Nevertheless, by virtue of its failure to dismantle the segregated system, Clark ruled against the state of Missouri. Accordingly, the judge ordered that plans be developed to remedy the Kansas City schools and restore the plaintiff school children to position that they would have occupied absent any constitutional violations.

Clark's instructions concerning possible remedies were rather broad, leaving the specifics to the professional educators in the Kansas City schools and the Missouri State Department of Education. He ordered that plans for establishing a unitary school system in Kansas City be drafted and submitted to the court within ninety days. In formulating the plans, Clark directed the district and the state to concentrate on those schools having enrollments in excess of 90% black. The judge also suggested that students should be permitted to attend the school nearest their home, provided that doing so did not detract from the effort to integrate the schools. Clark also alluded to possible educational improvements which might be necessary in order to "furnish quality education to its students." Finally, the judge instructed the school district and the state to "bear in mind cost factors" in developing their plans. This final recommendation is somewhat ironic in that, over the next ten years, Kansas City would implement the most expensive school desegregation plan in the nation's history, and Judge Clark would preside over the entire process. The expense of desegregating the Kansas City schools was bound to be considerable, and to the delight of school officials, Clark ruled in favor of the district's cross-claim against the state. "Much of the cost for preparing and implementing a plan to dismantle the vestiges of a dual school system in the Kansas City, Missouri School District," Clark wrote, "should be borne by the State." The financial obligations of the state and the school district were determined later with the state contributing roughly 75% of the necessary funds and the school district the other 25%.

Judge Clark's finding against the state was viewed by several of the attorneys involved in the suit as perhaps the single most significant aspect of the three sweeping rulings the judge announced in 1984. Jim Borthwick, the school district's lead attorney, interpreted the decision as "a clear victory for the school district." One of the school district's principle objectives in the suit – securing additional funding from the state – had been realized. Borthwick correctly foresaw that Clark's order meant that "millions of additional dollars will be coming into the School District to aid in the process of desegregation." Lawyers for the plaintiffs were also pleased with the decision against the state but continued to look toward the suburbs, which had been dismissed months earlier. Theodore Shaw, an NAACP attorney working with Arthur Benson, insisted that, "meaningful desegregation would require [the] suburban districts." Benson and the school district's attorneys believed Clark's ruling held open that possibility. They maintained that in finding against the state, Judge Clark could compel the state to pass legislation enabling the consolidation of suburbs and the Kansas City schools. Indeed, Clark had written that "such legislation is mandatory," if that was the only means by which the state could fulfill its equal protection obligations under the Fourteenth Amendment. Although Benson and the school district's lawyers placed great value on the judge's statement, attorneys for the state and suburbs did not. Chip Robertson, the deputy attorney general for the state, flatly dismissed the inclusion of the suburbs. Robertson concluded that the plaintiffs' attorneys, "have been dreaming since they filed this lawsuit and refuse to wake up even now."

Remedial Plans

Plans for addressing the constitutional violations in the Kansas City schools were developed as the suit entered its remedial phase following Clark's September 17 ruling. A chief concern among many Kansas City school district patrons was that, by ordering further desegregation of the city's schools, the proposed remedies might require additional forced busing and reassignment of students within the district. Benson, however, had no interest in more busing to racially balance the Kansas City schools. He emphasized that "we don't believe there are any advantages" in such a plan given the fact that the school district was almost 75% black. Conscious of the general public opposition, school district officials never considered plans for additional mandatory busing within the city's schools. This did not mean that the district was opposed to further busing, but rather to busing which was confined solely to the Kansas City schools. Indeed, in fashioning its proposed remedies, the school district explored several possibilities, including resurrecting plans for a consolidated metropolitan school district which would demand massive busing between the city and the suburbs.

Contrary to the cooperation that Clark had suggested in his September order, the state and the school district developed separate plans to remedy the constitutional violations found in the Kansas City schools. State officials from the Missouri Department of Elementary and Secondary Education concentrated exclusively on the Kansas City schools and pointedly omitted any inclusion of the suburbs. Attorneys representing the suburban school districts had made it clear when the remedial phase of the suit began that, having been dismissed from the suit, the suburbs had no interest whatsoever in participating in the remedy. Kansas City school officials, in consultation with the plaintiffs and a number of nationally recognized integration experts, took a much broader view of the remedial possibilities. The school district and the plaintiffs had every intention of drawing the suburbs into the remedy in some capacity. The first and most ambitious plan offered by the school district proposed the consolidation of the metropolitan area's school districts.

Kansas City and the state both submitted their first wildly different remedial plans to the court in mid-January 1985. Kansas City's initial plan proposed that the eleven suburban school districts dismissed from the suit earlier be consolidated with the city school district to create a single metropolitan district of nearly 120,000 students, of which about 27% were minorities. Under Kansas City's proposed remedy, each of the 139 elementary schools in the twelve districts would have a minority enrollment of between 20% and 40%, and all of the fifty-two of the secondary schools in the metropolitan area would have minority enrollments of 15-40%.

In order to achieve this degree of integration, school officials understood that massive busing between the city and the suburbs was necessary. In the school district's proposal, more than 15,000 blacks would be bused to suburban districts while nearly 18,000 suburban whites would be bused to the city's schools. Aside from the sweeping student reassignments proposed in the plan, the school district also urged that the court order funding for a host of educational improvements, so-called "*Milliken II*" programs. Educational enhancements proposed by the school district included: expanded summer school programs, full day kindergarten, additional programs for low achieving students, magnet schools, computerized instruction, upgrading of libraries, extensive staff development programs, and the hiring of more than 130 new teachers and counselors in order to reduce class sizes and restore the district to an AAA rating from the state. Moreover, the school district maintained that approximately $65 million was needed for capital improvements to the district's schools in order to eliminate safety and health hazards, improve the "attractiveness" and "comfort level," and create "a good learning climate." Finally, the school district urged the court to establish a committee to monitor the progress of integration in the consolidated district, and a "Housing Counseling Center" to promote residential integration in the metropolitan area. All together, the cost of the school district's plan was estimated at more than $100 million, excluding transportation costs. The school district proposed that the state assume approximately 90% of these expenses.

The initial plan submitted by the state was considerably more modest. Clearly, one of the state's primary objectives in the Kansas City remedy was to keep the cost of the plan under control. Already saddled with an expensive desegregation settlement in St. Louis, which was projected to cost more than $500 million over five years, the state had no desire to propose a similar plan for Kansas City. The state's plan for Kansas City focused exclusively on the city's schools, particularly on the twenty-four schools which remained more than 90% black. The state plan set out to "break down any remaining racially identifiable school," and adopted the goal of assuring that, "no student attends a school that is more than 82% black." Racial isolation, the state maintained, could be eliminated through voluntary transfers, revisions to attendance zones, and busing. Beyond the provisions aimed at racially balancing a district in which 73% of the students were minorities, the state proposed educational improvements for the disproportionately black schools and schools receiving African American students via the busing program. Expanded summer school, all day kindergarten, an aggressive testing program to identify low achieving students, an intensive "basic skills" math and language arts curriculum at the predominantly black elementary schools, and expanded in-service for teachers and staff were all included in the plan. The state plan, however, made essentially no provisions for programs aimed at junior high and high school students, made no mention of reducing class size, included no funding for capital improvements to the district's schools, and did not endorse taking steps to restore the Kansas City schools to an AAA rating. By fashioning its proposal so narrowly, the state had succeeded in keeping the expense down. Eliminating the vestiges of the segregated system and restoring the plaintiff school children to a position of equal educational opportunity, the state maintained, could be accomplished for less than $9 million. Moreover, the state proposed that much of the cost could be met through savings realized by cutting "non-essential items" in the school district's budget.

Judge Clark considered the two remedy proposals for a week before issuing another court order. During this period Clark also reviewed a response filed with the court by the American Federation of Teachers (AFT) local union, which had been granted status as intervenors in the suit in November 1984. AFT criticized the state's proposal as "so limited and stingy that there is no real hope it can remedy decades of its discriminatory conduct," while arguing that the school district's plan was not responsive to the judge's order to limit desegregation efforts to the Kansas City schools. Like the AFT, Judge Clark was not inclined to accept either plan. He found that, although the school district's plan could serve as a useful model for consolidation if a higher court should at some point rule against the suburbs, the proposal went "far beyond the nature and extent of the constitutional violation this Court found existed," and, therefore, exceeded the court's remedial powers. Nevertheless, while AFT characterized the plans as "separate and irreconcilable proposals," the judge chose to focus on those elements common to both plans. He recognized that despite substantial differences in terms of scope and cost, both plans included provisions for summer school programs, all day kindergarten, school reorganization and reform, and increased staff development. From these areas of consensus, Clark suggested that additional agreements might be reached, and ordered the school district to submit a new plan.

In formulating a second plan, school district officials and their legal advisors initially considered other means by which the suburbs could be compelled to participate in the desegregation remedy, but ultimately settled on a proposal limited to the Kansas City schools. Nevertheless, many school officials remained convinced that the only possibility for meaningful, long-term school integration in Kansas City was to include of the suburbs, and further attempts to incorporate the suburban school districts would be pursued in the appellate court.

The school district submitted a second plan in mid-February. Arguing that the state's plan to expand the busing program would "lead to an all-black school district," the school district plan concluded that, "there is no realistic possibility of achieving further meaningful desegregation within the Kansas City, Missouri School District through boundary adjustment or other methods of mandatory reassignment of students." Rather, the school district focused primarily on "systemic educational improvements." Much of the February plan simply expanded upon the educational improvements put forth in the metropolitan proposal. Those sections addressing expanded summer school, all day kindergarten, hiring additional staff, reducing class size, utilizing more computerized instruction, launching additional remedial programs, and taking steps to restore the district's AAA rating had all been recommended in the first plan. In all, the district plan called for some $44 million in "quality education programs," all of which should be borne by the state because, according to the school district's reasoning, the state was the "primary violator of the constitutional rights of black and minority students," in the district. Like its initial metropolitan plan, the district's new plan also proposed the creation of a committee to monitor desegregation in the Kansas City schools, and an organization to promote residential integration in the metropolitan area. The district also proposed that the court order $25 million in capital improvements to the city's schools for the coming school year in order to attract and maintain integrated enrollments.

Magnet schools, the district suggested, were another useful method of attracting integrated enrollments. The school district's February plan called for strengthening the district's three existing magnet school programs – the college preparatory magnet at Lincoln Academy, the Southwest Science and Math cluster at Cook, Hartman and Marlborough, and the Basic and Applied Skills magnet at Swinney-Volker. The plan also recommended the creation of two new magnet elementary schools, a Montessori magnet at Faxon, and a Basic and Applied Skills magnet at Knotts, both of which were more than 95% black, and one additional magnet secondary school, the High School for Visual and Performing Arts. Magnet schools had not figured prominently in the district's initial plan, and remained of secondary importance in the February plan. However, from the modest expansion of the magnet program suggested in the district's second plan, magnet schools rapidly became the preferred approach to promoting integration in Kansas City.

In March and April 1985, the state developed two new plans of its own. Both reiterated the essential points of the initial state submission, and both were much more frugal than Kansas City's proposal. The March plan contained practically no new material and the state continued to contend that school desegregation in Kansas City could be accomplished for less than $9 million. From the school district's perspective, the April plan was a bit of an improvement. The state's April plan offered a one-time commitment of $20 million for capital improvements and an additional $20 million for educational programs. Indeed, during April, attorneys for the state and school district very nearly reached a settlement on the remedy, but discussions collapsed when the two sides were unable to agree on financial aspects of the plan.

With the school district and state at odds over the remedy, Judge Clark, vowing to issue a remedial order by mid-June, convened a two-week hearing in late April. During the hearing, experts for the state and school district discussed at length the various aspects of each proposed remedy. Further complicating the consideration of an appropriate remedy, the plaintiffs' attorneys submitted a plan in late May. The plaintiffs' proposal was tailored along the lines of the settlement in St. Louis which provided for voluntary transfers between the city and suburbs, the creation of magnet schools and extensive educational improvements in the city. As Clark deliberated on the remedy, he had no less than five plans from which to choose.

Clark announced his first remedial order for the Kansas City schools on June 14, 1985. In fashioning the remedy, the judge relied heavily on the school district's second plan. Finding that segregation had caused a "system wide reduction in student achievement," Clark ordered a broad range of educational improvements. In order to restore the district to a AAA rating from the state, he ordered the hiring of eighteen school counselors, eighteen art teachers, eighteen music teachers, eighteen physical education teachers, thirty-one elementary teachers, thirty-one teachers' aides, twenty-two librarians, and $950,000 for library and media resources. Further achievement gains could be attained, Clark reasoned, through reductions in the class size so that students would receive more individualized instruction. The judge also suggested that smaller classes might aid the school district in "maintaining and attracting non-minority enrollment." For these reasons, he mandated hiring 183 more teachers over a three year period. Clark went on to order expansion of the district's summer school programs, before and after school tutoring programs, and full day kindergarten, which required the district to hire thirty-nine more teachers. Early childhood screening and developmental programs were also approved, as was an extensive staff development component. The judge also prescribed more than $17 million over a three year period in additional programs designed to raise student achievement throughout the district. To oversee the progress of desegregation and student achievement in the district, Clark ordered the creation of a ten member monitoring committee comprised of four whites, four blacks, and two Hispanics. The school district, state, plaintiffs, and AFT were all directed to submit the names of nominees for the committee.

Four other provisions of the remedy order were rather open-ended. Clark approved a modest expansion of the district's magnet school program, but also directed the school district to conduct an extensive survey of the metropolitan area in order to determine whether additional magnet themes would attract non-minority students to the district. Furthermore, the judge ordered the state to proceed with its study to determine whether racial isolation could be reduced in those schools which were more than 90% black. He further instructed the state to "actively seek the cooperation of each school district in the Kansas City, Missouri metropolitan area in a voluntary interdistrict transfer program," and report back to the monitoring committee. Finally, the judge found that "in order for other components of this plan to be effective, it is imperative that improvements be made in the [district's] facilities," and approved $37 million in capital improvements. Moreover, Clark directed the school district to conduct a thorough review of other capital improvements which would be necessary to make the Kansas City public schools comparable to neighboring suburban schools.

In all, Clark's first remedy order required expenditures totaling nearly $88 million, more than three-fourths of which fell to the state. Even so, Clark recognized that the school district would be unable to provide its share of just over $20 million. In light of the district's tight finances and "because of the extreme unlikelihood, due to the recent history of tax levy defeats and time constraints, that a tax levy proposal would be received favorably by two-thirds of the [district's] voting patrons," Clark ordered that the state's Proposition C tax levy rollback be enjoined for one year. Under Proposition C, Kansas City's $3.75 tax levy was to be rolled back to $3.26 in 1985, thereby reducing the district's operating budget by approximately $4 million. By enjoining the Proposition C rollback for a year, Clark hoped to assure that the district could pay its share of the plan while providing the district with sufficient time to secure approval for a tax levy increase.

The June 14, 1985 ruling was only the first of dozens of remedial orders issued by Judge Clark, but it is remarkable how clearly the order sketched the broad strokes of Kansas City's desegregation efforts for the next ten years. In particular, those sections of the order addressing educational improvements, voluntary transfers between the city and the suburbs, magnet schools, and capital improvements, became the framework of the desegregation plan. Over the course of the next several years, each of these components assumed larger proportions as the plan was expanded and more clearly articulated. Moreover, the plaintiffs, school district, and Judge Clark all came to the conclusion that these components were inter-related and addressed what the court had deemed to be the primary objectives of the remedy. Essentially, Judge Clark, as well as the attorneys for the school district and the plaintiffs, adopted the position that the remedy should accomplish three major objectives. First, it should erase the remaining vestiges of segregation in the district. Second, the remedy should improve the educational opportunities for all Kansas City students at least to the point where they were comparable to the surrounding suburban districts. Third, it should foster additional racial integration by drawing in white students from the suburbs and private schools, and providing opportunities for inner city black students to attend suburban schools. Improving facilities, offering specialized curricular themes, and enhancing the district's educational programs were essential to remedy the past effects of segregation and to promote equal educational opportunities for the city's students. Each of those remedial measures was also considered to be crucial to the effort to draw in additional white transfer students who would promote greater racial integration in the district.

In order for the remedial plans to realize their maximum potential for improving educational opportunity and promoting racial integration, Clark's first remedial order endorsed the notion that additional, system-wide improvements could be in order. In doing so, he tacitly encouraged the school district to develop fantastically expensive proposals for additional magnet schools and capital improvements. Furthermore, by enjoining Proposition C, Clark signaled his willingness to authorize the fiscal adjustments necessary to finance the plan. Attaining the three major objectives of the desegregation remedy would, of course, demand substantial financial commitments from the state and the school district. Securing funds for the school district's share of the remedy threatened to be the most significant obstacle to realizing the main goals of the remedy. In fact, the school district continued to experience extreme difficulty in meeting its fiscal obligations as the cost of the remedy rose. The provision enjoining the Proposition C rollback in the June 1985 order was but the first of several extraordinary fiscal measures imposed by Judge Clark. Ultimately, the question of what limits the constitution imposed on the judge's authority to ensure funding of the ever-expanding desegregation program in Kansas City would reach the United States Supreme Court in 1989.

Appeals

Following the June 1985 remedial order, the appeals phase of the Kansas City suit began in earnest. Throughout the trial and remedy hearings, attorneys on all sides of the case predicted that numerous elements of Judge Clark's 1984 and 1985 orders would be appealed to the Eighth Circuit Court in St. Louis. By November 1985, those predictions had been borne out. The plaintiffs and the Kansas City school district joined in appealing the dismissal of the suburban school districts and the denial of interdistrict relief in the suit. The plaintiffs also appealed the dismissal of HUD from the proceedings. The state appealed the scope of Clark's first remedy order and the provision that the state should bear roughly three-fourths of the cost of the remedy. Attorneys for the state sought a less expensive remedy which would be more evenly divided by the defendants. The Kansas City school district also appealed the remedy's scope and the division of expenses. Unlike Missouri, however, the school district sought the inclusion of additional programs in the remedy and argued that the state alone should provide funding for many of the remedial programs. Kansas City's appeal also sought once again to have the school district reinstated as a plaintiff in the case, this time in hopes of having their legal fees reimbursed by the state. In mid-November 1985, all of these issues were argued before the eight judges of the appellate court sitting *en banc*.

Judges of the Eighth Circuit Court had a reputation for being staunch defenders of civil rights claims. They had ruled on some of the nation's most difficult school desegregation cases, including the integration of the Little Rock, Arkansas, schools in the late 1950s. Faced with massive white resistance, obstruction and intimidation, the appellate judges had ordered that the integration plan in Little Rock proceed despite a year wrought with tension following the introduction of nine black students at Central High School. Between 1954 and 1984, the Eighth Circuit had continually reaffirmed its commitment to school integration, issuing nearly seventy opinions on desegregation plans. One attorney not involved with the Kansas City case characterized the Eighth Circuit as "hell on wheels," claiming that the judges "have a tendency to find violations much quicker than any other circuit in the country." Given the circuit's record on civil rights issues, Gary Orfield, a University of Chicago political scientist and an expert witness for the Kansas City plaintiffs, suggested there was "a very strong possibility that the dismissal of the suburbs will be overturned." A few years earlier, the Eighth Circuit had approved interdistrict remedies in the St. Louis area, and Conway County, Arkansas.

In the Kansas City's *Jenkins* suit, however, a majority of the eight appellate judges found no basis for ordering an interdistrict remedy. By a vote of five to three, the judges upheld the dismissal of the suburban school districts ruling, "there was no barrier of movement to blacks" in the suburbs. The majority also agreed with Judge Clark's finding that, within four years of the 1954 *Brown v. Board of Education* decision, the suburbs had eliminated vestiges of their former segregated systems, and that there was no evidence of interdistrict cause and effect in the Kansas City area. On the housing issues, the evenly split appellate court also affirmed the dismissal of HUD, finding that the department had pursued a policy of balancing federally assisted housing initiatives in the city with similar programs in the suburbs. Furthermore, the appellate court refused to realign the Kansas City school district as a plaintiff in the suit, agreeing with Clark's determination that a conflict of interest existed. Finally, the judges modified the remedy order in ruling that the cost of some programs included in the desegregation plan should be divided equally between the state and the school district. The Eighth Circuit's judgment became final when the United States Supreme Court declined to review the case.

During the summer months of 1985, while the attorneys prepared to argue the various appeals before the appellate judges in St. Louis, school officials in Kansas City began the complex task of implementing Judge Clark's remedial order. With just over two months before the start of the school year, the pressure to hire staff and implement the programs called for in the remedy order was extreme. These efforts were further complicated by the "less than enthusiastic" posture of the district's new superintendent, Dr. Claude Perkins, who, according to some observers, failed to grasp the importance of having the remedial components operational by the start of the school year. As a result, some of the educational components included in the remedy were not implemented fully during the 1985-86 school year. The school district's fiscal situation did not improve either. Three proposals to raise the district's tax levy failed during the remedy's first year. Each of these developments deeply troubled the ten members of the newly created Desegregation Monitoring Committee appointed in August 1985. There was growing concern that the district would fail to implement all of the elements of the remedy, or that, even after having been granted millions of dollars in additional funding, the district would lack the fiscal resources to do so.

The Initial Magnet Schools Plan

Under pressure from the desegregation monitoring committee and the plaintiffs' attorneys, school officials stepped up efforts to implement the educational improvement components ordered by the court and began work on a long-range magnet schools plan for the district. School planners were pleased with the results of the school district's survey, which according to Superintendent Perkins illustrated the community's "intense interest" in magnet programs. School district officials were encouraged further by the sizeable attendance at public hearings on magnet schools conducted during the early months of 1986. In May 1986, Perkins presented a magnet school proposal to the school board.

The Perkins administration's plan focused primarily on strengthening the district's existing magnet schools. Magnet programs at Lincoln, the Southwest elementary cluster, and Swinney-Volker had all begun under Plan 6-C in 1977, but were never fully implemented due to subsequent cuts in federal funding for magnet schools. Perkins suggested that the school district should initially concentrate on fully funding the existing magnet programs in order to ensure that these programs realized their maximum "desegregative drawing power." While the programs recommended in the plan were limited to just six schools, Perkins apparently saw no need to exercise restraint in developing the budget. He estimated that the personnel, resources, educational programs, and capital improvements necessary in order to maximize the desegregative drawing power at the six schools would require no less than $62 million. The school district subsequently presented the Perkins plan, with some revisions, to the court. The school district also requested that Judge Clark extend the deadline for the submission of a long-range magnet plan, allowing school officials, the plaintiffs, and educational consultants to develop jointly a more extensive proposal.

Hearings on the Perkins magnet school plan and revisions to the educational improvement components of the initial 1985 remedial order were held during late May and early June 1986. These issues were addressed in Judge Clark's second remedy order, announced in mid-June. Clark considered restoring the school district's AAA rating to be one of the most crucial objectives of the desegregation plan. Despite having hired 125 teachers and dozens of librarians, counselor, art, music, and physical education teachers in order to reduce class sizes and meet the state's AAA standards, the school district retained its AA rating due to deficiencies in its school libraries. In the second remedial order, Clark directed the school district to "take whatever steps are necessary" to meet AAA standards, specifically instructing the school district to expand its library and media resources. The state and school district were both ordered to budget more than $4 million in order to meet AAA standards for the 1986-87 school year. Clark further directed the state to redouble its efforts to seek the cooperation of the suburbs in voluntary interdistrict transfer arrangements. During 1985-86, the state had contacted the eleven suburban districts previously named as defendants in the suit, all had refused to participate. Clark also ordered minor modifications of the summer school, full day kindergarten, tutoring programs, and reaffirmed the state's $9.2 million obligation to provide funding for the district's effective schools projects and the salaries of personnel hired in order to reduce class sizes.

The heart of the second remedy order, however, dealt with magnet schools and capital improvements. By 1986, Judge Clark was convinced that magnet schools were the most promising means of desegregating Kansas City's schools. Magnet schools, he reasoned, would not only attract non-minority students but could also be an integral part of raising student achievement in the district. Accordingly, the judge ordered that nearly $13 million, divided evenly between the state and the school district, be devoted to fully implementing magnet programs at the six existing magnet schools. Moreover, Clark concluded that in order to attract non-minority students to the magnets, extensive capital improvements were required to alleviate safety and health hazards, improve the comfort level, and make the facilities more visually attractive. With these objectives in mind, Clark ordered the state to budget an additional $12.9 million for capital improvements at the magnet schools. Finally, Clark instructed the school district to submit its long-range magnet schools proposal and its assessment of additional capital improvement needs within the next year.

Judge Clark's second remedial order was an important turning point in the Kansas City case. The judge's emergent interest in magnet schools and his willingness to order extensive capital improvements necessary to make those schools effective tools for integration fundamentally changed the scope of desegregation in Kansas City. The school district was already in the process of developing a more extensive magnet school proposal and a sweeping plan of recommendations for capital improvement projects. Prior to the June 1986 remedy order, however, it was difficult to ascertain whether Clark would order such massive and expensive plans. The June 1986 order seemed to indicate that he would, and, of equal importance to the school district, that the state would be responsible for the lion's share of the funding. The estimated cost of the numerous programs and improvements called for in the June 1986 order totaled roughly $48.5 million, of which the state was responsible for $36 million. Moreover, in August 1986 Judge Clark again came to the aid of the school district in meeting its financial obligations under the remedy orders. Due to the district's inability to secure passage of a tax levy increase, Clark ordered that the Proposition C rollback be enjoined for another year in order to allow the district to raise an additional $6.5 million for desegregation.

The Pink Plan

A comprehensive long-range plan for magnet schools was presented to the school board in late July 1986. School officials, educational consultants, and the plaintiffs' attorneys worked together for months on several color-coded versions of the plan. Ultimately, the school district settled on the so called "Pink Plan," developed primarily by two consultants, Phale Hale and Daniel Levine. The Pink Plan rested upon the novel recommendation that magnet schools should constitute the organizing principle of the entire district. Under the plan, every high school and junior high school in the district would become a magnet school, as would approximately one-half of the elementary schools. By proposing to convert so many schools to magnets the hope was that the district could avoid establishing a "two-tier" system where the magnet schools would be viewed as elite while the remaining schools would be perceived as inferior. The plan's objective was to provide opportunities for as many students as possible, including suburban whites, to enroll in the magnet programs. In order to draw additional white students to the Kansas City schools, the plan was designed with careful consideration of the magnet themes most likely to attract whites and recommended placing those programs at sites "likely to be attractive to nonminority students." In addition to the college preparatory, science and math, and applied learning magnets already in operation, the Pink Plan suggested a number of other themes, including communications, fine arts, business, public service, environmental science, computers, engineering, foreign language, classical Greek, and Latin grammar. In all, eighteen different magnet themes were recommended, and fifty-three Kansas City schools would offer one or more of the proposed magnet themes. Such a plan was bound to be expensive. The cost of implementing the Pink Plan over a six year period was projected at nearly $143 million. Moreover, just as Judge Clark had concluded that magnet schools would be ineffective unless the programs were implemented in safe, comfortable, attractive schools, the Pink Plan proposed an additional $53 million in capital improvements for the district's schools.

The school district presented its long-range magnet plan to Judge Clark in August 1986, and hearings concerning the school district proposal were conducted during September and October. At the hearings, attorneys for the state argued that the plan was hastily drafted and too costly. The state favored converting fewer schools to magnets and implementing the programs more gradually. Clark, however, favored the school district plan.

Convinced that Kansas City students were entitled to "vindication of past denial of constitutional rights" beginning immediately, the judge ordered the entire plan implemented. Magnet schools, Clark surmised, would benefit all Kansas City students as well as draw white students from private schools and the suburbs into the district. He found the costs estimated in the Pink Plan to be acceptable, concluding that, "greater educational opportunity in an integrated environment is worthy of such an investment." The school district's share of the implementation costs totaled roughly $26.5 million, while the state was ordered to contribute $116 million plus an additional $53 million for capital improvements.

Although the financing approved in Clark's order clearly favored Kansas City, it was obvious to all involved with the case that the school district would not be able to meet its share of the expenses. With this in mind, Clark suggested that the state assembly "explore the possibility of enacting legislation that would permit a district involved in a desegregation plan more versatility than it presently has to raise funds with which to support the program." When the general assembly proved unwilling or unable to enact such legislation, Clark began to consider other means of assuring that the plan would be fully funded.

Officials from the state objected to what they perceived as an overly ambitious and expensive plan, and Missouri appealed the magnet schools order to the Eighth Circuit in 1988. The appellate court, however, affirmed Clark's ruling. In reaching their decision, the three- judge panel cited two of the state's own expert witnesses who had testified that converting most of the schools to magnets was "a step in the right direction," because such a comprehensive plan avoided the difficulty of creating the perception that the magnet schools were exclusive and available only to elite students. Moreover, the appellate court affirmed Clark's distribution of the costs for implementing the magnet schools. A year later, the United States Supreme Court denied the state of Missouri's petition for a review of the Eighth Circuit's opinion, and Kansas City's ambitious magnet plan was secure.

With the approval of the long-range magnet plan, one of the components unique to school desegregation in Kansas City was in place. No other city would attempt to convert the majority of its schools to magnets, and no other city would spend so much implementing magnet themes. Nowhere else would so many students have so many choices as to their curricular options. The magnet order also touched upon what Clark, the school district, and the plaintiffs considered to be the two most important unresolved issues in Kansas City's desegregation plan – capital improvements and financing. Clark would address both of those issues in 1987.

Capital Improvements and the Hunter Report

As prescribed by Judge Clark in his first remedy order, the school district had begun its assessment of capital improvement needs in 1985. The initial survey was conducted by E. Allen Roth, a local architect. Roth noted numerous serious problems in the nineteen buildings he assessed, ranging from peeling paint to faulty heating and cooling systems and dangerously old electrical wiring. Roth's preliminary findings convinced the school board that a comprehensive survey of all of the district's schools was in order. Toward that end, the school district contracted three architectural firms to report on the improvements necessary to eliminate safety and health hazards, improve the comfort level in the schools, and render the buildings more attractive. After examining seventy-nine schools and two athletic facilities, the architectural team presented the results of the second study in November 1985. The report recommended nearly $170 million in improvements. The district did not, however, seek approval of the capital improvements plans in 1985. Rather, attention was focused on the long-range magnet schools proposal, with the understanding that further capital improvements could be required should the court approve of the magnet proposal.

Judge Clark's order regarding the long-range magnet plan in November 1986 fundamentally changed the scope of the school district's capital improvement needs. Bearing in mind that the implementation of magnet programs required additional enhancements to the schools, the school district brought in another consultant, Dr. Richard C. Hunter, to update the 1985 study and to recommend additional improvements necessary to implement the magnet schools concept. Dr. Hunter was a professor of educational administration at the University of North Carolina who had previously worked as superintendent of schools in Richmond, Virginia, and Dayton, Ohio. He was a highly respected administrator with extensive experience in assessing the building needs of school districts such as Kansas City. As superintendent of the Richmond schools, Hunter had overseen the preparation of a comprehensive capital improvements plan for that district.

In preparing his report on the Kansas City schools, Dr. Hunter visited every school in the district and some twenty suburban schools for purposes of comparison. The architectural firms which had compiled the 1985 study updated their previous recommendations and cost estimates, and incorporated those additional improvements which Hunter deemed necessary in order to implement the magnet programs and bring the city's school facilities to a level comparable to the suburban districts. In early 1987, the revised capital improvement plan, the "Hunter Report," was completed.

Kansas City's schools were, in Hunter's assessment, "generally very old and in poor condition." He calculated the average age of the district's eighty-one school buildings to be fifty-four years, but noted that eleven schools had been in use for more than seventy-five years. Asserting that the report included "only those [improvements] deemed absolutely essential to the implementation of the [magnet schools] program," Hunter concluded that massive renovations and new construction were in order. After examining all of the district's schools and studying enrollment projections, the report recommended that seventeen schools be demolished, twenty-one new schools be constructed, and all of the remaining buildings undergo renovation. The cost of the plan was projected at roughly $265 million.

Dr. Hunter's school-by-school delineation of the improvements necessary in order to convert to magnet schools revealed just how comprehensive the district's make-over would be. For example, the Greek classical magnets, which would emphasize the development of both mind and body, would all require outdoor running tracks, larger gymnasiums, softball diamonds, soccer fields, and indoor swimming pools. The capstone of the Greek classical magnets, a new Central High School, would have a field house with an indoor track, basketball courts, racquetball and handball courts, and a natatorium with an Olympic size pool, a diving platform, and seating for 400 spectators. Those schools designated as computer magnets would have one computer for every student. Environmental science magnets would all have greenhouses, botany laboratories, animal storage facilities, an amphitheater, and, at East High School, a twenty-five acre farm. Science and math magnets would all have expanded laboratory rooms and planetariums at the junior high and high school levels. The fine arts magnets would all have dance studios, auditoriums, acoustically treated music rooms, and classrooms for art. The jewel of the fine arts theme was a new Paseo High School. Among other accouterments, the facilities at Paseo were to include studios for photography, painting, graphic design, and ceramics, an art gallery, two dance studios, facilities for movie screening and editing, a recording studio, two large rooms for instrumental and vocal music, a little theater, and a 1000 seat auditorium. Even the city's next generation of school desegregation litigators could begin their training in the Kansas City magnets. Capital improvements proposed for the district's public service magnet, Northeast High School, included a mock courtroom and law library.

After the school board approved the Hunter Report, it was submitted to the Desegregation Monitoring Committee. In agreement with Dr. Hunter's assessment, the committee found the district's schools to be desperately wanting. Conveying the report to Judge Clark, committee chairman Dr. Eugene Eubanks wrote that the condition of Kansas City's schools was a "painfully obvious" vestige of segregation. The committee concluded that the schools were "seriously deteriorated and dangerous," and impaired the educational process. Moreover, without improvements, Eubanks argued, the condition of the schools alone could "frustrate the desegregative goals of the Court." The committee agreed that the improvements suggested in the Hunter Report were essential to the desegregation effort. The report was approved unanimously and forwarded to Judge Clark in February 1987.

Hearings on the school district's capital improvements proposal convened in August 1987. As expected, the state strongly objected to the $265 million proposal. Attorneys for the state argued that any additional capital improvements in the Kansas City schools should be closely scrutinized, inasmuch as, Clark's previous orders had already approved more than $110 million in capital improvements. As an alternative to the school district plan, the state developed its own proposal which called for $61 million in improvements to the district's schools. The merits of the state and school district plans, as well as the means of financing the improvements, were argued for a week, and the hearing closed on August 12. One month later Clark announced his decision on the capital improvements plans.

As had been the case in Clark's previous remedial orders, his September 15, 1987 order favored the school district. Clark found the overall condition of the Kansas City schools to be "generally depressing," and that over the years, some of the city's schools had "literally rotted." He concluded that such facilities adversely affected the learning environment and discouraged parents from enrolling their children in the city's schools. Clark agreed with the state's argument that much of the deterioration of the Kansas City schools was attributable to deferred maintenance. He also found, however, that by failing to act affirmatively to eradicate the vestiges of segregation in the school district, the state had "contributed to an atmosphere which prevented the Kansas City, Missouri School District from raising the funds to maintain its schools." The judge concluded that correcting those deficiencies which stemmed from vestiges of segregation demanded massive district-wide improvements.

Clark found the state's plan inadequate because it failed to consider those measures necessary to make the Kansas City schools comparable to suburban facilities. He objected to the state's "patch and repair approach," concluding that such methods would not achieve the level of visual attractiveness that the court sought. Following the state's plan, Clark wrote, would result in "floor coverings with unsightly sections of mismatched carpeting and tile, and individual walls possessing different shades of paint." Moreover, Clark found that the state plan included no provision for those improvements needed in order to implement the magnet programs.

The school district plan, on the other hand, promised to erase the vestiges of segregation, provide for the implementation of the magnet schools plan, and raise the city's schools to a level comparable to the suburbs. Each of these objectives, Clark reasoned, were appropriate in order to assure the success of the desegregation plan and restore the plaintiff school children to the position that they would have occupied absent any constitutional violations. He found the school district's estimated costs to be reasonable for such extensive work, in fact he termed the proposal "conservative," given the enrollment projections for the following several years. Even so, the judge did not approve of the entire proposal, choosing instead to order only those improvements scheduled for completion within the next three years. Nevertheless, during that three-year period, the school district plan called for closing sixteen schools, building seventeen new schools, and renovations to twenty-eight more schools. The cost of these projects was estimated at roughly $187 million, and Clark ordered that those expenses be split evenly between the state and school district.

Financing the Desegregation Remedy

Having authorized nearly $190 million in capital improvements, the judge turned to the issue of financing the work. Clark fully understood the school district's desperate financial condition. Despite having twice enjoined the Proposition C rollback, the district continued to experience budget deficits and had been unable to fulfill its financial obligations in the previous remedy orders. In fact, the district was some $62 million short of the funds necessary to meet its share of the expenses already approved in Clark's remedial orders. Furthermore, when the district's financial obligations under the previously approved remedial measures, magnet schools, and capital improvements plans were projected over the next five years, the deficit grew to more than $280 million.

By September 1987, Judge Clark found the situation intolerable. He insisted that the desegregation remedy be fully funded, but also recognized that the school district had "exhausted all available means of raising additional revenue." The city's voters had proven most reluctant to approve measures which would have allowed the school district to fund the remedy. Between November 1986 and March 1987, four proposed tax levy increases and one bond issue had failed to win the approval of Kansas City voters. Weighing the constitutional rights of the taxpayers against those of the plaintiff school children, Clark found that "the balance is clearly in favor of the students who are helpless without the aid of this Court." He reasoned that the court was required to "exercise its broad equitable powers," and issue an order that would enable the school district to raise the revenue needed in order to finance the remedial measures.

Two fiscal measures designed to provide the school district with millions of dollars in additional revenue were included in the September 1987 order. A 1.5% state income tax surcharge was imposed on residents and nonresidents of Kansas City who provided services or conducted business within the boundaries of the school district. Revenue raised by the income tax surcharge was to be committed to retiring $150 million in capital improvement bonds, which the school district was ordered to issue. The second measure was aimed at the tax levy. When the rollback authorized under Proposition C was applied in Kansas City, the school district's tax levy plummeted to $2.05 per $100 of assessed valuation, the lowest rate in the metropolitan area. Clark found that the district required an additional $27 million annually in order to pay its share of the desegregation costs, excluding capital improvements, over the next five years. With these figures in mind, Clark ordered that the school district's tax levy be nearly doubled to $4.00 per $100 in assessed valuation through the 1991-92 fiscal year.

Clark's September 15, 1987 order is viewed by many legal observers as the most infamous of his many decisions in the Kansas City case. Not only did he authorize nearly $190 in additional capital improvements for the school district, but it could be argued that he trampled on the Constitution in providing for the financing of those projects. Overnight, taxpayers organized to fight the judicially imposed surcharge and levy increase, and state officials vowed to appeal both the massive capital improvements order and the fiscal measures imposed to finance the projects. The state's objection to the surcharge and the levy increase represented a reversal in the state's position on the fiscal issues involved in the remedy. Previously, attorneys for the state of Missouri had argued passionately that the school district pay its share of the costs for educational improvements, magnet schools, and capital improvements. However, just as the September order had provided Kansas City with the means of meeting its fiscal obligations, the state appealed the order. The appeals of the September order were heard by a three judge panel of the Eighth Circuit Court in March 1988.

The Tax Levy Appeal

The appeals of Judge Clark's tax orders revolved around the issue of whether a federal judge possessed the constitutional authority to order taxes. Attorneys for the state, as well as numerous *amicus curiae* briefs filed in opposition to the tax measures, plainly asserted that Clark had no authority in this regard. In part, the state offered an historical argument to support its position. Citing the Federalist Papers Number 78, which asserted that the judiciary "has no influence over either the sword or the purse," the state's attorneys insisted that the framers of the Constitution intended to restrict tightly the authority of the courts on revenue issues. By imposing the tax measures, the state argued that Clark had usurped the legislature's authority to levy taxes, and in doing so had violated the reserved powers of the state under the Tenth Amendment, the doctrine of separation of powers, and the principles of federal-state comity.

The appellate court announced its decision on the tax measures in August 1988. The three judge panel overturned the 1.5% income tax surcharge finding that it intruded upon local fiscal affairs. The tax had been imposed on a geographic area not consistent with any existing tax jurisdiction, and thereby had necessitated the use of new regulations, forms, and procedures, as well as the creation of a new tax collection agency. The judges of the Eighth Circuit reasoned that the imposition of a tax which required such extraordinary measures unconstitutionally interfered with the right of local jurisdictions to manage their own financial affairs. At the time of the judges' ruling, the surcharge was generating approximately $30 million annually, which then had to be refunded. Thus, although the state of Missouri had prevailed on appeal, the school district was unable to fully meet its share of the remedy's expenses. Consequently, the state's contributions to the desegregation plan increased commensurately as the appellate court ruled that should the school district be unable to fund its portion of the remedy, "the remainder must be paid by the State."

On the property tax issue, the Eighth Circuit dismissed the arguments that a judicially imposed tax measure violated the state's reserved powers under the Constitution. In *Milliken II*, the judges found that the Supreme Court had ruled that the Tenth Amendment could not be invoked to resist a court order properly imposed in order to remedy prior state actions which had violated the Fourteenth Amendment's equal protection clause. In short, the appellate court ruled that because the state of Missouri had violated the Fourteenth Amendment by failing to dismantle its segregated schools system, an appropriate remedy ordered by Judge Clark could not be construed to offend the reserved powers of the state under the Tenth Amendment.

The Eighth Circuit panel went on to address the state's arguments concerning separation of powers and comity. The judges found that several state laws "have imposed a unique fiscal disadvantage" on the

Kansas City school district. The panel concluded that the Missouri statute requiring two-thirds majorities in order to raise the tax levy above $3.75 per $100 of assessed valuation, the Proposition C rollback, and the Hancock Amendment, which provided that tax levies would not increase even after the value of property was reassessed to account for inflation, all had a substantial negative impact on the school district's finances. Because these laws strictly circumscribed the school district's ability to raise revenue, the Eighth Circuit judges reasoned that the district court would be powerless to implement a remedy, if it were compelled to operate within those limits. Such circumstances, the panel concluded, offended the supremacy clause in Article III of the Constitution. The supremacy of the United States Constitution, the judges asserted, superceded any state laws which impeded the implementation of a remedy designed to redress constitutional violations. Therefore, the Eighth Circuit affirmed the tax levy increase and found that Judge Clark had "clear authority" to impose the measure. Nevertheless, the Eighth Circuit suggested that in the future, the district court should strive to avoid imposing tax measures on its authority alone. The judges agreed with the state that the principles of federal-state comity required that the district court use "minimally intrusive methods to remedy constitutional violations." Bearing this in mind, the panel proposed that "a preferable method" of raising revenue in the school district would be to authorize the school board to submit a proposed levy to the agencies responsible for collecting taxes, and then the district court could enjoin those state statutes which would limit or reduce the levy below the amount submitted by the school board. Such an arrangement would permit the school district to fully fund its share of the remedy without offending the principles of comity.

Unsatisfied with the outcome of the tax question at the Eighth Circuit, the state of Missouri appealed to the United States Supreme Court. In its petition to the Court, the state reiterated its arguments concerning the Tenth Amendment, comity, and separation of powers. Moreover, the state argued that the tax issue was a product of the scope of the desegregation remedy in Kansas City and thereby sought review of Judge Clark's remedial orders as well. The state's attorneys insisted that, had Judge Clark not authorized the sweeping magnet schools proposal and capital improvement plan, the tax order would never have been necessary. The Court agreed to review the tax issue, but declined to hear the appeal on the scope of the desegregation remedy in Kansas City. By limiting its review to the tax measure alone, the Court allowed the implementation of the magnet schools and capital improvement plans to proceed. For the time being, the framework of Kansas City's desegregation remedy was safe. The tax issue was argued before the Supreme Court on October 30, 1989.

At the Supreme Court, the justices split five to four on the tax issue. Writing for the majority, Justice White adopted the same position that the Eighth Circuit Court had staked out in its ruling a year earlier. White found that the tax increase contravened the principles of comity and that the district court had "abused its discretion in imposing the tax itself." Nevertheless, White asserted that "a court order directing a local government body to levy its own taxes is plainly a judicial act within the power of a federal court." White cited "a long and venerable line of cases" in which federal courts had exercised such authority in compelling states to levy taxes and raise revenue in order to meet their debt obligations. The supremacy clause, Justice White wrote, demands that local and state governments "fulfill the requirements that the Constitution imposes on them." In this case, the obligations imposed on the school district and state by the Fourteenth Amendment demanded that desegregation plans be fully funded. In order to finance the remedy, the Supreme Court endorsed the Eighth Circuit's suggestion that the school district levy property taxes at a rate adequate to fund the desegregation plans while the district court enjoined those state laws which would have otherwise prevented the district from exercising this power. "Directing local government institutions to devise and implement remedies," White wrote, "protects the function of those institutions," and adhered to the principles of comity. Moreover, White asserted that such an arrangement removes the judiciary from the position of directly imposing a taxation measure and "places the responsibility for solutions to the problems of segregation upon those who have themselves created the problems."

Writing for the four dissenting justices, Justice Kennedy sought to lay bare the transparency of the majority opinion. Kennedy concluded that the majority's ruling which held that the direct imposition of taxes was beyond judicial authority, but which permitted the district court to order the school board to impose such taxes was "convenient formalism." He argued that the majority opinion had announced "an expansion of power in the Federal judiciary beyond all precedent." Kennedy asserted that the framers of the Constitution recognized that "taxation was not a proper area for judicial involvement." He maintained that confining taxation authority to the legislative branches "was not random," but rather reflected the "ideal that the power of taxation must be under the control of those who are taxed," as opposed to unelected, life-tenured federal jurists. By granting federal judges authority in the "sensitive" realm of taxation, Kennedy feared that the majority opinion "could threaten fundamental alteration of the form of government our Constitution embodies."

Justice Kennedy's impassioned arguments regarding the power of taxation and the federal judiciary notwithstanding, the Supreme Court's 1990 *Jenkins* decision assured that funding for Kansas City's desegregation remedy was secure. In essence, the Supreme Court's ruling on the tax measure chided Judge Clark for imposing the tax increase himself but also remanded the case to his courtroom so that he could direct the school district to raise the tax levy. The Court also upheld Judge Clark's authority to ignore the outcome of tax levy votes and enjoin the state laws requiring two-thirds majorities for levy increases. Not surprisingly, the school board voted in short order to comply with the Supreme Court's instructions and the revenue raised by the $4.00 tax levy continued to flow into the district.

Conclusions

In 1990, all of the elements that would characterize the desegregation plan for the Kansas City schools were in place. Hundreds of millions of dollars were devoted to educational improvements and raising student achievement in the district. In order to restore the district's AAA rating, scores of teachers and dozens of librarians, counselors, and support staff were hired, and millions of dollars spent upgrading school libraries. The process of converting the district's traditional schools to magnets was also well underway. Extensive capital improvements and new school construction projects had begun, and the tax levy had been raised to ensure that funding for the desegregation plan was secure. The plaintiffs and the school district may not have realized their initial goal of consolidating the metropolitan area's schools into a single district, but for a period of more than three years nearly everything else that the school district and plaintiffs argued was necessary in order to fashion an effective remedy in Kansas City had been approved by Judge Clark. In lieu of ordering a metropolitan solution, Clark had overseen the creation of the most expensive and expansive magnet school system in the country.

Clearly, the single most important and controversial figure in the creation of the sweeping remedial plan for the Kansas City schools was Judge Russell Clark. To his critics, Clark represented the worst excesses of school desegregation jurisprudence. Not surprisingly, he was roundly criticized for the tax measures imposed in order to finance the remedy, but numerous components in his other remedial orders were also disparaged. Clark's approval of the lavish designs for the district's magnet schools as well as his orders insisting that the comfort level and attractiveness of the district's schools be made comparable to suburban schools were frequently pointed to as examples of the judge's inclination to exceed the limits of what was necessary in order to correct the constitutional violations. Clark's defenders, on the other hand, tended to perceive the judge's orders as necessary steps in remedying what a great many Kansas City residents viewed as a depressingly unsatisfactory school system. Regardless of one's perspective on the appropriateness of some of the remedial measures ordered by the judge, there was no denying that, having dismissed the suburban districts from the suit, Clark was prepared to use his authority to fashion the most equitable remedy possible for the Kansas City schools. In doing so, the judge may have lost sight of his own caveat to "bear in mind cost factors." Nevertheless, the transformation of the Kansas City schools was nothing short of remarkable – an inner city school system that just seven years earlier had been awash with fiscal problems, crumbling schools, discontented teachers, serious deficiencies in materials and equipment, and substandard student achievement, was in the process of being remade by judicial order.

What remained to be seen was whether this fabulous creation could fulfill the lofty expectations which the judge and the attorneys for the school district and the plaintiffs had invested in it. By 1990, more than one-half a billion dollars had been committed to rebuilding and reorganizing the school district, and parties on all sides of the suit eagerly anticipated the results. In particular, student achievement was expected to rise and significant numbers of white students were expected to be drawn into the magnet schools from the suburbs and the city's private and parochial schools.

Having committed tens of millions of dollars to educational improvements in the district, Clark and the parties in the case sought some means of evaluating the progress being made in raising the distressingly low levels of academic achievement in the inner city. Standardized test results would emerge as the annual acid test of student achievement. The other primary means of assessing the success of the desegregation plan was the number of voluntary transfers between the city and suburbs. Transfer students in some respects became the measuring stick by which the attractiveness of Kansas City's magnet programs and facilities improvements were judged. Clark and the school district fully expected that as the magnet schools came on line, significant numbers of white students would transfer into the Kansas City schools. However, neither the expected gains in student achievement nor the expected number of white transfer students materialized as rapidly as had been anticipated. By the early 1990s, the entire magnet schools experiment and its profligate spending were again assailed by critics, and in 1995, the scope of the desegregation remedy for the Kansas City schools would be argued before the United States Supreme Court.

CHAPTER 8

Questionable Attraction

Kansas City's Magnet School System, 1985-1995

At precisely 9:00 in the morning on November 29, 1990, the explosives were detonated and the exterior walls at Paseo High School began to topple. For sixty-four years, Paseo had stood as one of the city's most cherished architectural monuments. Nicknamed "the Castle on the Hill," Paseo was a truly beautiful school. Its Gothic features were constructed of a type of limestone found nowhere else in the country, and the school's five-story tower offered a commanding view of midtown Kansas City. When Paseo opened in 1926, it was considered to be a state-of-the-art school, but by 1990 the rapidly changing Kansas City school district had little use for the building. Paseo High School had become a victim of the district's magnet schools and capital improvement plans. When the dust settled from the explosives, a roar went up from the sizable crowd of tearful protestors gathered for the event. Much of the front facade and the school's tower remained standing, but soon a wrecking ball brought down those sections as well. By the end of the week, little was left of Paseo but rubble and even that had diminished as former students carried off chunks of limestone from the demolition site as momentos.

By 1990, the school district's plans for magnet programs and capital improvements had become a juggernaut of sorts. By virtue of Judge Clark's decisions announced during the remedial phase of the desegregation suit, the school district's breathtaking plans for remaking the district and its ambitious timetable for completing the projects had been ordered. Resistance to the sort of institutional momentum that the desegregation plan had gathered was essentially futile. Organizations that attempted to compel the school district to reconsider the costs and direction of the desegregation plan were overwhelmed by Judge Clark, the school board, and the attorneys who had argued in favor of the plan.

In the case of Paseo, those opposed to the demolition of the school were well organized and relatively numerous. The "Friends of Paseo," an organization of students, alumni, and other supporters, had come together in the months following the school board's 1989 decision to tear down the school so that a new magnet high school and middle school for the performing and visual arts could be built on the site. Throughout the early months of 1990, the group lobbied the school board to reconsider its decision, and sought to block demolition of the school by having Paseo added to the city's registry of historic buildings. Paseo students also actively protested against the demolition of their school. The students staged sit-ins, circulated petitions opposing the school board's plans, held rallies, and organized protest marches. Eighteen Paseo students filed lawsuits in the federal and county courts seeking an order to prohibit the district from destroying the school. The plaintiffs named in the students' suits were members of the junior class who argued that by displacing the students prior to their senior year at Paseo, the school district's action threatened their opportunities of earning athletic and academic scholarships.

Despite opposition, the school district's plans for the Paseo site proceeded on schedule. Considerations of the historic and aesthetic value of a school, or whether the desegregation plan victimized certain students were clearly secondary to the crusade to remake the district. The students' lawsuits were dismissed in October, and the effort to place Paseo on the historic register failed to stymie the district. The school district had already demonstrated that it did not consider the historic registry sacrosanct. Booker T. Washington School was listed in the Kansas City Register of Historic Places, but the school was demolished to make way for the new Crispus Attucks Elementary, a communications magnet. As Arthur Benson, the attorney for the plaintiff school children in *Jenkins v. Missouri* put it: "The district's mission is education and desegregation, not historic preservation."

From the perspective of the school district, the most cost effective site for the new high school and middle school fine arts academies was Paseo. Although the school was an attractive building, Arthur Benson maintained that there were "mega-problems with [the existing] Paseo." Among other difficulties, Benson noted that the library was located in the school's basement and lacked accessibility for handicapped students, several classrooms were too small to be of practical use, and the limited capacity of the school's cafeteria located in a long, narrow room on the top floor necessitated that lunch shifts begin in the middle of the morning. If the new fine arts magnets were to be visually attractive and draw in additional white students, Benson and the school board maintained that Paseo had to be replaced, and Judge Clark agreed. The new Paseo Academy of Fine and Performing Arts, a beautiful school in its own right, opened in 1992.

The heavy-handedness which the school district and Judge Clark demonstrated with respect to Paseo was not an isolated incident. Clark's order raising the tax levy to $4.00 is perhaps the most obvious example of the lengths to which the judge was willing to go in order to implement the desegregation plan. On a smaller scale, however, there were numerous episodes where the plans developed by the school district and approved by the court wreaked havoc on the lives of individual citizens. For example, in 1987, the school district unveiled plans for a new magnet school, Gladstone Elementary, in the northeast section of the city. In order to expand the site for the school, the Gladstone proposal included a provision to demolish fifteen homes. Similarly, at Westport High School Judge Clark approved the razing of more than fifty homes and twelve apartment buildings in order to add athletic facilities and a parking structure at the school. In 1995, fifty-seven more homes were slated to be demolished so that the school district could add athletic facilities at the Foreign Language Middle School. Given the traumatic impact that the school district's magnet schools and capital improvement plans had on some Kansas City residents, it was not surprising that numerous critics of the desegregation plan emerged.

Criticism

Criticism of the objectives, implementation, and expense of the Kansas City desegregation plan began almost as soon as Judge Clark read the first remedial order. The numerous appeals of the judge's remedial orders and the taxation measures were clearly one vehicle for attacking the plans crafted by the plaintiffs' attorneys and the school district. Moreover, some of Clark's orders alienated patrons who otherwise supported the desegregation plan. The tax order in particular drew the ire of thousands of Kansas City residents. Clark, however, was by no means the lone target of criticism. Implementation of the desegregation plan in Kansas City also brought the school board and central administration under intense scrutiny.

The scope of the desegregation plan in Kansas City assured that the school district would experience some difficulty in efficiently managing and implementing the court ordered improvements. The components announced in the first remedial order alone placed a staggering burden on the school district. Judge Clark's June 1985 order required that the district hire more than 200 teachers, librarians, and counselors, distribute $17 million in effective schools grants throughout the district, upgrade the school libraries, manage $37 million in capital improvement projects, conduct extensive surveys of additional capital improvement needs and the potential drawing power of various magnet school themes, and undertake major expansions of the district's summer school, early childhood education, extended day kindergarten, and tutorial programs. In scrambling to initiate each of these components, several of the programs were delayed or poorly implemented, administrative oversight was haphazard, and the accounting was sloppy.

In its first annual report to Judge Clark, the Desegregation Monitoring Committee (DMC) made note of "a number of serious problems [which] have hampered implementation" of the desegregation remedy. According to the DMC report, many school principals were not well informed as to the objectives of the remedial programs, several desegregation programs were understaffed, a large portion of building administrators and staff were confused regarding the availability of effective schools grants, and the school district had "seriously underestimated" the deficiencies in the school libraries. These shortcomings, the DMC lamented, had deprived students of the full benefits of the desegregation plan and resulted in Kansas City retaining its AA rating from the state. The DMC concluded that perhaps the single largest problem was that the school district's administration lacked sufficient numbers of well organized and competent leaders to successfully implement the programs required in the judge's order.

In addition to the more grievous problems encountered in implementing the remedial programs, the DMC found the school district's accounting suspect. The committee's report indicated that the financial data supplied by the school district changed so frequently that "it was difficult to place any confidence in the information." A subsequent investigation by Margaret Kelly, the state of Missouri auditor, confirmed the DMC's suspicions. Kelly reported that in the first year alone, the school district misspent nearly $3 million and on occasion had shifted funds earmarked for desegregation into other accounts in order to cover operating expenses unrelated to the court ordered remedy. Although the school district convincingly rebutted many of the state auditor's allegations, Kansas City's accounting of the budget for the remedy remained highly suspect.

The massive expansion of the desegregation program approved in Judge Clark's magnet schools and capital improvements orders in 1986 and 1987 compounded the school district's difficulties in managing the financial aspects of implementing the programs. In its annual reports, the DMC budget subcommittee frequently complained that the district's accounting methods had grown "progressively worse," and maintained that school district had "undertaken a task which its current personnel was not capable of completing." On one hand, the DMC repeatedly expressed concerns regarding the school district's inability to exhaust the funding ordered by the court for educational improvements. The DMC found that over the course of the first six years of desegregation under the district court orders, Kansas City only spent approximately 85% of the money approved for educational components. By failing to exhaust the funds available for educational enhancements, the monitoring committee concluded that the district denied the plaintiff school children of the full benefits of the desegregation remedy.

On the other hand, the DMC also noted that some components of the desegregation plan were consistently well over budget. The capital improvements program was particularly worrisome in this regard. In its 1988-89 summary, the DMC reported that the improvements to the district's facilities were projected at almost $20 million over budget. Over-runs at certain schools were positively shocking. In the initial capital improvements plan, the new Central High School, with its dual themes of computers unlimited and classical Greek education, was projected to cost about $15.2 million. In order to accommodate design and program modifications, the budget for Central was subsequently revised and increased to almost $26 million. Even so, when Central opened in 1990, the final cost for the awe-inspiring school stood at $32 million. Although such cost over-runs may have troubled the DMC, the school district was somewhat less concerned. Judge Clark had ordered the state of Missouri to provide the balance of the funding when the school district was unable to finance its share. Such an arrangement, the DMC mused, assured that school officials in Kansas City had "little incentive to realistically control the desegregation plan costs."

In addition to accounting problems, more fundamental weaknesses in the district's plan were revealed in the monitoring committee's annual reports. The most damning of the DMC's criticisms involved the failure of the magnet schools to produce the dramatic results which the court and the monitoring committee had anticipated. In its 1987 summary, the DMC reported that its members were "generally optimistic" that the magnet schools, educational enhancements, and capital improvements approved by Judge Clark would fulfill the expectations of greater integration and higher achievement in the Kansas City schools. Just three years later, however, the DMC found that the magnets had "fallen far short of the ability to deliver on their promises." In the interim, the DMC had become aware of a multitude of problems with the magnet schools.

Attracting White Transfer Students

One of the stated objectives of Kansas City's magnet schools desegregation plan was that additional white students would be attracted to the district in order to promote integration. This consideration profoundly influenced the development of the school district's magnet schools proposal and capital improvements plans. In order to draw in significant numbers of white transfer students, school planners in Kansas City reasoned that the quality and attractiveness of the district's facilities must be comparable to those located in the suburbs, and the district's curriculum must offer unique and specialized opportunities unavailable elsewhere in the metropolitan area. Clark agreed and approved the plans fully expecting the number of white students to rise as non-minority students abandoned the suburban schools and the city's private schools in favor of the superior educational programs and facilities available in Kansas City's public schools.

As the magnets were implemented across the district, however, it became clear that the specialized schools were not attracting the number of white transfer students that had been anticipated. Between 1985 and 1989, the first four years of magnet schools in Kansas City, the white enrollment in the district actually fell by nearly 900 students, precisely the opposite effect that the magnets were designed to produce. School planners had projected steady increases in white enrollment as more families became familiar with the advantages of smaller class sizes and the specialized curriculum available at the magnets. Across the metropolitan area, however, interest in the magnets was tepid at best. One study conducted by an independent research team in 1989 revealed that just 12% of private school parents and 8% of suburban parents had ever considered sending their children to the Kansas City magnets. Consequently, non-minority transfer students were slow to materialize, and the school district consistently failed to meet its goals for drawing in white students. For the 1989-90 school year, the district established the goal of attracting 1,500 non-minority transfer students, but only 278 white students transferred to the district. Two years later, the number of non-minority transfer students attending in Kansas City was up to 715, but still well shy of the goal set at 2,100. By the mid-1990s, the district was more successful in attracting non-minorities. The number of white transfer students attending the Kansas City public schools peaked during the 1994-95 school year at 1,476. Even so, the racial composition of the district had not improved as a result of the desegregation plan. In 1983, the year in which the *Jenkins v. Missouri* desegregation trial began, minority students comprised 72.6% of the district's enrollment. Eleven years later, minorities accounted for almost 76% of the district's students.

The difficulty in attracting significant numbers of white transfer students was compounded by a complementary problem involving the failure of the magnet schools to retain transfer students from one year to the next. In the mid-1990s, only about 65% of the non-minority transfer students enrolled in the Kansas City public schools renewed their transfers and returned to the district the following year. School district data indicated that while more than 70% of the white transfer students at the elementary level returned the following year, less than one-half did so at the middle school level. Such evidence did not bode well for the school district's efforts to promote integration in the upper grades. Moreover, the school district's inability to retain roughly one of every three white transfer students year to year rendered progress toward meeting the goal of a 60% minority enrollment district-wide virtually impossible. On an annual basis, the school district was required to replace those transfer students who opted not to return to the district, as well as attract hundreds more whites. This proved to be a challenge too large for the school district's personnel.

In part, the school district's inability to attract and retain non-minority transfer students was related to the inadequacy of the recruitment effort. The 1990 DMC report noted that the district had not hired a coordinator charged with overseeing recruitment until July 1989, and that during one year the organizational responsibility for supervising the recruiting effort had shifted between three different offices within central administration. Moreover, the DMC found the recruiting department was understaffed, and that individual recruiters were frequently not well trained. In sum, the DMC found that the school district's designs for attracting additional white transfer students to the magnet schools were "haphazard, disorganized, and non-productive." To be sure, the performance of the recruiting office was disappointing at times, particularly during the first five years of the plan. Nevertheless, the failure to attract and retain white students cannot be attributed solely to the shortcomings of the recruiting department. A wide range of problems associated with the magnet school programs cumulatively discouraged thousands of whites from enrolling in the Kansas City public schools.

A Litany of Problems

In 1991, the DMC reported that students who were attracted to Kansas City's magnet programs were "likely to be disappointed by the experience that followed." Numerous difficulties involving the placement of students, the distribution of equipment and materials to the magnets, and the transportation system plagued the district. Of these three related problems, the DMC largely viewed student placement as the root of the others. Processing the magnet school applications for thousands of students and placing those students in programs after having given due consideration to the racial goals of the desegregation plan and the racial composition of each of the magnet schools was a lengthy and complicated process. Consequently, student placements were often not finalized until a few weeks prior to the beginning of the school year. The DMC maintained that the uncertainty surrounding the assignment of children to schools served to discourage some parents, especially non-minorities, from enrolling their children in the Kansas City schools.

Late summer decisions regarding student placements complicated several other activities which otherwise should have been completed prior to the opening of the school year. Late placements occasionally brought radical changes in the enrollment at certain schools. In 1987, the DMC observed that the enrollments in some schools increased by more than 50% in the weeks just prior to the start of school. Increases of this magnitude necessitated prompt adjustments across the district. Reassigning teachers and staff, and rushing to supply the schools with sufficient numbers of desks, books, and other materials were an annual rite of late summer in Kansas City. Invariably, some schools were forced to cope with shortages of teachers, books, furniture, and equipment during September. Furthermore, final plans for the school district's transportation program could not be developed until student placement decisions had been made. As a result, the district's busing program often was not functioning efficiently or providing the expected level of reliable service until a month or more of the school year had passed. Given these difficulties, it was not entirely unexpected when the DMC reported in one of its annual summaries that the busing program was operating at an "abysmal level." The transportation service improved with the use of a computerized routing system, but the cost of the busing program steadily increased to the point where transportation expenses rivaled those for capital improvements year to year. In 1985, before Judge Clark ordered the magnet schools plan, Kansas City's transportation program cost about $7 million. By 1988, those costs had risen to over $11 million, and in 1991 transportation expenses exceeded $27 million.

In addition to transportation problems, the Kansas City school district was bedeviled with construction problems related to the magnets. Delays in the capital improvements projects slowed the pace at which magnet programs could be implemented in newly constructed or renovated schools specifically designed for the magnet themes. In the late 1980s and early 1990s, numerous projects fell behind schedule due to difficulties in acquiring sites for new schools and problems encountered in attempting to incorporate modifications into the architectural designs. In 1989, DMC reported that of the thirty-five capital improvements projects underway in the district, just twelve were on schedule for completion. The remaining twenty-three schools were one semester or more behind schedule. One year later, the number of projects behind schedule had risen to twenty-nine.

Delays in the completion of capital improvements projects clearly hindered recruitment to Kansas City's magnet schools. While construction progressed on the projects, the magnet themes were implemented at temporary facilities, often vacant school buildings or annexes, which frequently were less than ideal and had "no desegregative attractiveness." For a great many students who began their experience with the Kansas City magnets in a school scheduled for a major renovation or new construction, it was possible that they could be placed in three different schools during a three or four year period. In such cases, students were introduced to the magnet theme at one school, moved to a temporary facility for a period of a year or more while construction progressed, and then returned to the renovated or newly constructed magnet school. The DMC concluded that dislocations of this sort had a negative impact on the educational program and surely dissuaded some parents from enrolling their children in the magnets, at least until the massive construction projects were finished.

The monitoring committee also found that at times the magnet schools failed to offer the complete theme and educational enhancements that had been advertised to the district's patrons and potential transfer students. In some magnets, the DMC reported that the school did not offer the full complement of advanced courses as promised because the curriculum had been skewed in order to accommodate lower achieving students. The monitoring committee believed that suburban whites were aware of this phenomenon and chose not to enroll their children. For some magnet themes, the recruitment of an appropriate teaching staff was an obstacle. This was especially true for those magnets which offered a foreign language component. In 1987, the DMC reported that staffing was an "enormous problem" at the foreign language magnets as some of those teachers whom the school district had recruited overseas experienced difficulty entering the country and obtaining certification to teach in Missouri. One year later, the DMC found that the district was unable to locate and hire qualified Latin teachers for the Latin Grammar middle school magnet until the midway through the second semester. At still other magnet sites, equipment shortages precluded the implementation of the school's theme. For instance, the students who arrived at the Computers Unlimited Middle School and High School in 1988 were certainly disappointed to find that neither school had computers for much of the school year. In 1990, similar material shortages frustrated the implementation of other magnet programs ranging from the language development program at Holliday Montessori, to vocational laboratories at the Metropolitan Advanced Technical High School, and the business computer laboratory at Westport's Business and Communications Technology High School.

To some degree, these deficiencies with the magnet schools were attributable to the school district's inefficient system of purchasing and distributing equipment and educational materials to the schools. On an annual basis the DMC blasted the school district's purchasing department, finding that it was not uncommon for six or seven months to pass between the submission of a requisition and the delivery of the materials to a classroom. Moreover, the school district did not simply have trouble delivering equipment and supplies to the correct destinations, but had difficulty keeping it there as well. In 1990, the DMC found that several hundred thousand dollars of equipment had "mysteriously disappeared" in the preceding few years and that improved security was in order across the district. Tighter security measures involving the installation of alarms, more officers, better communications, and routine patrols helped to alleviate these concerns somewhat in subsequent reports. The problem persisted, however. A school district review in 1995 confirmed that $3.3 million in equipment was missing from the district, including some 2,700 computers.

Given the litany of problems associated with Kansas City's magnet schools system, the members of the monitoring committee annually questioned whether the school district possessed personnel and the expertise needed for the desegregation program to succeed. Year after year, the DMC's reports expressed grave doubts as to the competence of the school district's administration to implement a desegregation plan of such sweeping magnitude. The DMC and many school district patrons concluded that the school board and central administration were ultimately responsible for the numerous shortcomings of the magnet schools. That conclusion was difficult to refute. The district's administrative structure and the school board were deeply troubled throughout the period between 1985 and 1995. Incompetent administrators, poor decision-making, squabbling and divisiveness among school board members, and transient leadership within central administration all coalesced to seriously damage the district's desegregation plan.

Administrative Problems

Without question the rapid turnover within the ranks of central administration adversely affected the implementation of the magnet schools system. In several of its annual reports, the monitoring committee noted the alarming turnover rate in the district's administrative apparatus. For example, between 1987 and 1989, the newly hired members of central administration included: the superintendent, three assistant superintendents, the director of public relations, the director of personnel, and a number of key employees in the finance and personnel departments. Moreover, the tenure of several of the administrators in these positions was disturbingly short. In 1990, the constantly changing list of vacancies for administrative posts in the district included: two assistant superintendents, the director of marketing and recruitment, the director of personnel, and the director of transportation. That year the district was also searching for its fourth superintendent in six years. Moreover, the "revolving door" in central administration did not stop in 1990. The DMC's 1993 report noted that between 1991 and 1993, along with numerous other changes in personnel, the school district had employed three deputy superintendents, three associate superintendents for instruction, and two assistant superintendents for instruction. The monitoring committee concluded that a "sense of impermanence, transition and crisis," accompanied the continual turnover at the highest levels of the administration. The constant shifting of administrators, in turn, resulted in poor implementation of the district's programs and a "less than full commitment to the desegregation [plan's] goals by a significant number of personnel" in the district.

In filling administrative vacancies the DMC found that the administration was often pressured by the school board and local organizations to hire individuals "for reasons other than their qualifications." The monitoring committee lamented that too often vitally important positions within central administration were filled internally, rather than conducting national searches to locate the most qualified applicants. Bowing to considerations of seniority within the district and calls to increase minority representation in the administration, the district frequently filled administrative posts with individuals who were not equal to the task of competently carrying out the responsibilities which came with the position. Indeed, the Governor's Task Force to Study the Management of the Kansas City School District concluded in 1989 that some administrators were promoted through the ranks of the administrative hierarchy so rapidly that they scarcely had an opportunity to become familiar with the duties of their position before they were promoted again to a different post with an entirely different set of responsibilities.

An equally, if not more serious administrative problem was the rapid turnover within the middling ranks of the central administration. The DMC concluded that to some degree the instability and lack of continuity at the highest levels of the administration engendered feelings of frustration among mid-level administrators. "In several cases," the DMC noted in 1990, "qualified and competent individuals have, in effect, thrown in the towel in the face of what they see as a lack of coordination and administrative knowledge, vision, and support at the highest levels." The loss of mid-level administrators was particularly distressing because these individuals typically worked more closely with principals and teachers at the building level in refining magnet theme offerings, developing curriculum, coordinating effective schools programs, and carrying out a host of other functions essential to the daily operation of the desegregation plan.

Turnover at individual schools in the district was another substantial problem. The DMC's annual reports cite several instances in which certain schools operated for a year a more without a principal, while other schools had three or more different principals in a matter of one or two years. As a result of the absence of consistent leadership at the building level, oversight of the magnet programs often suffered as did the necessary evaluation of individual teachers involved in the development and implementation of the specialized curriculum for the magnet school.

Moreover, the monitoring committee was concerned with the manner in which administrative and staff vacancies were filled in the magnets.

In order for the magnet schools to succeed, the DMC emphasized that teachers and administrators at those schools should be selected based on their "proven interest, education, and background in the magnet theme," as well as evidence of their commitment to faithfully implement the theme and to provide students with the unique learning opportunities which the magnets promised. In practice, however, the school district frequently departed from those guidelines and relied on established procedures in considering the assignment of staff members and administrators. Seniority tended to be the most significant factor in the assignment of teachers and administrators to magnet schools. An individual's academic expertise or unique qualifications for making a meaningful contribution to the magnet's theme were often secondary considerations. For instance, the DMC noted in 1988 that none of the building administrators in the science and math magnets had sufficient "academic depth" in those subject areas to competently oversee the development of the math and science programs. Among teachers, the DMC found that those who used their seniority to gain more attractive assignments in the magnet schools too frequently compromised the uniqueness of the theme by continuing to teach subjects in precisely the same manner as they had in the traditional schools. The inability or reluctance of some teachers and building administrators to commit themselves to the successful implementation of the district's magnet themes undermined those unique qualities which were intended to set the magnets apart from other schools in the metropolitan area. Indeed, "the attitude very common among administrators," the DMC noted, was that "the desegregation plan is another source of funds to finance what it has been doing all along and in the manner in which it has been doing things."

Successes

To be sure, the monitoring committee's concerns and criticisms of the magnet school system did not apply to every school. In each of its annual reports, the DMC applauded the effort being made throughout the district in implementing the desegregation plan. The committee frequently cited several of the magnet schools which had developed outstanding curricular programs through the efforts of the school's teachers, administrators, advisory committees, and coordinators of instruction. In part, the DMC found that these successful programs had benefited from a high degree of community participation in the development of the desegregation plans. In 1989, almost 5,000 Kansas City residents were active in the various task forces, planning teams, and advisory committees related to the desegregation effort. Moreover, some 150 business partnerships with the schools had been established. The DMC also noted that many schools did not experience the sort of rapid turnover in their teaching staff and administration that plagued other buildings. Furthermore, a few schools, such as Lincoln College Preparatory Academy, were cited for their rigorous academic standards and the high levels of student achievement. Indeed, some students in the magnet system were achieving at extremely high levels, and school district publications proudly acknowledged dozens of Kansas City students who were recognized for their outstanding achievements at state, regional, and national competitions for the arts, engineering, and academics.

On a district-wide level, the monitoring committee noted many positive developments in Kansas City. The early childhood education program was consistently applauded by DMC for the exemplary manner in which the program addressed the needs of disadvantaged children prior to their entry into the school system, and for the level of cooperation exhibited by officials from the state and the school district in managing the program. The monitoring committee credited the full day kindergarten program with helping to raise student achievement in the primary grades. The DMC was also relatively pleased with the operation of the district's summer school and tutoring programs, despite the fact that the DMC tended to view these programs as an eclectic mixed-bag of enrichment and remediation. The district's success in regaining its AAA rating from the state in 1986 and retaining that level of quality with each passing year clearly satisfied the committee as well. Finally, the DMC frequently made note of the beautiful and functional schools which were completed under the capital improvements program. The district's sweeping plans for renovations and new school construction slowly came to fruition over the course of nearly a decade and refashioned the school district in a manner which was scarcely imaginable ten years earlier. The capital improvements program succeeded in transforming a school district comprised of aged and crumbling facilities into a showplace of exemplary school architecture. In 1993, the monitoring committee proudly asserted that the district had "the best equipped and [most] attractive physical plants in which to conduct education in the area."

The DMC's annual reports, therefore, were not an indictment of the entire school system, but they did bring to light some of the more vexing problems which faced the school district. Members of the monitoring committee generally agreed that the numerous difficulties which the district experienced in implementing the magnet schools and capital improvements plans had an adverse impact on the desegregation plan and the attainment of the district's integration and educational goals. The committee also recognized, however, that some of the difficulties that the school district encountered could not be prevented. The capital improvements plan, for instance, was certain to cause some dislocation of students while the construction projects proceeded. Although the rebuilding of the school district may have dissuaded some parents from enrolling their students in the Kansas City schools, the district had little choice but to embark on the construction projects. Renovations and new construction on a massive scale were necessary for the implementation of the magnet themes, and to improve facilities such that the schools were attractive learning environments for both minority students and the much hoped for non-minority transfer students.

Lingering Problems

Other difficulties, however, were viewed by the DMC as inexcusable. The annual reports are laced with references to the poor organization and ineffective leadership within the district. Particularly troubling to the members of the monitoring committee was the school district's apparent reluctance to attack aggressively some of the chronic problems which adversely affected the desegregation plan. Although the district made some headway in notifying students of their placement in the magnet programs at an earlier date, the DMC found that after more than three years of operating magnets, the uncertainty and lengthy delays which accompanied the placement process continued to discourage some parents from enrolling their children. The inefficiency of both the transportation system and the distribution of equipment to the schools also persisted until the early 1990s. Furthermore, the DMC frequently lamented the reluctance of administrators and teachers to fully commit themselves to the development of innovative and attractive magnet programs at some of the schools. The DMC often recommended the reassignment of staff and administrators in order to address this sort of entrenched resistance to change, but typically found that the district's central administration lacked the resolve to take such steps. Consequently, the requirements that teachers and administrators be certified for the magnet themes in which they were employed were enforced inconsistently, and at some schools, never enforced.

Most discouraging for the DMC was the instability of the district's central administration. Turnover within the administration undeniably conveyed the impression that the district lacked consistent leadership and that the direction of the desegregation effort was constantly in flux. Administrators, overwhelmed by the responsibilities of managing a desegregation plan of such broad scope and complexity, abandoned the district with startling regularity. Such turnover clearly damaged the public's perception of the school district and convinced some parents that their children would be better served by the suburban districts or private schools. Moreover, the inability of the constantly changing administration to solve problems with the magnet program led the DMC, school district patrons, and the state of Missouri to question whether school officials in Kansas City were capable of competently overseeing the court ordered remedial measures.

Concerns about the district's ability to manage the desegregation plan mounted with each passing year. By 1991, the DMC recommended that Judge Clark revise the district's overly ambitious schedule for implementing the magnet programs and capital improvements in the hope that "some deliberate slowing of the pace ... might result in a higher quality educational product." Two years later, the DMC voted unanimously not to support the school district's long-range magnet renewal proposal. The district's plan, which would have supported the magnet system through 2002, proposed the implementation of new magnet themes and converting the remaining traditional elementary schools to magnets. From the DMC's perspective, the district already had enough magnet schools and needed to focus its resources on refining the existing programs rather than experimenting further with unproven themes, for which there was minimal community support.

At the state level, questions about the school district's ability to oversee the desegregation plan tended to focus most directly on the school board. The 1989 report of the Governor's Task Force and the 1990 report of the House Select Committee on the Kansas City Schools both found that the district's school board had lost the confidence of its patrons. Indeed, a 1988 survey of school district patrons, staff, and students revealed that the lowest ratings and most negative responses concerning the operation of the school district were related to the leadership of the school board. The Governor's Task Force maintained that the school board was "plagued by provincialism, bickering, posturing, and mistrust of fellow board members, administrators and residents of the district." In some respects, the divisions within the school board were related to the magnet schools and capital improvements programs. On occasion during the late 1980s and early 1990s, the school board was bitterly divided by the narrow interests of individual board members seeking to secure magnet programs, facilities improvements, and educational enhancements for the sub-districts which they represented. Discussions concerning the implementation of magnet school themes and awarding contracts for capital improvements frequently smacked of parochialism and favoritism which was not in the best interest of efficient, cost-effective management of the district, and occasionally ran counter to the district's desegregation goals.

The House Select Committee found that the school board contributed to the problem of turnover in central administration. All too often individual school board members used their position to influence personnel decisions regarding the hiring and placement of employees in the administration. The reports of both the Governor's Task Force and the House Select Committee recommended new legislation to change the composition of the school board. Although neither of the legislative proposals was approved by the General Assembly, the legislature and the governor's office continued to monitor closely the cost and management of desegregation in Kansas City.

By the early 1990s, various components of Kansas City's desegregation plan were assailed by a growing number of critics. It was to be expected that any desegregation plan, particularly one as broad and expensive as Kansas City's would meet with some opposition. Furthermore, any school district would likely have experienced difficulty in managing so sweeping a plan with the sort of precision that the district's critics seemed to demand. What was disconcerting about Kansas City's situation was the manner in which individuals and groups who initially supported the district's objectives had abandoned its cause. Taxpayers, many of whom favored increased integration, had grown extremely critical of the expense of the desegregation program and the court ordered tax levy increase imposed in order to fund the plan. State officials, who initially had supported several components of the court ordered remedy, also objected to the expense of the plan and were highly critical of the district's administrative leadership. The initial optimism of the Desegregation Monitoring Committee had faded as well. Each of the committee's annual reports brought to light serious reservations as to the school district's ability to manage the plan competently, and consistently expressed great concern over the lack of significant progress toward the dual goals of greater integration and higher student achievement.

Supporters of the desegregation plan were dwindling by the early 1990s. Yet, despite all of the criticism, many of the school officials and attorneys who had crafted the desegregation remedy remained confident that the district could solve the problems associated with the magnet program and meet the goals of improving student achievement and promoting greater racial integration. The linchpin in realizing these objectives, it was argued, lay in establishing an interdistrict student transfer program with the suburbs.

The Elusive Voluntary Interdistrict Transfers (VIDTs)

Judge Clark's first remedial order, issued in June 1985, endorsed a wide range of measures designed to draw more white students into the Kansas City public schools. Among the numerous provisions of the order, Clark directed the state of Missouri to "actively seek the cooperation of each school district in the Kansas City, Missouri metropolitan area in a voluntary interdistrict transfer program." The judge noted that agreements between the city and suburbs on voluntary student transfers were an integral element of the St. Louis desegregation plan, and he expressed hope that similar cooperative arrangements could be forged in Kansas City. In order to make voluntary transfers more attractive to both the suburbs and the Kansas City schools, Clark included financial incentives to encourage transfers. He ordered that the state pay the transportation costs for transfer students, as well as pay both the city and suburban districts the full allotment under the state's education foundation formula for each transfer student.

The inclusion of a voluntary interdistrict transfer (VIDT) component in the first remedial order was widely applauded by school officials in Kansas City and the attorneys for the plaintiff school children. Although Judge Clark had dismissed the suburbs from the trial and rejected the arguments pleading for consolidation of the metropolitan area's school districts, the discussion of VIDTs in the remedial order held some promise that the suburbs would perhaps be compelled to cooperate in the desegregation of Kansas City's schools. Should the suburban districts be persuaded to participate in a VIDT program, officials in Kansas City foresaw that the number of minority students attending the inner city schools could be reduced while the non-minority enrollment increased. Such an arrangement could render the district's goal of a 60% minority enrollment attainable and stabilize the racial composition in Kansas City's schools as the transfers were renewed each year. Moreover, it was generally assumed that the introduction of suburban white students into the Kansas City schools would produce a positive effect on student achievement levels in the district. Similarly, achievement levels were expected to rise for inner city school children who transferred to suburban schools.

For school planners in Kansas City, a VIDT program was an attractive proposition. Indeed, some officials in Kansas City, including the members of the DMC, argued that it would be impossible for the school district to meet the goal of a 60% minority enrollment without a VIDT program involving the suburbs. However, in order to meet that goal, the VIDT program would require a level of participation from the suburban school districts that could be viewed as optimistic in the extreme. Reducing the minority enrollment in Kansas City from roughly 75% to 60%, would require the transfer of some 8,500 white suburban students to the city's schools, or about 10,000 minority student transfers to suburban schools, or some combination of those figures. Given the animosity which existed between Kansas City and the suburban districts as a result of the metropolitan desegregation suit, the likelihood of the suburbs agreeing to participate in a VIDT program which involved thousands of students was remote.

Not surprisingly, the initial discussions regarding a VIDT plan were fruitless. From 1984 to 1988, administrators in the suburban school districts and their legal advisors refused even to discuss the possibility of developing a VIDT plan with the Kansas City schools. Officials from the state contacted school administrators in the suburban districts on several occasions seeking to open discussions regarding VIDTs. In each instance, the suburban school officials replied that they would not consider VIDTs while the final resolution of the metropolitan case was still pending on appeal. Frustrated with the failure to make any headway on a VIDT agreement during the first four years of the court ordered remedy in Kansas City, the DMC complained, "the State of Missouri has not in any meaningful way exerted the power, authority, and influence of the state to actively seek the cooperation of the suburban school districts." Perhaps the state could have been more aggressive in its dealings with the suburban districts, but it was unlikely that any agreement could be forged while the suburban districts were defending their very existence in the appeals of the metropolitan case. The first indications that the suburbs would consider cooperating in a VIDT program came in 1988, after the Supreme Court declined to hear the appeal of Clark's 1984 ruling which dismissed the suburbs from the metropolitan suit.

In July 1988, the suburban school districts of Independence and North Kansas City contacted the State Board of Education concerning a VIDT program with Kansas City. The letter from administrators in the North Kansas City district laid out the conditions under which it would possibly accept transfer students from Kansas City. The letter marked a starting point for negotiations, but a firm VIDT plan involving the North Kansas City schools would take months to develop. Independence, however, submitted a complete plan for consideration by the state. The plan proposed building one new elementary school with a capacity of approximately 450 in Independence. The school would enroll 210 black students from Kansas City and 210 white Independence students, would have a racially balanced staff, and would offer a number of specialized programs. Construction costs for the school were estimated at $3.4 million, while the annual operational expenses for the school were estimated at roughly $3 million, all of which would be borne by the state for as long as the school was in existence.

The state of Missouri was not prepared to adopt the Independence VIDT plan as it was in 1988 without significant revisions. State officials considered the expense of the proposal to be excessive and objected to the provision that the state alone would be responsible for funding the project. Nevertheless, the submission of the Independence plan signaled the first firm commitment that a suburban district might cooperate in a VIDT program with the Kansas City schools. However, just as the first promising developments regarding VIDTs materialized, the suburban districts again grew wary of becoming involved in such proposals.

While the Independence proposal was under consideration by officials from the state, three suburban Kansas City school districts, including Independence and North Kansas City, were again named as defendants in a desegregation suit. In June 1988, Arthur Benson posted letters to the attorneys for several suburban school districts in the metropolitan area in which he raised the issue of those districts accepting minority transfer students from the Kansas City schools. Although Benson insisted that he and his clients had "no interest whatsoever in any future litigation against any surrounding school district," the threat of a new lawsuit was plainly implied. Two months later, after having been informed by each of the suburban districts that they had not yet decided whether to participate in a transfer program, Benson mailed a second letter to the attorneys for the school districts of Lee's Summit, North Kansas City, and Independence. In his second letter Benson informed the suburban districts that if they did not accept the transfer students from Kansas City he was prepared to file suit with the court, and a draft of the complaint was enclosed in each letter. Benson's clients then applied for transfers to the suburban districts. When each of the 134 black students who applied for transfers from Kansas City to the Lee's Summit, North Kansas City, and Independence schools received notice that they would not be admitted to the suburban districts, Benson filed his complaint in Kansas City's federal district court. The suit was styled *Naylor v. Lee's Summit Reorganized School District R-7*, and was assigned to Judge Joseph E. Stevens.

Benson's strategy in *Naylor* was reminiscent of the NAACP's desegregation strategy a half century earlier. Just as Thurgood Marshall and Charles Houston had filed suits in Maryland, Missouri, Oklahoma, and Texas after their clients had been denied admission to graduate school programs at state universities on racial grounds, Benson sought to prove that the suburban school districts had denied the students' transfers for reasons of race, thereby violating the Fourteenth Amendment. In *Naylor*, Benson argued that the suburban districts accepted white transfer students who were in need of special educational services, but rejected Kansas City's black transfer students who also demanded a specialized educational setting – namely, a racially integrated school environment. Therefore, he concluded that the rejection of the black students' transfer requests was evidence of the racial selectivity of the suburban districts and a violation of the students' constitutional rights. Benson's argument hinged on a novel interpretation of what sort of conditions characterize a child who has special educational needs. While educators would generally agree that children with emotional problems, learning disabilities or physical disabilities required specialized educational arrangements, some would likely wince at Benson's assertion that attending a racially isolated school constituted a similar handicap. At any rate, one section of Benson's complaint against the three suburban school districts pursued this line of reasoning.

Aside from arguments concerning the special educational needs of the plaintiff black students, Benson stated that the suburbs had not discussed the subject of VIDTs in good faith with the state. He asserted that Judge Clark's initial remedy order implied that the suburbs had a duty to cooperate in the development of a VIDT plan with the Kansas City schools. As was true of Benson's previous argument, his reading of Clark's remedial order was unique. Although the judge plainly favored VIDTs as one aspect of the desegregation remedy, it was less clear whether he imposed any duty on the suburbs to cooperate with such a plan. Benson asserted that Clark had, and that the four years which had passed without a VIDT plan were *prima facie* evidence that the suburbs had defied the judge's order. Furthermore, Benson pointed to the Eighth Circuit's 1986 opinion on the appeal of the original *Jenkins* decision. A footnote in the majority opinion raised the issue of whether the refusal of the suburban districts to participate in a VIDT program could be considered evidence of discriminatory intent and "thus be an independent basis for further relief and mandatory participation." Although the circuit court reasoned that it "should not anticipate" these circumstances and did not elaborate upon the issue, the majority implied that it might consider such an argument. Three years later, Arthur Benson presented precisely this argument before the district court.

The three attorneys for the suburban districts in *Naylor*, insisted that none of the language in Judge Clark's initial remedial order imposed a duty on the suburbs to cooperate in a VIDT plan. Essentially, they maintained that Clark's 1984 *Jenkins* decisions exonerated the suburbs and placed no constitutional obligation upon the suburbs to remedy the violations found against the state and the Kansas City public schools. Citing the first remedial order in the *Jenkins* suit, the suburban lawyers insisted that Clark had emphasized the *voluntary* nature of VIDTs recognizing that any mandatory participation imposed on the suburbs would reach "far beyond the nature and extent of the constitutional violations" found by the court. Moreover, the suburban districts' legal counsel pointed to the very same footnote which Benson used in his argument. One sentence prior to the section that raised the tantalizing issue of suburbs which refused to cooperate in a VIDT plan, the Eighth Circuit conceded that, based on the record in *Jenkins*, Clark was correct in ruling that "such a program cannot be mandatorily imposed."

At the district court, Judge Stevens was unconvinced by Benson's arguments concerning the special educational needs of racially isolated minority students or the alleged duty imposed on the suburban districts by Judge Clark. Rather, Stevens viewed the issue narrowly, weighing whether the defendant school districts had rejected the minority students' transfer requests for racial reasons or that the districts had refused the transfers in accord with their own established policies for reviewing non-resident transfer applications. Although Benson argued that the Kansas City students were refused admission because they were black and the districts' guidelines for non-resident transfers were merely a pretext, Judge Stevens concluded otherwise. Stevens found that under each districts' non-resident transfer policy, the plaintiffs "failed to establish any evidence that black students are treated any differently than white students." Moreover, he rejected Benson's contentions of discriminatory intent by noting that at the time of the complaint both Independence and North Kansas City were in the process of developing VIDT proposals. In ruling in favor of the suburbs, Stevens concluded that the denial of the Kansas City students' transfers was not the result of racial animus but was thoroughly consistent with the criteria established by the suburban districts for evaluating transfer applications.

The plaintiffs appealed to the Eighth Circuit, a court which Benson believed was more inclined to accept his theories. He was not disappointed. A three judge panel at the Court of Appeals in St. Louis reversed Judge Stevens's finding for the suburbs. In a brief opinion written by Senior Circuit Judge Gerald W. Heaney, the panel found that "one thing is clear from the record": in the five years which had passed since Judge Clark's first remedial order not a single black student from Kansas City had been transferred to the suburban districts under a VIDT plan. While the circuit court judges did not rule out the possibility that the state and suburbs would at some point agree to a plan, the panel concluded that "further delay cannot be countenanced," and remanded *Naylor* to Judge Clark's courtroom with instructions for the district court to formulate and implement a VIDT plan.

When *Naylor* was remanded to Clark's courtroom, another VIDT plan was already under consideration. Missouri City, a small rural school district of 110 students located twenty miles northeast of the city, agreed in 1990 to accept ten minority transfer students from Kansas City. Clark approved the arrangement and ordered that the state of Missouri pay all expenses associated with the plan. The VIDT program with Missouri City was the first such plan approved in the Kansas City case, and, as it turned out, the only one. Ten black Kansas City students attended the Missouri City schools during the 1990-91 school year, and one of the transfer students graduated from the district at the end of the year. In its 1990 report to Clark, the Desegregation Monitoring Committee hailed the first year of the Missouri City VIDT program a "huge success." However, the 1990 report also expressed the DMC's concerns that additional VIDT programs might not materialize. In particular, the members of the monitoring committee fretted over the disposition of the *Naylor* case.

In late 1990 and early 1991, Clark reviewed the Independence VIDT proposal and a new plan which Arthur Benson had negotiated with the North Kansas City school district. Under its proposal, North Kansas City agreed to accept sixty kindergarten students and sixty first grade students from the Kansas City schools during the 1991-92 school year. Each year thereafter, sixty kindergarten students would be transferred to the North Kansas City district so that by the plan's twelfth year 780 Kansas City students might attend schools in North Kansas City. The plan provided for the transfer students to be dispersed throughout the district, but also envisioned that new construction would ultimately be needed to accommodate the rising enrollment. Therefore, the plan also called for one new school at an estimated cost of roughly $4.4 million. Like the Independence plan, North Kansas City's proposal stipulated that the state of Missouri pay construction costs, as well as numerous additional expenses including transportation, teacher and staff salaries, staff development programs, and tuition.

In May 1991, Judge Clark issued his first order on the Independence and North Kansas City VIDT plans. Citing objections by the state and the Kansas City school district, Clark rejected both plans. Surprisingly, considering that Clark had already approved more than $500 million in improvements to the Kansas City schools, the judge's primary criticism of both plans was that they were too expensive. Roughly $7.5 million in new construction in the two districts and millions more in annual operating expenses were more than Clark was willing to commit to VIDTs. He also noted that in the plans there was no foreseeable end to the state's responsibility to fund the programs. Clark further objected to the manner in which both plans excluded the DMC from any involvement in administering the plans. With respect to the Independence plan, he balked at the proposal to build another magnet school and questioned the constitutionality of creating one 50% minority school in a district that otherwise was predominantly white. The judge instructed Arthur Benson to renew talks with the two suburban districts and submit revised plans which addressed the infirmities cited in the opinion.

Benson again appealed to the Eighth Circuit. The appellate court's 1992 opinion, however, affirmed Clark's decision. The three judge panel agreed with Clark's findings that the plans were too expensive, and that the Independence plan calling for a newly constructed magnet school to serve as a lone minority student outpost in an overwhelming white school district was constitutionally suspect. The circuit court also found that the VIDT plans were not tailored to remedy the constitutional violations. The panel reasoned that the new construction proposed in both plans created a windfall for the suburban districts. The new schools proposed for Independence and North Kansas City, the court argued, would benefit suburban students as much as the minority transfer students. Such a situation was objectionable in light of the state's contention that there was sufficient space available in the two suburban districts to accommodate the transfer students without any new construction. Nevertheless, the circuit court's desire to see a VIDT program in operation in Kansas City remained strong. The case was again remanded to Judge Clark with instructions to examine the two plans further and consider bringing in outside consultants to assist with the negotiations.

In the end, Judge Clark never approved a VIDT plan involving the Independence or North Kansas City schools. A North Kansas City plan was resubmitted to the district court in 1993 but Clark rejected the proposal because of the expense and the inclusion of provisions which called for new construction in the suburban district. On appeal, the Eighth Circuit Court upheld the decision, and the efforts to develop a VIDT program involving a substantial number of transfer students were largely abandoned.

The failure to secure a VIDT agreement involving the physical transfer of students between the city and suburbs led to a somewhat bizarre proposal for electronic desegregation. In 1993, the DMC presented a SHARE NET plan for VIDTs to Judge Clark. The SHARE NET proposal suggested that selected students in Kansas City and the suburbs could participate in something akin to a VIDT plan by communicating via electronic mail or fax transmissions. These students would then take joint field trips every other week and participate in summer camp sessions as part of the VIDT plan.

SHARE NET was roundly attacked at the district court by the black plaintiff class, the state, and the Kansas City school district. Despite these objections, Judge Clark approved the $1.2 million plan finding that it was an important initial step in establishing a productive dialogue between students, teachers, and administrators in the city and suburbs. On appeal the circuit court reversed Clark's SHARE NET order reasoning that there was "simply not evidence in the record . . . that the establishment of such a plan and its successful implementation would remedy any constitutional violations." The circuit judges conceded that electronic communication between students in the city and those in the suburbs could be a positive development. The judges also recognized, however, that SHARE NET provided minimal desegregation in a "physical sense," and that the reality was that the plan involved students "sitting before computer screens miles apart."

The reversal of the SHARE NET program in 1994 brought a close to the efforts to establish VIDTs in the Kansas City area. Despite nearly nine years of cajoling from Judge Clark and the Eighth Circuit Court, no VIDT plan involving a substantial number of students was developed. In large part, the failure to establish a VIDT program can be attributed to the inability of the state, the suburban districts, the Kansas City school district, and the plaintiffs' attorneys to settle on an acceptable framework for such a program. School officials in Kansas City were interested in VIDTs provided that such exchanges with the suburbs did not come at the expense of programs or funding already committed to the remedy in the city. The state, conversely, argued that funds committed to a VIDT plan should be deducted from the state's obligations to Kansas City because the city's schools would serve fewer students. Administrators in the suburbs it seems were motivated by two concerns. The suburban districts sought to avoid any arrangement which threatened to entangle them in additional litigation. Fear of entering into an agreement which might result in future litigation helps to explain why the great majority of Kansas City's suburban school districts expressed no interest whatsoever in VIDTs, particularly after the filing of the *Naylor* suit. Administrators in Independence and North Kansas City, however, saw VIDTs as an opportunity to demonstrate good faith in assisting with the desegregation of the Kansas City schools while also incorporating clauses into the agreements which would benefit the suburban districts and cost the suburbs nothing. For these two districts, the lure of new school construction financed by the state and additional state aid were attractive incentives in proposing a plan. Without those provisions, however, the suburban districts consistently demonstrated in the early 1990s that they were not interested in VIDTs.

The suburbs' insistence that VIDT plans include new school construction proved to be single largest obstacle to the state's endorsement of these plans. Officials from the state consistently attacked provisions that the state would fund these programs exclusively, and argued throughout the lengthy litigation and negotiation process that the suburban districts could absorb the minority transfer students without any new construction. These irreconcilable differences cumulatively doomed the two most promising proposals involving Independence and North Kansas City and ultimately led the courts to reject both plans.

One decade after Judge Clark's initial remedy order had suggested VIDTs as an important element of Kansas City's desegregation plan, only one small-scale VIDT program was in operation. The lone success of that ten-year effort was the agreement with the Missouri City schools. In that arrangement, the Missouri City school district accepted a total of ten minority transfer students from Kansas City each year from 1990 to 1994, and then doubled this figure to twenty students per school year. Although Arthur Benson, the DMC, and others applauded the Missouri City VIDT agreement as a tremendous success, the reality remained that the African-American students involved in this one program represented approximately one-five hundredth of the number of transfers necessary for the Kansas City schools to reach the goal of a 60% minority enrollment.

Without a VIDT component any possibility of reaching the 60% minority enrollment goal in the Kansas City schools was lost. Coupled with the failure of the magnet schools to attract the anticipated number of white students, the inability to negotiate large-scale VIDT plans with suburbs insured that the Kansas City schools would remain approximately three-fourths minority at the very best. Although these trends may have been distressing to school officials, Arthur Benson, the DMC, and Judge Clark, it plainly was of less concern to the students and families in the district. Many Kansas City blacks considered the district's goals for attracting white students and establishing transfer programs with the suburbs to be quixotic and unrealistic. Indeed, a growing number of black patrons had begun to question whether the entire point of the desegregation remedy had been turned on its head. The Kansas City school district's black patrons were much more interested in efforts to improve the city's schools than in VIDT programs which would bus their children out to the suburbs. For many Kansas City blacks the discussions regarding VIDTs were perceived as a serious threat to the objective of improving the schools for the district's largely black student population. Moreover, the school district's efforts to attract additional white students to the city's schools troubled some members of the black community. By focusing part of the desegregation effort on "chasing white kids," who did not attend the city's public schools, there was growing concern among the city's minorities that the principle of restoring the black students to the position that they would have occupied absent any unconstitutional discrimination was being sacrificed.

Thus, as the remedial phase progressed in Kansas City something curious began to happen. School district officials and the attorneys for the plaintiff school children assumed that they could always rely on the black community to support the objectives of the desegregation plan. By the early 1990s, however, the solid backing of the African American population was beginning to show cracks as well. In part, the dissatisfaction of the black community hinged on the numerous problems associated with the magnet program and the district's failure to document any significant growth in academic achievement as a result of the desegregation program.

African American Dissatisfaction with the Magnet Plan

For a large portion of the district's black patrons, the primary goal of the desegregation program was to improve the educational opportunities for the victims of the segregation – the district's minority students. Yet, what many of these parents perceived in the magnet school system troubled them. By the late 1980s and early 1990s, it was not uncommon for black parents in Kansas City to believe that their children were being victimized by the magnet system. Racial quotas imposed on the magnet schools functioned in such a manner that black applicants were often turned away from a magnet program because the minority percentage approved for that school had already been met. In essence, several magnets operated substantially below capacity during the late 1980s as desks sat vacant waiting for white students who were not there and were not coming.

In the middle schools and high schools, black students who were denied admission to their first choice of the magnet schools due to the quotas, had to settle for their second or third choice, something that rarely happened to white students. At the elementary level, black students who were turned away from the magnets often were consigned to the remaining traditional schools. The traditional schools frequently enrolled the most disadvantaged children in the district because their parents were often not well informed about the magnets and tended to apply to the programs too late to gain admission to the magnet schools, which were filled on a first-come basis. Moreover, the traditional schools were more racially isolated than the magnets. In 1989, twelve of the district's twenty-four traditional schools were located in the black residential corridor, and ten of those schools were more than 90% black. Six years later, due to closures and conversions, the number of traditional schools in the district had been trimmed to seventeen, eleven of which were more than 90% minority. In 1995, more than 25% of Kansas City's minority elementary school students received their education in the racially isolated traditional schools.

In much the same way that white parents in the 1950s and 1960s had manipulated the transfer policy to gain admission for their children to different schools, some black parents found a way to circumvent the racial quotas. In order to gain admission to the magnet programs, some black parents falsified the racial information on the magnet school application and their children were subsequently admitted as "white" students. Although it is impossible to establish precisely how many minority students used this ploy to gain entry to the magnets, the practice was not uncommon. The necessity of defying school authorities with false enrollment information was removed in July 1990 when Judge Clark relaxed the quotas, thereby allowing additional minority students to gain placements in the magnet schools. Even so, the experience with the quota system left many blacks wary of the motives behind the magnet schools, and disenchanted with the direction of desegregation in Kansas City. Indeed, the growing dissatisfaction among black patrons with the magnet system produced another lawsuit in 1989.

In October 1989 a group of black Kansas City students filed a complaint with the district court alleging that the desegregation plan for the city's schools had failed to eliminate the vestiges of the former segregated school system. The suit was styled as *Rivarde v. Missouri*, and was initially assigned to Judge Joseph Stephens who transferred the case to Judge Clark. The plaintiff students in *Rivarde* did not seek any modification of the desegregation plan, rather they sought to be removed from the plan altogether. They maintained that the magnet schools plan had failed to remedy the racial isolation of minority students in the district, and they did not foresee any possibility of the plan effectively addressing this concern in the future. For these reasons the plaintiffs sought relief through educational vouchers that would permit them to enroll in private schools of their choice.

At the district court Judge Clark dismissed the *Rivarde* complaint on procedural grounds. Clark ruled that because the students were enrolled in the Kansas City schools they were already members of the certified class of "all present and future students" in the *Jenkins* litigation, and therefore could not seek relief in a separate suit. The judge concluded that the plaintiffs could file a motion to intervene in the on-going *Jenkins* litigation and seek to have its proposed remedy incorporated into those orders, but the court could not consider an alternative remedy in a suit separate from *Jenkins*. On appeal, the Eighth Circuit affirmed Clark's ruling and the educational vouchers proposed in *Rivarde* were rejected.

Although the students in *Rivarde* did not win the option of enrolling in private schools at the state's expense, the suit is significant as one expression of the frustration that some black patrons felt in the magnet system. For some Kansas City blacks, the massive reconstruction of the district, its innovative magnet themes, new materials, smaller class sizes, and so on, did not effectively alter their perception that the city's public schools remained inferior and unappealing in comparison to private schools. To the chagrin of many Kansas City blacks, racial isolation remained a problem in the district in spite of the magnet schools. Moreover, dissatisfaction among minority patrons continued to mount as other objectives of the desegregation plan, such as raising student achievement levels, went unrealized. Indeed, all the shortcomings of the magnet desegregation plan may have been forgiven had it not been for the district's inability to document any substantial growth in student achievement. For many Kansas City residents, the figures on the annual achievement tests taken throughout the district were the most telling evidence of whether the magnet schools and educational improvements were in fact remedying the deficiencies in the city's schools.

Student Achievement

Numerous components of Kansas City's court ordered desegregation plan were designed to promote student achievement. Smaller class sizes, new materials and equipment, innovative curricular themes, more attractive and comfortable learning environments, expanded tutorial and enrichment programs, and millions of dollars in effective schools grants were all supposed to produce higher levels of student achievement across the district. Achievement levels, however, proved to be stubbornly resistant to the sort of gains that school officials, Judge Clark, and the district's patrons expected. In 1991, the DMC noted that while Kansas City ranked as "one of the best equipped school districts in the region, if not the country," when academic achievement was measured by standardized tests, the district "continues to offer the worst of education in the metropolitan Kansas City area."

Year after year, the school district's standardized test results remained significantly below national and state norms. Although scores rose incrementally in some subjects, such as science, improved test scores in other curricular areas, such as math and reading, were much more sluggish and revealed little or no progress. Essentially, between 1984 and 1995, the district's results on standardized tests were characterized by four general trends, none of which were very encouraging.

First, while Kansas City public school students in the primary grades generally tended to score at or above national averages, students from third grade through high school typically fell below the national averages. However, before condemning the school district's performance from third grade onward, a few cautionary notes are in order. Declines in achievement, which are apparent in Kansas City's scores after second grade, occur in most school districts. Across the country, scores drop after the primary grades because the test is no longer read to students. Also, given the wide range of problems that face urban school districts serving larger percentages of students from disadvantaged backgrounds, it could be considered unrealistic to expect Kansas City's students to perform at or above national norms for all grade levels. Nevertheless, in 1985 Arthur Benson and others associated with the desegregation suit predicted that within four years Kansas City's scores would meet or exceed the national norms. Some progress was made in raising Kansas City's achievement levels from one year to the next, but in many cases such growth was nominal and did not approach national norms. Essentially, the trend in Kansas City was a continuation of the pattern of performance which had characterized the district before the introduction of magnet schools and educational enhancements. Kansas City's problem, then, was not so much that achievement in the district was falling as it was that nothing had changed. The success which Kansas City students experienced through second grade may in part be attributable to the early childhood education and full day kindergarten programs that were initiated as part of the desegregation remedy. But the school district's performance on the tests did not reveal any substantial growth that could be attributed to the magnet schools and millions of dollars spent on effective schools programs.

The second general trend revealed in Kansas City's standardized achievement tests was that in the results for most years, the sharpest declines were apparent at the middle school level. Although Kansas City students consistently dropped below the national norms after second grade, they typically scored higher than the averages for other large cities through fifth grade. In sixth through twelfth grade, however, Kansas City's students fell behind the average for other large cities. Given the massive district-wide improvements made to the facilities and educational programs, virtually everyone associated with the *Jenkins* case anticipated that the district's scores would surpass those of other large cities. However, as Kansas City's scores in the upper grades continued to lag behind those of other urban districts, troubling questions arose regarding the validity of the desegregation plan and the ability of school district personnel to foster achievement gains. Furthermore, the district's disappointing test results in comparison to other cities undermined the argument that Kansas City students scored poorly on standardized tests because of cultural bias in the exams. Surely the Iowa Test of Basic Skills was no more biased against Kansas City students than those in other cities, yet from sixth grade onward Kansas City's median scores fell below the median for other urban school districts.

The third trend apparent in the school district's standardized testing results revealed significant differences in achievement for white and minority students, particularly at the middle school level. In its 1993 report, the DMC noted that in all subject areas, black middle school students consistently scored one academic year or more below their white counterparts. For some observers, the racial disparity in the test scores confirmed the perception that the test instrument was culturally biased against minority students. But what was more troubling to the members of the DMC and the attorneys for the school children was that a significant achievement gap existed at all. Under the terms of Judge Clark's June 1985 remedy order, schools which were predominantly black received a 50% larger share of the effective schools grants than those schools which were not racially isolated. Yet, despite the reductions in class size, revisions to the curriculum, millions of dollars worth of new equipment and supplies, and expanded services for low achieving students, the racial disparity lingered. As far as increased achievement was concerned, the plaintiff black students, whose suit against the school district had spawned the massive desegregation remedy in Kansas City, did not appear to be benefiting accordingly. By the mid-1990s, as achievement levels in the district continued to show little improvement and the gap between the races persisted, Arthur Benson and a growing number of skeptics grew increasingly critical of the school district's ability to effect meaningful educational change as part of the remedy in Kansas City.

A final trend which was apparent in the school district's standardized test results involved the magnet schools. School officials and the members of the monitoring committee were clearly dismayed by the minimal progress made in student achievement district-wide, and the results from the magnet schools were especially disappointing. Essentially, the district's test scores illustrated little or no correlation between magnet themes and increases in achievement. In 1989, the DMC reported that students in the district's math and science magnet schools did not score any higher on the math and science subtests than students enrolled in other magnet programs. Indeed, at the middle school level, students at the Middle School for the Arts scored significantly higher on the math and science subtests than those students enrolled in the three math and science middle school magnets. Moreover, Northeast High School, the law and public service magnet, scored higher on the math and science subtests than Southwest High School, the math and science magnet. Two years later, the DMC again found that on average, students in the math and science magnets scored no higher on those subtests than students enrolled in other magnet programs. Similarly, students at the communications magnets did not score appreciably higher on the reading and language arts subtests than students in other magnets. Even ten years after the advent of the magnet schools system in Kansas City, the lack of any significant correlation between magnet programs and higher achievement in certain subject areas was apparent in the district's 1995 school achievement profiles. The lone exception to this trend was the college preparatory magnet at Lincoln Academy, which year after year produced standardized test scores significantly above the state and national averages in virtually all subject areas. Lincoln, however, was also the only school in the district where students had to meet or exceed criteria based on standardized test scores in order to be eligible for admission to the school. Aside from Lincoln, any connection between magnet themes and significantly higher achievement proved to be elusive.

In spite of the extensive efforts to remodel the district's facilities and improve the educational programs available to Kansas City's public school students, achievement in the district did not approach the levels that many patrons expected. Although a handful of schools met or exceeded national norms, the majority of the district's students continued to score below national averages. The elusive data demonstrating significant improvement in student achievement was an annual source of concern to all of the parties involved in the *Jenkins* suit. In light of the substantial financial commitment made in order to improve the educational and physical quality of the Kansas City public schools, the yearly test results brought little reason for celebration. Indeed, the announcement of another year's languishing scores frequently brought the school board and central administration under intense criticism. For some observers, such as Arthur Benson, the consistently substandard performance on achievement tests confirmed the suspicion that the school district lacked enough competent and committed personnel at all levels to fully implement the educational components of the remedy.

Conclusions

By the early 1990s, officials from the state of Missouri as well as a broad cross-section of Kansas City residents and patrons, including the plaintiffs, were openly critical of the school board's management of the district, central administration's management of the desegregation plan, and Judge Clark's judicial reign over the district. Having created the most expansive and expensive magnet school system in the country, Kansas City had few positive results to report. Despite the fabulous reconstruction of the district, and the millions of dollars committed to reducing class sizes, hiring more teachers, implementing innovative magnet themes, expanding remedial and enrichment programs for students, and a host of other initiatives, the school district had made precious little progress toward meeting the goals established for the desegregation plan. In 1995, the enrollment in the school district remained more than three-fourths minority, and achievement levels had not improved significantly. Indeed, by the mid-1990s, critics of the desegregation plan increasingly questioned whether the court would fund the remedy indefinitely in light of the lack of progress toward the objectives of increased integration and higher student achievement. Ten years after Judge Clark's initial remedial order in *Jenkins v. Missouri*, the magnet schools experiment in Kansas City appeared to be running against the clock.

CHAPTER 9

The Good Times End

Jenkins at the United States Supreme Court and the Aftermath, 1995-1999

In October 1994, Missouri Attorney General Jay Nixon and his staff were busy drafting the final copy of the state's latest appeal to the United States Supreme Court for a writ of certiorari in the *Jenkins* case. On seven previous occasions the state had appealed orders in the Kansas City desegregation case to the Supreme Court. Twice the nation's highest court had heard the state's appeals – first in 1989 when the Court affirmed an order requiring the state to reimburse Arthur Benson and the NAACP legal defense team some $4 million in compensation for their legal fees under the Civil Rights Attorney's Fees Act of 1976, and again in 1990 when the Court upheld Judge Clark's court-ordered tax increase. Once again, the Supreme Court would agree to hear the state's appeal, and the outcome of the 1994 appeal would fundamentally change the course of desegregation for Kansas City. Moreover, the Supreme Court's decision would eventually influence more than two hundred school districts across the nation operating under court ordered desegregation. For Jay Nixon, the Supreme Court's decision in the Kansas City case would be arguably the single most important victory he achieved as Attorney General.

The son of a wealthy lawyer, Jay Nixon was born in DeSoto, Missouri, and attended the public schools of Jefferson County. He graduated from the University of Missouri in 1978 with a degree in political science, and earned his law degree there as well in 1981. In 1986, at the age of thirty, Nixon was elected to the Missouri Senate. Following an unsuccessful bid for the United States Senate in 1988, Nixon was re-elected to the state Senate in 1990. Midway through his second term in the legislature, Nixon won election to the Attorney General's office, running on a platform vowing to reduce crime, clean up corruption in state government, protect consumers, and enforce Missouri's environmental laws. Resolving the state's two desegregation cases, in Kansas City and St. Louis, were not among the various objectives that Nixon promised to pursue as Attorney General and his reasons for doing so are uncertain. What is clear is that Nixon had always proven eager to undertake high visibility cases which promised extensive media coverage. A former colleague in the Missouri Senate called Nixon "the greatest press hound" he had ever known, and it was at times difficult to determine whether Nixon pursued cases because of his desire to fulfill aggressively the responsibilities of his office or because he enjoyed being at the center of the media coverage. Moreover, it was widely speculated that Nixon's appetite for media exposure was driven by his aspirations for higher office. As a politician, Jay Nixon had an innate sense for the importance of self-promotion, and, in 1994, an appeal in the Kansas City desegregation case was a sure bet to capture the attention of the media.

In 1994, the desegregation remedy in Kansas City was in its ninth year of operation. Although the plan had been disappointing in its ability to attract non-minority students to the district or raise achievement levels, many of those closest to the case, including Arthur Benson, fully expected the desegregation plan and the massive infusions of state funding to continue for years to come. There were, however, a growing number of critics of the plan who were eager to see the remedial phase and the disproportionate funding for the Kansas City magnet system end. By 1994, the cost of Kansas City's desegregation remedy had risen to more than $1 billion and school districts across Missouri suffered to varying degrees as educational funds that otherwise would have been distributed throughout the state flowed into the Kansas City schools. For many Missouri residents there was no foreseeable end to the Kansas City desegregation plan, or to the manner in which the city school district's programs were approved and funded at the expense of legitimate educational needs elsewhere in the state. Given the growing opposition, the attorney general's decision to appeal various aspects of the remedy and seek limits to the soaring expense of the plan won the support of a broad cross-section of Missouri residents. Accordingly, the state's appeal to the Supreme Court in 1994 was widely supported.

Throughout the *Jenkins* litigation, attorneys for the state of Missouri had contested various aspects of the desegregation remedy. In most instances, the state was unsuccessful in its attempts to pare away at the breadth and expense of the Kansas City plan. Judge Clark had consistently approved sweeping proposals reasoning that such steps were necessary in order to insure that the magnet themes and capital improvements in the district would be comparable or superior to the programs and facilities in the suburbs. Moreover, on appeal, the judges of the Eighth Circuit Court typically affirmed Clark's orders and endorsed the position that desegregating the school system in Kansas City might require extreme measures that flirted with the constitutional limits of the court's remedial authority.

For a time, the state's arguments in opposition to the remedial measures gave the impression that the government's approach to the Kansas City case was driven by budgetary concerns far more than by considerations of sculpting an appropriate remedy for the constitutional violations. However, by the early 1990s, the state's objections to some of the remedial measures had attracted new converts. As the wildly expensive magnet schools programs, capital improvements, and educational enhancements in Kansas City failed to approach the lofty objectives endorsed by the courts for the desegregation plan, more critics of the school district emerged. A growing number of Missouri residents and patrons of the Kansas City public schools, both black and white, questioned the goals of the magnet plan, its expense, and the competence of the district's leadership to make the magnets work. Gradually the perceptions of the school district and the state in the *Jenkins* case were transformed. The state's objections to the remedy appeared to be more reasonable, while the school district's ability to effect meaningful integration and higher levels of student achievement was roundly criticized.

Beyond the local arena, developments in Kansas City began to attract national interest during the early 1990s. In magazine articles and television segments the media typically underscored the profligate spending on the Kansas City schools and the meager returns, and portrayed the case as a glaring example of judicial excess. Kansas City's desegregation plan also attracted the attention of the Republican Party in its 1994 "Contract with America." Among the policy statements articulated in the contract, Republicans vowed to restrict "unfunded mandates" – obligations imposed on state and local governments without federal funds to assist in paying for them – and pointed to Kansas City as a prime example of how the judiciary's authority in these fiscal matters should be curtailed. Prominent Republicans argued that in Kansas City the judiciary had abused its authority first by mandating the creation of the magnet system without due consideration of how to finance the plan, and then by imposing new tax measures upon the citizenry when the school district could not meet its share of the costs.

More ominous for Kansas City's desegregation plan was the shift which had occurred within the Supreme Court. Bolstered by the appointment of five conservative justices during the Reagan and Bush presidencies, the Court began to show signs of abandoning school desegregation in the early 1990s. In particular, the Court demonstrated greater inclination to find that school districts had remedied their constitutional violations and achieved "unitary status," thereby facilitating the removal of judicial oversight of the schools and the restoration of local control. In this shifting context, attorneys for the state of Missouri grew increasingly confident that the remedy in Kansas City was vulnerable.

Missouri's 1994 Appeals to the U.S. Supreme Court

In 1994, the state decided to challenge two more of Judge Clark's orders in the Kansas City case. The appeals contested the judge's decisions regarding the state's obligation to provide funding for increases in teacher and staff salaries, as well as an extension of the state's funding for educational improvements, the so-called *Milliken II* programs. These appeals were ultimately heard by the United States Supreme Court in January 1995, and the Court's decision brought radical changes for the magnet schools desegregation plan in Kansas City.

For the state's attorneys, Judge Clark's orders providing salary increases for school district personnel were characteristic of the excesses of the remedy. Reasoning that the school district's ability to hire and retain high quality teachers rested in part on the competitiveness of the district's salary schedule, Clark had approved salary increases as elements of the remedy on three separate occasions. Clark maintained that high quality teachers were essential to the magnet programs and the quality of education in the district generally. Therefore, the judge concluded that the salary increases were part of the underpinnings of improving the desegregative attractiveness of the district. The first round of salary increases were included in the sweeping September 15, 1987 order that funded the capital improvements program and provided for the doubling of the district's tax levy to pay for the improvements. That relatively modest $7.15 million increase was followed by more substantial increases in 1990 and 1993. In all, the cost of the salary increases between 1987 and 1993 totaled more than $200 million. After the 1993 increases were implemented, virtually every employee in the district had benefited from one or more of the salary orders. Not only did all administrators and teachers enjoy salary increases, but so too did garbage handlers, custodial personnel, food service workers, and a host of others. All told, all but three employees in the Kansas City school district had benefited from a court ordered salary increase between 1987 and 1993. For teachers in the Kansas City schools, the salary orders cumulatively raised the base pay by 44% from $17,000 a year to $24,500.

Not surprisingly the salary measures imposed a hefty burden on the state and the school district. Between 1991 and 1995, the state contributed a total of more than $130 million to pay its share of the salary orders, while the school district funded its share by raising the tax levy. In order to finance the new salary structure, the district, with Clark's approval, increased the levy by almost a dollar to $4.96 per $100 of assessed property valuation.

In each of the three court imposed salary increases, the state's attorneys argued that salary increases for school district personnel were unrelated to the desegregation remedy and beyond the remedial authority of the court. In particular, the state argued that the increases ordered for non-instructional personnel had nothing to do with desegregation. Moreover, the state's attorneys maintained that low salaries in the Kansas City schools were not vestiges of the former segregated system and did not stem from the constitutional violations found by the court. Nevertheless, in each instance, the increases ordered by Clark were affirmed by the Eighth Circuit Court.

Judge Clark's orders providing for the extension of educational improvements were also appealed by the state to the Eighth Circuit Court in 1992. The state maintained that after having infused more than $220 million into the *Milliken II* programs over a seven-year period, the state had fulfilled its obligation to improve educational opportunities in the district. In other words, the state argued that the remedial and enrichment programs ordered in 1985 had effectively restored the quality of education in the Kansas City schools to the level that it would have been without the constitutional violations. In support of its argument that the vestiges of segregation had been eliminated, the state pointed to the fact that since 1986 the Kansas City school district had achieved a AAA rating, the state's highest rating, and that Kansas City spent more money per pupil than any other district in the state. In short, the state maintained that the lone objective of the educational improvements had been full implementation of the programs, and that there was no requirement that the *Milliken II* components result in increased integration or higher levels of student achievement. Indeed, attorneys for the state insisted that standardized test scores were an inappropriate means of evaluating whether the state had satisfied its obligations. Clark disagreed, finding that educational improvements were central to the larger goal of promoting greater racial integration, and that, as measured by standardized test scores, the *Milliken II* programs in the district had not yet erased the vestiges of segregation. He ordered that the educational improvement components be renewed as part of the 1992-93 desegregation budget. On appeal, the Eighth Circuit affirmed Clark's decision.

Following its unsuccessful appeals to the Eighth Circuit Court on the salary and educational improvements issues, the state appealed to the United State Supreme Court. In 1994, the Supreme Court agreed to review those two components of Kansas City's desegregation plan. It is important to note that the Court did not agree to render a decision on the scope of the remedy, nor, indeed, had the state petitioned the Court to do so. In its 1990 appeal of the tax levy order, the state had petitioned for a review of the scope of the remedy, and although the Court agreed to hear the taxation issue, the justices declined to grant certiorari on the broader issue of the remedy's scope. Basically, by seeking a review of the scope of the remedy, the state in 1990 had requested that the Court examine those objectives of the remedial plan which could be construed as extending beyond the limits of the Kansas City school district. Throughout the remedial phase of the *Jenkins* litigation, the state argued that various elements of the remedy approved by Judge Clark and affirmed at the circuit court level reached beyond the authority of the court and exceeded the scope and nature of the constitutional violations. Specifically, the state objected to the goal of attracting additional white students to the district, and to those orders which underwrote the objective of creating a school district in Kansas City which would be comparable or superior to the surrounding suburban districts.

The Court's refusal in 1990 to review the scope of the remedy led some observers of Kansas City's case to believe that the basic tenets of the remedy were secure. Essentially, some of those close to the desegregation plan were convinced that the Court's refusal to grant certiorari on the scope of the remedy in 1990 was tantamount to an affirmation of the remedial plan's objectives. That was not the case, however. The justices' denial of certiorari in 1990 had been neither an affirmation nor a reversal of the scope of the remedy, and the state planned to raise the issue again before the Court when arguments commenced before the justices on January 11, 1995. Moreover, by 1995 the Court was more inclined to examine critically the scope of the remedy. Indeed, the most significant element of the Court's 1995 decision would address the scope and objectives of the remedy despite the fact that the state had not sought a review of those issues, nor had the Court granted certiorari on those issues.

Prior to arguments before the Court, Missouri Attorney General Jay Nixon expressed his hope that the justices would define "the end game" for Kansas City's desegregation case. Nixon maintained that school desegregation suits were notoriously difficult to conclude and viewed Kansas City as an ideal opportunity for the Court to clarify the standards which should be met in order to facilitate a "responsible, effective wind-down of the state's involvement" in such remedies. The state of Missouri's interest in bringing an end to the remedial phase was underscored by the fact that, at the time the Supreme Court heard arguments in the case, the total cost of the remedy in Kansas City stood at just under $1.45 billion.

Among school officials in Kansas City there was quiet concern that the Supreme Court might radically refashion the desegregation remedy. In particular, they feared that the educational improvements ordered by

Judge Clark might be overturned and the district would lose millions of dollars in state funding flowing into Kansas City's schools. Attorneys for the school district and plaintiff school children sought to convince the justices that the remedy was consistent with standards established in previous school desegregation cases, and that the remedy should continue to be fully funded until the objectives of greater integration and higher student achievement were realized. Arthur Benson optimistically maintained that even if the Court should overturn the Eighth Circuit's decision, the state's contributions to educational programs funded by the desegregation orders would not necessarily end. Some school district officials, however, took little solace in that possibility. "My gut reaction," school board member John Still said, "is that it will be the beginning of the end."

Missouri v. Jenkins at the Supreme Court

At the Supreme Court, Missouri was represented by John Munich, the state's assistant attorney general. Munich was native of the St. Louis area and a 1981 graduate of the University of St. Louis law school. He had worked in the litigation division of a Washington D.C. law firm before joining the attorney general's offices in 1993. His counterpart representing the plaintiff school children was Theodore Shaw, the associate director counsel for the NAACP's Legal Defense and Education Fund. Shaw was a graduate of Columbia law school with extensive experience in civil rights and school desegregation litigation. Prior to joining the NAACP's Legal Defense staff, Shaw had worked for eight years in the Civil Rights Division of the United States Justice Department before resigning in 1987 in protest of the Reagan administration's civil rights policies.

The opposing sides' arguments before the Court centered largely upon the remedy ordered in Kansas City. Specifically, much of the debate focused on the degree to which the objectives of the desegregation plan had been attained, and whether the state should be relieved of its obligations to fund the remedy. Although the Court had granted review only on the two narrow questions concerning the salary increases and state funding for educational improvements, Munich questioned the entire scope of the remedy. He insisted that in order to resolve the educational improvements and salary issues, it was necessary for the Court to review Judge Clark's rationale in ordering those components. In particular, Munich argued that Clark's reliance on "desegregative attractiveness" and "suburban comparability" as justification for numerous elements of the remedy was nebulous, unsupported by law, and patently open-ended. Munich emphasized, however, that although the state considered much of the remedy excessive; it did not seek to have the entire plan overturned. Rather, he pleaded that the Court compel Judge Clark to adopt more tangible criteria for evaluating the progress of the plan in Kansas City and ultimately define the point at which the state of Missouri might be relieved of funding a disproportionate share of the remedy. The assistant attorney general's arguments won at least one supporter on the Court. At one point, Justice Anthony Kennedy merely shook his head and stated, "I just see no end to it."

Theodore Shaw argued that the remedy had brought massive change for the better in Kansas City, but maintained that much remained to be done. Shaw told the justices that he had "no doubt that there will be an end to this remedy," but insisted that a link existed between desegregation and student achievement. He asserted that the changes which Judge Clark had ordered in the district were thoroughly consistent with the objectives of improving the educational opportunities available to students in Kansas City and restoring the victims of segregation to the position that they would have occupied absent the constitutional violations. Yet, Shaw maintained that substandard achievement levels in the district were a vestige of segregation which demanded continuation of the state's funding for the remedy. Justice Stephen Breyer agreed and asked hypothetically if the state would ask the Court to abandon the remedy even if the district's students could not read.

Both Munich and Shaw left the Court expressing their satisfaction with the reception that their arguments received from the justices. Nevertheless, clear divisions within the Court were readily apparent, and many observers concluded that the case would be decided by a narrow majority. For more than two hundred school districts nationwide operating under court ordered desegregation plans, the Court's decision in *Missouri v. Jenkins* was certain to be its most significant ruling in recent years, perhaps providing further guidance as to determinations of "unitary status," and the criteria by which the Court measured whether a school district had remedied its constitutional violation thereby allowing for the resumption of local control. Five months passed before the Court announced its decision.

Chief Justice William Rehnquist delivered the majority opinion for the Court on June 12, 1995. As predicted, the Court was split, returning a five to four decision in favor of the state of Missouri on each of the issues presented for review. For the majority, Rehnquist was joined by Justices Sandra Day O'Connor, Antonin Scalia, Anthony Kennedy, and Clarence Thomas, with O'Connor and Thomas filing concurring opinions. Justice David Souter filed a dissenting opinion in which Justices John Paul Stevens, Ruth Bader Ginsburg, and Stephen Breyer joined. Ginsburg also filed a separate dissenting opinion.

In the majority opinion, the chief justice began by briefly reviewing the eighteen-year history of Kansas City's desegregation case, the capital improvements program, the magnet school system and the two issues under consideration by the Court. Having established the basic framework of the case, Rehnquist's opinion proceeded to undermine the very foundation of the desegregation remedy ordered by Judge Clark. The majority opinion ruled not only on the two issues presented for review but also examined the scope of the remedy. Adopting the approach suggested by the Missouri assistant attorney general, the majority concluded that "an analysis of the permissible scope of the District Court's remedial authority is necessary" in order to determine whether the salary increases and the extension of the educational improvement programs were legitimate remedial measures. On the critical issue of the scope of the remedy, Rehnquist and the majority found that Clark had overstepped his authority in ordering the plan implemented in Kansas City. The justices concluded that when Clark issued the first remedial order in 1985 he must have believed that desegregation confined solely to within the school district would have been insufficient to integrate a district that at the time was almost 70% minority. Nevertheless, the Court maintained that the remedy should have focused more directly on the Kansas City schools. In particular, the majority opinion reiterated the remedial goals developed by Judge Clark in 1985: the elimination of the 90% minority schools in the district, bolstering student achievement, and eradicating the vestiges of segregation within the city's schools.

The Court noted that neither Clark nor the Eighth Circuit Court had found constitutional violations beyond the boundaries of the Kansas City school district. Thus, according to *Milliken v. Bradley*, an interdistrict remedy which included the suburbs exceeded the remedial authority of the court. By ordering the magnet schools plan with the intent of attracting non-minority students from outside the school district, a majority of the Court found that the district court judge had gone too far. Chief Justice Rehnquist asserted that Judge Clark had "devised a remedy to accomplish indirectly what [the district court] admittedly lacks the remedial authority to mandate directly: the interdistrict transfer of students." Although it is debatable whether attracting non-minority transfer students was the lone, or even the primary objective of the remedy, the majority opinion characterized it so, and concluded that plan implemented in Kansas City exceeded the scope and nature of the constitutional violations.

Having dealt the scope of the remedy a mortal blow, the majority opinion went on to examine the issues of salary increases and the continuation of the state's funding for educational improvements. With respect to salary increases, Rehnquist's opinion was especially critical of

Judge Clark's use of "desegregative attractiveness" as justification for various components of the remedy. Such an objective, Rehnquist wrote, "cannot be reconciled with our cases placing limitations on a district court's remedial authority." Operating under the rationale of desegregative attractiveness, the Court's majority found that Clark had "limitless authority" to impose additional measures as part of the remedy. The majority opinion held that, "Each additional program ordered by the District Court – and financed by the State – to increase the 'desegregative attractiveness' of the school district makes [the school district] more and more dependent on additional funding from the State." Moreover, Rehnquist asserted that as the school district's dependence on state funding increased, its reliance on continued supervision by the district court grew proportionately. For the Court's majority, the spiraling dependence of the school district on ever larger infusions of state funding for salary increases was both unacceptable and characteristic of the manner in which Judge Clark had abused his broad discretion in overseeing the remedy in Kansas City. "Salary increases," Rehnquist's opinion concluded, were among the "many imponderables" that were "simply too far removed" from the tasks of eliminating racially identifiable schools and remedying the effects of previous segregation. Like the interdistrict aspects of the remedy, the salary increases were determined to be beyond the authority of the district court.

The majority opinion also sided with the state of Missouri on the question of the state's continued funding of the remedy's educational improvement components. With respect to the school district's *Milliken II* programs, the majority emphasized that many of the remedial goals had been attained. Specifically, the Court pointed to the district's AAA rating from the state and the exemplary school facilities in Kansas City as evidence of what had been accomplished during the remedial phase. Moreover, the Chief Justice's opinion faulted Clark for failing to have established the extent to which the substandard levels of student achievement in Kansas City were attributable to the constitutional violations. Such determinations, the justices maintained, were important in defining the ultimate goals of the educational programs and measuring the success of those components. The majority opinion further criticized the manner in which Judge Clark justified the continuation of state funding for educational improvements on the basis of test scores which remained at or below national averages. "Insistence upon academic goals unrelated to the effects of segregation," Rehnquist wrote, "unwarrantably postpones the day when [the school district] will be able to operate on its own." The Court's majority opinion did not, however, go so far as to rule that the educational components had achieved "unitary status." Rather, the question of continued funding for *Milliken II* programs in Kansas City was remanded to Clark's courtroom with instructions to reevaluate the goals of those components and to determine whether those elements of the remedy could be terminated. The majority opinion also instructed Clark to sharply curtail or abandon his reliance on test scores as justification for further spending on the remedy. Finally, Justice Rehnquist's majority opinion reminded Clark that one of the goals of desegregation cases such as Kansas City was to bring an end to the period of judicial oversight and restore state and local authorities to control of the school system.

In the concurring opinions, Justices O'Connor and Thomas underscored various elements of the majority opinion. Justice O'Connor's concurrence attempted to defuse criticism from the dissenting justices that the Court had ruled on the scope of the remedy without having granted certiorari on that issue or having given notice to the attorneys for the school district and the plaintiff school children that the Court would consider the scope of the remedy in its decision. O'Connor maintained that "the propriety of desegregative attractiveness as a remedial purpose ... is presented in the question itself [of salary increases]," and that the Court "appropriately and necessarily" considered the scope of the remedy in ruling on the salary issue. O'Connor went on to assert that the attorneys for the school district and the school children would have ignored the state's arguments regarding the scope of the remedy "at their own peril." She noted that fully twenty-five pages of the state's brief were devoted to discussion of "suburban comparability" and "desegregative attractiveness" as the underpinnings for much of the remedy. Apparently O'Connor believed that the lengthy arguments concerning the scope of the remedy contained in the state's brief were sufficient notice for the opposing attorneys that the issue would be presented before the Court. Nevertheless, it is important to note that in granting certiorari on the salary and educational improvement issues the Court had not informed either party that the scope of the remedy was at issue.

Beyond those arguments defending the ruling on the scope of the remedy, O'Connor's opinion served largely to elaborate upon how the majority opinion was consistent with *Swann* and *Milliken*, two of the Court's previous decisions involving metropolitan school desegregation, as well as an important housing discrimination case involving metropolitan Chicago, *Hills v. Gautreaux*. In particular, O'Connor reiterated the central point in the majority opinion that there had been no constitutional violations of an interdistrict nature which could support Clark's imposition of a remedy that was interdistrict in scope. Remedial measures designed to reverse "white flight" and attract white students back to the school district were impermissible, Justice O'Connor asserted, because there was no evidence that the exodus of white students from the Kansas City schools stemmed from the constitutional violations found by the district court. O'Connor also urged Judge Clark to re-evaluate the propriety of other remedial measures in light of the Court's decision that those elements of the remedy designed to draw non-minority students back to the district or to promote desegregative attractiveness and suburban comparability were invalid.

More than any other part of the decision in *Missouri v. Jenkins*, Justice Thomas's concurrence underscored the conservative constitutionalism of the Rehnquist Court. The ultraconservative Thomas had been appointed to the bench in 1991 by President Bush to fill the seat vacated by Thurgood Marshall. His appointment vividly illustrated the essence of the conservative shift within the Court. Thomas replaced one of the architects of the NAACP's legal assault on school segregation and one of the Court's staunchest defenders of civil rights. Whereas Marshall had consistently sided with his more liberal fellow justices and was a passionate defender of school desegregation, Thomas was devoutly conservative and committed to limiting, if not dismantling, the liberal jurisprudence of the 1950s, 1960s and 1970s, including school desegregation. Clarence Thomas's concurring opinion in *Jenkins* is a classic example of the Court's conservativism.

Thomas argued that not only was the remedy in Kansas City suspect, but that the district court's findings of liability against the state of Missouri were questionable as well. He insisted that the racial isolation evident in the Kansas City schools was a product of "larger social forces" and "personal decisions" rather than discriminatory state action. Without convincing proof of unconstitutional state action, Thomas maintained that the entire desegregation remedy in Kansas City was unjustifiable. Underscoring his doubts regarding the liability of the state, Thomas insisted that Judge Clark based the decision exclusively on the existence of racially isolated schools in Kansas City. "When a district court holds the State liable for discrimination almost 30 [sic] years after the last official state action," Thomas wrote, "it must do more than show that there are some schools with high black populations." Racial isolation alone, Thomas asserted, was not sufficient justification for a desegregation remedy, and he urged district court judges to abandon the stereotypical notion that schools which were predominantly black were necessarily the product of unconstitutional state action. Moreover, Thomas expressed profound resentment at what he perceived as the tendency among district court judges to view predominantly black schools as inferior and in need of remedial measures.

Aside from Thomas's conclusions regarding the state's liability, he lamented the manner in which federal district court judges, such as Judge Clark, had come to dominate school systems operating under desegregation orders. At length, Thomas pleaded for greater restraint in the use of the judiciary's broad equitable powers. Federal courts, he maintained, were ill-equipped to oversee the operation of school systems, and Kansas City was a prime example of a federal judge continually modifying and expanding upon the remedy in order to attain "some broad, abstract, and often elusive goal." The courts, he argued, should devise a "unified remedy in a single decree," whenever possible, thereby avoiding the protracted litigation in a case such as Kansas City. Like the majority opinion, Thomas embraced the principle that desegregation remedies were temporary measures and that one goal should be returning the school district to the control of local authorities.

Rehnquist's majority opinion coupled with the concurring opinions written by O'Connor, and Thomas illustrate the conservative perspective of the Court's majority. The five justices in the majority were all inclined to view the developments in Kansas City as evidence of the excesses of school desegregation. From this perspective, the majority undermined the foundation of the desegregation plan in Kansas City and reversed Judge Clark's orders on the two specific issues presented for review. Moreover, the concurring opinions written by O'Connor and Thomas expressed the strong reservations about other aspects of the remedy. Indeed, by ruling that the remedy in Kansas City was interdistrict in scope, the Court had essentially rendered the entire remedy suspect. According the majority opinion, remedial measures which had been approved in order to promote desegregative attractiveness, achieve suburban comparability, or attract white students from outside the district were unwarranted and beyond the authority of the district court. Such an interpretation promised to bring profound changes to the magnet system. In one respect or another, virtually all of the remedial components approved in Kansas City touched upon these objectives. Consequently, although the majority opinion had not expressly overturned the remedy in Kansas City, the ruling in effect did precisely that. In essence, Judge Clark's instructions from the Court were to bring the remedial phase to an end and oversee the process of weaning the school district from the massive infusions of state aid that had flowed into the district under the court ordered remedy.

Four members of the Court refused to join the majority opinion in *Missouri v. Jenkins*, and Justices Souter and Ginsberg wrote dissenting opinions. Justice Ginsberg's dissent was a rather novel approach which placed the Kansas City desegregation case in historical perspective. Ginsberg addressed none of the points of law presented in the case, but rather recounted the "more than two centuries of firmly entrenched official discrimination" in Missouri, dating back to the 1724 French slave codes issued for the Colony of Louisiana. Against that historical backdrop Ginsberg considered the ten-year effort to remedy racial segregation in the Kansas City schools. "Given the deep, inglorious history of segregation in Missouri," Ginsberg wrote, "to curtail desegregation at this time and in this manner is an action at once too swift and too soon." Compared to centuries of discrimination, Ginsberg argued, "the experience with the desegregation remedies ordered by the District Court has been evanescent." Ginsberg's brief dissent laid bare one of the fundamental questions at the heart of school desegregation: given centuries of discrimination, how much history could be redressed through the courts? Although Justice Ginsberg did not elaborate, her dissent clearly suggested that ending a remedy which had only been fully implemented for a handful of years was hardly an equitable solution.

In contrast to Justice Ginsberg's brief dissent, Justice Souter offered a comprehensive dissenting opinion which disputed the majority's conclusions point for point. He boldly declared, "The Court's process of orderly adjudication has broken down in this case." Specifically, Souter challenged the majority's conclusion that in order to resolve the issues of salary increases and the state's funding for educational improvements it was necessary to consider the scope of the remedy for Kansas City. First, Justice Souter noted that the state had not petitioned for certiorari on the issue of the remedy's scope, and he argued that the Court had failed to give notice to either party that the "foundational issue" was at stake in the arguments before the justices. Indeed, Souter endorsed the position that the Court's refusal to grant certiorari on the scope of the remedy in the state's 1990 appeal was tantamount to an affirmation of the remedial measures.

Second, Souter argued that if it was necessary to review the remedy in order to resolve the two issues before the Court, the majority's characterization of Kansas City's desegregation plan was erroneous. He asserted that in previous cases, the Court had consistently defined interdistrict remedies as desegregation measures that were *imposed* on adjacent school districts, and mandated adjacent districts to participate in the remedy. In *Jenkins*, Souter recognized that there had been no constitutional violations of an interdistrict nature in Kansas City and agreed that the district court had no authority to impose an interdistrict remedy on the suburbs. However, Souter asserted that Judge Clark had not abused his authority in fashioning the remedy for Kansas City because the remedy was confined to the city's school district, did not consolidate or restructure the suburban districts, and imposed no remedial obligations on the suburban districts.

Third, Justice Souter disputed the majority's conclusion that, by seeking to attract white students to the Kansas City schools, Clark had overstepped his authority. Souter defended Clark's finding that the decline of the school system in the 1970s and 1980s was attributable in part to white families removing their children from the district. Souter emphasized that white flight did not warrant the imposition of an interdistrict remedy on the suburbs. However, he maintained that white flight exacerbated the racial segregation of the Kansas City public schools. Thus, Souter argued that the objective of halting or reversing white flight was a legitimate remedial goal and was consistent with the nature and extent of the constitutional violations found in the school district. Furthermore, Souter disagreed with the with the majority's assertion that in seeking to halt or reverse white flight, the desegregation plan was aimed exclusively at attracting non-minority students from the surrounding suburbs. Rather, Souter asserted that "a substantial impetus for the District Court's remedy" was to attract white students who lived in the city and who attended private or parochial schools. He suggested that much of the remedy "does not consider the world beyond district boundaries at all," therefore, much of the majority opinion, "is of little significance to the case."

Finally, Souter reiterated that those components of Kansas City's desegregation plan which could be construed as being interdistrict were strictly voluntary and did not require the participation of any surrounding suburban school district. No students were forced to enroll in the city's schools, nor were any suburban school districts compelled to accept minority transfer students from the city. He maintained that, with the exception of the small, voluntary transfer arrangement worked out with Missouri City, the interdistrict components of Kansas City's plan did not involve other school districts. Rather, the students drawn to the Kansas City public schools had enrolled based upon choices made within their own families. Individuals, not school district officials, had chosen the Kansas City schools voluntarily because of the specialized curricula and superior facilities, not because of any mandatory, court-imposed interdistrict desegregation provision. What set Kansas City's situation apart from other interdistrict desegregation plans was its voluntary nature. Souter agreed that Clark did not have the authority to impose an interdistrict plan on the suburbs, but maintained that there was nothing objectionable about a plan which attracted voluntary transfers.

Having thoroughly attacked the majority opinion's conclusions regarding the scope of the remedy, Souter considered the salary and educational improvement issues. In particular, Souter demonstrated how both of those issues could be resolved independently of any inquiry into the scope of the remedy. With respect to the court-ordered salary increases, Souter noted that the Eighth Circuit Court had specifically affirmed the salary increases finding that, the most qualified personnel were essential to the success of the desegregation effort. Souter argued that salary increases were necessary in order to attract the most qualified personnel to the district which, it was assumed, would in turn promote higher levels of student achievement. Therefore, salary increases could be viewed exclusively as an appropriate remedial measure designed to restore educational opportunities to the victims of prior segregation.

On the issue of the state's continued funding of the educational improvements Souter argued that by focusing upon Judge Clark's reliance on test scores the majority had essentially ignored the critical issue of whether the *Milliken II* programs had remedied the reduction in student achievement in Kansas City. Souter emphasized that the state had not made a claim that the educational improvements had remedied the declines in achievement, but rather "simply argued that various *Milliken II* programs had been implemented." Justice Souter concluded that according to the state's logic, once the programs were in operation, "the state was at liberty to walk away from them, no matter how great the remaining consequences of segregation for educational quality or how great the potential for curing them if state funding continued." Finally, Souter doubted the "good faith" commitment of the state to promote desegregation and educational improvement in Kansas City. He maintained that, throughout the remedial phase, the state had consistently been antagonistic toward the school district's plans while offering no tenable alternatives. Justice Souter conceded that after ten years in operation it was conceivable that the educational improvement programs in Kansas City had remedied the reduction in student achievement to the extent practicable, but he insisted that there was nothing in the record before the Court that supported such a conclusion. He did not discount the possibility of relieving the state's obligation to fund the *Milliken II* programs, but maintained that do so with the meager record that was before the Court was premature.

Despite Justice Souter's passionate dissent, it was clear from the Supreme Court's ruling that the state would begin to be relieved of its obligations to finance part of the remedy in Kansas City. A majority of the Court was in agreement with the state that the remedy implemented in Kansas City included unwarranted interdistrict components which were beyond the authority of the district court judge. Although the majority opinion did not overturn the entire remedy, the Court's instructions to Judge Clark made clear that the time had come for the district court to remove itself from the management of the Kansas City schools, wean the district from the massive infusions of state aid that it had been receiving under the district court's orders, and restore local and state authorities to control over the district. The Supreme Court's decision signaled an end to the ten-year remedial phase in Kansas City, and underscored the Court's inclination in school desegregation cases to emphasize the return of local control.

Reaction

As might be expected, Attorney General Jay Nixon was quite pleased with the Supreme Court's 1995 *Jenkins* decision. Although Nixon maintained that the state was "still formulating its legal strategy" as to how it might proceed, he hinted at a slew of possible cuts in the district's budget and suggested that there were certain aspects of the desegregation plan, such as the salary increases, which the state would no longer fund. However, he also assured the school district's patrons that the state would remain "very responsible" in its role of providing funds for quality education in the city.

Despite the setback at the Supreme Court, Arthur Benson remained optimistic that much of the desegregation plan could be retained. Benson recognized that the district had lost and was "going to have to pay for it," but, he also believed that the state would not insist on a "scorched earth policy" where the state would seek to abandon immediately all its commitments to the desegregation plan. Indeed, Benson argued that the state was not in position to do so. He maintained that the Court "actually decided far less than it first appeared," and that by sending the case back to Judge Clark much of the magnet plan and state funding could still be salvaged.

Among those most critical of the Supreme Court's decision were the editors of the *Kansas City Star*, who had supported the desegregation plan throughout. One editorial characterized the majority opinion as "slapdash" and a "make-it-up-as-we-go-along approach" to school desegregation. Nevertheless, the editors also expressed hope that the basic framework of the magnet schools plan could be preserved through negotiations with the state. Others in Kansas City welcomed the Supreme Court's ruling. In particular, some black parents were pleased that the Court invalidated the objective of attracting white suburban students to the district. A substantial part of the city's black community had come to resent the district's crusade to attract white students, many of whom did not remain in the district for more than a year. Minority patrons viewed the Court's instructions to refocus the desegregation effort on the students living in the district as a most positive development. Beyond the city limits, the decision was widely applauded across the state, especially in smaller, rural districts. The superintendent of a rural district outside Joplin, stated that over the past ten years it had been "a pretty bitter pill to swallow to watch them spend so much money on one school district." With respect to the majority opinion, he adequately summed up the feelings of many Missouri taxpayers, stating "it is about time."

Outside of the state of Missouri, the Court's decision to some degree reflected the mood of a substantial portion of the nation in 1995. The broad support outside the South that school desegregation had enjoyed in the 1950s and 1960s, when the objective was to reform the blatant discrimination in southern school systems, had been sapped during the 1970s and 1980s when desegregation and forced busing came to the

North and West. By the 1990s, the national will to desegregate schools, if there had ever been such a thing, had largely evaporated. Across the country, desegregation suits which had been managed by district courts for decades were under assault. Moreover, school integration was no longer an issue that demanded the nation's attention. Whereas, school desegregation and forced busing had incited emotional, white-hot debates in cities across the country two decades earlier, a certain ambivalence had set in by the mid-1990s. To some degree, school desegregation had been replaced in the public consciousness by other issues, and much of the country was prepared to declare school desegregation a success and move on to other concerns. With respect to the Kansas City case specifically, it seems reasonable to suggest that many Americans had come to the conclusion that ten years and $1.5 billion in improvements should have been sufficient to eradicate the vestiges of segregation in the school system. *Time Magazine* characterized the Supreme Court's decision in *Missouri v. Jenkins* as the "Waterloo" of school desegregation, and it seems that, given the propensity of other cities to seek the termination of their court-ordered desegregation plans since the 1995 ruling, it was precisely the sort of defeat that some locales had been anticipating. Indeed, prior to the announcement of the Supreme Court's decision, officials from the state and Kansas City were preparing for a ruling that could call for the gradual termination of the desegregation plan. In February 1995, just one month after the *Jenkins* case was argued at the Supreme Court, state officials had begun meeting with school district officials and the attorneys for the plaintiff school children to negotiate a settlement in Kansas City's eighteen year suit. Although these preliminary negotiations failed to resolve any of the major issues, they were a starting point from which discussions continued after the Supreme Court announced its decision in *Jenkins* in June.

Fallout and Negotiations

In the negotiations that resumed following the *Jenkins* decision, discussions largely centered on the necessity of trimming the school district's $140 million desegregation budget in light of the high court's ruling. The first group directly affected by the fallout from the Supreme Court's ruling was comprised of non-minority suburban transfer students. State funded transportation for suburban white students attending the city's schools was dropped in July. By eliminating the private taxi rides for suburban students, the district trimmed about $6.4 million from the desegregation budget. The state payments to the school district for each suburban transfer student were also cut. Suburban students seeking to attend the Kansas City schools in September would need to arrange their own transportation and pay tuition, which was set at $3,800 a year for elementary and middle school students and $4,448 for high school students.

For many suburban parents, the inconvenience of organizing car pools or making other transportation arrangements and paying thousands of dollars in tuition outweighed the appeal of the magnet schools. Despite the appeals of acting superintendent Willie Giles urging suburban parents "not to withdraw their students and not to panic," a new variety of white flight began. Hundreds of suburban families chose not to enroll their children in the Kansas City schools. Whereas nearly 1,500 non-minority transfers attended the city's schools the previous year, fewer than 800 enrolled in Kansas City following the Supreme Court's decision. Accordingly, the district's racial composition shifted. During the 1995-96 school year white students accounted for just 22% of the district's enrollment, a new low.

Discussions continued through the summer as the state pressed for additional budget reductions. Jay Nixon and other state officials argued that the offices within central administration were among those areas which the school district could significantly cut. More importantly, a majority of Kansas City's Board of Education agreed. School board member Patricia Kurtz suggested that the *Jenkins* decision provided Kansas City with an opportunity "to get rid of a top heavy administrative bureaucracy" bloated with what fellow school board member John Rios described as "'make work' type of positions."

Few people associated with the school district disputed that the district's central administration was filled with redundant and non-essential positions. In late June, school officials trimmed an additional $14 million from the desegregation budget by eliminating some 148 school based personnel and 170 positions in central administration. Within the central offices the deepest cuts were made to the departments of business, instruction, and maintenance which combined accounted for about 60% of the positions eliminated. However, because many of the central administration positions tabbed for cuts were vacant, the brunt of the lay-offs fell on curriculum coordinators and resource teachers working in the district's schools. Cutting the coordinator positions was a particularly ominous development. Coordinators were among the most important contributors to the creation of the magnet programs, and the elimination these positions heightened suspicion that the magnet programs would be significantly modified. Among the coordinators whose positions were cut was Paul Garcia. A foreign language specialist with twenty-eight years experience in the district, Garcia described the cuts and the effect that it would have on the magnet programs as "turning back the clock."

Although some of the specialist and resource teacher positions were subsequently restored, the magnet programs still suffered. School principals were instructed by central administration to cut approximately 25% of each school's magnet budget. The reductions in the magnet budget were necessary in order to retain the salary raises in light of the Supreme Court ruling which relieved the state of funding the salary measures.

Following the announcement of the additional $14 million in cuts, negotiations stalled. Despite the state's prodding for additional savings through further cuts to the central administration structure, reconfiguration of the magnet programs, or school closings, district officials balked at committing to such measures. September 1, the initial deadline, passed without a settlement. Judge Clark granted two extensions allowing the settlement talks to continue through late October, but still no agreement could be forged. When the final deadline passed without a settlement, school board member Edward Newsome suggested that the lawyers be "taken out of the equation," and that the discussions continue. In late October, however, the attorneys were not bowing out of the dispute, but instead they were preparing to resume litigation.

With the settlement talks at an impasse, Missouri's Attorney General returned to court seeking an end to the state's involvement in the Kansas City desegregation remedy. On October 26, Jay Nixon filed a motion in federal district court seeking enforcement of the Supreme Court's decision. Specifically, Nixon wanted a firm timetable and budget for the state's withdrawal from the desegregation plan, an end to the state's obligations to fund school construction projects, and restitution for $78 million which the state had contributed for the salary packages ordered by Judge Clark.

Predictably, Nixon's motion prompted strongly worded rebuttals from the school district's defenders. Arthur Benson decried the motion arguing that it would "bankrupt the district," and "drive away black and white middle class taxpayers." School board member Edward Newsome was even more damning. He asserted that, "now that white suburban students are no longer the focus, the state does not appear to care what happens to blacks and other minorities in the district." Newsome also lamented the wastefulness of the state's motion. In light of the substantial cuts that the district had already initiated in order to cope with the shifting fiscal reality of the desegregation plan, Newsome maintained that the district "can't afford to go back to court and spend another million dollars in legal fees." For other observers, Nixon's motion confirmed suspicions that he had sabotaged the negotiations from the start, seeking to use the case to promote his personal ambitions. Kansas City mayor Emmanuel Cleaver suggested that Nixon was "running for higher office on the backs of the people in Kansas City."

Despite the criticism, Nixon argued that the Supreme Court had clearly ruled that the remedy was too broad. He reassured that the state would continue to fund magnet programs which promoted desegregation during a transition period while the state's funding obligations were reduced. He made clear, however, that, in the taxpayers' interest, the state would seek to end its obligations to fund magnet programs which were not performing well and did nothing to promote additional desegregation, and those components of the remedy designed to attract non-minority students to the district. Nixon believed that the weight of the Supreme Court decision strongly favored the state, and he hoped that the threat of further litigation would compel school district officials to reconsider settling the case out of court.

To Nixon's chagrin, the motion filed in October 1995 seeking a gradual withdrawal of the state from Kansas City's desegregation plan resulted in neither a firm timetable for relieving the state nor a quick settlement. As negotiations and litigation proceeded in March 1996, Kansas City's school board approved a proposed budget for the 1996-97 school year calling for $74 million in state assistance to support the magnet system. In developing the budget, the school district trimmed an additional $36 million from the state's share of the funding the previous year. Among the cost-cutting measures incorporated in the budget were the elimination of 350 staff position across the district, termination of after school programs, the discontinuation of some magnet programs, a return to a neighborhood schools concept at several schools, reconfiguration of grade levels in some sections of the city to allow for more efficient use of school facilities, and the closure of two middle schools.

The proposed budget reduced the state's share of the desegregation funding to less than $100 million for the first time in eleven years. Still, Nixon maintained the cuts did not go far enough. In particular, the state's attorney general criticized the decision not to close any of the district's ten high schools. Closing one or more high schools had been under discussion since November 1995 and had proven to be arguably the most controversial means of trimming the district's budget. In 1995, Kansas City's ten high schools had a combined capacity of roughly 14,000 students but enrolled just 8,000 students. Because the high schools were operating at less than 60% of capacity, closing one or more of the schools appeared to be a reasonable cost cutting measure. The school district estimated that for each high school closed, the district would save between $1 million and $1.5 million annually. Moreover, some school officials argued that at the high school level, certain magnet themes were not popular and that across the district there was a groundswell of support for a return to more traditional neighborhood schools. A rash of fights and fires deliberately set during the school day at Southwest High School were commonly cited as examples of the students' dissatisfaction with the science and math magnet program and their lack of allegiance to the school. Cumulatively, these various considerations made closing one or more high schools a relatively attractive cost cutting measure, but deciding which schools to close was far from simple.

Over the course of two months the school board narrowed its options. Three high schools – Lincoln, Central, and Paseo – were untouchable. Lincoln High School was secure because it was unquestionably the greatest single success in the magnet system. Lincoln had been the district's lone black high school in the segregated system and had remained virtually all-black during the first twenty years of integrated schooling in Kansas City. During that time the facilities at Lincoln had deteriorated terribly from neglect and the school was among the most unattractive sites in the district to attend. The magnet system had dramatically transformed Lincoln. The building underwent extensive renovations and became a racially balanced school with the introduction of the college preparatory magnet theme. In 1995, Lincoln was among the most integrated schools in the district and was the highest achieving high school in the city by a wide margin. Paseo and Central were safe for a different reason. Both offered popular magnet themes, but more importantly, both were new facilities which together had cost more than $50 million to build. Closing Paseo or Central was out of the question simply because of the investment made in constructing the schools. The seven remaining high schools were all under consideration although some were perceived as being less likely candidates for closure. Of these remaining schools, Northeast was generally considered safe because its public service theme was among the more popular magnet programs and the school was one of the more integrated high schools in the district. East was also relatively secure because of the school board's determination that no magnet themes would be lost in the event that a school was closed. District officials generally agreed that the twenty-five acre farm which was part of the school's agribusiness theme would be impossible to replicate elsewhere. Thus, the school board limited the possible closures to five schools, and held a series of public forums in January 1996 to discuss the options.

Ultimately, the school board agreed unanimously not to close any of the city's high schools. At the public forums it had become clear that each high school had a sizeable contingent of defenders determined to keep their school open. Moreover, no school board member was willing to concede to closing a school in their subdistrict. Each of the high schools also offered a unique program that could not easily be relocated to a different site. Finally, each school had undergone significant renovation or new construction in order to house its magnet theme and it seemed foolish to close buildings to which so much money had been committed. Of the five high schools which the school board considered closing, the cost of the renovations already completed at each school ranged from a high of nearly $13 million at Metro to a low of $8.6 million at Southeast.

The alternative to closing one or more high schools was to find some means of making more efficient use of the vacant space in the high schools. With this objective in mind the school board unveiled its plans for reconfiguration of grade levels in the district. Under the proposed plan, four high schools would be converted into centers serving grades six through twelve, three middle schools would be reconfigured into kindergarten through eighth grade centers, two high schools would revert to being traditional schools, two middle schools would close, and several of the elementary schools would drop their magnet themes and return to traditional schools. The proposal met with massive opposition. For some patrons, the plan seemed to be another attempt by the school board to avoid making difficult decisions which affected a relatively small number of students, such as closing a high school, and instead concocting a plan filled with sweeping changes and unproven approaches to education which affected thousands of students across the district. Arthur Benson likened the district's plan to an airplane whose engines had stalled, commenting that "rather than restarting the engines, they're telling the passengers to all change seats." Clinton Adams, an outspoken critic of the district, also objected to the plan. He maintained that with thorough planning and strong leadership the reconfiguration of the district could succeed, however, he also added that "proper planning and effective administrative leadership have never been strong points in this district."

Nevertheless, the school board filed a slightly modified version of its proposal with the district court in late March. One week later, however, three supporters of the plan were unseated in school board elections and replaced with new board members who harbored serious reservations about the proposal. Moreover, in mid-April attorneys for the teachers' union, the state and the school children all filed motions in district court calling for the closure of one or more high schools, as well as other substantial changes to the magnet system. Faced with these difficulties, the school board began to reconsider its March plan and reopened discussions regarding the closure of high schools and long-term plans for the magnet system. In late April, a majority of the school board appeared to have agreed that the district should close two high schools, Van Horn and Metro, and two middle schools, Bingham and Robeson, as well as convert Southwest High School to a middle school. They also seemed to agree to eliminate the foreign language and Greek classical magnet themes at several elementary schools. Like many of the proposals which preceded it, the April plan met with something less than universal enthusiasm, and like many of those proposals which preceded it, the April plan was quickly revised.

In early May, the school board reversed course again announcing that no high schools would close for the 1996-97 school year. Although the announcement appeased some district patrons, Jay Nixon found the decision unacceptable. Just one week earlier, Nixon had stated that the district was "moving in the right direction" and that it was encouraging to note that the school board had come to the understanding that "it doesn't benefit the education of kids to heat empty classrooms." The school board's reversal, however, compelled Nixon again to seek a resolution of the case in district court. The Missouri attorney general filed a motion with Judge Clark seeking a declaration of "unitary status" in the Kansas City case. A ruling of unitary status would essentially affirm that the vestiges of segregation in the district had been remedied to the greatest practicable extent and that the state would be relieved of its obligations to fund Kansas City's desegregation plan. Arthur Benson called the motion "Jay Nixon's death wish for the school district." Nixon, however, maintained that the state's goal again was to seek a settlement, which finally was reached nearly a year later.

Settlement

On March 25, 1997 Judge Clark approved a settlement in the *Jenkins* suit. Considering the complexity of Kansas City's desegregation litigation, the terms of the settlement were simple. Over a three-year period, from the 1996-97 school year through the 1998-99 school year, the state would be required to contribute $320 million to the school district in addition to the district's allotment under the state's educational foundation formula. Following the 1998-99 school year, the state was excused from any further court-ordered obligations to finance the city's desegregation efforts. During the three-year transitional period, Judge Clark mandated that the school district achieve two challenging objectives. First, the school district was instructed to formulate and implement a comprehensive instructional plan designed to measurably reduce the achievement gap between white and black students. Second, the judge urged the district to "come to grips with fiscal reality" and make further revisions to its budget in preparation for the day when the state's court-ordered financial obligations to the district would end. It was a telling commentary on Clark's two decades of experience in working with the district that he was not overly optimistic that either objective would be achieved. In approving the settlement, the judge made note of the numerous improvements that had been made as a result of the desegregation effort, but also reiterated numerous chronic difficulties which continued to hound the district.

Clark's opinion expressed great satisfaction with some of the developments in Kansas City. "The Court," he wrote, "remains proud of the innovations it ordered," and noted that, "the large amount of money spent in the district has indeed resulted in tangible benefits." Among the benefits the judge cited the district's low pupil-teacher ratio, the increased number of computers and greater access to technology available to students across the district, the intervention programs implemented for at-risk students, and the beautiful new and renovated facilities made possible through the capital improvements program. Indeed, Clark insisted that the court had "afforded the district an opportunity ... unimaginable in most school districts." However, he also lamented that having been given an extraordinary opportunity to rebuild, reform, and revitalize the district, a host of perennial problems had frustrated the goals of the desegregation plan.

Above all, Clark faulted the administration and school board for the district's inability to manage its fiscal affairs, effect meaningful reforms, improve test scores, or narrow the achievement gap between white and minority students. Foremost among the district's chronic difficulties, the judge maintained, was the lack of stable leadership in the district. He observed that between 1988 and 1997, the school district had employed ten different superintendents. Moreover, scores of positions within central administration had high rates of turnover, and numerous individual schools were seemingly in a constant state of flux as building principals were replaced. Clark concluded that the administrative instability had resulted in "a lack of accountability for deficiencies," and that "essential programs for improvement attain only a continual state of limbo, awaiting the next administration to modify the plans." The cumulative effect of these shortcomings, Clark asserted, was that the district's "recent performance had been dismal at best." In particular, the judge noted that on the Missouri Mastery and Achievement Tests, just five elementary schools, one middle school, and one high school had met or exceeded the statewide average.

Clark also expressed serious concern that, having agreed to the settlement relieving the state of its extraordinary obligations to the district, administrators in Kansas City would be unable to "get its financial affairs in order" and cope effectively with the reductions in state aid. The judge commented that "the purpose of a budget is to plan for upcoming expenses and only deviate from that budgeted amount for good cause." He noted, however, that the district's lax accounting inexplicably continued "to simply throw large sums of money into various accounts, allowing departments to either exceed the budgeted amount by a huge sum, or not use significant portions in that account." Such practices, Clark maintained, "makes identifying how much money the district actually needs to operate extremely difficult." Nevertheless, the judge reminded school officials that "within a very short time frame" the district would be forced to operate within its means, and he suggested additional cuts to central administration. Clark asserted that in the past two years, the district "has found much to cut in the way of school services, but little in the areas of administration." During the transition period, the judge suggested that district officials critically examine the "lavish" expenditures budgeted for the administrative superstructure.

In the end, Clark concluded that, when confronted with the challenges of narrowing the achievement gap between white and minority students and devising a workable operational budget, "the administration of the [district] is not up to the task." By his own assessment, Clark found Kansas City's school system to be, "floundering and in desperate need of educational expertise," and flatly asserted that, "the district has lost the confidence of many of its staff, students, parents and community at large." Accordingly, he appealed to Robert Bartman, Missouri Education Commissioner, "to provide guidance through this transition period." Should Bartman decline the court's request, Clark suggested that another "special master" be appointed to monitor the transition and approve the district's budget decisions.

The March 26 order was Judge Clark's final ruling in Kansas City's desegregation case. Having overseen the twenty years of litigation which had passed since the initial suit seeking the creation of a metropolitan school district was filed, Clark excused himself from the case. The judge's final order was a fitting capstone to his two decade tenure as the arbiter for the Kansas City school district. Clark's concern for the district's students is evident throughout the opinion, and he cited approvingly some of the accomplishments made possible by his orders from the bench. However, the judge also expressed his profound disappointment with the results of the desegregation effort. Many Kansas City residents viewed Clark – for good or ill – as the primary architect of the magnet schools desegregation plan, but in the March order, he attempted, in some respects, to distance himself from the district's plan. In large measure, the judge's ruling was a scathing indictment of the school district's inability to manage and implement effectively the substantial financial and educational resources which the court ordered. Clark's frustration with the school district is palpable throughout much of the ruling, but, having approved the settlement, the judge stepped down knowing that numerous difficulties lingered and that the goals of higher student achievement and increased desegregation remained elusive.

The case was reassigned to Judge Dean Whipple, who oversaw the litigation during the transitional period, and true to Clark's observations, many of the chronic problems which had long plagued the district persisted. By late 1998, the district was again searching for a new superintendent. In October 1998, at the urging of the three-member panel appointed by Judge Whipple to monitor the transition, the school board voted to buy out the remainder of Superintendent Henry Williams's contract. Williams had been hired as superintendent just two years earlier but had proven unable to work effectively with the school board or to demonstrate convincingly that achievement in the district would improve under his leadership. While the school board conducted a nine-month search for Williams's successor, two high ranking members of central administration shared the responsibilities of the superintendent's office. The torturous search for a new superintendent plainly illustrated the lingering problems in Kansas City and the negative perception which many school administrators held of the district.

Potential candidates for the superintendency were wary of assuming administrative leadership in a district replete with as many problems as were present in Kansas City. The new superintendent would be forced to contend not only with vexing budgetary decisions in light of the imminent end of the state's desegregation funding, but would also be called upon to provide guidance in addressing a host of additional concerns. In 1999, achievement levels in Kansas City continued to lag behind state and national averages, the achievement gap between the races persisted, the dropout rate remained nearly double the state average, the number of district schools with minority enrollments of more than 90% was again rising, and the future of the magnet schools remained uncertain. Moreover, the district's enrollment was declining precipitously as more than 3,000 students who had attended district schools the previous year opted to enroll in state-funded charter schools. Conscious of the substantial challenges present in Kansas City, several candidates for the superintendent's office withdrew from consideration and two finalists refused the school district's contract offers. Ultimately, Benjamin Demps, a former administrator with the Federal Aviation Administration, accepted the post in July 1999.

Demps inherited a beleaguered school district, and despite his optimism that a plethora of problems could be overcome with effective leadership and organization, the district's standing declined further. The cruelest blow came in October 1999 when the Missouri State Board of Education voted unanimously to strip the school district of its accreditation. Officials from the state found that Kansas City's schools failed to meet any of the eleven mandatory state performance standards for accreditation, including attendance, dropout rates, standardized test scores, reading achievement, and college entrance exam scores, among others. Moreover, one month later Judge Whipple declined the school district's pleas that the state's decision be declared void. In his November 17 order, the judge concluded that, "the state board's accreditation decision holds the Kansas City, Missouri School District accountable for its educational failures," and that to overturn that decision would allow the district "to further shirk its educational responsibilities to the state of Missouri and the children of Kansas City."

The school district's desperate situation was compounded further by Judge Whipple's surprise ruling to dismiss the desegregation case. In dismissing the suit, the judge found that "the retention of judicial control may be more disruptive than beneficial." He reasoned that further judicial oversight was likely to impede Superintendent Demps's determination to provide the leadership necessary to overcome the district's ills. Moreover, Whipple maintained that the time had come for the elected school board to solve the district's problems rather than embroiling the district in more costly litigation, and using the court as a shield against accepting greater responsibility for the school system's affairs. Most crucially, although he acknowledged that the district remained deeply troubled, the judge found that the school district was indeed providing equal educational opportunities for all students regardless of their race. Thus, Whipple's ruling laid bare one of the curious ironies of school desegregation law. The constitution guarantees that all students should be provided with equal educational opportunities, but it is silent as to the quality of that education. Indeed, coupled with the state's decision to strip Kansas City of its accreditation, Whipple's decision in essence found that all students in the district were provided with thoroughly equal opportunities to receive a substandard education.

Conclusions

Judge Whipple's November 1999 order dismissing the case brought an end to the nation's most expensive desegregation plan. After twenty-two years of litigation and the implementation of a remedy which cost nearly $2 billion, Whipple determined that the vestiges of segregation in Kansas City had been eradicated to the maximum extent practicable and that the school district was providing equal educational opportunities for all its students. Whipple's decision brought closure to the process that the Supreme Court had set in motion four years earlier. The Court's 1995 ruling had fatally undermined the foundation of the remedial plan by finding that the objective of attracting additional white students to the district was invalid. That decision signaled the beginning of the abandonment of desegregation in Kansas City. Judge Whipple's 1999 decision simply finalized the process of gradually reducing the amount of financial assistance the district received from the state and returning Kansas City's school system to local control. With the end of the transition period, the school district was declared unitary, and Kansas City joined a number of school systems around the country in gradually terminating their desegregation plans.

Developments in the Kansas City case during the mid-1990s not only radically reshaped and redirected the school district, but also reverberated through school systems across the country. Indeed, the Supreme Court's 1995 decision in *Missouri v. Jenkins* can be viewed as an important turning point in the history of school desegregation. That decision, in part, illustrated the high court's inclination to withdraw from school desegregation. In *Jenkins*, the Court's majority emphasized the temporary nature of remedial plans and underscored the Court's desire for school districts to be released from judicial oversight and returned to local control. After forty years of defining the constitutional context of school integration, passing judgment on appropriate remedial measures, and leading the nation's schools toward greater social equality, a majority of the Supreme Court was prepared to abandon the issue. Moreover, the significance of the Court's *Jenkins* ruling was not lost on school administrators, attorneys, or federal judges. Since the 1995 decision, numerous cities have been released from court-ordered desegregation remedies, including some of those most readily identifiable as battlegrounds in the legal struggle for integrated schooling. Denver, Boston, and Charlotte-Mecklenburg, among a great many other cities, began to dismantle their court-ordered desegregation plans between 1995 and 1999.

In Kansas City, the gradual transition from judicial oversight to local control was rife with difficulties. The timetable and the state's fiscal contributions were significant obstacles to the initial settlement negotiations. Having won at the Supreme Court, officials from the state pressed for a relatively rapid and inexpensive exit from its commitments to Kansas City. School officials, on the other hand, sought a much more gradual transition, and at times appeared most reluctant to remove the school district from the security of judicial oversight. Pressure from the state and the federal district court eventually compelled the school district to settle and begin the process of weaning itself from the massive infusions of state assistance. In the end, the budget reductions necessary throughout the district in order to adjust for the loss of the state's desegregation aid left the Kansas City schools a shell of what had they had been just five years earlier. Educational enhancements were slashed dramatically, magnet programs were dropped at numerous schools, building maintenance suffered because of budget reductions, and class sizes rose in many buildings due to cuts to the teaching staff. Moreover, the administrative instability, budgetary indecision, and maddening uncertainty regarding school closures and the future of the district's magnet programs brought the school board and central administration under intense criticism. Still further, during the transitional period, student achievement levels lagged behind state and national averages, the white enrollment declined, and the number of racially isolated schools increased. In some respects, the Kansas City public schools of 1999 were bedeviled by the same problems which existed when the desegregation suit was initiated twenty-two years earlier. In fact there were many school district patrons and employees who would agree with Judy Morgan, the president of the teachers' union in Kansas City, who commented after Judge Whipple's dismissal of the case, "there was a period when things were better, but I don't think they are now."

Conclusion

Judge Whipple's November 1999 order dismissing the desegregation suit ended more than two decades of litigation in Kansas City. Twenty-two years had passed since the last time that school officials in Kansas City made policy decisions free of the distractions presented by a pending desegregation lawsuit. Moreover, the district would be operating without judicial oversight for the first time in fifteen years. While Superintendent Benjamin Demps and others welcomed the opportunity to chart the district's course without the intervention of a federal judge, the dismissal of the desegregation suit was hardly cause for celebration. As the nation stood on the threshold of a new millennium, the immediate future of the Kansas City public schools looked rather bleak. Whipple's refusal to enjoin the state education department's decision denying accreditation to the school district assured that school officials would face substantial challenges for some time to come.

Whipple's decision not only brought an end to the *Jenkins* litigation but also brought a sense of closure to a roughly fifty year period in which racial considerations and racially-oriented issues figured most prominently, and, at times, dominated the policy decisions made by school officials. The Kansas City public schools were radically transformed over the course of this period and the school system in 1999 bore little resemblance to that of five decades earlier. In 1954, Kansas City's segregated schools were more than 80% white, enrolled about 60,000 students, and offered arguably the finest public education available in the metropolitan area. At a time when many smaller surrounding communities offered little or no education for black students beyond elementary school and only rudimentary high school programs for white students, Kansas City boasted of a comprehensive educational program for all students, black and white, through high school. While it was not uncommon for surrounding school districts to employ teachers with little formal education beyond high school, every teacher in the Kansas City schools held a college degree, and much of the district's staff had completed graduate school course work. Moreover, in 1954,

Kansas City students attended classes in some of the finest school facilities in the area. The city's residents took pride in their schools and had proven willing to invest in the improvement of the school district. Kansas City voters had a long history of routinely approving tax levy increases and bond issues in order to bolster the operating budget and provide funding for new school construction or renovations to existing buildings. It would seem safe to conclude that in 1954, residents of the metropolitan area generally considered the Kansas City public schools one of the better, if not the best, districts in the area.

By 1999, the Kansas City public schools enrolled 31,200 students, approximately 80% of whom were minorities, and the general perception of the Kansas City public schools was much less favorable. Whereas fifty years earlier, the school system was an institution in which most Kansas City residents took pride, in 1999, Kansas City was the only unaccredited school district in the state of Missouri. Student achievement in the district was below state and national averages, and the school district had the highest drop-out rate in the area. Although some schools, such as Lincoln Academy, boasted of student achievement levels well above state and national norms, the district, when measured by standardized achievement test scores, generally offered what Desegregation Monitoring Committee had earlier described as "the worst of education in the metropolitan Kansas City area."

In 1999, the school district had wonderful facilities but not because of any groundswell of support from the city's residents. The fabulous make-over of the district's schools accomplished during the 1980s and 1990s was entirely attributable to Judge Clark's court orders. Clark authorized the massive capital improvements plans knowing just how unlikely it was that the city's voting population would approve the fiscal measures necessary to finance the projects. After a handful of unsuccessful attempts to gain the required support from the district's patrons at the polls, Clark imposed the tax levy measure on his own authority. Moreover, the public's continued indifference to the school system's declining financial standing following the termination of the state's obligations under the desegregation orders threatened to compound many of the school district's most basic problems.

The school district's precarious financial position in 1999 was testament to the tepid support of the city's voters. Since the 1995 *Jenkins* decision, school officials had drastically cut away at the district's bloated budget by eliminating hundreds of staff positions, trimming or terminating numerous programs, and slashing countless other expenses. Even so, the district's fiscal situation remained dubious and school officials looked more toward the state legislature than the city's residents for the financial assistance the district desperately required.

Between 1954 and 1999, Kansas City residents witnessed a dramatic reversal in the reputation and educational standing of the city's public school system. The question, then, is how to account for what happened to Kansas City's public school system over this roughly fifty year period. Of course, any answer to this question is certain to be incomplete; however, in part the answer lies in basic local problems, such as the transient leadership of the school district, the inability of the school district to address adequately the concerns of its diverse patron base, and the lack of sufficient financial support on a consistent basis from the voting public since the late 1960s. In part the answer lies in larger issues concerning the city itself. Fluid demographic patterns, the exodus of the middle class from the city, the growth of the suburban ring, and the concentration of what William Julius Wilson has termed "the truly disadvantaged" population in the central city, all contributed to the difficulties of managing the school system. Furthermore, part of the school district's decline is plainly attributable to the inability of school officials to keep pace with the changing legal standards. The downfall of the Kansas City schools, then, is in part the result of the complex interaction of several factors, some of which were beyond the control of school officials in the city. All of these factors, however, were related in some degree to issues of race.

Formulating public policies that dealt with racial issues in a manner that was acceptable to the diverse interests affected by those decisions is without question one of the defining problems in American history during the last half of the twentieth century. Racial implications steadily became larger considerations in numerous aspects of American social and political life, including the management of the public schools. Managing racial issues in the public schools was a vexing problem for hundreds of cities, and Kansas City's experience was no exception. Indeed, it can be argued that the great failure of the Kansas City public schools in the last half of the twentieth century was the inability of school officials and the public school system to deal effectively with racial concerns.

Beginning in the 1950s, school officials in Kansas City were compelled to evaluate racial considerations as a part of the policy making process in a way which they had not been forced to do previously. Changes in constitutional law propelled racial issues to the forefront of the policy making process in Kansas City. Moreover, racially specific demographic shifts in the city and metropolitan area increasingly became part of the calculus of formulating policy for the district. Still further, school officials were obliged to evaluate the interests and relative influence of the district's racial constituencies, neighborhood associations, community groups and civil rights organizations in the school district's policy making process. In Kansas City, race indisputably became a much more significant consideration in the school district's policy decisions from 1954 forward, and the inability of the school district and its leadership to adjust effectively to a rapidly changing set of circumstances in the last half of the twentieth century helps to explain the district's ignominious downward spiral.

Prior to the 1950s, race was a relatively minor consideration in the formulation of school district policy. On a few occasions in the 1920s and 1940s, demographic changes compelled the school board to convert a school from white use to black use. Similarly, the school board at times addressed the need to renovate some of the district's segregated black schools or build a new school for black students. Aside from these considerations, the school board meeting minutes reveal few instances where racially-oriented issues were discussed. This is not to suggest that Kansas City's black population was thoroughly satisfied with the school system, but the paucity of references to issues involving the district's segregated black schools suggests at least a certain level of tolerance or acceptance for the manner in which the system met the interests of black families.

The delicate process of balancing the competing interests of different racial and community groups grew increasingly difficult as the district converted to integrated schools in 1955. Following the *Brown* decision, school planners in Kansas City followed the letter of law and dismantled the segregated system in 1955. The initial desegregation plan based on a neighborhood schools format assured that the great majority of Kansas City's students would continue to attend the same school as they had previously and that integration would only occur at those schools where the lines defining the attendance zones crossed the lines of residential segregation. Dissolving the segregated system resulted in relatively little racial mixing in Kansas City's public schools, but the law required nothing more in the 1950s. In fact, by simply dismantling its racially segregated dual attendance zones, Kansas City was a leader among cities implementing the *Brown* decision and was widely hailed as a model of compliance.

However, while school officials congratulated themselves for their prompt compliance with the Supreme Court's edict and the racially neutral manner in which the attendance zones were drawn, the plan belied hints of catering to the interests of white patrons. School officials had compelling reasons for considering how the white population might react to the integration plan. At the time, white students comprised more than 80% of the enrollment in Kansas City's public schools. Moreover, white residents accounted for more than 80% of the city's population, and provided the bulk of the tax revenue that financed the school district. White support was absolutely critical to the operation of the school district, and white reaction against an integration plan which brought too much change too soon could have potentially borne serious consequences for the district. With these considerations in mind, school planners in Kansas City developed the 1955 desegregation plan which assured that the majority of the white population would not be immediately affected by school integration.

The initial desegregation plan itself included some evidence that the interests of white patrons figured prominently in the development of the district's plan. In some sections of the city, the newly fashioned attendance zones followed the prevailing lines of residential segregation, and in at least one instance, there appears to be evidence of gerrymandering. In the Dunbar area, the peculiarly shaped attendance zone strictly adhered to the prevailing lines of residential segregation and the school remained exclusively black until the early 1970s. A second indication of the school district's deference to the interests of white patrons was the continuation of the school district's long-standing policy of granting student transfers. Indeed, the copies of the desegregation plan that were distributed to the public included a six-page section that reaffirmed the district's liberal student transfer policy. The transfer policy permitted students who, for any reason, were dissatisfied with their neighborhood school to be placed in another school having space available to accommodate them. In effect, the transfer policy provided an avenue by which one could avoid attending an integrated school, and hundreds of white students did just that. The problem of evading integration through the transfer policy was initially confined to relatively few schools. During the 1960s and 1970s, however, as the process of racial transition began to accelerate in those neighborhoods south and east of the central black residential area, the use of the transfer policy to evade integration became a more significant problem for school officials.

The desegregation plan adopted in 1955 foreshadowed some of the problems which would plague the school district over the next twenty years. By adopting a neighborhood schools model as the integration plan, school officials shackled the school district to the pronounced patterns of residential segregation in the city. Moreover, when coupled with the liberal transfer policy, the desegregation plan in effect meant that avoiding integration was relatively simple. Thus, in 1955, Kansas City school officials, perhaps to some degree unwittingly, had created the system which would later haunt the district. The conversion to integrated schools was widely applauded and thoroughly in compliance with the legal standards, but the plan established a framework for subsequent problems. Over the course of the next two decades, as numerous crises arose concerning the state of integration in the Kansas City public schools, school leaders proved exceedingly reluctant to veer from the policy choices made in 1955. Indeed, the dogged reluctance of school officials to scuttle the neighborhood schools plan and the transfer policy, and to begin thinking of integration in broader terms spelled disaster for the district. After considering what school officials perceived to be the interests of the various racial constituencies and neighborhood groups affected by policy decisions, the school district typically reaffirmed its commitment to integration through a neighborhood schools concept. Addressing isolated crises in a piecemeal fashion that inconvenienced or alienated as few district patrons, especially whites, as possible proved to be the preferred method of managing the school system for the next twenty years. In doing so, however, school officials consistently neglected to address in a forthright way the larger causes, such as demographic change, which lay at the root of the crises.

Among Kansas City's public school patrons, attitudes toward school integration and the proper course for the district during the 1960s and 1970s covered a broad spectrum. The bulk of the district's patrons, however, fell into two large constituencies, and with respect to racial issues, school officials' options were essentially narrowed to choosing between two competing interests. On one hand, was a large cross-section of the black population and residents in transitional neighborhoods, such as the Paseo High School area and later in the southeast corridor. These patrons argued that rather than reacting to demographic changes, the school district should assume a pro-active role in promoting more extensive integration in the city's schools and urged school officials to use the influence of the district to stabilize neighborhoods undergoing racial transition. These patrons pressured the school district to integrate the black students involved in the initial busing program, and advocated that the new schools built to relieve crowding in the black residential area be constructed at sites which would stimulate further integration. These patrons were also early supporters of pairing and clustering schemes which would cut across the lines of residential segregation and facilitate increased racial mixing in the schools. Furthermore, they were among the first to suggest that the school district revise the long-standing liberal transfer policy, which they correctly recognized was being used to evade integration. Finally, although these patrons were not staunch supporters of busing, they were not firmly opposed to it provided that their children were safe and attended good schools.

On the other hand, were those residents who preferred that the school district continue to react to the changing circumstances in the city rather than attempt to influence developments. Many of these patrons lived far enough removed from the growing black residential area that their children were generally unaffected by school district policy decisions announced for the transitional areas. It was possible for these patrons to view the racial issues involving the core black area and the transitional neighborhoods as someone else's problem. They had no objection to the manner in which the schools were organized, were satisfied with an integration program confined largely to those schools in the transitional areas, and were generally unconcerned about whether the transfer policy was being used to avoid integration. Furthermore, assuming that those neighborhood groups which appeared before the school board were representative of these communities, these patrons were not eager to see the school district employ busing or other schemes to promote additional integration.

During the 1960s and early 1970s, members of the Board of Education and central administration for the Kansas City schools were also divided, albeit unevenly, over the proper course for the school district on issues of racial integration. As evidenced by the policy choices that administrators recommended to the school board, the bulk of Kansas City's central administration was inclined to support measures that dealt with racial crises in an isolated manner while facilitating the continuation of the neighborhood schools concept with limited racial mixing as the primary organizational model for the district. It was not until twenty years after the implementation of the original desegregation plan that the district's central administration developed Plan 6-C, the first district-wide plan that contemplated substantial revisions to the neighborhood schools plan.

There were indications, however, that a small group within the district's central administration at times advocated a more pro-active approach to the district's racial concerns. These administrators were led by Superintendent James Hazlett. In the 1960s, Hazlett and others recommended that student transfers out of Paseo and Southeast high schools be sharply curtailed in an effort to stabilize those transitional neighborhoods. More importantly, Hazlett's "Concepts for Changing Times" proposed several policy options that would have extended school integration beyond the neighborhood school. The pairing, clustering, magnet schools, and metropolitan desegregation proposals discussed in Hazlett's pamphlet clearly suggest openness to innovative schemes for promoting greater integration.

Superintendent Hazlett's support for pro-active policies on racially-oriented issues was, however, inconsistent at best. He was equally capable of recommending measures that reflected a more reactive stance. In the early 1960s, he supported the initial intact busing arrangement that segregated black students transported out of the overcrowded schools in the expanding black residential area. Only when the district was threatened with legal action by the city's civil rights organizations did Hazlett advocate integrating the bused black students. In the mid-1960s, he also rejected the recommendations made in Dr. Robert Havighurst's study that the three new schools to relieve crowding in the black corridor be built at sites that would draw an integrated enrollment. Hazlett favored building the schools at sites which were more cost effective despite the fact that the new schools would be exclusively black. Furthermore, Superintendent Hazlett supported the busing arrangement made for the largely black student body at Manual High School. In a policy reminiscent of the intact busing policy of the early 1960s, the entire Manual enrollment was bused for eight years to the vacant junior college building and never integrated with the majority white Westport High School, located across the street from the junior college.

On issues of integration, the policies that Hazlett recommended fluctuated wildly between the pro-active and reactive positions. Although he supported sweeping changes to the integration program in his "Concepts for Changing Times" pamphlet, Hazlett tended to react to more immediate crises in a conservative manner which reinforced the neighborhood schools concept. Hazlett's shifting position on racial issues further demonstrates the conflicting pressures that shaped the district's integration policy. Demographic shifts, such as the growth of the central black neighborhood and the rapid pace of racial transition along the southeast corridor, compelled the superintendent to formulate policies that addressed immediate crises. Indeed, between 1955 and 1965, Hazlett's first ten years as superintendent, the black student population grew by 19,000. In weighing the competing interests of black and white patrons, Hazlett often tended to show greater deference to whites. His support for the intact busing plans and his reluctance to restrict transfers on a more extensive basis, both demonstrate an advocacy for adhering to the principles of the initial desegregation plan. Furthermore, his understanding of the school district's budgetary limitations persuaded him to reject the recommendations in the Havighurst study. Hazlett did, however, recognize that radical changes in the way in which the school district was organized were necessary in order to create a lasting solution to the district's integration problems. Nevertheless, during the 1960s and early 1970s, school board members did not share his vision.

The ultimate responsibility for the district's integration plan and its modifications lay with the school board, and during the 1960s and 1970s, Kansas City's school board was not a very representative group. Until 1970, board members, almost without exception, were residents of the affluent, overwhelmingly white, southwestern part of the city. Because of the curious composition of the school board, one suspects that individual members were perhaps more fully informed of the perspective of upper class whites who lived in areas far removed from the growing black neighborhood and the transitional corridor. Indeed, one would suspect that, although not completely ignorant of the interests of the black community in school district affairs, the board members were certainly less familiar with the interests and expectations of the city's African-American population. After all, while the affluent white segment of the population was often represented by six members, only one black, Dr. John Ramos, served on the school board prior to the 1970s. Moreover, the 1970 reorganization of the board into a nine member body designed to be more representative of the city's population did not fundamentally shift the balance of power. Beginning in 1970, black students comprised a majority of the district's enrollment, but the school board remained majority white.

In managing the direction of the school district on racial issues, school board members generally opted for what they perceived to be the safer course. Almost without exception, the school district embraced the familiar role of reacting to changing circumstances in a conservative manner which typically reinforced the city's patterns of residential segregation and reflected what the school board perceived to be the will of the city's white majority. In spite of overwhelming evidence that the demographic bases of the school district were changing dramatically and that traditional models of school organization might no longer be applicable in light of the evolving legal standards regarding school desegregation, school officials relied on annual adjustments to attendance zones and modifications to the busing program as the preferred tools for addressing the population shifts affecting the district. Other options, such as those presented in Hazlett's "Concepts for Changing Times," were deemed to be too radical of a departure from the existing neighborhood schools system. Moreover, school officials proved most reluctant throughout the 1960s to adopt any change in the transfer policy despite documentation indicating that thousands of patrons used transfers to evade integration. The district's conservative policy choices were roundly criticized by black patrons and residents living in the transitional areas, but were generally supported in those sections of the city removed from the core black neighborhood and the southeast corridor.

Typically, the district's policy choices during the 1960s and early 1970s bowed to the interests of a white majority which was generally comfortable with the segregated nature of the city's residential patterns and schools. In short, one must conclude that district officials were attempting to comply with the bare minimum requirements of the prevailing legal standards while preserving the status quo to the maximum extent possible. In practice, school district policy choices had the effect of producing minimal racial mixing confined almost exclusively to those schools which served neighborhoods undergoing racial transition and to those schools involved in the district's modest busing program.

In adopting this position school district officials were motivated to some degree by the fear of losing white students to the suburbs or the city's private and parochial schools. By the late1960s, the Kansas City public schools were losing almost 2,000 white students each year, and concerns over additional losses figured prominently in the district's policy choices. In most instances, it seems clear that the fear of fueling the white exodus from the school district overrode the interests of other groups in policy decisions. Most damaging was the benign neglect of the district's black patrons. Throughout the 1960s, the black community's pleas for more extensive integration, an end to the evasion of the transfer policy, further relief for the overcrowded condition of the schools serving the expanding black neighborhood in the southeast, and access to a higher quality education went unanswered. The consequences of the school district's choices were profound. Whereas the Kansas City schools had been in the vanguard of school integration in the mid-1950s, fifteen years later the school board had abandoned any pretext of aggressively promoting additional integration. Feelings of alienation and frustration grew in the black community while the district's policy choices failed to stem the white exodus.

School district policy choices designed to preserve the status quo were doomed, in part, by the rapidly changing nature of the city in the 1960s and 1970s. Massive highway construction and urban renewal projects refashioned the city and displaced thousands of residents. Moreover, residents who were not displaced by construction projects were also highly mobile. On one hand, it is difficult to conceive of any school district policy measure which would have halted the white exodus from the city. During the 1960s, the white population living within the school district's boundaries declined by more than 31,000 and the white school enrollment fell by almost 16,000. Undeniably, whites were moving away from the city, frequently to the growing suburban ring, and school officials were essentially powerless to reverse the trend. On the other hand, Kansas City's black population grew at an unprecedented rate. Between 1960 and 1970, the city's black population increased by almost 29,000 and the number of black students enrolled in the city's public schools grew by 15,000 students, an increase of nearly 75%.

The same demographic trends which characterized the 1960s continued in the 1970s. During the 1970s, the white population within the school district declined by more than 86,000 and the white student enrollment in the city's public schools fell by nearly 25,000. In 1970, the Kansas City public schools became majority black, and by the end of the decade black students comprised more than two-thirds of the district's enrollment. The growth of the black residential area in the southeast corridor continued unabated during the 1970s, and by 1980, the process of residential transition had reached the southeast fringes of the city. A continuous line of neighborhoods, three to four miles wide, occupied almost exclusively by black residents stretched for more than ten miles from the downtown area toward the southeast.

As the number of white students attending the Kansas City public schools declined, support for the fiscal measures which financed the district declined as well. It is important to remember that although Kansas City's public schools were two-thirds black by the late 1970s, the population of the city remained majority white. It seems clear that in some sections of the city, particularly the working class areas north and east of downtown, the white majority refused to support fiscal measures that benefited a predominantly black school district. Arthur Benson and others have noted that it hardly seems coincidental that the last time the public approved a school district fiscal measure was in 1969, the last year in which white students comprised a majority of the district's enrollment. After the approval of the 1969 tax levy increase, nineteen consecutive bond issues and levy increases were defeated, and the consequences for the school district were catastrophic.

The school district's desperate fiscal condition in the early 1970s generated innumerable problems for the school system. Building maintenance was cut drastically and the city's public schools became by degrees increasingly less pleasant environments for education. Teaching positions were eliminated and class sizes rose concomitantly. Educational programs, such as art, music and physical education, were cut. Support personnel, including school nurses, custodians, and teachers' aides, were radically reduced as well. Twice during the 1970s, the district's teachers went on strike seeking higher salaries and expanded benefits from a district which was teetering on the verge of insolvency. By the mid-1970s, because of the public's failure to provide adequate financial support, the district had deteriorated to the point that few patrons were satisfied. Facilities were literally crumbling, the academic program had been cut to the core, and the school district's AAA rating from the state had been dropped to AA.

Beyond those problems related to the school district's fiscal situation were a host of lingering racially-oriented difficulties. Racial isolation in the city's public schools remained an enormous problem. In the early 1970s, more than three-fourths of the district's black students attended schools which were more than 95% black. Black activists in the city expressed their profound concern that most schools in the district could be easily identified as either overwhelmingly black or virtually all-white, while very few schools were integrated to any significant extent. The integration that was achieved at certain schools tended to be fleeting, and most schools resegregated in a matter of a few years. In addition to the problem of racial isolation among students, in the early 1970s, Kansas City's NAACP office began to challenge the district's hiring practices and raised questions concerning the paucity of minorities who held positions in central administration. Finally, during the early 1970s, Hispanic activism in school affairs increased significantly. Patrons living on the West Side aggressively pressed for school programs that more adequately met the interests of the city's Latino population.

The late 1960s and early 1970s were pivotal times for the school district in Kansas City. During this period, school officials were confronted with the growing activism of the district's black and Hispanic patrons, the withdrawal of white students from the district at a staggering rate, and a desperately poor fiscal situation. Furthermore, a growing number of school officials realized that the school district was no longer in compliance with the legal standards governing school integration. The sheer number of racially isolated schools in Kansas City clearly violated the Supreme Court's 1968 admonition in *Green v. County School Board* that segregation must be dismantled "root and branch." It would appear that the time was ripe for change in the district, but little changed. School officials continued to pursue a policy of school integration within a neighborhood schools concept despite the recognition that such a policy, tied to the city's rigidly segregated residential patterns, produced little integration. Indeed, when the SCLC filed the *Scott* suit in 1973 seeking increased integration in the city's public schools, the district was in its eighteenth year of integration within the neighborhood schools concept, and there was no indication that central administration intended to revise the integration plan in the immediate future. The reluctance of school officials to aggressively address the interests of the district's minority patrons in seeking more extensive integration ultimately led to the protracted struggle with the federal department of Health, Education and Welfare in the mid-1970s.

Under the crushing weight of the school district's financial problems coupled with the on-going racial difficulties, school officials appealed to the federal government for relief. The school district's application for federal funds available under the Emergency School Assistance Act immediately brought increased scrutiny of the district's desegregation program. Under pressure from HEW, school leaders grudgingly began to address some of the chronic racial problems in the district. The use of the liberal student transfer policy to evade integration ended at the insistence of HEW, and the district was compelled to reassign hundreds of teachers and building principals in such a way that the schools were not racially identifiable on the basis of their staffs alone. Furthermore, at the insistence of HEW, school officials developed the first district-wide integration plan. After more than two decades in which integration occurred solely by the geography of chance in those neighborhoods where the racial composition was in transition, the school district adopted Plan 6-C, a massive busing plan for integration.

In the contentious relationship with HEW, school leaders in Kansas City finally abandoned the original desegregation plan and began to consider integration in dramatically different terms. To be sure, forsaking the neighborhood schools concept was not a choice that school officials made willingly. Only after years of negotiation, prodding and threats of losing federal funding did school officials implement a busing plan for integration. Plan 6-C also marked the first time in which the school district adopted an integration measure that was wildly unpopular with the district's white patrons. Although Plan 6-C solved the school district's racial integration problems to the satisfaction of HEW, the plan actually promoted white flight from the district. The year after the plan went into effect, the school district lost more than 3,000 white students.

The school district's relationship with HEW marks an important turning point for the Kansas City public schools. Not only did HEW compel school officials to address forthrightly the issue of racial isolation in the schools but the federal department also persuaded the school district's policy makers to begin considering other models for integration. Although Plan 6-C was largely a forced busing scheme, the plan also contained school clustering and magnet schools components. The introduction of magnet schools in particular would be influential in shaping the school district's approach to integration in the 1980s and 1990s. Finally, the relationship with HEW convinced many school officials in Kansas City that the only long-term solution to the district's integration problems was a metropolitan approach that incorporated the largely white suburban school districts.

As the exodus of white students continued unabated under Plan 6-C, school district leaders resorted to litigation, filing the metropolitan suit in 1977. Having finally abandoned the neighborhood schools concept, the metropolitan lawsuit is indicative of how school officials were thoroughly converted to broader models for integration. The metropolitan complaint proposed the consolidation of school districts on both sides of the state line, an unprecedented remedial measure. The defendants named in the school district's metropolitan suit can be viewed as a snapshot of where school officials in Kansas City believed blame for the school district's integration problems should be placed. The suburban districts, it was alleged, were liable because they were havens that had excluded blacks while welcoming white families fleeing the city. The states of Kansas and Missouri were at fault, the school district alleged, for having tacitly supported the growth of the predominantly white suburbs, and in Missouri's case for not having provided Kansas City with adequate assistance in eradicating the vestiges of segregation that plagued the district. The school district complaint also maintained that the federal departments of Housing and Urban Development, and Transportation were liable because of the way in which federal housing policies and the relocation of families displaced by urban renewal and highway construction projects had reinforced the patterns of residential segregation in the city. Finally, school district attorneys maintained that the reforms HEW demanded were capricious and forced school officials to adopt the busing plan that exacerbated white flight from the Kansas City public schools. In this context, school officials maintained that the district was essentially blameless for the failure to integrate.

Although the school district's arguments against some of the defendants contained kernels of truth, the complaint was riddled with allegations that could not be adequately substantiated. Moreover, the district's questionable record on integration raised serious doubts as to the appropriateness of the school district pursuing the suit on behalf of its students and virtually assured that the school district would be realigned as a defendant. Indeed, from the 1950s until the mid-1970s, there appeared to be a clear pattern in which school officials bowed to the interests of white patrons when dealing with racial issues. In the final analysis, the school district's metropolitan suit should be viewed as an act of desperation on the part of a school district beleaguered with difficulties in satisfying the diverse interests of its patrons, unable to conceive of a plan that would promote stable integration, struggling with enormous fiscal uncertainties, and still vulnerable to further litigation.

In the *Jenkins* litigation that grew out of the metropolitan suit, the transformation of the school district's position on racial integration was complete. Nothing illustrated this shift more clearly than the level of cooperation between school officials and the attorneys for the black plaintiffs. School district officials readily admitted to the shortcomings of the original desegregation plan and acknowledged that vestiges of the segregated system lingered in the Kansas City schools thirty years later. School district officials cooperated with the black plaintiffs because the remedy initially sought in the *Jenkins* litigation remained metropolitan. With the dismissal of the suburbs, however, the school district adopted a compelling new motive for working with the plaintiffs: the remaking of the school district largely at the expense of the state of Missouri.

The legal standards concerning school integration had changed dramatically during the 1970s, and during the remedial phase of the *Jenkins* litigation, Kansas City took full advantage. Prior to the mid-1970s, school integration focused almost exclusively on the degree of racial mixing that various plans could produce in the schools. Little attention had been paid to the victims of segregation, other than to try to assure that they would attend schools in which white students were also enrolled. Following the Supreme Court's 1977 *Milliken v. Bradley II* decision, educational enhancements were commonly incorporated into desegregation remedies in order to address the specific needs of the victims of segregation. In *Jenkins*, the educational improvements proposed by the plaintiffs, endorsed by the school district, and ordered by Judge Russell Clark included millions of dollars in effective schools grants to every school in the district, enrichment and remedial programs, early childhood education, and a host of other initiatives. By 1995, the cost of these programs totaled more than $220 million.

Of course, the remedy also mandated that the Kansas City schools would promote additional integration, and school officials again looked toward the white population. By the mid-1980s, white students comprised one-fourth of the school district's enrollment, and most administrators agreed that meaningful, stable integration was impossible with so few whites. Recapturing white students lost to the suburbs or the city's private and parochial schools became a pivotal consideration in the formulation of the desegregation remedy, and one of the primary objectives of the magnet schools plan was to attract additional white students to the district. Magnet themes were selected in part based upon the projected drawing power that a theme would have among white students. School officials also maintained, however, that no matter how attractive a particular theme might be to white students, they would not attend the Kansas City public schools until the district's facilities were substantially improved. With this argument, the school district found an enthusiastic advocate in Judge Clark. Under the nebulous rationale of "suburban comparability" and "desegregative attractiveness," Clark authorized new construction or extensive renovations for every school in the district. Over the first ten years of the remedial period, the cost of the magnet schools programs and capital improvements totaled more than $1 billion.

For a time, the school district's desegregation plan based on educational improvements, magnet schools, and capital improvements seemed to hold promise for overcoming some of the district's most grievous problems. The school district's initial marketing studies indicated that white students enrolled in suburban districts or the city's private and parochial schools would seriously consider transferring to some of the district's magnet programs. Although the number of white transfer students consistently fell well short of the school district's goals, the white enrollment in the Kansas City public schools did slowly increase. Moreover, the magnet schools concept seemed to provide a solution to the district's chronic inability to satisfy the diverse interests of its patron base. The smorgasbord of curricular programs available through the magnet schools offered something for everyone and every section of the city. Despite their seemingly great potential on paper, Kansas City's magnets, in practice, never approached the lofty goals established in Judge Clark's remedial orders.

In large part, the failings of the magnet system in Kansas City are attributable to the district's leadership. One significant problem was the constant turnover in the superintendent's office. During the fourteen year remedial phase between 1985 and 1999, eight different men served as superintendent. Without consistent leadership from the superintendents, the remedy was continually tainted by a sense of impermanence. Beyond the lack of consistent leadership from the superintendent's office, other departments within Kansas City's central school administration amply demonstrated that they lacked the expertise to manage competently so sweeping a plan. District administrators frequently failed to meet the ambitious time line established for implementing the remedial plan. Consequently, curricular programs were not fully implemented, the assignment of students to magnet programs was often delayed, school construction projects fell behind schedule, student transportation was haphazard, and valuable equipment was misplaced. Moreover, under the intense pressure, administrators resigned and were too often replaced with personnel who lacked the experience and expertise to manage the responsibilities of their position. With each small administrative failure, the school district's critics grew in number.

Dissatisfaction with the school district and its management of the desegregation remedy ranged far beyond the administrative shortcomings. Many blacks viewed the plan's goals for attracting thousands of white students as both optimistic in the extreme and largely irrelevant to the objective of remedying the effects that past segregation had upon minority students. Moreover, conceptual problems, such as the quota system which initially limited the number of black students admitted to the magnet programs, alienated some patrons. Support for the desegregation plan among black patrons diminished further as the programs failed to meet the established educational goals. In spite of millions spent on educational improvements, the desegregation remedy did not close the achievement gap between black and white students. While some Kansas City blacks argued that another year's substandard test scores demonstrated the need to commit additional funding and resources to the educational improvements and the magnet schools, others maintained that the city's black students would be better served by a return to neighborhood schools that focused intensively on the core curriculum. By the early 1990s, the solid support of Kansas City's black community for the magnet schools system and other components of the remedial plan was crumbling.

Aside from the flagging support among the city's black population, the school district's plan was besieged by other critics from both within and outside the school district. Perhaps more than any other single factor, the expense of the remedial phase disaffected school patrons in Kansas City, particularly following Judge Clark's doubling of the tax levy. Individuals who otherwise supported the desegregation plan balked at the judicially imposed levy increase to fund the remedy. Moreover, beyond the city, the expense of the desegregation plan was widely criticized. The fiscal impact of the Kansas City remedy was felt most acutely in the state's smaller school districts. For small districts, the disproportionate level of state spending on the remedy in Kansas City meant that desperately needed state funds were channeled to the city while smaller districts coped with less. Budget shortfalls forced numerous districts to make significant adjustments and consider the termination of programs. Indeed, in some school districts in the metropolitan Kansas City area, a portion of the athletic budget came from parents who volunteered to work as vendors at Kansas City Royals games.

Criticism of the remedy's expense grew with each additional funding order mandated by Judge Clark. Particularly irksome were those orders which provided state funding for salary increases, and the extensions of state funding for the educational enhancements in the district. Many Missouri taxpayers perceived the objective of raising employees' salaries in Kansas City to a level comparable to surrounding school districts as thoroughly unrelated to integration or the task of remedying the constitutional violations. Similarly, Judge Clark was pilloried for his extensions of the state's obligations to fund the school district's educational enhancements. In particular, officials from the state objected to the manner in which the state's obligations continued indefinitely while Kansas City's standardized test scores remained largely stagnant. Clark had ruled that educational improvements should continue in Kansas City until the achievement gap between black and white students was narrowed appreciably, and until the district's standardized test scores improved to the point that they were equal to the national averages. Attorneys for the state maintained that Clark's achievement standards were arbitrary and had little relationship to the harm minority students had suffered as a result of the constitutional violations. The state's appeals on these points found a sympathetic majority in the United States Supreme Court.

When the state's appeals reached the Supreme Court in early 1995, school integration was clearly in retreat. Gone were the justices who had been the long-time defenders of school integration. In their place were seated a younger generation of more pragmatic jurists, a majority of whom tended to be inclined toward bringing a close to four decades of judicial oversight and experimentation with social engineering in the country's public schools. The Court's 1991 *Board of Education of Oklahoma City v. Dowell* and 1992 *Freeman v. Pitts* decisions clearly signaled a change in direction within the high court. In both cases, the Court specified the requirements to be met in order for a school district to be released from its court-ordered desegregation plan. By emphasizing that desegregation was intended only as a temporary measure to remedy past discrimination, the Court placed its imprimatur on the objective of restoring local authorities to the control of school systems. The 1995 decision in *Jenkins v. Missouri* further underscored the Court's withdrawal from school integration.

By 1995, school integration had ceased to be an issue which held captive the nation's attention as it had in decades past. According to opinion polls, a majority of nation's whites believed that educational opportunities available to blacks were equal to or superior to those for whites. Although relatively few blacks shared that conviction, a majority of the Supreme Court in a growing number of cases did. Despite the fact that the Court did not speak directly to this point in its 1995 *Jenkins* decision, the essence of the opinion embraced the notion that Kansas City's magnet schools system and capital improvements had accomplished the objective of providing minority students with educational opportunities equal to their white counterparts and had succeeded in restoring the black victims of segregation to the position that they would have occupied absent any constitutional violations. By ruling that the scope of the remedy in Kansas City exceeded the scope of the constitutional violations, the Court dealt the continued operation of the magnet schools desegregation plan a mortal blow. Moreover, by finding that Judge Clark could not justify the continuation of state funding for educational improvements on the basis of standardized test scores which remained below national norms, the Court undermined another aspect of the remedy. On the issue of continued state funding for educational improvements, the Court's decision had the effect of ruling that those programs had remedied the constitutional violations to the greatest extent practicable.

The Supreme Court's 1995 decision signaled the end for the remedial phase in Kansas City. For many of the plan's critics, the Court's ruling was a welcome change from the ever-expanding remedial orders issued from Judge Clark's bench. Indeed, for some observers, Kansas City had come to represent the flagrant excesses of school desegregation remedies. By 1995, about $1.5 billion had been spent on the desegregation remedy, and that figure rose to nearly $2 billion before the suit was dismissed in 1999. Much of that total had been committed to the implementation of magnet themes at newly constructed or extensively renovated schools, many of which operated at about 50% of capacity, and led some observers to conclude that the massive investment in the Kansas City magnet schools system had borne only meager returns.

Many of the problems that the school district faced in late 1999 were familiar ones. Student achievement in the district remained below national and state averages in most grade levels, and the racial disparity in student achievement lingered. The percentage of minority students attending racially isolated schools was again rising, while white enrollment in the district was declining. The district's fiscal standing was also uncertain as school officials lobbied the state legislature for additional funds and considered new taxation measures to bolster the operating budget. Finally, turnover within central administration remained a chronic problem. The latest superintendent had been on the job just five months.

The litany of problems facing the Kansas City public schools in 1999 looked eerily similar to those in 1977, when the metropolitan desegregation suit was initially filed in federal court. More than two decades of litigation had resulted in dozens of beautiful newly constructed or extensively renovated schools, millions in new equipment, some innovative magnet themes, more enrichment and remediation programs, but had failed to solve many of the school district's most basic problems. With the dismissal of the suit, school officials in Kansas City began anew the delicate process of balancing the interests of the district's diverse patron base while formulating policy measures in order to adjust to demographic shifts, changing legal standards, and the fiscal limitations of the school district.

Bibliography

Primary Sources

Kansas City, Missouri School District (KCMSD) Documents and File Groups

Abend-Singleton and Associates, Lintecum Architects, and Tognasioli, Gross, and Jarvis Architects, "Kansas City, Missouri School District Desegregation Capital Improvements Study," November 25, 1985, filed in Richard C. Hunter, "Kansas City, Missouri School District Long-Range Capital Improvement Plan," ("Hunter Report") February 1987, Appendix I, Hunter Report File, KCMSD Archives.

Benson History of Kansas City Desegregation File, KCMSD Archives.

Blair, Reverend James, Spokesman for CUA, Statement to Board of Education, filed in *BOE Minutes*, September 8, 1966, Doc. 307646.

Blim to Students of Kansas City Junior College, August 16, 1954; "Desegregation -- Junior College, Progress Report," August 18, 1954, Junior College File, KCMSD Archives.

Board of Education Meeting Minutes. Office of Board Services, KCMSD.

"Bond Proposal: Recapitulation of Wards and Blue Township," filed in *BOE Minutes*, April 25, 1969, Doc. 315507.

"Bond Proposal: Recapitulation of Wards and Blue Township," filed in *BOE Minutes*, June 5, 1969, Doc. 315590.

"Bond Proposal: Recapitulation of Wards and Blue Township," filed in *BOE Minutes*, July 28, 1969, Doc. 315697.

Borthwick, James and Shirley Ward Keeler, "Desegregation Summary," Borthwick-Keeler History of Kansas City Desegregation File, KCMSD Archives.

Brooks, Marvin to Ruth R. Kempton, "Hardship Cases," September 5, 1973, Teacher Integration, Sept-Oct 1973 File, KCMSD Archives

Busing Files, KCMSD Archives.

Central High School File, KCMSD Archives.

Civil Rights Act of 1964 File, KCMSD Archives.

Clymer, Lewis, Statement to Board of Education, May 25, 1954, filed in *BOE Minutes*, June 3, 1954.

"Compensatory Education Programs of the Kansas City, Missouri Public Schools: The Lincoln Plus and Manual Plus Projects, Report for the Years 1963-1965," Compensatory Education File, KCMSD Archives.

Council of Thirty, "Fiscal Report: Concepts for Changing Times," filed in KCMSD, *BOE Minutes*, August 28, 1968.
--------. "Report of the Subcommittee on the Creation of Master Elementary Districts," January 3, 1969, Council of Thirty File, KCMSD Archives.
--------. "Revised Report of the Council of Thirty Subcommittee on Elementary School Pairing," January 28, 1969, Council of Thirty File, KCMSD Archives.
--------. "Progress Report #1," July 1969, Council of Thirty File, KCMSD Archives.
--------. "Progress Report #2," July 1969, Council of Thirty File, KCMSD Archives.
Dalton, John M., Attorney General for the State of Missouri, to BOE President Ray Joslyn, June 30, 1954, Desegregation File, KCMSD Archives.
Daniels, Fletcher, representing the Community Committee for Social Action, Statement to the Board of Education, filed in *BOE Minutes*, August 25, 1966, Doc. 304039.
Desegregation – 1955 File, KCMSD Archives
Desegregation – Annual Reports File, KCMSD Archives.
Desegregation Correspondence Files, KCMSD Archives.
Desegregation – Miscellaneous File, KCMSD Archives.
Desegregation Monitoring Committee (DMC), "Report of the Desegregation Monitoring Committee for the Kansas City, Missouri School District for the Period of June 14, 1985 - June 30, 1986," (1985-86 Report), August 17, 1986, Offices of the Desegregation Monitoring Committee, KCMSD Board of Education Building.
--------. 1986-87 Report.
--------. 1987-88 Report.
--------. 1988-89 Report.
--------. 1989-90 Report.
--------. 1990-91 Report.
--------. 1991-92 Report.
--------. 1992-93 Report.
--------. 1993-94 Report.
--------. 1994-95 Report.
ESAA 1973 Files, KCMSD Archives.
ESAA, First Plan – 1973 File, KCMSD Archives.
ESAA 1973 Study File, KCMSD Archives.
"Field Reports Concerning the Disorder in Schools, April 1968," (various authors), Martin Luther King Riot – April 1968 File, KCMSD Archives.
Governor's Task Force to Study the Management of the Kansas City, Missouri School District, "Final Report to the Governor, the General Assembly, and the Citizens of the Kansas City Missouri School District," April 1989, 7, Governor's Task Force File, KCMSD Archives.
Grievance letters, Teacher Integration – August 1973 File, KCMSD Archives.
Hale, Phale D. and Daniel U. Levine, "Kansas City, Missouri School District Long-Range Magnet School Plan," (Pink Plan), July 28, 1986, Pink Plan File, KCMSD Archives.

Havighurst Integration File, KCMSD Archives.

Havighurst Study File, KCMSD Archives.

Havighurst, Robert J. "Problems of Integration in the Kansas City Public Schools," Havighurst Integration File, KCMSD Archives.

Havighurst, Robert J. and Daniel U. Levine, "Negro Population Growth in Kansas City and the Problems of Residential Segregation," May 1966, Havighurst Study File, KCMSD Archives.

Havighurst and Levine, "The Feasibility of Maintaining Integration in the Proposed Middle School," April 17, 1967, Havighurst Study File, KCMSD Archives.

Hazlett, James A. "Concepts for Changing Times: Proposals Offered for Public Examination, Dealing with Educational Equality in the Kansas City, Missouri, School District" March 1968, James A. Hazlett File, KCMSD Archives.

HEW Brief File, KCMSD Archives.

HEW Desegregation Order Book I, KCMSD Archives.

HEW Desegregation Order Book II, KCMSD Archives.

HEW Desegregation Order Book III, KCMSD Archives.

HEW Desegregation Order Book IV, KCMSD Archives.

HEW Desegregation Order Book V, KCMSD Archives.

HEW Files, KCMSD Archives.

HEW Suspension of ESAA Funds File, KCMSD Archives.

History of Individual Schools Files, KCMSD Archives.

Holmes, Paul, Desegregation Advisory Office, to Superintendent Medcalf, "Racial Isolation and Racially Identifiable School in Attendance Area Plans A, B, and C," Tables 1 and 2, May 7, 1975, filed in *BOE Minutes*, May 9, 1975, Doc. 321285.

Human Relations Task Force on Civil Disorder, "Three-Year Report: The Quality of Urban Life," October 1971, Kansas City Commission on Human Relations File, KCMSD Archives.

Hunter, Dr. Richard C. "Kansas City, Missouri School District Long-Range Capital Improvement Plan," ("Hunter Report") February 1987, Hunter Report File, KCMSD Archives.

Hunter Report – Capital Improvements File, KCMSD Archives.

Independence Public School District, "Collaborative Schooling: An Independence Public Schools Program for the Superior Education of Students from the Independence Public School District and the Kansas City Public School District," July 1988, filed in House Select Committee, "Report to the Speaker," Appendix Q.

Infante, Henry, President of the Mexican-American Organization for Progress, Statement to the Board of Education, filed in *BOE Minutes*, August 25, 1966, Doc. 304039.

Integrated Pupils, Faculties and Schools File, KCMSD Archives.

Kansas City Commission on Human Relations. "Report from the City Manager on the Economic Implications of the Civil Disorder in Kansas City," April 18, 1968, Kansas City Commission on Human Relations File, KCMSD Archives.

KCMSD. "Achieving Excellence: 1989 Report to the Community," District Communications Office, KCMSD.
--------. "Affirmative Action Plan," filed with *BOE Minutes*, July 30, 1974, Doc. 320501.
--------. Building Needs, Bond Issues, School Building, 1952-54, "A Survey of Circumstances Relevant to the Current and Projected Increases in School Membership in the Booker T. Washington Elementary School," Booker T. Washington School File, Histories of Individual Schools Files, KCMSD Archives.
--------. "Building Our Future through Diversity: 1990 Report to the Community," District Communications Office, KCMSD.
--------. "Busing 1966-67," Busing -- Transportation of Pupils File, KCMSD Archives.
--------. "Capacity-Membership Study of Elementary Schools Involved in Transportation 1966-67," Busing File, KCMSD Archives.
--------. Chronological Record of NAACP Correspondence, NAACP Reports File, KCMSD Archives.
--------. "Desegregation Remedy Plan," Desegregation Plan 1996 File, KCMSD Archives.
--------. Emergency School Aid Act, Basic Project, Project No. F7059TA, December 27, 1973, KCMSD Archives
--------. Emergency School Aid Act, Pilot Project, Project No. F7060TB, December 1973, ESAA First Plan – 1973 File, KCMSD Archives.
--------. "Integration and the Kansas City, Missouri, Schools: A Statement of the Board of Education of the School District of Kansas City, Missouri, Acknowledging Requests Made by the Kansas City Congress of Racial Equality," August 1, 1963, CORE File, KCMSD Archives.
--------. Operating Budgets for Fiscal Years 1953-54 through 1980-81, Financial Records Files, KCMSD Archives;
--------. "Plan for Implementation of Settlement Agreement Pertaining to Compliance with ESAA Funding Assurances," February 1975, HEW Suspension of ESAA Funds File.
--------. "Plan to Reach the 15% Non-Minority Enrollment as Specified in the Agreement Received February 22, 1978 from the Office for Civil Rights," HEW Desegregation Order Book IV, KCMSD Archives.
--------. "Plan for Remedying Vestiges of the Segregated Public School System," January 18, 1985, KCMSD Plan 1 File, KCMSD Archives.
--------. "Policies for the Transition from System of Separate Schools to a Desegregated School System," (Kansas City: KCMSD, March 3, 1955).
---------. "Present Capacities of Elementary School Buildings, 1964," School Capacities File, KCMSD Archives.
--------. "Project Head Start: Submitted to the Human Resources Corporation under the Provisions of Title II-A of the Economic Opportunity Act of 1964," April 8, 1965, Economic Opportunity Act – 1964 File, KCMSD Archives.
--------. "School Profiles, 1994-95," Research and Assessment Offices, KCMSD.

KCMSD. "Some Highlights of District Desegregation," undated, Desegregation Highlights File, KCMSD Archives.

--------. "Summary of Meeting with Westport High School Patrons," April 17, 1969, Manual-Westport Situation Report, KCMSD Archives.

--------. "Summary of Meeting with Manual Patrons," April 21, 1969, Manual-Westport Situation Report.

--------. "Teachers -- Distribution by Race, by School, 1954-55 - 1973-74," Integrated Pupils, Faculty, and Schools File, KCMSD Archives.

--------. "Transcript of Proceedings, Tuesday, July 2, 1963 in Auditorium of Kansas City Library," Howard Rittmaster and Associates, KCMSD Archives.

KCMSD and Community Desegregation Task Force, "Plan 6-C: School Integration Program for the School District of Kansas City, Missouri," March 20, 1977, Plan 6-C File, KCMSD Archives.

KCMSD Research Department, "Integration Data: Actual Occurrence of Integration Compared With Predicted Outcomes;" Integrated Pupils, Faculties and Schools File, KCMSD Archives.

--------. "A Study of the Problems Involved in the Desegregation of the Public Schools of Kansas City, Missouri," July 15, 1954.

--------. "A High School in the Manual District," 1965-66, Manual File, KCMSD Archives.

--------. "A Proposal Concept: West Community High School," filed in *BOE Minutes*, August 14, 1980, Doc. 326692; *BOE Minutes*, August 14, 1980, Doc. 326693; September 1, 1980, Doc. 327483.

--------. "Pupil Reassignment Survey," July 1970, Transfers File, KCMSD Archives.

--------. "Study of School Attendance Area Boundaries, Comparison of Minority Group Percentage in Plans A, B, C, and D," May 1975, filed in *BOE Minutes*, May 7, 1975, Doc. 321281

Levine, Daniel U. "School Facilities Decisions in the Kansas City Public School District," 1967, Havighurst Study File, KCMSD Archives.

Manual School File, KCMSD Archives.

Maya, Agapito, Statement to the Board of Education, filed in *BOE Minutes*, February 7, 1966, Doc. 302330.

Mexican American Organization for Progress, Statement to Board of Education, May 26, 1966, filed in *BOE Minutes*, May 26, 1966, Doc. 303041.

Midwest Center for Race and Sex Desegregation, "Yet Another West Side Story," November 1979, West Side Studies - Various File, KCMSD Archives.

Miscellaneous Correspondence 1984-85 File, KCMSD Archives.

Missouri School District Reorganization Commission, "School District Organization for Missouri: A Plan to Provide Equal Access to Educational Opportunity for All Children," Spainhower Report File, KCMSD Archives.

--------. "Equal Treatment to Equals: A New Structure for Public Schools in the Kansas City and St. Louis Metropolitan Areas," June 1969, Spainhower Report File, KCMSD Archives.

Northeast High School File, KCMSD Archives.

NAACP Correspondence 1973-1975 Files, KCMSD Archives.

NAACP Reports File, KCMSD Archives.

Office of the Superintendent, "Fall Membership Report, 1954-55," Integrated Pupils, Faculties and Schools File, KCMSD Archives.

--------. "Kansas City, Missouri School District Enrollment By School, 1954-55 – 1983-84," Integrated Pupils, Faculties and Schools File, KCMSD Archives.

--------. "Negro and White Memberships, September 16, 1955," Desegregation, 1955 File, KCMSD Archives.

--------. "Students Lost in Strike," Teachers' Strike – 1974 File, KCMSD Archives.

Paseo High School File, KCMSD Archives.

Perkins, Dr. Claude G. "Kansas City, Missouri School District Magnet School Plan," May 8, 1986, Original Magnet Plan File, KCMSD Archives.

Pink Plan File, KCMSD Archives.

Plan E File, KCMSD Archives.

Plan 6-C File, KCMSD Archives.

Report to the Speaker from the House Select Committee on the Kansas City Schools, January 1990, KCMSD Archives.

Results of May 26, 1964 Bond Election, filed in KCMSD, *BOE Minutes*, June 18, 1964, Doc. 299089.

Results of February 23, 1965 Bond Election, filed in KCMSD, *BOE Minutes*, March 11, 1965, Doc. 300329.

Roleke, James W. "1988 Parent, Student and Staff Opinion Survey Report: District Summary," cited in Governor's Task Force, "Final Report," Governor's Task Force File, KCMSD Archives.

Runnells and Winholtz, "West Side Study," December 4, 1968, West Side Study File, KCMSD Archives.

Smith, Dr. G. Dewey, Dr. Richard A. Ball, and J. Glenn Travis, "Northwest Senior High School as Recommended by Dr. Havighurst," January 19, 1966, Havighurst Study File, KCMSD Archives.

Southeast High School File, KCMSD Archives.

Southwest High School File, KCMSD Archives.

Spainhower Report File, KCMSD Archives.

Strike Material – 1974 File, KCMSD Archives.

Teacher Integration – August 1973 File, KCMSD Archives.

Teacher Integration – Sept-Oct 1973 File, KCMSD Archives.

Teachers' Strike – 1974 File, KCMSD Archives.

Teachers' Strike – 1977 File, KCMSD Archives.

Title I Files, KCMSD Archives.

Transfers Files, KCMSD Archives.

Travis, J. Glenn. *Historic Report*, Office of Board Services, October 1987.

--------. "A Study of Extent of Integration Pupils, Faculty, and Schools, 1965-1966," Havighurst Study File, KCMSD Archives.

--------. "Historical Development of Regulations Dealing With Pupil Transfers," October 15, 1965, Havighurst Study File, KCMSD Archives.

--------. "Comments Regarding Operation of Historic Transfer Policy," (undated) Havighurst Study File, KCMSD Archives.

West High School File, KCMSD Archives.
West Side Educational Advisory Committee, Presentation to Board of Education, filed in *BOE Minutes*, June 26, 1973, Doc. 319479.
West Side Information File, KCMSD Archives.
West Side Schools File, KCMSD Archives.
West Side Study File, KCMSD Archives.
West Side – Various File, KCMS Archives.
Westport School File, KCMSD Archives.
Wheeler, Robert, James W. Newell and Glenn Travis, "Model (Demonstration) Cities Application Material," September-December 1966, Model Cities File, KCMSD Archives.
Wolkey, Eugene, Administrative Asst., to Superintendent Wheeler, "Weekly Reporting of Enrollment in the Magnet School Programs," February 8, 1979, HEW Desegregation Order Book IV, KCMSD Archives.
Wolkey, Eugene to Wheeler, "Reporting of the Enrollment in the West Business/Management School Program," April 17, 1979, HEW Desegregation Order Book V, KCMSD Archives.
Zimmer, Louise, Dr. Gordon Wesner, Dr. Richard Ball, James Newell, Dr. Dewey Smith, "Committee Report Relative to a Proposed Middle School in the Kansas City, Missouri School District," January 31, 1967, Havighurst Integration File, KCMSD Archives

Court Cases and Legal Documents

Adams v. Richardson, 356 F. Supp. 92 (1973).
Adams v. Weinberger. 391 F. Supp. 269 (1975).
AFT, "Intervenors' Initial Response to Defendants' Proposed Remedies," Intervenors' Response to Initial Plans File, KCMSD Archives.
Alexander v. Holmes County Board of Education 396 U.S. 19 (1969).
Black v. State of Missouri, 492 F. Supp. 848 (W.D. Mo. 1980).
Board of Education of Oklahoma City v. Dowell 498 U.S. 237 (1991).
Bradley v. Milliken 338 F. Supp. 582 (E.D. Mich. 1971).
Bradley v. Milliken 345 F. Supp. 914 (E.D. Mich. 1972).
Bradley v. Milliken 484 F.2d 215 (6th Cir. 1973).
Brown v. Board of Education of Topeka, 98 F. Supp. 797 (1951).
--------, 347 U.S. 483 (1954)
--------. 349 U.S. 294 (1955).
Carter v. West Feliciana Parish School Board 396 U.S. 290 (1970).
"Decision of Administrative Law Judge Rollie D. Thedford," HEW Administrative Decision File, KCMSD Archives.
Freeman v. Pitts 503 U.S. 467 (1992).
Green v. County School Board, 391 U.S. 430 (1968).
HEW Brief on Behalf of General Counsel, In the Matter of Kansas City, Missouri School District and State Department of Education, Missouri,

Administrative Proceedings in the Department of Health, Education, and Welfare, March 30, 1975, No. S-92, *HEW Brief* File, KCMSD Archives.

Jesaitis, et al. v. Kansas City Missouri School District, et al., Docket No. CV75-0701 in the Circuit Court of Jackson County, HEW Suspension of ESAA Funds File, KCMSD Archives.

Jenkins v. Missouri 460 F. Supp. 421 (W.D. Mo. 1978).

--------. 593 F. Supp. 1485 (W.D. Mo. 1984).

--------. 639 F. Supp. 19 (W.D. Mo. 1985).

--------. 807 F. 2d 657 (8th Cir. 1986).

--------. 672 F. Supp. 400 (W.D. Mo. 1987).

--------. cert. denied 484 U.S. 816 (1987).

--------. 855 F.2d 1295 (8th Cir. 1988).

--------. 904 F.2d 414 (8th Cir. 1990).

--------. 981 F.2d 1009 (8th Cir. 1992).

--------. 11 F.3d 755 (8th Cir. 1993).

--------. 13 F.3d 1170 (8th Cir. 1993).

--------. 38 F.3d 960 (8th Cir. 1994).

--------. 73 F. Supp. 2d 1058 (W.D. Mo. 1999).

Jenkins v. Missouri, June 5, 1984, unreported slip opinion, Judge Clark's Desegregation Orders Files, June 5, 1984 File, KCMSD Archives.

--------. July 16, 1984 Order, unreported slip opinion, Judge Clark's Desegregation Orders Files, July 16, 1984 File, KCMSD Archives.

--------. January 25, 1985 Order, unreported slip opinion, Judge Clark's Desegregation Orders Files, January 25, 1985 File, KCMSD Archives.

--------. June 16, 1986 Order, unreported slip opinion, Judge Clark's Desegregation Orders Files, June 16, 1986 File, KCMSD Archives.

--------. August 25, 1986 Order, unreported slip opinion, Judge Clark's Desegregation Orders Files, August 25, 1986 File, KCMSD Archives.

--------. November 12, 1986 Order, unreported slip opinion, Judge Clark's Desegregation Orders Files, November 12, 1986 File, KCMSD Archives.

--------. April 20, 1989 Order, unreported slip opinion, Judge Clark's Desegregation Orders Files, April 20, 1989 File, KCMSD Archives.

--------. July 3, 1990 Order, unreported slip opinion, Judge Clark's Desegregation Orders Files, July 3, 1990 File, KCMSD Archives.

--------. July 23, 1990 Order, unreported slip opinion, Judge Clark's Desegregation Orders Files, July 23, 1990 File, KCMSD Archives.

--------. September 4, 1990 Order, unreported slip opinion, Judge Clark's Desegregation Orders Files, September 4, 1990 File, KCMSD Archives.

--------. May 24, 1991 Order, unreported slip opinion, Judge Clark's Desegregation Orders Files, May 24, 1991 File, KCMSD Archives.

--------. June 17, 1992 Order, unreported slip opinion, Judge Clark's Desegregation Orders Files, June 17, 1992 File, KCMSD Archives.

--------. June 25, 1992 Order, unreported slip opinion, Judge Clark's Desegregation Orders Files, June 25, 1992 File, KCMSD Archives.

--------. June 30, 1993 Order, unreported slip opinion, Judge Clark's Desegregation Orders Files, June 30, 1993, KCMSD Archives.

--------. December 22, 1993 Order, unreported slip opinion, Judge Clark's Desegregation Orders Files, December 22, 1993 File, KCMSD Archives.

--------. January 10, 1994 Order, unreported slip opinion, Judge Clark's Desegregation Orders Files, January 10, 1994 File, KCMSD Archives.

--------. July 15, 1994 Order, unreported slip opinion, Judge Clark's Desegregation Orders Files, July 15, 1994 File, KCMSD Archives.

--------. March 25, 1997 Order, unreported slip opinion, Judge Clark's Desegregation Orders Files, March 25, 1997 File, KCMSD Archives.

Jenkins v. Missouri, Plaintiffs' Trial Brief, 1-22, Plaintiffs' Brief File, KCMSD Archives.

KCMSD, "Intradistrict Plan Submitted by the School District of Kansas City, Missouri in Response to the Court Order of January 25, 1985," February 19, 1985, KCMSD Intradistrict Plan File, KCMSD Archives.

--------. "Voluntary Interdistrict Transfer Plan," (undated), filed in court February 19, 1985, Voluntary Transfer File, KCMSD Archives.

--------. "Memorandum Responding to Order of January 25, 1985 and Commenting on state Defendants' Plan," February 19, 1985, KCMSD Intradistrict Plan File, KCMSD Archives.

Liddell v. Missouri 731 F. 2d 1294 (8th Cir.), cert. denied, 105 S. Ct. 82 (1984).

Missouri State Constitution, art. 9, sec. 1.

Memorandum in Support of Motion to Stay -- Or in the Alternative to Dismiss -- Action Because of Failure to Join Parties Under Rule 19, *Scott, et al v. Kansas City, Missouri School District, et al*, Scott Case File, KCMSD Archives.

Milliken v. Bradley 418 U.S. 717 (1974).

Milliken v. Bradley (*Milliken II*) 433 U.S. 267 (1977).

Missouri v. Jenkins, 491 U.S. 274 (1989).

--------. 495 U.S. 33 (1990).

--------. 515 U.S. 70 (1995).

Morrilton School District No. 32 v. United States 606 F.2d 222 (8th Cir. 1979), cert. denied 444 U.S. 1071 (1980).

Motion to Dismiss Complaint for Failure to State a Claim Properly Maintainable as a Class Action, *Scott, et al v. Kansas City, Missouri School District, et al.*, Scott Case File, KCMSD Archives.

Naylor v. Lee's Summit Reorganized School District R-7 703 F. Supp. 814 (W.D. Mo. 1989).

--------. 904 F.2d 414 (8th Cir. 1990).

North Kansas City VIDT plan discussed in *Jenkins* 981 F.2d at 1011-1012.

Revised Statutes of Missouri, 1949, sec. 163.130.

Revised Statutes of Missouri, sec. 165.393.

Rivarde v. State of Missouri (unreported slip opinion), November 28, 1989, Judge Clark's Desegregation Orders Files, November 28, 1989 File, KCMSD Archives.

--------. 930 F.2d 641 (8th Cir. 1991).

Taylor v. Board of Education of New Rochelle, 250 F. 2d 36 (1961)

School District of Kansas City, Missouri v. State of Missouri 438 F. Supp. 830 (W.D. Mo. 1977).

School District of Kansas City, Missouri v. State of Missouri 460 F. Supp. 427 (W.D. Mo. 1978).

School District of Kansas City, Missouri v. Missouri, 592 F.2d 493 (8th Cir. 1979).

Scott, et al v. Kansas City, Missouri School District et al, No. 73 CV 40-W-2, in the United States District Court for the Western District of Missouri, Western Division, Scott Case File, KCMSD Archives.

Singleton v. Jackson Municipal Separate School District 348 F.2d 729 (CA5 1965)

Singleton II 355 F.2d 865 (CA5 1966).

State Defendants, "Remedial Plan of the State Defendants and Summary Memorandum," January 17, 1985, State Plan 1 File, KCMSD Archives.

--------. "Desegregation Implementation Plan," March 26, 1985, State Plan 2 File, KCMSD Archives.

--------. "KCMSD Desegregation Implementation Plan," April 29, 1985, State Plan 3 File, KCMSD Archives.

State of Missouri, "A Chronology of the Kansas City, Missouri School District Desegregation Case," Department of Elementary and Secondary Education, State of Missouri, Jefferson City, MO.

--------. "Kansas City, Missouri School District Total Desegregation Program Expenditures," September 30, 1994, Department of Elementary and Secondary Education, State of Missouri, Jefferson City, MO.

--------. "Kansas City, Missouri School District Total Desegregation Program Expenditures," November 3, 1995, Department of Elementary and Secondary Education, State of Missouri, Jefferson City, MO.

--------. "Kansas City Desegregation Case Total Expenditures," November 8, 1994, Department of Elementary and Secondary Education, State of Missouri, Jefferson City, MO.

--------. "Kansas City Desegregation Fact Sheet," Department of Elementary and Secondary Education, State of Missouri, Jefferson City, MO.

--------. "Kansas City Missouri School District September Enrollments," November 1994, Department of Elementary and Secondary Education, State of Missouri, Jefferson City, MO.

--------. "State's Payments Under Joint and Several Liability, Salary Account," November 3, 1995, Department of Elementary and Secondary Education, State of Missouri, Jefferson City, MO.

Swann v. Charlotte-Mecklenburg Board of Education 402 U.S. 1 (1971).

United States v. Jefferson County Board of Education 372 F.2d 836 (CA5 1966).

United States v. Missouri 515 F.2d 1365 (8th Cir. 1975), cert. denied 423 U.S. 951 (1975).

United States v. Montgomery County Board of Education 395 U.S. 225 (1969).

Newspapers

Denver Post
Kansas City Call
Kansas City Star

Kansas City Times
St. Louis Post-Dispatch
Washington Post
Wednesday Magazine
U.S.A. Today

Government Documents

Department of Commerce, Bureau of the Census, *U.S. Census, 1950, Census Tracts, Kansas City SMSA*. Washington D.C.: U.S. Government Printing, 1951.

--------. *U.S. Census, 1960, Census Tracts, Kansas City SMSA*. Washington D.C.: U.S. Government Printing, 1961.

--------. *U.S. Census, 1970, Census Tracts, Kansas City SMSA*. Washington D.C.: U.S. Government Printing, 1972.

--------. *U.S. Census, 1980, Census Tracts, Kansas City, SMSA*. Washington D.C.: U.S. Government Printing, 1983.

--------. *U.S. Census, 1990, Census Tracts, Kansas City, MSA*. Washington D.C.: U.S. Government Printing, 1994.

Emergency School Aid Act, Public Law 92-318, 20 U.S.C. 1601-1619 (1973).

Kansas City, Missouri City Planning Commission. "Negro Residential Areas, 1950." Kansas City: City Planning Office.

--------. "Negro Residential Areas, 1960." Kansas City: City Planning Office.

Interviews and Email Correspondence

J. Glenn Travis, administrator in KCMSD for more than forty years, interview by author, Kansas City, MO, June 23, 1992.

John Duncan, KCMSD historian, interview by author, June 12, 1996.

Shirley Ward Keeler, KCMSD legal counsel 1970s-1990s, interview by author, Kansas City, MO, June 16, 1999.

Arthur A. Benson II, plaintiffs' attorney in *Jenkins* litigation, e-mail correspondence with author, August 19, 1999.

Arthur A. Benson II, e-mail correspondence with author, September 16, 1999.

Secondary Sources

Books and Articles

Armor, David J. *Forced Justice: School Desegregation and the Law*. New York: Oxford University Press, 1995.

Bailey, Stephen K. and Edith K. Mosher, *ESEA: The Office of Education Administers a Law*. Syracuse: Syracuse University Press, 1968.

Bass, Jack. *Unlikely Heroes: The Dramatic Story of the Southern Judges of the*

Fifth Circuit Who Translated the Supreme Court's Brown Decision into a Revolution for Equality. New York: Simon and Schuster, 1981.

Benson, Arthur A. "Fragarach: A Brief Outline of the History of Litigation Concerning KCMSD to Achieve Racial Integration and Improve Educational Opportunities," (unpublished manuscript) Arthur Benson and Associates, Kansas City, MO.

--------. "School Segregation and Desegregation in Kansas City," (unpublished manuscript) Arthur Benson and Associates, Kansas City, MO.

Berke, Joel S. and Michael W. Kirst, *Federal Aid to Education: Who Benefits? Who Governs?* Lexington, MA: Lexington Books, 1972.

Billington, Monroe. "Public School Integration in Missouri, 1954-64," *Journal of Negro Education*, XXXIII, No. 3 (Summer, 1964), 252-262.

Blaustein, A.P. and C.C. Ferguson, *Desegregation and the Law*. New Brunswick: Rutgers University Press, 1957.

Brantley, George D. "Present Status of Integration in the Public Schools of Missouri," *Journal of Negro Education*, XXIV, No. 3 (Summer, 1955), 293-309.

Cataldo, Everett F. *School Desegregation Policy: Compliance, Avoidance and the Metropolitan Remedy*. Lexington, MA: Lexington Books, 1978.

Clotfelter, Charles T. *After Brown: The Rise and Retreat of School Desegregation*. Princeton, NJ: Princeton University Press, 2004.

Coleman, James S., et al, *Equality of Educational Opportunity*. Washington, D.C.: U.S. government Printing Office, 1966.

Conant, James B. *The American High School Today*. New York: McGraw-Hill, 1959.

--------. *Slums and Suburbs*. New York: McGraw-Hill, 1961.

Congressional Quarterly. *Congress and the Nation: A Review of Government and Politics, Volume IV, 1973-1976*. Washington D.C.: Congressional Quarterly, 1977.

--------. *Congress and the Nation: A Review of Government and Politics, Volume V, 1977-1980*. Washington D.C.: Congressional Quarterly, 1981.

Dimond, Paul R. *Beyond Busing: Inside the Challenge to Urban Segregation*. Ann Arbor: University of Michigan Press, 1985.

--------. "School Segregation in the North: There is but One Constitution." *Harvard Civil Rights-Civil Liberties Law Review* 7 (January 1972): 1-55.

Eagles, Charles W. (ed.). *The Civil Rights Movement in America*. Oxford, MS: University Press of Mississippi, 1986.

Freyer, Tony. *The Little Rock Crisis: A Constitutional Interpretation*. Westport, CT: Greenwood Press, 1984.

Gordon, William M. "School Desegregation: A Look at the 70s and 80s." *Journal of Law and Education* 18, 2 (Spring 1989): 189-214.

Graglia, Lino. *Disaster By Decree: The Supreme Court on Race and the Schools*. Ithaca, NY: Cornell University Press, 1976.

Hirsch, Arnold R. *Making the Second Ghetto: Race and Housing in Chicago, 1940-1960*. Chicago: University of Chicago Press, 1998.

Irons, Peter. *Jim Crow's Children: The Broken Promise of the Brown Decision*. New York: Viking Press, 2002.

Jackson, Kenneth T. *Crabgrass Frontier: The Suburbanization of the United States.* New York: Oxford University Press, 1985.

Jackson, Reid E. "The Development and Character of Permissive and Partly Segregated Schools," *Journal of Negro Education*, XV, No. 3 (Summer, 1947), 301-310.

Johnson, Daniel M. and Rex R. Campbell, *Black Migration in America.* Durham, NC: Duke University Press, 1981.

Johnston, R.J. *Residential Segregation, The State and Constitutional Conflict in American Urban Areas.* New York: Academic Press, 1984.

Jones, Leon. *From Brown to Boston: Desegregation in Education, 1954-1974.* 2 vols. Metuchen, NJ: Scarecrow Press, 1979.

Kalodner, Howard. *Limits of Justice: The Courts' Role in School Desegregation.* Cambridge, MA: Ballinger Publishing, 1978.

Kluger, Richard. *Simple Justice: The History of Brown v. Board of Education and Black America's Struggle for Equality.* New York: Alfred A. Knopf, 1976.

Kunen, James. "The End of Integration," *Time Magazine* 147, 18 (April 29, 1996): 40-45.

Leiberson, Stanley. *Ethnic Patterns in American Cities.* New York: The Free Press, 1963.

--------. *A Piece of the Pie: Blacks and White Immigrants Since 1880.* Berkeley: University of California Press, 1980.

Lemann, Nicholas. *The Promised Land: The Great Black Migration and How It Changed America.* New York: Vintage Books, 1992.

Levine, Daniel. "America's Worst Judges," *Reader's Digest*, 155, 927 (July 1999): 92-93.

Lewis, Anthony. *Portrait of a Decade: The Second American Revolution.* New York: Random House, 1964.

Lukas, J. Anthony. *Common Ground: A Turbulent Decade in the Lives of Three American Families.* New York: Oxford University Press, 1985.

Marshall, Albert P. "Racial Integration in Missouri," *Journal of Negro Education*, XXV, No. 3 (Summer, 1956), 289-298.

Metcalf, George R. *From Little Rock to Boston: The History of School Desegregation.* Westport, CT: Greenwood Press, 1983.

Monti, Daniel J. *A Semblance of Justice: St. Louis School Desegregation and Order in Urban America.* Columbia, MO: University of Missouri Press, 1985.

Muse, Benjamin. *Ten Years of Prelude: The Story of Integration Since the Supreme Court's 1954 Decision.* New York: Viking Press, 1964.

Nieman, Donald G. *Promises to Keep: African-Americans and the Constitutional Order, 1776 to the Present.* New York: Oxford University Press, 1991.

Orfield, Gary. *Must We Bus?: Segregated Schools and National Policy.* Washington D.C.: Brookings Institute, 1978.

Orfield, Gary, Susan Eaton and the Harvard Project on School Desegregation. *Dismantling Desegregation: The Quiet Reversal of Brown v. Board of Education.* New York: The New Press, 1996.

Parrish, C.H. "Desegregation in Public Education -- A Critical Summary," *Journal of Negro Education*, XXIV, No. 3 (Summer, 1955), 382-387.

Peach, Robinson, and Smith (eds.); *Ethnic Segregation in Cities*. London: Croom Helm, 1981.

Peltason, J.W. *Fifty-Eight Lonely Men: Southern Federal Judges and School Desegregation*. New York: Harcourt, Brace and World, 1961.

Presser, Arlynn Leiber. "Broken Dreams," *American Bar Association Journal* 77 (May 1991): 60-64.

Raffel, Jeffery A. *The Politics of School Desegregation: The Metropolitan Remedy in Delaware*. Philadelphia: Temple University Press, 1980.

Read, Frank T. and Lucy McGough. *Let Them Be Judged: The Judicial Integration of the Deep South*. Metuchen, NJ: Scarecrow Press, 1978.

Rose, Alvin W. "The Impending Crisis," *The Antioch Review*, XIV, No. 4 (December, 1954), 421-430.

Rossell, Christine H. *The Carrot or the Stick for School Desegregation Policy: Magnet Schools or Forced Busing*. Philadelphia: Temple University Press, 1990.

Schwartz, Bernard. *Swann's Way: The School Busing Case and the Supreme Court*. New York: Oxford University Press, 1986.

Sitkoff, Harvard. *The Struggle for Black Equality, 1954-1992*, rev. ed. New York: Hill and Wang, 1993.

Smith, Robert C. *They Closed Their Schools: Prince Edward County, Virginia, 1951-1964*. Chapel Hill: University of North Carolina Press, 1965.

Swanson, Austin D. and Richard A. King. *School Finance: Its Economics and Politics*. White Plains, NY: Longman Publishing, 1991.

Taeuber, Karl E. and Alma F. Taeuber. *Negroes in Cities: Residential Segregation and Neighborhood Change*. Chicago: Aldine Publishing, 1965.

Time Magazine, 66, 12 (September 19, 1955), 25.

Trotter, Joe William (ed.). *The Great Migration in Historical Perspective: New Dimensions of Race, Class and Gender*. Bloomington, IN: Indiana University Press, 1991.

Tushnet, Mark V. *The NAACP's Legal Strategy against Segregated Education, 1925-1950*. Chapel Hill: University of North Carolina Press, 1987.

Wasby, Stephen, et al. *Desegregation from Brown to Alexander: An Exploration of Supreme Court Strategies*. Carbondale: Southern Illinois University Press, 1977.

Weinberg, Meyer (ed.). *Integrated Education*. Beverly Hills, CA: Glencoe Press, 1968.

Wilkinson, J. Harvie. *From Brown to Bakke: The Supreme Court and School Integration, 1954-1978*. New York: Oxford University Press, 1979.

Williams, Juan (ed.). *Eyes on the Prize: America's Civil Rights Years, 1954-1965*. New York: Viking Press, 1987.

Wolf, Eleanor Paperno. *Trial and Error: The Detroit School Segregation Case*. Detroit: Wayne State University Press, 1981.

Woodward, C. Vann. *The Strange Career of Jim Crow*, rev. 3d ed. New York: Oxford University Press, 1974.

Index